Ideologies of Hispanism

HISPANIC ISSUES • VOLUME 30

Ideologies of Hispanism

Mabel Moraña

EDITOR

Vanderbilt University Press
NASHVILLE, TENNESSEE
2005

This book is printed on acid-free paper.
Manufactured in the United States of America

The editors gratefully acknowledge assistance from the
College of Liberal Arts and the Department of Spanish
and Portuguese Studies at the University of Minnesota.

*The complete list of volumes in the
Hispanic Issues series begins on page 335.*

Library of Congress Cataloging-in-Publication Data

Ideologies of Hispanism / Mabel Moraña. — 1st ed.
   p. cm.   —   (Hispanic issues ; v. 30)
   Includes bibliographical references and index.
ISBN 0-8265-1471-5 (cloth : alk. paper)
ISBN 0-8265-1472-3 (pbk. : alk. paper)
   1. Civilization, Hispanic. I. Moraña, Mabel.
II. Hispanic issues; 30.
CB226.I345 2005
305.868—dc22

                                        2004022806

Contents

◆ **Introduction:**
Mapping Hispanism

Mabel Moraña

In the context of current debates on postcolonialism and multiculturalism, a collective reflection on *ideologies of hispanism* seems to be in order. And yet, this is a daunting task, given the ambiguities and complexities involved both in the mere definition of the topic and in the demarcation of its theoretical and epistemological boundaries. Indeed, the extension and transformation of cultural and ideological practices associated with Hispanism suggest the impossibility of confining the analysis to a specific period or modality. It indicates the need to explore, from multidisciplinary and transnational perspectives, the various ways in which Hispanism has functioned as a dominating political force, as an interpretive and representational cultural model, and as an epistemological paradigm, throughout the entire development of Spanish America's and Spain's cultural histories.

At the same time, the topic points to the disciplinary level in which the different perspectives on Hispanism articulate. Within Spanish, Latin American, and U.S. academies, disciplines constitute localizing spaces for the appropriation, legitimization, and institutionalization of Hispanism, as well as sites from which the global dissemination of knowledge related to this field is actually implemented. A collective reflection on the *ideologies of hispanism* entails, then, the examination of the intertwined connections between power, cultural institutions, and cultural production, as well as an analysis of the changing role played by writers and scholars in the production of critical discourse related to the categories of colonialism, national formation, modernity, and identity politics that constitute the basis of the post-colonial debate.

Without a doubt, the project of hispanization evokes, in the first place, the historical experience of imperial expansion in the so-called New World, and the strategies of resistance implemented by the colonial subject in order to counteract the violence of material and symbolic domination. The array of problems associated with what Aníbal Quijano has called the *coloniality of power* are inextricably related to linguistic colonization, that is, to the imposition and dissemination of the predominant imperial language for the purposes of control and submission of dominated cultures, the reduction of differences, and the symbolic appropriation of autochthonous imaginaries. Intertwined with the project of Christianization, as well as with the overarching purposes of economic profit and political legitimization, the Spanish language became, from the first stages of colonization, one of the most refined and versatile technologies of power in America.

In the Iberian Peninsula, the consolidation of Castilian hegemony over all other cultural identities also indicates the crucial role of enforced monolingualism in the projects of political unification and cultural dissemination of imperial Spain within its own primary territories. But far from being limited to the period of imperial expansion, the project and practices of hispanization have also played a key role in the postcolonial scene, both in Spain and Spanish America, throughout the process of the formation and consolidation of national states, and nowadays in the context of globalization.

Over the centuries, the Spanish language has constituted, both in Spain and in Spanish America, a distinct space for symbolic struggle, for the construction of collective memories and subjectivities, and for the perpetuation of a cultural and economic linkage between the old metropolis and the former colonies. The transnational impact of Hispanism can also be traced at the academic level, in the disciplinary fields associated with the transmission of Spain's cultural heritage or with the study of cultures derived from the Spanish conquest. Factors as diverse as the rapid expansion of the Spanish language, particularly in the United States, the focus on social and cultural migrations promoted in the framework of postcolonial and cultural studies, and the articulation of Spain to the European Community, have considerably contributed to increasing the attention on Hispanism, from different perspectives, and to reinvigorating transnational debates about its political content, cultural value, and political significance.

The use of language both as a pragmatic and a symbolic device of domination—as well as a key element of cultural resistance—is one of the most important issues studied in this book. In the Spanish American colonies, *translation* is not only the main procedure for transculturation but also is one of the most important recourses for the appropriation and subjugation of subaltern imagination. Lydia Fossa analyzes in this volume the manipulation of linguistic codes in the Andean region, and the uses of hispanization—and latinization—as political procedures implemented for the reduction of cultural differences. The *invincible ignorance* of the Indians and members of colonial *castas* was the final frontier conquered by European epistemologies. For this reason, colonial domination depended, to a great extent, on the proliferation of communicative strategies designed to complement, and often to replace, linguistic colonization. Fossa's study shows that Hispanization was often confronted with the challenge of going well beyond the limits of the language, which became only one of the elements of the complex and effective cultural semiosis that accompanied imperial domination in America. The use of interpreters, iconography, and performances for the transmission of religious dogma, the adoption of teaching techniques differentially applied to children and adults as well as to members of different social strata, the construction of dictionaries, glossaries, and grammatical treatises that transformed Quechua and Aymara into linguistic oddities even in their own cultural realm, and the elimination in these books of all cultural and linguistic components considered superfluous to the purposes of pragmatic appropriations of indigenous cultures, were some of the strategies used for the implementation of the paradoxical "evangelization without language" that, as Fossa indicates, took place in America during the sixteenth century.

With the advancement and consolidation of colonialism, the Spanish language was also crucial to the organization and transmission of a *creole archive* that would define the cultural parameters of a new, emerging American elite which, in spite of its subaltern position to Peninsular sectors, would claim the right to re-discover, register, and interpret pre-Hispanic cultures as part of the process of the "invention of traditions" initiated by Spanish missionaries and men of letters soon after the "discovery." But the recovery and interpretation of indigenous cultures that survived the dismantling processes of the conquest and colonization of America was a project that also found its way in the new Spanish American republics, playing an important and, at times, contradictory role in the articulation of national discourses. Ignacio M. Sánchez-Prado analyzes the rediscovery of pre-Hispanic cultures carried out in Mexico by Miguel León Portilla, as well as his loose utilization of archival materials, and the operations of cultural and linguistic translation used for the construction of an indigenous past that could be productively integrated into the conflictive realm of modern Mexican culture. Within this framework, Hispanism constitutes the institutionalizing and legitimizing space for a nationalist appropriation of pre-Columbian history. The Spanish language is defended by León Portilla as the unifying and cohesive force—the *lingua franca*—that could articulate and bring together all the components of Mexican diversity. Sánchez Prado's study poses the question of the limits and merits of transcultural appropriations (use of historic sources, textualization of oral discourses, translation of indigenous languages into dominant codes), indicative of the epistemological violence inherent in the interpretation and representation of subaltern cultures in postcolonial scenarios.

The discursive and ideological reappropriation of the past has been an obsessive pursuit in modern historiography. As Joan Ramón Resina indicates, the territorial loss that resulted from Spanish American independence is strategically compensated during the ninetheenth century by the gradual promotion of a trans-Atlantic *Hispanic* culture articulated around the congregant power of the language, and the communion of customs and beliefs.

The manipulation of social memory and, as Resina reminds us, the *fabrication of oblivion,* is thus one of the main dispositions of modernity. The construction of knowledge in the specific field of Hispanism had its point of departure in the universalistic and ahistorical concept of *Hispania* as a spacial and temporal extension of what once was Spain's imperial dominion. The suppression of diversity and particularism, and the repression of all references to the colonial origins of the concept, has promoted Hispanism as a program of cultural and linguistic dissemination in modern times. As Resina indicates, *historical violence* is codified as *symbolic violence,* and the superior value of tradition absorbs all the political connotations of the historical concept.

In spite of the fact that, as Nicolas Shumway rightfully indicates, many of Spanish America's "enlightened" liberators—particularly Simón Bolívar—considered the "Spanish legacy an impediment to be overcome rather than embraced," in Latin America nationalism included the components of Spanish language and Christian religion as unifying forces for the homogenization of diverse and conflictive populations strongly rooted in their own indigenous traditions, and for the construction of consensus and citizenship in the new Republics. It is also true that the role then played by Hispanism was certainly articulated with—and often limited by—the forces of progress and political change. The dazzling effect of new cultural models (i.e., France, Northern Europe, the United States) gradually overshadowed most vestiges of the old Empire, which was seen by liberal leaders of the nineteenth century as a declining, retrograde and peripheral nation within the much more promising realm of Western modernity.

As an ideologically charged cultural practice, Hispanism produced different results and managed to define very diverse political agendas, depending on the project to which it was articulated, the international conjuncture in which it was immersed, and the goals pursued by intellectual sectors connected to its discursive field, both in the Peninsula and abroad. Yet the colonial past, and the ways in which history was recovered and interpreted from different political perspectives over the centuries, has always been the most conflictive and enduring issue in these debates.

The ideological tensions which characterized the cultural relations between Spain and the Americas from the beginning, manifested new and often contradictory political dimensions during the twentieth century, in response to the challenges posed by the transformations that were taking place in the international arena.

The development of Hispanism reached one of its most notorious and productive stages with the Spanish exile, which brought a large diaspora of scholars and writers who would be crucial to the dissemination of Spanish culture in the Americas across the Atlantic Ocean in the 1930s and 1940s. Sebastiaan Faber's study focuses on the underlying ideological tensions that dwell within the concept of Hispanism, and identifies three major events that contributed to the international re-definition of this field: the Spanish Civil War, Roosevelt's Good Neighbor Policy and consequent U.S.-sponsored Pan-Americanism, and World War II, after which the Americas were perceived by many as the only repository of Western civilization. While some of the movements emerging from those events were directly linked to fascism, others were embedded in the cultural and "spiritual" mission to disseminate the Spanish culture in both North and Latin America, particularly at the academic level. Faber's article illustrates the redefinitions and transformations of Hispanism in three journals founded in Mexico City between 1938 and 1940 (*Revista Iberoamericana, Romance,* and *España Peregrina*). Based on the study of these publications, his essay focuses on some of the contradictions that are inherent to the field. Among other things, Faber mentions that "in spite of Hispanism's transnational ambitions, it is simply too tied up with cultural nationalism," and that the idea of Hispanic studies proposes, to a large extent, the assimilation of heterogeneous cultural realities. Multicultural studies could be, according to Faber, a way of counteracting the rigid, expansionist, and homogenizing orientation of most traditional Hispanic studies.

During some of the processes that I have described thus far, cultural politics has often invoked the linguistic realm as a space for encounter and communion, while in other cases language has been emphasized as one of the most sophisticated and efficient tools used in the project of effacing cultural differences and consolidating political supremacy. Nevertheless, monolingualism has always been, in fact, at the core of Spain's hegemonic projects, both within its Peninsular territories and abroad. Thomas Harrington's article analyzes the terms in which Castilian supremacy was constructed, established, and perpetuated in Spain, over Basque, Galician, and Catalan cultural identities. Harrington traces the cultural process of the standarization of Spanish as part of a political project initiated in the late-Medieval period, which included a definition of the "nation" equalized to the affirmation of Castilian exceptionality and superiority with respect to both non-Christian populations and all other cultures, such as, according to Nebrija, "vizcainos, navarros, franceses, italianos, y todos los otros que tienen algún trato y conversación con España" (Biscayans, Navarrese, French, Italians, and all others who have dealings and are conversants with Spain). Joan Ramón Resina also makes reference to this supposedly self-constitutive foundation of Hispanism, which assumed since the Middle Ages the superiority and "intrinsic universality" of the Castilian language as a point of departure for the definition of a "spiritual" and, without a doubt, political mission of cultural dissemination.

Several articles included in this volume focus on the disciplinary and academic aspects of Hispanism, not only as a field related to the teaching of the language—in this respect, closely connected to the cultural and educational market—but also as a space for the study of history and cultural production. Anthony Cascardi's contribution resides primarily in the analysis of several key moments that can be identified in the development of Spanish literary and cultural studies and proposes some ways in which traditional perspectives on Hispanic literature could be refurbished, both critically and theoretically. Based on his *critique* of both Américo Castro's existential and vitalistic historicism and José Antonio Maravall's political and cultural perspective, Cascardi elaborates on the theoretical avenues opened by the Althusserian notions of ideology, interpellation, and subject formation, and offers the examples of *El Lazarillo de Tormes,* and Cervantes' *Don Quixote* to illuminate the idea of a "fractured mimesis" in Imperial Spain, and to shed light on the often overlooked interconnection between discursive strategies and institutional structures in canonical literary works.

The essays included in this book are not only concerned with the revision of disciplinary aspects related to the field of Hispanism, but are also penetrated by many of the issues and theoretical problems currently debated with respect to identity politics, collective subjectivity, and multiculturalism. In some cases, the authors of these articles have chosen to focus on specific topics where the tensions of aesthetic and ideological representation are particularly evident. Among them, the category of magic realism and the readings of Spanish American Baroque and Neo-Baroque that have been, for several decades, at the center of critical debates.

Sylvia Molloy's article takes into consideration the specificity of Latin American history and culture, in order to illuminate what she calls "a discomfort, an ideological blind spot in the construction of 'Latin America' by the U.S. academy and by the public at large." In particular, she makes reference to the homogenizing postcolonial model elaborated mainly by intellectuals located at American universities, and to the application of exoticizing critical categories generally used to evaluate Latin American literary production. Molloy focuses on the reception of magic realism in the United States, as a prominent example of reductionist interpretations which often disregard the theoretical, critical, and political density of this and other Latin American representational strategies, thus preventing the possibility of a productive and non-stereotypical integration of Latin American cultural practices in transnational debates.

The speculative essay offered by Alberto Moreiras focuses on what Carlos Rincón has called "the returns of the Baroque" and on the attention given to this model by critics such as John Beverley and Roberto González Echevarría. Following Spinoza's concept of "sad passion," Moreiras defines academic practices in the U.S. as a self-dominating, localizing, disciplining, and anti-political passion, and wonders if there is "an exteriority to university discourse." He also refers to Hispanism as an epistemic "site of expropriation" with respect to a slippery object of study that can neither be totally captured by critical practice, nor fully resist its partial appropriation. As an identitarian expression of the Hispanic experience of modernity, the Baroque—and the Neo-Baroque—have become fields of theoretical and representational struggle and, in a way, a symbolic commodity that gives evidence of the practices of transculturation and hybridity in regional spaces of cultural production. Moreiras proposes to overcome both the view of literature "as state apparatus or hegemonic identity" and "anti-literature as a subalternist reading practice," and reflects on the possibility of an alternative form of *critique* that, by de-localizing knowledge, could allow for "a general practice of reading" that might shed new light on regional cultural and literary productions.

However, Moreiras's own critical practice of what could be defined as an intricate philosophical and self-reflective critical approach to Latin American literature is also questioned in this volume. Brad Epps' article titled "Keeping

Things Opaque: On the Reluctant Personalism of a Certain Mode of Critique" is an exhaustive attempt to explore the question of *locality:* the place from where we speak, work, and write. Yet by exploring *intellectual location,* Epps refers not only to the geopolitical or institutional place, but also to the rhetorical site of (self) production, the space of the critical or theoretical "I" often transfigured in a self-reflecting "we" that maintains an evanescent but insistent presence throughout the course of textual and/or cultural analysis. Moreiras' personal writing style—which Epps considers "representative of a certain mode of critique"—as much as some of his elaborations around the topics of Latin Americanism (regional or not, *first* or *second*), subalternism, and the like, are articulated by Epps through an inquiry into the role of U.S. universities as privileged spaces for academic exchange and knowledge production, and as contradictory battlefields that frame—sometimes in more than one sense—our work and mark our intellectual and ideological agendas. In addition, while discussing location and locality, Epps' article touches on the strategies of *displacement*—somehow, the exodus or *peregrinaje* alluded to by Moreiras in his essay on the Baroque, included in this volume—as a central proposition of "a nameless, groundless, radical thinking" destined to counteract what Moreiras calls the "salvaging movement" of neo-Arielist tendencies. Epps' critique of de-localization is an attempt to recuperate an awareness of the determinations—disciplinary, as well as national and institutional—that influence our work, the disregard of which contributes to the opacity of theoretical and critical discourse.

Even with the understanding that intellectual struggles and academic conflicts within the field of Latin Americanism, Hispanism, and Peninsularism will not be resolved by the mere confrontation of individual or even representative positions and polarized agendas (universalist theorization *versus* historically and regionally-grounded critical thinking, self-reflective intellectualism *versus* experience-based critical subjectivities, academic performativity *versus* cultural and political activism, global epistemological dissemination *versus* local knowledge), the disclosure of alternative and even divergent standpoints brings to light some of the impulses that traverse disciplinary practices dealing with ideologically and politically-charged fields of study. At the same time, current emphasis on cultural studies over more traditional close readings and hermeneutical or historiographical approaches have contributed to impel methodological transformations in the field of Hispanism and to promote new disciplinary articulations that pose unseen challenges to scholars working both in Peninsular and Latin American studies. Academia is today, more than ever, a contradictory space where the production and reproduction of critical knowledge receive the impact of political, economic, and social conditions that modify pedagogical practices and intellectual exchanges in a globalized yet strongly regionalized transnational space.

The illusion of the existence of fixed and ahistorical identities that shaped, both culturally and ideologically, the enlightened modernity where Hispanism consolidated some of its most salient ideological features, has been gradually replaced by a much more volatile, porous, temporary experience of *the social,* where *otherness,* heterogeneity, and diversity are the conspicuous protagonists of cultural exchanges and epistemological explorations. While the challenges posed by the recognition of social, political, and cultural *differences,* as well as the complex problems associated with the real implementation of democracy, are today inescapable, the tensions and inequalities that characterize the dynamics of globalization, have intensified defensiveness, discrimination, and fundamentalism, in different cultural and institutional domains around the world.

As Idelber Avelar shows in his article on "Xenophobia and Diasporic Latin Americanism," the concept of the *foreign* is the underlying and probably most conflictive category in the vast realm of cultural studies and particularly in the field of Hispanism. The definition of the boundaries that connect the Spanish language and its *others*—such as the previously mentioned imposition of Spanish over both dominated cultural identities in the Peninsula and indigenous cultures in Latin America, besides the tense coexistence of English and Spanish in the Unitd States—has always depended on economic and political forces, from which situations of cultural predominance emerge and perpetuate themselves, supported by legitimizing discourses and institutional arrangements in their particular domains. The notion of cultural *difference,* conceived as the unrepresentable site of *otherness* that empowers and consecrates the self-image of dominating subjectivities, is an ever-changing battlefield where ideological negotiations take place, in a balancing act that manifests not only the strength of the political powers at work, but also the vulnerability of both dominant and subaltern positions.

In the United States academy, Latin Americanism occupies an *in-between* space strongly affected by the existence of ideological and political agendas constituted as fields of symbolic struggles for the representation of Latino and Hispanic constituencies which have always existed intertwined with the dominant Anglo-Saxon culture. This *in-between* locality occupied by Latin Americanism in the U.S. academy, the struggle of Latino studies to acquire recognition in this country even within the space opened by current theories on multiculturalism, identity politics, and ethnic studies, and even the most recent attempts to put forward not only the political value but also the aesthetic merits of bilingualism and hybridity have, without a doubt, managed to gain space within the horizons of dominant cultural ideologies. Nevertheless, they have been insufficient to eradicate the notion of *foreignness* that crosses over academic practices, intellectual debates, and everyday life, as a ghostly feature of the new world order.

As Avelar indicates in his article, the destruction of the World Trade Center has radicalized the positions around the idea of *foreignness,* and made even more vulnerable all academic and critical domains dealing primarily with the diverse cultures that exist outside and within the United States. These cultures are increasingly perceived as a potential threat, and could become the target of discriminatory policies masquerading as security considerations. Avelar demonstrates how the academic practice of Hispanism is directly affected by the standards imposed at the academic level to faculty and students working in this field, and by the universalization and imposition of criteria applied to the evaluation of intellectual performance, without consideration for the diversity upon which scholarly work has always depended. Today more than ever, this imperative must be emphasized, particularly in all disciplines dealing with foreign cultures, within the context of globalization.

Closing the reflections of this volume, Román de la Campa's article on "U.S. Hispanism and Its Lines of Flight" analyzes the critical scenarios that followed the advent of deconstructive paradigms after the 1960s, particularly in the U.S. academy. The fields of Hispanism, Latin Americanism, and Latino Studies that had evoked until then distinct spaces of research and specific pedagogical practices in departments of Spanish, Modern, and Foreign Languages, have experienced radical transformations in the last few decades. De la Campa's article is an attempt to assess the disciplinary flux that characterizes current humanistic approaches to Hispanic literatures and cultures in the realm of what he has called the "discursive communities" dealing with Latin American studies. According to De la Campa, it would be impossible, in future years, to disregard the disciplinary changes that have impacted the academic world, as well as the pressures of cultural markets that have created a postnational production and consumption of knowledge in these fields. Comparative approaches will be necessary to articulate the new constellation of critical and theoretical practices that should include Latino studies as an integral part of the cultural agenda.

While several articles included in this book focus on the clarification of the origins and different stages of consolidation of Hispanism at the academic level, others elaborate on the drastic transformations that have been affecting the field, particularly since the end of the Cold War. Without a doubt, the advancement of the European Union has propelled the redefinition of Spain's international role in Europe, as well as with respect to Spanish American nations and Spanish-speaking communities in the U.S. Based on its historic nexus with Latin America, Spain is still perceived as the natural mediator for the economic rearticulation of Spanish American countries to Europe in the post-colonial era. At the same time, the rapidly growing Spanish-speaking population in the U.S. has also opened up unseen scenarios for Spain, thus renewing a trans-Oceanic connection, now with Anglo American cultures, via research programs and cultural exchange. At the economic level, the financially troubled Latin American countries have already received the impact of Spanish investments, which recognize in trans-Atlantic markets the opportunity for entrepreneurial and financial expansion within the framework of neoliberalism. Again, as Madrid places itself at the center of international arrangements, the language is reaffirmed as the primary and legitimizing vehicle for intercultural relations, and the expectation of profitable business paves the road for the re-entry of Spanish capitals in the old colonies. Even though the terms and rhetoric of the new exchanges have obviously been modified, the renovated relations between Spain and Latin America are—needless to say—still marked by the sign of economic asymmetry and cultural condescension.

Under these circumstances, the study of the variety of cultures that are connected to or exist in the periphery of the Spanish language, either in Spain or in the Americas, requires innovative trans-disciplinary and transnational approaches that take into consideration the political, social, and cultural transformation of the international arena. Within this context, it is possible to predict that the highly politicized field of Hispanic studies will maintain its legitimacy and specificity at the academic level, particularly in view of the undeniable need to maintain the study of past colonialisms as one of the main foci of academic research. Furthermore, cultures and societies of Hispanic origin continue to be located at the margins of global arrangements, a position of obvious disadvantage that provides, nevertheless, a strategic critical perspective on dominant models, and calls for a strong political and cultural agenda for mobilization and research. The same can be said with respect to communities that speak nondominant languages both in Spain and in Spanish America, which continue the struggle to survive the effects of national colonialism, and to challenge the predominance of the Spanish language as well as the epistemological paradigms that are still being imposed upon them in order to assimilate them at theoretical, critical, and historiographical levels.

Finally, in yet another battlefield of Hispanic studies, it should be mentioned that literary and cultural studies conducted in Spanish or Portuguese in the United States and abroad are also receiving the impact of a more trendy and strongly institutionalized Latin Americanism or Peninsularism that finds in the

English language its primary vehicle for production and dissemination of theories and critical approaches on the literatures and cultures that constitute their field of study. In his polemic last article titled "Mestizaje e hibridez: el riesgo de las metáforas" (*Revista Iberoamericana,* 63/180 [1997]: 341–44) Antonio Cornejo Polar elaborated on this issue and its impact on Hispanic studies. The concerns expressed by the Peruvian critic, as well as the positions discussed in some of the responses triggered by his provocative piece, are implicitly echoed in many of the articles included in this volume. As Cornejo Polar suggested, the problem posed by the receding position of Spanish in Hispanic studies is far from being restricted to the use of the language. This fact also entails the application of epistemological paradigms created for other cultural realities, which are often forced upon Latin American and Spanish productions with little consideration for their historical, social, and cultural *differences* and, for that matter, for the subaltern position that those cultures still have in the global design. This occurs despite the fact that concepts such as difference, subalternity, and the like, constitute an integral part of current theoretical agendas that, nevertheless, frequently fail in identifying them when imbedded in their own practice and critical discourse. Non-dominant languages—indigenous and regional languages as well as Spanish and Portuguese (and the cultures they represent)—are then placed in secondary or tertiary positions with respect to English, which dominates, at least in the U.S., the scholarly production and reproduction of knowledge in the highly polemic fields of Hispanism, Peninsularism, and Latin American studies. By the same token, critical or theoretical approaches produced in languages other than English are often overlooked or ignored in transnational debates. These situations create obvious imbalances in the production of knowledge, and constitute some of the most flagrant and inexcusable contradictions affecting our field.

As we have seen, and as the articles included in this book thoroughly demonstrate, the predominance or subordination of the Spanish language and the particular ideologies embedded in the field of Hispanism are a shifting reality that varies depending on the historic, political, and cultural contexts considered in each case, and on the particular agendas to which academic practices and intellectual debates related to this field actually articulate. Far from diluting our political or professional responsibility, this position must keep us alert with respect to the forces at work in our field, the transnational parameters it involves, and the academic and pedagogical implications of our work. In my opinion, the tensions, contradictions, and paradoxes that cut across the field are precisely what keep it alive, connected to both the social communities that produce its objects of study, and the political and cultural processes that these communities continuously challenge and reshape. I hope that this book will contribute to the understanding of our academic practices and to the strengthening of liberating political agendas connected to them.

In closing, I would like to thank the contributors of this volume for their generous and patient cooperation. This book belongs to them. Special thanks to the editors of *Hispanic Issues* for the warm encouragement they gave to this project. Finally, I am very grateful to Nicholas Spadaccini for writing the final words that close this book and open it to new, constructive debates in our field.

Part I
Constructions of Hispanism:
The Spanish Language and Its Others

◆ 1

Spanish in the Sixteenth Century:
The Colonial Hispanization of Andean Indigenous
Languages and Cultures

Lydia Fossa

Evangelization was the main justification for the Spanish colonization of the Indies, but it could not be carried out without a common language. I will explore the circumstances of this seemingly focused religious activity from the perspective of its attached language policies and their application, and examine their disproportionate consequences for the survival of the Andean languages and cultures.

When first approaching the study of Andean hispanization, we see on the one hand that there were several royal decrees and laws requiring the teaching of Spanish to all inhabitants of the *New World* to facilitate their conversion; on the other hand, the evangelization in indigenous languages was happening prior to or in place of that teaching. I will analyze those simultaneous and apparently contradictory movements in linguistic colonization that characterize the fifty-year period between 1526 and 1576 in the Andes. The association between evangelization, hispanization, and the teaching of "good manners" will also be acknowledged, as well as the dramatic effects hispanization had on indigenous languages.

Evangelization, the Main Justification for Invasion

The Pope had the mission of promoting the dissemination of the New Testament throughout the world (Vitoria 227). If he so wished, he could transfer this responsibility to royalty. The Spanish Kings received it by way of the *Patronato.*[1] Through this Institution they received funding to exercise the missionary activities they entrusted to the religious orders and diocesan clergy in the Indies.

One of the first indications of the crucial economic and religious importance of the evangelization of the Indies is found in the Instructions of the King and Queen of Spain to Christopher Columbus, in 1497:

> Item: se debe procurar que vayan a las dichas Indias algunos religiosos e clérigos, buenas personas, para que allá administren los Santos Sacramentos a los que allá estarán, e procuren de convertir a nuestra santa fe católica a los dichos indios naturales de las dichas Indias . . . (Morales Padrón 79)

> (Item: it should be stressed that those going to the Indies be religious men, and clerics, good people, so they can administer the Sacraments to the ones that are already there. They should also endeavor to convert to our sacred Catholic faith the said natural Indians of the said Indies . . . (translation mine)

In 1509, in an Instruction to Admiral Diego Colón, issued by the Catholic King, Don Fernando V, the first paragraph instructs the Admiral on what to do in Hispaniola regarding "las cosas del servicio de Dios Nuestro Señor" (the things needed for the service of God Our Lord). This Instruction was issued to ensure that churches recently built were being used by the appointed clerics and friars who cared for the spiritual needs of both Christians and newly converted peoples. In the same Instruction, the King expressed his main wish:

> . . . mi principal deseo siempre ha sido y es en estas cosas de las Indias que los indios se conviertan a nuestra santa fe católica para que sus ánimas no se pierdan, para lo cual es menester que sean informados de las cosas de nuestra santa fe católica; ternéis muy gran cuidado cómo sin les hacer fuerza alguna, ansí las personas religiosas como aquellas a quien los dieren en nuestro nombre en encomienda, los instruyan e informen en las cosas de nuestra santa fe católica con mucho amor, para que los que se han ya convertido a nuestra santa fe, perseveren en ella y sirvan a Dios como buenos cristianos, y los que no se hobieren convertido hasta agora se conviertan lo más presto que ser pueda . . . (81)

(. . . my main wish has always been, and is, in these things related to the Indies, that indians be converted to our sacred Catholic faith so that their souls will not be lost. For that purpose it is necessary that they be informed of all things pertaining to our sacred Catholic faith. You, religious persons or those who receive them in *encomienda,* have to instruct them. You will be very careful in their instruction, teaching them without pressure. As for those who are already converted, inform them of our faith with love, to persevere in it and serve God as good Christians, and those who have not been converted yet, should be converted as fast as possible . . .)

Friars and *encomenderos* shared the responsibilities of converting indigenous populations in the *New World.* The conversion was not to be carried out under force or stress; infidels were to be informed and instructed in the Catholic religion. Conversion and the consolidation of the Christian faith were of equal importance, so the responsibilities Spaniards had did not disappear once the new peoples were converted. In order to organize these two activities better, the King of Spain ordered:

> . . . debéis mandar que en cada población haya una persona eclesiástica, cual convenga, para que esta persona tenga cuidado de procurar como sean bien tratados según lo tenemos mandado, y que tenga ansimismo especial cuidado de los enseñar las cosas de la fe; y a esta persona mandaréis hacer una casa cerca de la iglesia, de la parte donde habéis de mandar que se junten todos los niños de la tal población, para que allí los enseñen esta dicha persona las cosas de nuestra santa fe . . . (81)

(. . . you should order that a clergyman be in each village, as be fit, so that this person takes into himself that the Indians be well treated as we have commanded. He should also be very careful in teaching things of faith. You will have a house built for this person close to the church, in the section where the children of the village will get together so that this person will teach them the things of our sacred faith . . .)

The idea that indigenous peoples needed to be protected by a clergyman is clearly documented as early as 1509. The formal appointment of an officer for this purpose had to wait until 1538 in the Andes, but that need was felt early in the history of the Spanish presence in the Indies.

The order " . . . y trabajarán que los niños hablen y sepan nuestra lengua . . ." (. . . and you will work towards the goal of children speaking and knowing our language . . .) (Lisson Cháves 139) reminded the clergy in New Castile in a 1541 *Instrucción.* Children were the primary targets for early simultaneous acts of hispanization and evangelization.[2] They were ordered to be put under the supervision of a clergyman in houses built for that purpose near every church in the Andes. This religious contact at an early age meant isolating them from their kin in order to train them as instructors of their own people and preparing them for a life of close relationships with the Spanish community. The arguments used to support the evangelization of children included their docility as well as their ability to quickly learn the new language and concepts: " . . . los que son ya hombres con mucha dificultad la tomarán [la lengua] . . ." (. . . those who are already men will take [the language] with great difficulty . . .) (139). Fray Vicente de Valverde wrote in 1537 that the linguistic and religious project was destined, first, to the children of native lords: "Que los hijos de los caçiques y señores siendo pequeños estén cierto tiempo en las casas de los religiosos hasta que sean enseñados para que ellos enseñen a los otros en sus pueblos" (That the children of *caciques* and lords while they are small, should spend some time in clergymen's houses until they are taught so they, in turn, will teach others in their villages) (20). Spaniards believed that conversion of the children of the native nobility in a Spanish context would foster a rapid integration. This belief, and the lack of monasteries in the early Sixteenth century in the Andean region, spurred religious and civil authorities to send or take children and young men to the Iberian Peninsula to learn Spanish, as the same friar stated in his 1539 letter to the King (115). Valverde also expressed the need to designate a special location in the Spanish towns in the Indies in order to have alternative indoctrination to that carried out in houses adjacent to churches (21). The idea was to educate, within Catholic principles, the future lords of indigenous communities (Solano 1993, 295).

Spanish historian Paulino Castañeda boldly states that: "La lengua siempre fue considerada como indispensable para dar un paso en el mundo infiel. He dicho *siempre*. No sólo en 1492. En cualquier preparación misionera el conocimiento de las lenguas fue fundamental" (Language was always considered essential to advance in the infidel world. I said *always*. Not only in 1492. In any missionary preparation the knowledge of languages was fundamental) (29). The experience with Muslim as well as Jewish communities in the Iberian Peninsula was decisive in approaching the Indies' multilinguism.[3] Linguistic policies were implemented in the Indies following those applied to other ethnic and linguistic groups living in the Peninsula, such as Catalans and Basques: "Trato y escuelas para los niños y niñas indios, a cargo de sacristanes alfabetos que les enseñen a leer y escribir: facilitando la difusión del castellano y la erradicación de sus lenguas y costumbres. El castellano, así, sería una lengua general, tal como se efectuó en España con áreas catalanas y vascas" (Manners and schools for indian boys and girls in charge of literate sacristans who teach them to read and write, facilitating the spread of Castilian and the eradication of their languages and customs. In this way, Castilian would end up being a general language, in the same was as it was in Spain with Catalan and Basque areas) (Solano 298–99). The Spanish experiences in Africa and the Canary Islands, where similar linguistic situations were found, were also considered valuable.[4]

The way of dealing with the lack of linguistic communication in the Andes speaks of previous similar activities in other places. This is evident when observing how the matter was approached, either by individual Spaniards, or by corporate entities such as the Royal administration, or by religious orders. Invariably, everyone knew what to do. They were simply repeating what they had done before: impose the Spanish language and customs while battling the *other's* languages and customs on every front.

The group of young men who underwent indoctrination were known as "los muchachos de la doctrina" or "los muchachos que enseñan la doctrina" (the doctrine boys or the boys who teach doctrine) (Husson 265). Children were drawn into church schools not only to evangelize and hispanicize them, but also, and mainly, to turn them into auxiliary clergy: " . . . sirviendo la escuela para la promoción elitista de una parte de la población indígena [los hijos de la nobleza] así como a la formación de personal auxiliar en las iglesias" (. . . school serving for the elitist promotion of one part of the indigenous population [children of nobility] as well as for the preparation of auxiliary personnel for the churches) (Solano 295).

The first addresses or *Requerimientos* were read in Spanish by either soldiers or priests, to speakers of indigenous languages in the early Sixteenth century.[5] In the 1530s, there was a special *Requerimiento* written for the Peruvian territory, a document known as "Requerimiento que se ha de hazer a los yndios del Peru" (The *Requerimiento* that should be done to the Indians of Peru) (Lisson Cháves 22). In this case, Spaniards counted on the assistance of indigenous interpreters when available, even though the "lenguas" scarcely knew Spanish or even the languages into which they were interpreting (Castañeda 30).[6] Friars resorted to symbols like the crosses they were carrying, and later to drawings, pictures, and theater. They seldom transmitted their religious messages in the way it was supposed to be done, peacefully and lovingly, so that Spanish authorities had to insist for centuries on this matter as evidenced by their numerous decrees.[7] A blatant example of the way these first communications were implemented is the *Requerimiento*,[8] written following *Patronato* directives "en virtud de ser territorios reconquistados al Islam" (by virtue of being territories reconquered from Islam) in the late Fifteenth and early Sixteenth centuries (Garrido 21), and later because the Indies were believed to be territories conquered from the devil.[9]

Spaniards had dealt before with infidel communities who spoke other languages, as their Reconquest experiences show us. They were amply aware that in order to evangelize properly, a language common to cleric and catechumen had to be used. They also knew that mutual language knowledge was not a short-term project, and that indigenous individuals had to be evangelized before they died. Having no language in common, Spaniards resorted to violence. One of the first steps taken by clerics and laymen alike was to destroy the natives' temples and adoratories as well as their idolatrous images.[10] The second was to outlaw their religious customs and ceremonies as evidenced in the 1509 *Instrucción* given to Diego Colón by King Ferdinand V:

> ... habéis de dar orden que los indios no hagan las fiestas ni cerimonias que solian hacer si por ventura las hacen, sino que tengan en su vivir la forma que las otras gentes de nuestros reinos, y esto se ha de procurar en ellos poco a poco y con mucha maña, sin los escandalizar ni maltratar. (Morales Padrón 82)

> (. . . you should mandate that Indians do not celebrate the festivities or the ceremonies they used to if they celebrate at all. They should incorporate in their living the ways of other peoples in our kingdoms, and this should be little by little and pursued with great tact, without scandalizing or mistreating them.)

Under papal authority, any Christian Spaniard could command infidels or barbarous peoples under tyrannical rule to abstain from their rites and customs when they were not in accordance with the Catholic faith (Vitoria 231). In addition to changing their ceremonies and celebrations, King Fernando V informed Diego Colón in 1509 of the way in which the Indies' inhabitants should live:

> Ansimismo, porque Nos hobimos mandado al dicho comendador mayor que entendiese con mucha diligencia en que los indios de la dicha isla Española viniesen [sic for viviesen] juntamente en poblaciones como los nuestros naturales viven en estos reinos y que cada uno tenga su casa aparte y mujeres e hijos, y heredad conocida; sabréis lo que está hecho en esto, y si estuviere algo por cumplir dello, trabajad que se haga lo más presto que pudiéredes, mandando hacer las poblaciones donde mejor vos paresciere para el bien de los pobladores de ella . . . (82)

> (Also, we ordered the said *comendador mayor* to take diligent care in that the indians of the said island of Hispanola come [sic for live] together in towns as our nationals live in these kingdoms, having each of them a separate house with women and children and known property. You should be informed what has been done on this matter, and if anything were still to be done regarding this matter, you

will work towards it as fast as you can, ordering the towns to be built where in your
opinion would be better for the benefit of their inhabitants . . .)

One aspect which differs from those of the Reconquest was the absence of
towns or populated areas in America. In the "New World," indigenous peoples
was scattered, *derramados,* all over the land. The concept of *civitas* was foreign
to them, as well as that of *poliçia. Poliçia* was the appropriate way to live in a
"republic of Christians," that is, in a society formed by families that lived in a
specified location and that had economic bonds to a specific land or to the land
of the lord who ruled it. Thus, in order to enable evangelization when the Conquest had just ended, towns had to be built according to the Spanish style.

Along with these requirements, came the way Indians should dress and
carry themselves: " . . . ansimismo ha de procurar la persona suso dicha que
los indios se vistan e anden como hombres razonables" (" . . . also the person
just mentioned should make certain that the Indians dress and carry themselves
as reasonable men) (82). Even the food they ate was put into question, and
Spanish food was mandated: " . . . por ser nuevamente convertidos a la fee y
no tener tantos manjares como los xpianos se les permite que puedan comer
carne y huevos queso etc [leche, manteca] en todo el otro tiempo de la qua-
resma y vigilias . . ." (. . . since they are new converts to the faith and do not
have as many delicacies as Christians do they are allowed to eat meat and eggs,
cheese, etc. [milk, lard] during the remaining time of Lent and vigils . . .)
(Lisson Cháves 141). The 1509 Instruction commanded that Indians should follow "reasonable" (meaning Spanish) customs in dress, and should also behave
in an appropriate manner, that is, as Spaniards.

The *Leyes de Burgos* (1512), known as the ordinances for the treatment of
the Indians, dictated by Ferdinand, the Catholic King were designed to attain
success in the evangelization of natives in the Caribbean. The reasons given by
the King made evident the need for the establishment of strict norms of social
behavior:

> . . . el principal estorbo que tienen para no se enmendar de sus vicios y que la
> doctrina no les aproveche ni en ellos imprima ni la tomen es tener sus asientos y
> estancias tan lejos como los tienen y apartados de los lugares donde viven los espa-
> ñoles . . . porque al tiempo que los vienen a servir [a los españoles], los doctrinen
> y enseñen las cosas de nuestra fe como después de haber servido se vuelven a sus
> estancias con estar apartadas y la mala inclinación que tienen, olvidan luego todo
> lo que les han enseñado y tornan a su acostumbrada ociosidad y vicios y cuando
> otra vez se vuelven a servir está tan nuevos en la doctrina como de primero, . . . y
> viendo que esto es tan contrario a nuestra fe y cuanto somos obligados a que por

todas las vías y maneras del mundo que ser pueda se busque algún remedio . . . (Morales Padrón 312–13)

(. . . the main barrier they have for not amending their vices, allowing doctrine to be useless to them since they do not adhere to it, is having their living quarters too far from the places where Spaniards live . . . When they come to serve [Spaniards], and be taught the doctrine and other things of our faith after having served, they return to where they live, and since they are so far away, and with the evil inclination they have, they soon forget everything they were taught and go back to their usual laziness and vices. When again they return to serve, they are as new in the doctrine as they were the first time, . . . and seeing that all this is so contrary to our faith and since we are obliged to look for a remedy to this in all ways and manners in the world . . .)

The ways of life found in the Indies, utterly different from those of the invaders, were the source of numerous legal dispositions written with the goal of transforming indigenous customs into what Spaniards believed were "good manners," the ways used in the Iberian Peninsula. A later Ordinance from Charles I, dated in 1526, reiterated that the first thing to be done upon arrival in new lands was "procurar, por lenguas de intérpretes que entiendan los indios . . . cómo Nos les enviamos para los enseñar buenas costumbres . . ." (your endeavor should be that Indians have to understand, through interpreters' tongues, how We send you to teach them good manners . . .) (Solano 16). The Crown's urgency was not only that natives had to be evangelized quickly, but that they also had to transform the way they lived by adopting Spanish customs. Christianity thus was not only a faith; it was also a way of life. New Christians had to adopt both the faith and the mores.[11]

In 1526 new Ordinances regarding the appropriate treatment of natives were made public. King Charles I admonished the men in charge of "entries" and "new discoveries" that:

. . . los descubrimientos y poblaciones que de aquí adelante se hubieren de hacer, se hagan sin ofensa de Dios y sin muertes ni robos de los dichos indios y sin cautivarlos por esclavos indebidamente de manera que el deseo que habemos tenido y tenemos de ampliar nuestra santa fe y que los dichos indios e infieles vengan en conocimiento della se haga sin cargo de nuestras conciencias y se prosiga nuestro propósito y la intención y obra de los Reyes Católicos, nuestros abuelos y señores . . . (Morales Padrón 375)

(. . . the discoveries and settlements should be undertaken from now on without offending God, and without the killings and robberies of the said Indians, and without holding them captive as slaves unlawfully, in a way that the wish we have had and have of extending our sacred faith and that the said Indians reach their knowledge should be done without charging our consciences, continuing with our purpose and the intention and deeds of the Catholic Kings, our grandfathers and lords . . .)

It goes on to specify, in very clear terms, that further killings, enslavements, and other forms of oppression of the Indians would not be tolerated. The King insisted that the true intentions of the Conquest were "enseñar las buenas costumbres . . . y a instruirlos en nuestra santa fe . . ." (teach good manners . . . and instruct them in our sacred faith . . .) (Morales Padrón 377).[12] He clearly indicated that the two issues were interrelated and also that the first was the prerequisite for the latter. Learning the appropriate behavior would open up the way to Catholicism. In this early period, the use of interpreters was expected and encouraged as the best means for religious instruction.

In Francisco Pizarro's Capitulation signed by the Queen of Spain in 1529, the need to take priests with him was reiterated.[13] Spanish authorities had by then realized that priests were needed to temper the greed of newcomers and the subsequent violence that surged if gold was withheld from them in any way, imagined or real.[14] The riches were not only anticipated by soldiers and sailors; the *Hacienda,* or Spanish tribute agency, was also in pursuit of wealth. Officers from the Real Hacienda were mentioned before the clergymen, underscoring their importance and the fact that no expedition would be complete without them. The Crown wanted the riches and was willing to exchange evangelization efforts, through the *Patronato,* for gold. In this Spanish equation, the Crown won (riches) and the indigenous peoples won (salvation) while the clergy and the soldiers were left to manage with the surplus, usually independent Indian labor. For the secular man, this was not negligible, while the religious communities would thrive on native labor and *diezmos* as they fulfilled their obligations of delivering the true faith to the locals.

By 1541, Spaniards had been in the area for almost ten years. Archbishop Jerónimo de Loayza, O.P., continued reminding them that in order to justify their presence in the Indies all of them, laymen and clerics, had to contribute to make the evangelization pledge a reality:

" . . . Por quanto el título y fin del descubrimiento y conquista destas partes a sido la predicación del evangelio y conversión de los naturales dellas al conoscimiento de dios nuestro señor y aunque esto generalmente obliga a todos los xpianos que acá han pasado, especialmente y de oficio yncumbe a los perlados en sus diocesys . . ." (Lisson Cháves 134)

(. . . Since the title and end of the discovery and conquest of these parts has been the preaching of the gospel and the conversion of natives into the knowledge of God our Lord and even though this generally obliges all Christians who have passed here, it especially and professionally concerns the bishops in their dioceses . . .)

This insistence on the same objectives was due in part to the fact that new *heathen* ethnic groups were being *discovered* by Spaniards and new territories were being incorporated into the Viceroyalty of New Castile.

The *Nuevas Leyes,* written in 1542 and made public in 1543, delineated the same objectives of the discoveries and colonization, stressing a protective approach towards indigenous populations.[15] They spoke in an admonishing tone towards those who failed to treat Indians well. This document encompasses an interesting difference with respect to previous ones: it exhibits a clear intention to accept some of the natives' customs regarding land tenure, as if to compensate for previous totalizing prohibitions and interdictions:

. . . que no se den lugar a que en los pleitos de entre yndios o con ellos se hagan proçessos ordinarios ni aya alargas, como suele acontesçer por la maliçia de algunos abogados y procuradores sino que sumariamente sean determinados, guardando sus usos y costunbres no siendo claramente ynjustos . . . (Morales Padrón 434)

(. . . it should not be allowed that disputes between Indians or against them turn into ordinary legal processes nor they should be overly extended, as happens through the wickedness of some lawyers and solicitors, but those disputes should be summarily determined, in keeping with their uses and customs when they are not clearly unfair . . .)

This modification of the attitude observed in previous documents owes its presence to the indefatigable efforts of some outstanding Dominican friars such as Bartolomé de Las Casas and Francisco de Vitoria. These two men, and other members of the Order, such as Domingo de Santo Tomás, and Tomás de San Martín, as well as educated laymen such as Polo Ondegardo and the self-taught historian Pedro de Cieza de León, supported the idea that indigenous customs not interfering with Catholicism were to be allowed as long as they did not "scandalize" or alienate clergy in particular, and Spaniards in general. This change in attitude gave indigenous peoples more opportunities to continue celebrating some of their festivities. This tendency to permit some ceremonies that were not immediately identified as sacred or "infidel" had an important impact on judicial standards through the acknowledgement of Indians' *fueros,* especially those regarding land tenure and possession, and the ensuing Spanish litigation.

Evangelization without Language

It soon became evident that land and gold could be obtained without much linguistic difficulty. However, when it came to evangelizing, things were completely different.[16] The first contacts with Andean indigenous populations in the 1530s had been made with the intervention of interpreters, with a modest level of success (Fossa, *Narrativas*). Those first interactions consisted mainly of the Spanish presenting themselves as vassals of the Spanish King and followers of the Church of Jesus Christ.[17] Some objects were exchanged, and large meals regularly provided by the "hosts" were lavishly enjoyed by both locals and foreigners.[18] Thereafter, Spanish soldiers only wanted to know where the gold was and how they could obtain it:

> " . . . [Candia] dixo que vio cantaros de plata y estar labrando a muchos plateros y que por algunas paredes del tenplo avia planchas de oro y plata y que las mujeres que llamavan del Sol, que heran muy hermosas. Locos estaban de plazer los españoles de oyr tantas cosas; esperavan en Dios de gozar su parte dello." (Cieza 60)

> (. . . [Candia] said he saw silver pitchers and many silversmiths doing their craft, and that some walls in the temple were gold- and silver-plated, and that the women who were said to be of the Sun were very beautiful. The Spaniards were mad with pleasure of hearing so many things, and they waited in God to have their share of it . . .)

After 1533, when the soldiers had settled in the Andean region, few members of the clergy were available in Ciudad de los Reyes (Lima) to perform the desired and ordered evangelization. Vicente de Valverde, the Dominican friar who accompanied Pizarro in Cajamarca, was his cousin (Pérez 44) and political ally (Pérez 54). He was one of the few clergymen active in those years, though his activities were reduced to destroying natives' idols and temples:[19]

> Y como los Ingas reynaron en esta tierra y señorearon este valle aunque por ellos fue mandado edificar en él templo del sol tan grande y principal como solian en las demas partes no dexaron de hazer sus ofrendas y sacrificios a este Guaribilca. Lo qual todo assi lo uno como lo otro esta deshecho y ruynado y lleno de grandes hervaçales y malezas porque entrando en este valle el governador don Francisco

Piçarro dizen los indios que el obispo fray Vicente de Valverde quebro las figuras y los ydolos. (Cieza 244)

(And as the Incas ruled in this land and were lords of this valley, even though they had had the large and important temple of the Sun built as they used to do in other parts, they did not stop making their offerings and sacrifices to the Guaribilca. All that, this as well as the other, is now destroyed and ruined and all covered by tall weeds and brush because upon entering this valley Governor Francisco Pizarro, Bishop Vicente de Valverde tore down the figures and the idols, Indians say.)

A second source, Fray Juan Meléndez of the Dominican Order (Pérez 67), confirms Cieza's information and adds: " . . . ni fue sola en este genero esta hazaña del padre Fr. Vicente que cuantas huacas hallaba por el camino las pisaba y echaba por el suelo (llaman huacas los indios no solamente a los idolos sino a todos los lugares adonde los adoran . . .) levantando su celo en todas partes el estandarte santisimo de la cruz . . ." (. . . this deed of father Fra Vicente was not an isolated event in this category, since every *huaca* found on the road was taken down and stomped over [Indians call *huaca* not only the idols but also all the sites where they adore them . . .] raising with his zeal everywhere the most sacred banner of the cross . . .) (Pérez 67). Other religious orders were aware of these activities. An Augustinian friar wrote *circa* 1561: "No por esto digo que las otras órdenes como el Señor Santo Domingo y Sant Françisco no an travaxado muncho y sacado munchos ydolos y en la predicaçión del evangelio hecha como varones apostólicos" (This is not to say that other orders such as that of Lord Saint Dominic and Saint Francis have not worked much and removed many idols, or that their preaching of the gospels has been done as one would expect of apostolic men) (San Pedro 9). [20]

In addition to temple destruction and image desecration, Valverde was performing his evangelical duty through sermons that were translated by interpreters.

Fray Vicente va derecho a *coricancha,* casa hecha por los incas antiquísimos para el hacedor. Al fin la ley de dios y su santo evangelio tan deseado entró a tomar posesión de la nueva viña, que estaba usurpada por los Enemigos antiguos. Allí predica todo el tiempo como otro santo Tomás el apóstol, patrón de este reino, sin descansar, con el celo de ganar almas haciéndolos convertirse, bautizando a los curacas con hisopos no más, porque no pudieron echar agua a cada uno. Que si hubiera sabido la lengua hubiera sido mucha su diligencia, mas por intérprete hablaba. (Santa Cruz 129; Pérez 67)

(Friar Vicente goes directly to the Coricancha, a house built by the very ancient Incas for the Maker. Finally, the law of God and his so desired sacred gospel entered and took possession of the new vineyard that had been taken by the ancient Enemies. There he preaches all the time, as a second Saint Thomas the Apostle, patron of this kingdom, tirelessly, with the zeal of gaining souls, converting them, baptizing the kuraka only with hyssops because they could not pour water on each one. Had he known the language his diligence would have been great, however he spoke only through an interpreter.)

In 1534 Fray Vicente Valverde traveled to Spain (Araníbar 870), and arrived in September 1535 (Pérez 97). His application to be a bishop, whose seat would be in Cuzco, was presented at that time although he stayed in the Peninsula until November 1537. While in Spain, Valverde recruited a group of eight Dominican priests who arrived in Peru in May or June 1537 (Pérez 97). Bishop Valverde arrived in Cuzco in November 1538 (Pérez 97). During his absence, another Dominican priest had visited Peru.

Bishop Tomás de Berlanga arrived in Lima in 1535 with two missions: to check the accounting systems of the Conquerors to ensure that the King had received what he was due of the conquest's pillage, and to observe to what extent Pizarro had complied with the *Capitulación* he had received in 1529 regarding the Catholic instruction of the natives as established by the *Patronato*. Once he had finished his investigation, Bishop Berlanga wrote a *Requerimiento* for Pizarro, admonishing him for not having distributed the Indians to their *encomenderos,* except within his own family and for not having established the tax they had to pay. He also stated that "se ha descuidado la instrucción de los indios en la fe y urge llevarla a efecto, pues 'los padres de San Francisco han dicho que, si no dan que hagan, que se irían'" (the instruction of Indians in the faith has been neglected and it urgently needs to be undertaken, for the Franciscans fathers have said that they would leave if it is not made to happen) (Pérez 63). No real evangelization had taken place in New Castile, as far as high-ranking church officers were concerned.

Most of the information available regarding evangelization in the second half of the 1530s revolves around the figure of Fray Vicente Valverde. There are few documents that cover his years in Spain during this decade or in the New World except for letters he sent to Spain when he was in Cuzco as a Bishop in 1538 and 1539. By that time, he had also been named *Protector de Indios* (Lisson Cháves 20) as had been included in his selection of manuscripts from the Archivo de Indias, a *Memorial* attributed to Valverde. It is undated and unsigned, but bears a note saying: "esto para quando el obispo de los Reyes vino y órdenes que dio para la doctrina" (this for when Bishop of Los Reyes came and orders he gave for the doctrine). This note suffices to date the document around 1536 and to identify Vicente Valverde as the one who had written and presented it to Spanish authorities. This *Memorial* was most likely written in anticipation of what Bishop Berlanga would find in Los Reyes:

> –Que se embien luego Religiosos de las hordenes mendicantes para que hagan monasterios y enseñen a los yndios.
> –Que los hijos de los caciques y señores, siendo pequeños, esten cierto tiempo en las casas de los religiosos hasta que sean enseñados para que ellos enseñen a los otros en sus pueblos.
> –Que en los pueblos de los xpianos aya, junto a la yglesia, una casa que sea como escuela, donde esten y residan tambien los hijos de los caciques y que aya una persona particular que los dotrine y enseñe alli porque seria posible que ubiese tantos que no se pudiesen tener en los monesterios.
> –Que los que tuvieren copia de yndios sean obligados a tener con ellos quien los doctrine en las cosas de nuestra sancta fee catolica y, a los que tuvieren pocos, que tengan todos juntos un clerigo en comarca de sus yndios, donde todos se lleguen a ser doctrinados de manera que por toda la tierra aya aparejo para que los yndios sean enseñados. Ay mucha necesidad desto en todas las tierras de los yndios como vemos que entre los xpianos que aca son en España la tienen, con ser xpianos. (Lisson Cháves 20–21)

> (–Clergymen of the mendicant orders should be sent soon to build monasteries and teach Indians.
> –Children of Caciques and Lords, while small, shall remain for a period of time in the clergymen's houses until they have been taught, so they can teach others in their towns.
> –In Christian towns there should be a house to be used as school next to the church where the children of *caciques* will stay and live. An appointed person should indoctrinate and teach them because there might be so many that the monasteries will not be large enough to house them.
> –Those who have numerous Indians should be obliged to have someone indoctrinate them in the things of our sacred faith, and, those who have few, should come together to have a cleric where their Indians live, and where all of them can go to be indoctrinated in such a way that in all the land there be arrangements for teaching the Indians. There is a great need of this in all Indian lands in the same way that among Christians who are here in Spain)

This document spelled out the policy that would guide evangelization and hispanization activities in the Andean region. It was a plan of action that first stated the need to have more priests. Those priests would have monasteries built where doctrinal lessons could be imparted to the children of *prinçipales*.

Then, he mentioned that in every Christians town, adjacent to the church, a house should be built for the same indoctrination tasks, always singling out children as their students. Thirdly, Valverde indicated that those who had Indians in their charge had to evangelize them. *Encomenderos* could do this in two ways: explaining the dogmas of the Church and teaching the prayers to the natives under their care if they were few, or hiring a cleric to do it if the Indians were numerous. The responsibility of Catholic indoctrination was then shared by *encomenderos* and clerics. In the 1530s, there were very few clerics and a large number of *encomenderos,* so it was mainly the responsibility of the latter to indoctrinate native populations.

Valverde did not mention languages in his plan, but since he wanted children to live with Catholic priests fresh from Spain and learn the doctrine from them, one can infer that he meant evangelization in Spanish to native children. Valverde himself never learned native languages and was compelled to resort to interpreters to translate his sermons and to aid him in hearing confessions.

In a letter Valverde wrote to the King in 1539, he recalled that in his trip to Spain in 1534 he took "ocho o nueve indios ansi chicos como grandes para lenguas . . . y con poner toda la diligencia posible en curallos no me quedo sino uno . . ." (eight or nine Indians, both young and old to be interpreters . . . and despite being diligent in caring for them, only one was spared . . .) (Lisson Cháves 115). Besides the information regarding the transport of Indians to the Peninsula, I wish to underscore the interest of Valverde in having interpreters trained and taught in Spain. At the end of that same paragraph, Valverde told the King that there was no more need to take natives abroad to teach them Spanish because "aca se pueden enseñar sin que se lleven a esas partes, no se devria sacar de la tierra" (they can be taught here without taking them to those parts [Spain]; they should not be taken from the land) (115). Priests needed interpreters to evangelize adults, for the translation of sermons, and to hear confessions. These early sermons in Spanish are barely comprehensible today. One can only imagine them "translated" into native languages by unskilled *lenguas* who were also new to Catholicism, and wonder about the impact those strange advocations/admonitions had on recent converts. Sermons were preached using theatrical and rhetorical strategies to people who had a different protocol for the spoken word.[21]

What Valverde's message meant was that the regular clergy would be responsible for the indoctrination of children in Spanish while secular clergy or *doctrineros* would do the work for *encomenderos.* Thus, he separated his flock into two sections, that of the children and that of adults, each with a different linguistic approach.[22] Within the group of children or young men, there was another differentiation, that of class. Children of *principales* would attend daily classes in houses adjacent to churches or live with the friars; children of the commoners would be indoctrinated by clerics or *encomenderos* in church atria. Secular clergy and *encomenderos* would deal with adult evangelization in native languages through the intervention of interpreters until they themselves learned local languages. The same had been done before in New Spain, where the Franciscan friars developed this policy (Garrido 56–58), adapting it from their experience with the Moorish population in Granada.

Valverde also had good news regarding evangelization in his 1539 letter to the King: "aca ay fundadas iglesias y muchos christianos y se enseñan las cosas de Dios con toda diligencia y cuidado . . ." (here there are founded churches and many Christians and the things of God are taught with all diligence and care . . .) (Lisson Cháves 115). However, he is contradicted by the Licentiate Martel de Santoyo, who wrote in 1542 that nothing had been done in regard to catechization (conversion and indoctrination) by clerics who had not even learned the indigenous languages.[23]

The famous Dominican Francisco de Vitoria, in 1536, asked the members of the academic milieu of Salamanca, in his Relection *De Indiis,* quoting Saint Paul: "¿Acaso, dice, no han oído?" (Perchance, he says, you have not heard?) (Vitoria 206). Those who had not heard were the indigenous populations. Vitoria was saying that understanding is another way of interpreting "hearing." Further, that not having heard or understood is not the listeners' fault, but rather the fault of those who tell. Lack of hearing and understanding are in the same category of causes for the *invincible ignorance* attributed to the natives: "Esos tales que nunca oyeron hablar de la fe, por muy pecadores que por otra parte sean, ignoran invenciblemente, luego su ignorancia no es pecado . . . si no se les ha predicado la fe, ignoran invenciblemente, porque no pueden conocerla" (Those ones who never heard about faith, as sinners as they can otherwise be, ignore invicibly, thus their ignorance is not a sin . . . if faith has not been preached to them, they invincibly ignore because they cannot know it) (Vitoria 206). He was also referring to the fact that there were no priests in the Indies before Columbus and to the poor communication between priests and non-believers afterwards. Vitoria stressed the importance of determining in which language people were going to be evangelized because their hearing and understanding and then accepting the word of God depended on that choice. If the word of God was spoken in a language foreign to those hearing it, how could they be held responsible for believing, or even understanding, what was said?[24]

This is the position most religious orders would hold dear along the first half of the Sixteenth century: teach the natives in their language so they could hear and understand.[25] That is why Duverger affirmed:[26]

> La primera decisión estratégica tomada por los misioneros es la de recurrir, sistemáticamente, a las lenguas indígenas. Se podrá objetar que se trata de una elección puramente pragmática, dictada por las necesidades de la comunicación. Eso es absolutamente falso. Se trata de una opción que contiene toda una filosofía del apostolado. Los religiosos hubieran perfectamente podido hacer como los conquistadores: hablar en castellano con los indios. Eligiendo expresarse en las lenguas del país, los franciscanos se distinguen netamente de los españoles presentes en México y se construyen así una 'imagen' cuidadosamente diferenciada. (163)

> (The missionaries' first strategic decision is to systematically resort to indigenous languages. This fact can be contested, saying that it is a purely pragmatic choice dictated by communication needs. That is absolutely false. It is an option that contains an apostolic philosophy. Clergymen could very well have done as conquerors did: speak Spanish to the Indians. In choosing to express themselves in the languages of the country, Franciscans appear as distinct from other Spaniards present in Mexico, thus constructing a carefully differentiated 'image.')

This is also true of the Dominicans, the order that had the most friars in the Andean region between 1536 and 1556. In order to overcome that *invincible ignorance,* priests should speak the word of God in the language of the Incas. This was the position of the Dominican clergy, followers of Vitoria, and other great thinkers within their Order. From this position, they built their argument of first learning the language of the inhabitants of the Indies to evangelize the adults:

> D'une façon générale, les missionnaires espagnols aux Indes préféraient apprendre les langues de leurs ouailles indigènes plutôt que de leur enseigner le castillan. Pour les Dominicaines, qui avaient plus que d'autres le souci d'une évangélisation patiente, progressive et approfondie, la connaissance de ces langues était indispensable en vue de l'administration des sacrements, notamment du baptême et de la pénitence. (Saint-Lu 42)

> (In a general sense, the Spanish missionaries in the Indies preferred to learn the languages of their indigenous flock more than teach them Castilian. For the Dominicans, who cherished more than others a patient, progressive and deep evangelization, the knowledge of those languages was utterly important, considering the sacraments' administration, especially Baptism and Penitence.)

Concurrently, Dominicans evangelized the children of the *principales* in their convents or their dwellings and taught them Spanish. Some of those children were taken to Spain to be catechized in Spanish. In this respect, Milhou suggests that evangelization in indigenous languages is a transitory situation that whould progressively retreat in favor of hispanization. He adds: "C'est pourquoi le Conseil des Indes continua, sans se faire probablement trop d'illusions, de préconiser à la fois l'enseignement du castillan, but ultime, et d'encourager l'apprentissage des langues indienne par les religieux et les curés *doctrineros*" (That is why the Council of the Indies continues, probably without harboring too many hopes, supporting simultaneously the teaching of Castilian, their ultimate aim, and encouraging clergymen and *doctrinero* priests to learn indigenous languages) (35–36). I agree that the ulterior aim is hispanization, but I believe evangelization in Spanish and indigenous languages was a double-sided policy that simultaneously worked to achieve results in the minimal amount of time possible.

Nonetheless, it was soon evident that spreading the word of Christ in languages other than Spanish caused great confusion among the indigenous catechumens, for their languages had no words for the main Christian conceptualizations and dogmas. This apparent deficiency provoked that: " . . . les constitutions synodales et mandements épiscopaux de l'Espagne des XVIème and XVIIème siècles insistaient sur la nécesité de la cathéquisation et de la prédication dans les langues vulgaires de la péninsule" (. . . the Synod constitutions and bishop instructions of Sixteenth- and Seventeenth-century Spain insisted on the need of cathequization and preaching in the vulgar languages of the Peninsula) (37). In the 1540s, it was still quite difficult for priests to communicate with "Indians" despite their efforts to learn native languages and to hispanize the recent converts.

In 1541, in Ciudad de los Reyes, Archbishop Loayza instructed his clergy, and Christians in general, to impart the teachings of the Church in any way possible: " . . . en la dicha yglesia se junten para . . . dotrinalos en las cosas de nuestra santa fee y conoscimiento de dios nuestro señor; por manera que a los dichos indios se les dira como lo entiendan que . . ." (. . . in the said church they should get together for . . . indoctrination in the things of our sacred faith and knowledge of God our Lord; the said Indians should be told in a way they understand that . . .) (Lisson Cháves 136). And also: " . . . les hagan entender en la mejor manera que se pudiere la general obligacion que los hombres tenemos a dios por su suma bondad . . . platicandoles el misterio y razones de la encarnacion . . ." (. . . they should be made to understand in the best possible way the general obligation that as men we have towards God for His supreme good-ness . . . talking about the mystery and reasons of the encarnation . . .) (136). In the early days of the first half of the Sixteenth century this meant evangelizing through drawings and paintings shown to natives, and later through theatrical exhibitions would complete the range of teaching materials utilized. As late as the Seventeenth century, Guaman Poma de Ayala believed it was necessary to convey religious ideas through paintings: " . . . y así en las iglesias y templos de Dios haya curiosidad y muchas pinturas de los santos, y en cada iglesia haya un juicio pintado alli, muestre la venida del Señor al juicio, el cielo y el mundo y las penas del infierno para que sea testigo del cristiano pecador" (. . . and so in the churches and temples of God there should be particular care and diligence and many paintings of the saints, and in each church there should be a Final Judgement painted there to show the coming of our Lord to the Judgement, the heavens, and the world, and the suffering in Hell so that He [el Señor] can be a witness of the Christian sinner) (547–48).[27] There were still very few "lenguas" friars could count on.

Loayza instructed those who undertook the task of teaching Christianity to the natives to transform those people of "poor understanding"—"los naturales de estas partes son gentes de poco entendimiento" (—indigenous peoples of these parts are people of little understanding) (Lisson Cháves 138)—into active Christians through the use of any and all means accessible to them.

The Colonial Hispanization of Indigenous Languages

Dominican priests, following Saint Paul's lead in the practice of evangelization in maternal languages, a time-honored Church tradition, started learning those languages to be able to instruct natives in their own tongues (Milhou 36). This project, though urgent, was long-term. Priests soon observed that Tawantinsuyu was a "mosaic" of languages (Mannheim 2), and that some of those languages, three or four, were used and could continue to be used as "general languages."[28] Those common languages were the ones Dominicans and Mercedaries started learning. Augustinians and Jesuits would later follow suit. The urgency of the matter and its importance for Spain and for Rome sanctioned this avenue as adequate and practical.

By 1541, many *cartillas* (primers) in native general languages, Quechua, Aymara, and Puquina, were being used in evangelization. In his Instruction of that year, the Dominican Archbishop Loayza ordered *doctrineros* to stop using the *cartillas* in the general languages. They were to be replaced with the ones then in use in Spain, until a model *cartilla* in native languages could be developed:

> . . . somos ynformados que con santo y virtuoso zelo se han hecho algunas cartillas en las lenguas de los naturales donde se contienen los principios de nuestra fee y porque aun no nos consta que las dichas cartillas o algunas dellas este traduzida y corregida conforme a la propiedad y sygnificacion de la lengua latina o de nuestro Romance castellano; por ende, queriendo proveer en lo susodicho como en cosa que al servicio de Dios nuestro señor y al descargo de nuestra conciencia y officio tanto ymporta, mandamos, so pena de excomunion mayor *latae sententie* a todos los que, como dicho es, al presente estan doctrinando los naturales o adelante fueren nombrados para ello asi en esta cibdad de los Reyes como en todo nuestro Arçobispado que doctrinen y enseñen los dichos naturales en el estilo general que es en la lengua latina o en Romance castellano conforme a lo contenido en las cartillas que de españa vienen ympresas y por el presente no husen de las dichas cartillas hechas en su lengua fasta tanto que por nos juntamente con los autores dellas y otras personas que entiendan bien su lengua sean vistas y examinadas y de las que asi estan hechas se reduzgan y hagan una. (Lisson Cháves 138–39)

> (. . . we have been informed that with saintly and virtuous zeal some reading primers where the principles of our faith are contained have been prepared in the languages of the natives, and since we cannot certify that the said reading primers or some of them have been translated and proofread according to the propriety and significance of our Latin language or our Castilian romance, thus in the interest of providing in the above said as in something that is of so much importance in the service of God our Lord and in the relieving of our conscience and office, we rule, under penalty of major excommunication latae sententie to all who, as said, at present are indoctrinating locals or would be appointed to that task in the future in this city of Los Reyes as in all our Archbishopry to indoctrinate and teach the said natives in the general style which is in Latin or in Castilian romance according to the content of the reading primers that are printed in Spain and that at the present time should not use the primers in their [indigenous] language until they have been seen and examined by us with their authors and other persons who understand well their language, and all doctrinal primers that have been made should be reduced to only one.)

This was one of the first official briefings in which the quality of translations was questioned. More importantly, with the doubt of having or not having an orthodox version of Christian dogma in native languages, there emerged an attitude of suspicion towards indigenous languages. This suspicion rested on the perception of their intrinsic limitation to faithfully express Christian ideas. This dubious feeling was corroborated and sanctioned as true when clerics studied indigenous languages and acquired a sizable vocabulary.

Fray Domingo de Santo Tomás, another member of the Dominican Order, arrived in Peru in the late 1530s. Shortly thereafter, he started compiling his Quechua *Vocabulary,* and composing his Quechua *Grammar.* He had been working on these books for several years when Pedro de Cieza met him in 1548–49, and mentioned the work in his *Primera Parte.*[29] Santo Tomás' *Lexicon o vocabulario de la lengua general del Perú* was published in 1560 in Seville, followed that same year by the *Arte y Grammatica.* In his "Introduction" to the latter, he stated that he had been writing for fifteen years, between 1540 and 1555 (1995, 6). Santo Tomás was called *El Nebrija indiano* (Cerrón-Palomino vii), and compared favorably to the prestigious Fifteenth-century author Gregorio Martínez, another Dominican (Cerrón-Palomino xv). His effort was enormous, since fifteen years after the Conquest and ten years after his arrival in Andean lands, he completed a bilingual *Vocabulary* of 354 pages long with approximately 30 entries per page.

Santo Tomás was also the first of many who "translated Spanish ideas into Quechua" (Itier 1995: 321). Thus, he and others who followed put together a "repertoire d'équivalences sémantiques à l'usage des prédicateurs" (repertory of semantic equivalences which preachers use) (323), forcing Quechua to express concepts and ideas that had no representation in that language. Santo Tomás utilized paraphrases, which incorporated unprecedented uses of roots and suffixes; similes, which changed the speaker's perspective from Andean to European; and loans, which replaced undesired native lexical items. All these translation strategies were utilized to convey Catholic ideas in that "heathen" language. In many ways, "general Quechua," as spoken by missionaries, turned into a different language.[30] A "manipulated language" is how César Itier describes it, calling it *Colonial Quechua* to stress its differentiation from the administrative language of Inca times.[31]

Santo Tomás advised on the absence of many indigenous words from his *Lexicon,* explaining the reasons for it as follows:

> Item. Ay en este nuestro vocabulario falta de muchos terminos de arboles, de semillas, de fructas, de aves, de pexes, de animales, de officios, de instrumentos dellos, de generos de armas, diversidad de vestidos, de manjares, de las cosas de nuestra sancta fe catholica, de ornamentos de yglesias, de atavios de casas, de diversidad de vasijas. Y brevemente, carecen los Indios de todos los vocablos de las cosas que no tenian ni se usavan en aquellas tierras, como assi mismo nosotros no tenemos

terminos de las que no ay en la nuestra y ay en otras. Y assi como en este caso nosotros usamos de los terminos proprios de las otras naciones para significar aquellas
cosas, assi ellos usan de los nuestros . . . (14–15)

(Item: In this our vocabulary many terms are lacking, those that refer to trees, to
seeds, fruits, fowl, fishes, animals, crafts and their instruments, types of weapons,
diversity of dresses, of foods, of the things of our sacred Catholic faith, of church
ornaments, of house decorations, of the diversity of bowls. Briefly, Indians lack all
the terms of the things they did not have or use in those lands, the same as we do
not have terms for those which we do not have in ours and exist in others. And, as
in this case, we use the proper terms of other nations to mean those things, in the
same way they use ours . . .)

He also announced that he was including words of other indigenous languages that had current use in the "general language":

Item como esta lengua (aunque es usada y general por toda la tierra) no es natural
en toda, como esta dicho, estan mezclados con los terminos della y recebidos y usa-
dos ya generalmente quasi de todos, muchos terminos de provincias particulares,
de los quales tambien pongo yo algunos en el vocabulario porque assi se usan ya
comunmente. (15)

(Item. As this language [even though it is used and general in all the area] is not
natural in all of it, as said before, there are terms received from other particular
provinces, mixed with those of this language that are used generally by almost
every one. I am including some of them in the vocabulary because they are thus
used commonly.)

Spanish terms were used for Spanish ideas that could not be conveyed with
Quechua words[32] without risking undesirable associations with former deities.
These loans, coming from a synthetic language, were subjected to Quechua's
agglutinant syntax, making it sound awkward, foreign.

The *Vocabulario* had a curious effect on indigenous readers, especially
those hispanicized and indoctrinated, such as Felipe Guaman Poma de Ayala:
" . . . compuso otro libro y lo escribió el maestro fray Domingo de Santo Tomás
de la Orden de Santo Domingo . . . libro de vocabulario de la lengua del Cuzco,
Chinchaysuyo, Quichiua todo revuelto con la lengua española . . ." (. . . [he]
composed another book and it was written by Master Fra Domingo de Santo
Tomás of the Order of Saint Dominic . . . book of vocabulary of the languages
of Cuzco, also of Chinchaysuyo, Quichiwa, all mixed up with the Spanish lan-

guage . . .) (876). This commentary speaks of the awkwardness of the "Quechua misionero," as felt by native speakers of indigenous languages. One can only imagine the additional effects of this kind of artificial mingling of two or more languages when used in sermons. Vicente Rafael has studied these issues in the Philippines, and some of his conclusions can be applied to the Andes: "Missionary discourse produces in the native devotees a series of mild shocks that they attend to in a state of distraction. They give in to colonial authority, but they do not give up. Yet they are able to dodge the priest's message only to the extent that they are able to acknowledge words and things Spanish at the horizon of their own thoughts" (213). Reluctance or laziness to speak native languages correctly in front of indigenous audiences, or simple ignorance of those languages on the part of missionaries and *doctrineros* alike had the added impact of further estranging the audience: "The result, however, was a kind of untranslatable discourse that produced not interest but an interminable oscillation between boredom and random violence" (214).

The author of the *Lexicon* unequivocally stated that he followed Antonio de Nebrija, not his *Gramática castellana* (1492) as was hastily inferred by many researchers and critics,[33] but rather his *Gramática latina* (1481): " . . . como el Antonio de Nebrissa, varón eruditísimo y de gran ingenio, dize en el prólogo del suyo que de la lengua latina hizo . . ." and more explicitly: " . . . este arte se haze para ecclesiasticos que tienen noticia de la lengua latina;[34] va conforme a la arte della [de Nebrissa]" (. . . as Antonio de Nebrissa's, man of great erudition and inventiveness, says in the prologue of the one he made of the Latin language . . . and more explicitly: . . . this art is made for clergymen who have knowledge of the Latin language; it conforms the art of that one [Nebrissa's]) (Santo Tomás 15). The fact is that the *Gramática* follows a Latin pattern that molds the language: "premunidos del esquema, que funciona como anteojera, se tiende a ver, en los hechos lingüísticos por describir, sólo aquello que cabe dentro de la horma. Lo que no encaja dentro de ella o es simplemente silenciado (y a veces ni siquiera advertido) o, lo que es peor, acomodado de modo que encuentre cabida" (having conceived a plan, it functions as a blinder that forces the author to see, in the linguistic facts to be described, only those who fit in it. That which does not fit in the plan is simply silenced [sometimes it is not even noticed] or, what is worse, it is accommodated in a way that allows for its fitting) (Cerrón-Palomino xix). This is why Franz Boas in 1940 observed "la modification syntaxique des langues amerindiennes sous l'influence de l'espagnol . . ." (the syntactic modification of Amerindian languages under the influence of Spanish . . .) (Adnès 59). It should be noted that this hispanization was carried out through the filter of Latin.

The *Vocabulario* is a paradigmatic case in which "Le dictionnaire devient instrument théologique" (The dictionary becomes a theological instrument) (De Certeau 232). And, I may add, *politique* (political). De Certeau's words are a categorical description of what Domingo de Santo Tomás had written and intended. Castañeda-Delgado describes the book as an instrument, synthesizing the conflation of evangelization and indigenous languages with these words: "Y así fue como aparecieron gramáticas, artes, vocabularios, sermonarios, confesonarios . . . que son indudablemente joyas para la lingüística y la etnología, que fueron instrumentos de evangelización" (That is how grammars, arts, dictionaries, collections of sermons, treatises, and rules for confession appeared, which undoubtedly are jewels for linguistics and ethnology, that were instruments of indoctrination) (41).

The Dominican friar's aim was not to know the language *per se;* it was to reduce this language[35] into a vehicle of Christianization.[36] The vocabulary was chosen as the best way to aid friars in their evangelization tasks: " . . . mi intención principal en este arte no es enseñar a hablar cosas superfluas y curiosas en esta lengua, sino solamente las necessarias para la predicación y publicación del Evangelio y declaración de los misterios de nuestra redempción . . ." (. . . my main objective in this art is not to teach how to say superfluous or curious things in that language, but only those necessary for preaching and the dissemination of the Gospel, and for the declaration of the ministries of our redemption . . .) (Santo Tomás 145). To comply with this aim, Quechua was simplified: " . . . ay algunos términos de que los indios usan que no se pueden bien explicar ni declarar en el vocabulario desta lengua donde no se sufre adnotar ni poner términos complexos, más de los términos incomplexos y senzillos y las significaciones dellos . . ." (. . . there are some terms that the Indians use that cannot be fully explained or declared in the vocabulary of this language, where it is not acceptable to annotate or include complex terms besides those terms that are not complex, that are simple, with their significations . . .) (138). Coincidentally, "superfluous" and "complex" terms were the ones used to refer to indigenous sacrality, areas of knowledge used at first in sermons and prayers by Catholic priests to convey Christian ideas: "reinterpretación cristiana" (Christian reinterpretation) in words of Itier (130). Where the Dominicans included any such words because of polysemantism, Itier's only cited the meaning furthest from the sacred. Nevertheless, his selection offers insight into many indigenous cultural aspects: "Desde el punto de vista semántico . . . son muchísimos los aspectos tocantes a la civilización prehispánica que emergen al conjuro de vocablos y expresiones que no siempre han sido suficientemente definidos o explicados en el *Lexicon,* dada la naturaleza práctica de éste" (From a semantic point of view . . . there are many aspects referring to pre-hispanic civilization that emerged upon entreatment of words and expressions that have not always been sufficiently defined or explained in the *Lexicon,* given its *ad hoc* nature) (Cerrón-Palomino liii).

According to Cerrón-Palomino, "La lengua general habría sido, pues, una variante del quechua hablado en la costa centro-sur peruana, localizable en el antiguo señorío de Chincha" (The general language would then have been a variant of the Quechua spoken in the South-central Peruvian coast, localized in the old fiefdom of Chincha) (xii). It is coincidental that Fray Domingo de Santo Tomás erected two of the first convents of his order in that same place, one in Chicama, and one in Chincha (Cieza 1984: 316) during the 1540s.

When this was the Incas' administrative language, it had not drowned out "particular" languages: "Porque puesto que ay en ella [la tierra de los Indios] otras muchas lenguas particulares que quasi en cada provincia ay la suya, pero esta es la general y entendida por toda la tierra y mas usada de los señores y gente principal y de muy gran parte de los demas Indios . . ." (Because as there are in it [Indians' land] so many particular languages that almost each province has its own, but this is the general one, which is understood in all the area and is mostly used by lords and notable people and a large part of the rest of the Indians . . .) (Santo Tomás 8). Santo Tomás also explained that this "general language" was not as widely used then as it had been in his day:

> . . . Y nunca esta lengua en los tiempos antiguos fue tan generalmente usada quasi de todos como el dia de oy. Porque con la communicacion, tracto y grangerias que al presente tienen unos con otros y concurso en los pueblos de los christianos y mercados dellos, assi para sus contractaciones como para el servicio de los españoles para entenderse entre si los de diversas provincias usan desta general . . . (8–9)

> (. . . And never this language in the old times was as commonly used by almost everyone as it is today. With the communication, relationship, and profit that at the present moment have those of different provinces with one another, and with the towns of Christians and their markets, for their commercial contracts as well as for the service of the Spaniards in order to understand each other, all use this general [language] . . .)

The spread of Quechua is owed to the missionaries who obliterated other languages and dialects. Previous Spanish experience with multilingualism showed them that the most prestigious dialects or languages were the ones to spread the fastest and had a sharper imprint on its users. Their hispanicizing noble children had an unacknowledged intention: to utilize their social prestige for purposes of linguistic and religious dissemination.

Indigenous languages were modified under the imprint of Spanish in all its aspects, becoming hispanicized versions of them. In particular, Quechua, the "general language" was then "colonized" from within and from without, importing Spanish concepts and Spanish words, and its syntax adapted to that of Spanish through Latin. Evangelization and hispanization also have to account for the ample diffusion of this language created by missionaries to the detriment of other indigenous languages.

Conclusions

The ideology behind hispanization was the drive to evangelize. Part of the ideology of colonization is control which was actualized through religious indoctrination and assimilation to Spanish *poliçia*. Spanish linguistic policy in the Andes was unambiguously attached to evangelization and was twofold: hispanization of the young, and quechuization of clerics to reach mature populations with a "manipulated" language.

I believe that the Spaniards' former experience with Moors and Jews was paramount in putting into practice specific linguistic policies in the Andes. They had a clear vision of what they wanted and how to obtain it. The Spaniards had the Reconquest and its subsequent experiences to inform their new position in America. For the Andes, the previous experiences in the Caribbean and in Mexico was crucial for the development and implementation of the evangelization/hispanization policy. The millennialist conception and management of time that pervaded Catholic thinking supported a long-term dedication to a long-term project: Spaniards were in the Andes to stay, and they had the certainty that they would prevail.

Their linguistic invasion is a dual movement in which two branches that radiate from a center form a circle of influence. The center is evangelization based upon the Reconquest and the American experiences. One of the branches is dedicated to the hispanization of the young, the other to adult indoctrination in an artificial language, perversely transformed to suit colonization and evangelization. The indigenization of Catholicism reclaimed the adaptation of Quechua, Aymara, and Puquina, languages that had previously been recognized as "general languages," and used as such. Spaniards knew what to do in situations that asked for hispanization and conversion as a means of religious uniformity.

Evangelization is so entrenched in Spanish and European culture that without having some characteristics of European daily life, Catholicism proves difficult to be spread. As far as has been understood, indigenous people were transient. These movements of people did not correspond to the more stationary concept of Spanish clerics and laymen who wanted to know how many people had been baptized and who had paid his *diezmo*. People in constant change of location rendered those determinations impossible. The later territorial reorganization initiated by Viceroy Francisco de Toledo in 1570 transformed the social panorama in the Andes and facilitated taxation and indoctrination of newly settled individuals organized in nuclear or extended families.

Catholicism holds this kind of family to be a basic social component: it is a unity and a focus of religious irradiation. As indigenous peoples had a different conception from that of a monogamous marriage for life, this fact played against the desired *poliçia* that the Spaniards needed to better administer the religion. When one considers these facts, it is easier to understand the numerous references of the need to impart *poliçia* to the native population.

Language colonization went farther than linguistic change. It required indigenous peoples not just to behave as Spaniards, but also to live, speak, dress, and eat like them, in order to better absorb Catholic dogma. If these peoples had not quite become Spaniards, language colonization required that the Andeans cease being themselves.

Notes

1. The *Patronato Indiano* was granted to Fernando, King of Spain in 1508 (Garrido 29). As a consequence of conquering heathen territory, the Pope granted the King funding to build churches and monasteries in the new lands, and to appoint members of the clergy to key Church positions. "Es importante resaltar el ambiente fin-reconquistador, junto con la política de acercamiento a la Santa Sede que imprime un carácter reinstaurador de la perdida fe cristiana a la organización eclesiástica granadina. Cuando se descubre un Nuevo Mundo bastará llevar a esas tierras el esquema jurídico de la Iglesia de Granada, por la que el rey se constituía en director (patrono) de las tareas organizativas misionales indianas" (It is important to highlight the end-of-reconquest atmosphere that, together with the politics of rapprochement towards the Holy See, imprints a restorative character to the Granadine ecclesiastical organization, vis-à-vis the lost Christian faith. When the New World is discovered it will suffice to transfer to those lands the juridical organization of the Church of Granada, through which the King is constituted as the director (patron) of the organization of missionary tasks in the Indies) (Garrido 29–30).

2.   " . . . todos quantos yndios ay en todas las Yndias . . . facilisimamente deprendieran nuestra lengua castellana si se pone por obra el aviso y orden que aqui doy . . . [que] los yndios de veynte años para avaxo que el saçerdote los recoxa a todos en vajo de su mano y que a bueltas de mostrarles la doctrina les muestre y haga deprender la lengua nuestra . . ." (. . . all of the indians in the whole Indies . . . will learn our Castilian language very easily if the recommendation and order that I will give here is put into action . . . [that] indians 20 years old or younger should be gathered under a priest's care, and at the same time he imparts them the doctrine, he should show and make them learn our language . . .) (Ares 140).

3.   "En 1526 se reúne en Granada una junta de funcionarios y personalidades con el fin de reglamentar las oportunas directrices para integrar, de forma rápida, a la población musulmana que vivía, según los tratados diplomáticos, acorde con sus propias costumbres. Se trataba de forzarla a una rápida castellanización: una etapa distinta de aquella que había seguido a la reconquista (1492), que contemplaba la catequesis en las antiguas mezquitas, así como enseñanzas para los hijos de los alfaquíes y notables en colegios y escuelas. Estas didácticas (en lengua árabe) se mantuvieron durante sólo un par de décadas; en 1526 se pretendía, sencillamente, la erradicación de la lengua árabe, la recogida de libros escritos en esta lengua, así como la prohibición de formular contratos y escrituras en árabe, y en caso de hacerlo, 'fueren ningunos, de ningún valor y efecto'; además de la eliminación de vestidos a la moda arábiga, destrucción de los baños turcos y prohibición del uso de nombres y apellidos árabes" (In 1526 a council of officers and dignitaries met in Granada to establish the regulations to integrate, as swiftly as possible, the Muslim population that lived according to diplomatic treaties in accordance with their own customs. The idea was to force it to a quick Castilianization; a different stage from the one that followed the reconquest (1492), which contemplated catequization in the old mosques, teachings for the children of *alfaquies* and notables in schools and colleges. These teachings (in Arabic) were imparted for about twenty years; in 1526 the aim was, simply, the eradication of the Arabic language, the collection of books written in that language, and also the prohibition of preparing contracts and deeds in Arabic. In case they were done, they would be considered 'null, without any value or effect.' Besides, Spanish authorities would eliminate clothing in the Arab fashion, destroy Turkish baths, and forbid the use of Arab names and surnames) (Solano 294).

4.   " . . . ces 'nations barbares' qui apprendrait le castillan: *moros* de Grenade ou d'Afrique du Nord, *guanches* des Canaires . . ." (. . . those 'barbaric nations' that learned Castilian; *moros* from Granada or the North of Africa, *guanches* from the Canary Islands . . .) (Milhou 33).

5.   " . . . debían hallarse ausentes el miedo y la ignorancia que vician toda elección [elección voluntaria de nuevos señores y de la fe]. Pero esto es precisamente lo que más interviene en aquellas elecciones y aceptaciones, pues los bárbaros no saben lo que hacen, y aún quizá ni entienden lo que les piden los españoles. Además, esto lo piden gentes armadas a una turba desarmada y medrosa y rodeada por ellas" (fear and ig-

norance should be absent [from voluntary election of new lords and faith] since they vitiate all election. But this is precisely what intervenes most in those elections and acceptances because barbarous peoples do not know what they are doing, and maybe they do not even understand what Spaniards are asking from them. Besides, those who ask are armed men, to an unarmed and fearful horde surrounded by them) (Vitoria 215–16).

6. Fossa, in press.

7. " . . . y ansi escusan açotes palos coçes que se les dan a los otros yndios *chontales* que no saven nuestra lengua que por su rudeza y poco entendimiento no vienen a la doctrina y misa como son obligados . . ." (. . . and in this way they permit whippings, clubbings, kickings that are given to the other *chontales* Indians who do not know our language and who, because of their coarseness and little understanding, do not come to the doctrine and Mass as they are obliged to do . . .) (Ares 140).

8. *Requerimiento* fragment: "E sy no lo hizieredes [reconocer a la iglesia por señora e superiora del universo mundo e al sumo Pontifice llamado Papa, en su nombre y al Emperador e Reyna doña Juana, nuestros señores, en su lugar, como a sus superiores e señores y reyes de esas yslas y tierra firme por virtud de la dicha donacion e consintays e deis lugar que estos Padres Religiosos os declaren e prediquen lo susodicho] o en ello dilacion maliciosamente pusieredes certificoos que, con el ayuda de Dios, nosotros entraremos poderosamente contra vosotros, e vos haremos guerra por todas las partes y maneras que pudieremos, e vos subjetaremos al yugo e obediencia de la yglesia y de sus magestades e tomaremos vuestras personas y de vuestras mugeres e hijos y los haremos esclavos y como tales los venderemos e dispornemos de ellos como sus magestades mandaren e vos tomaremos vuestros bienes e vos haremos todos los males y daños que pudieremos como a vasallos que no obedecen ny quieren recibir a su señor e le resisten e contradicen e protestamos que las muertes y daños que dello se recrecieren sea a vuestra culpa y no de sus magestades ni nuestras ny destos caballeros que con nosotros vienen . . ." (*Requerimiento* fragment: "And if you would not comply with it [recognizing the Church as Superior Lady of the universal world and the Supreme Pontiff called Pope, in his name and in that of the Emperor and Queen Doña Juana, our lords, in their place and unto them as your superiors and lords and kings of these islands and continental lands in virtue of the said donation and you would consent and allow these religious men declare and preach the above said] or if you will exert malicious delay in your consent, I certify to you that, with God's help, we will enter powerfully against you, and we will wage war on you from all parts and in all ways possible, and we will subject you under the yoke and obedience of the Church and their majesties, and we will take you and your women and children and we will make slaves, and as such we will sell them and dispose of them as their majesties will command, and we will take your goods and we will do all kind of evil and harm that we possibly can as disobedient vassals who do not want to receive their lord and resist and contradict him, and we declare that the death and harm that from this will happen be your fault and not their majesties' nor ours nor of these gentlemen that

come with us . . .") *Requerimiento que se ha de hazer a los yndios del Peru* (Lisson Cháves 24).

9. " . . . the more the natives were perceived to be under the power of Satan [a European construct], the more urgent the European presence became" (Cervantes 9).

10. "Y luego Cortés mandó que los despedazásemos y echásemos a rodar [los ídolos] unas gradas abajo, y así se hizo" (And then Cortés ordered that we tear them [the idols] apart and topple them down some steps, and so it was done) (Díaz del Castillo 45).

11. "Para López Medel, castellano nuevo de Guadalajara, las medidas para que arraigue el español entre los indios deben orientarse hacia el fomento del trato entre indios y blancos, siempre en castellano, a pesar de los posibles errores diplomáticos, porque la comunicación fomentará educación y buenas costumbres: ' . . . y con la continua conversación aprenderían nuestra policía de comer, de beber, de vestir, de limpiarnos y de tratar nuestras personas. Y nuestras cortesías y ceremonias en el hablar y nuestras crianzas y, finalmente, nuestra lengua'" (For López Medel, new Castilian from Guadalajara, the measures handed down Spanish to take root among the Indians should be oriented towards the fostering of relationships between Indians and whites, always in Spanish, notwithstanding the possible diplomatic errors, because communication would result in education and good manners: ' . . . and with the continuous conversation they would learn our way of eating, drinking, dressing, washing ourselves, and treat our persons. And our courtesies and ceremonies in speaking and our manners, and finally, our language') (Solano 298).

12. " . . . mandamos que la primera y principal cosa que después de salidos en tierra los dichos capitanes y nuestros oficiales y otras cualesquier gentes hubieren de hacer, sea procurar que por lenguas de intérpretes que entiendan los indios y moradores de la tal tierra o isla les digan y declaren como nos les enviamos para los enseñar buenas costumbres y apartarlos de vicios y de comer carne humana y a instruirles en nuestra santa fe y predicársela para que se salven . . ." (. . . we order that the first and main thing that after arriving on land the said captains and our officers, and whichever person should do, is to procure that through tongues of interpreters understood by Indians and dwellers of the said land, they should be told and declared how we send them to teach good manners and to steer them from vices and eating human flesh and to instruct them in our holy faith and preach it to them so they can be saved . . .) (Morales Padrón 377).

13. "yten. Con condición que quando salieredes destos nuestros reynos e llegaredes a la dicha provincia del peru ayays de llevar e tener con vos a los oficiales de nuestra hazienda que por nos estan y fueren nombrados y asi mismo las personas Religiosas e eclesiasticas que por nos seran señaladas para ynstrucion de los yndios y naturales de aquella provincia a nuestra santa fee catolica . . ." (Item. On condition that when you leave our kingdoms and arrive at the said province of Peru you should have taken and have with you our financial officers who represent us and have been thus appointed, and also the religious and ecclesiastical persons that will be indicated by us in order

to instruct the Indians and naturals of that province in our holy catholic faith . . .)
(Morales Padrón 239).

14. " . . . se ha hecho tan notable daño [a estos ynfieles] con los malos exemplos de los
cristianos y Prelados y personas de doctrina que los an consentido sean robados,
privados de su libertad, maltratados de muchos señores, muertos a tormentos porque
no daban oro, despojados de sus mujeres y adulteradas; y de sus hijas, corrompidas
y sus hijos, puestos en servidumbre y todos desterrados de sus propias casas, tierras
y heredades. . . ." Así lo expresa el Licenciado Martel de Santoyo a Su Magestad en
1542 (. . . such notable harm has been done [on these infidels] with bad examples
from Christians and prelates and persons of doctrine that have allowed they be robbed,
deprived of their freedom, mistreated by many lords, killed under torment because
they would not give gold, stripped of their women and they, adulterated, their daugh-
ters, corrupted, and their sons placed in serfdom and all of them exiled from their
own houses, land and estates. . . . That is how Licenciate Martel de Santoyo expressed
himself in a letter to His Majesty in 1542) (Lisson Cháves 99).

15. "Y porque nuestro principal yntento y voluntad siempre ha sido y es de la conservaçion y augmento de los yndios y que sean ynstruidos y enseñados en las cosas de
nuestra sancta fee catholica y bien tratados como personas libres y vasallos nuestros
como lo son, encargamos y mandamos a los del dicho nuestro Consejo [de Indias]
tengan siempre muy gran atençion y espeçial cuydado sobre todo de la conservaçion
y buen govierno y tratamiento de los dichos indios . . ." (And since our main intent
and wish has always been and is that of conservation and augmentation of Indians,
that they be instructed and taught the things of our holy Catholic faith, and be well
treated as free persons and our vassals, as they are, we entrust and command those in
our said Council [of the Indies] always to have great attention and special care on all
matters referring to the conservation and good government and treatment of the said
Indians . . .) (Morales Padrón 431).

16. " . . . ni dadose a saber vocablos de la lengua natural para Ello [conversión y doctrina]
ni desto a avido mas memoria que de una cosa digna de abominacion aunque vocablos
para pedirles oro e negociar en los casos que arriba digo no ay poca destreza." (. . .
nor having been inclined to know words of the natural language for that [conversion
and indoctrination]; of this, here has been no other memory than that of something
worthy of abomination, but words to ask them for gold or to negotiate in the above
said cases, there is no little ability). Relación del Licenciado Martel de Santoyo, 1542
(Lisson Cháves 99).

17. "Francisco Pizarro le respondio que venian de España donde eran naturales en cuya
tierra estava un rey grande y poderoso llamado don Carlos, cuyos vaçallos y criados
eran ellos y otros muchos, porque mandava grandes tierras; y quellos avian salido
a descubrir por aquellas partes como vian y a poner debaxo de la sujeçion de aquel
rey lo que hallasen y prinçipalmente y ante todas cosas, a dar notiça como los ydolos
en que adoravan heran falços y sin fundamento los sacrifiçios que hazian y como
para salvarse avian de se bolver cristianos y creer en el Dios que ellos adoravan, que

estava en el çielo llamado Jesucristo, porque los que no lo adoraren y cunplieren sus mandamientos yrian al ynfierno, lugar oscuro y lleno de fuego, y los que conoçiendo la verdad le tuviesen por Dios, solo Señor del çielo, mar y tierra con lo mas criado, serian moradores en el çielo donde estarian para siempre jamas" (Francisco Pizarro answered him that they came from Spain and were natives of that land, where there was a great and powerful king called Don Carlos, and they and many others were his vassals and servants because he ruled over immense lands; and that they had left their country to discover around those parts as they saw fit, and to place under the rule of that king whatever they found, and above all things, to notify how the idols they adored were false, and their sacrifices unfounded, and how in order to save themselves they had to turn Christian and believe in the God they adored, that was in heaven, called Jesus Christ, because all those who did not adore him or did not comply with his commandments would go to Hell, a dark place full of fire, and those who know the truth would accept him as God, only Lord of heaven, sea and land and with all things created they would will live in heaven where they would stay forever and ever) (Cieza 1989: 56).

18. "Y como estuviese la comida aparejada les dieron de comer mucho pescado y carne de diferentes maneras con muchas frutas y del vino y pan que ellos usan. Como ovieron comido los prencipales yndios que alli estaban con sus mugeres por hazer mas fiesta al capitan [Pizarro] vaylaron y cantaron a su costumbre" (And as the food was ready they fed them lots of fish and meat in many ways with many fruits and the wine and bread they use. As the Indian lords that were there with their women had eaten, in order to better honor captain [Pizarro], they danced and sang according to their customs) (Cieza 1989: 67).

19. See Pérez, 1989: 67.

20. "Teniendo en cuenta estos escasos elementos, el religioso que más se ajusta a ellos resulta ser Fr. Juan de San Pedro. Los datos son precarios pero resulta factible la hipótesis, por cuanto éstos encajan perfectamente con la vida de aquel religioso" (Taking into consideration these few elements, the priest that adheres better to them happens to be Friar Juan de San Pedro. Data is scarce but the hypothesis is feasible since the evidence matches perfectly the life of that friar) (Castro de Trelles xii).

21. " . . . el habla y el silencio estaban estrictamente reglamentados en los Andes" (. . . speech and silence were strictly regimented in the Andes) (Fossa, In press).

22. "In Robert Robins and Eugenius Uhlenbeck's *Endangered Languages,* languages are termed 'moribund' if they are spoken only by a small group of older people and are not being learned by children. In contrast, a 'safe' language has, at a minimum, 'a community of 100,000 speakers' and the 'official support of a nation-state'" (Fennelly 65).

23. "Primeramente toca a nuestra Magestad ser ynformado del cuydado que se ha tenido e tiene, doze años ha, que se descubrió e pobló esta tierra, de la conversion de los ynfieles naturales, e del cuydado que se ha tenido e tiene en doctrinarlos, asy en buenas costumbres e virtudes naturales como en cosas de nuestra santa fee, pues de la con-

ciencia de vuestra magestad, primero que otra alguna, depende el cumplimiento desto. Y lo que en este caso ay que avisar es que fasta oy, principio del año de quarenta y dos, no solamente se a dexado tan noble provecho en el camino de la salvacion destos ynfieles, pero por este fin se ha hecho tan notable daño con los malos exemplos de los cristianos y Prelados y personas de doctrina . . ." (First, it is in our Majesty's interest to be informed of the care that has been taken for the last twelve years, or since this land was discovered and populated, to instruct them in good manners and natural virtues as well as in those of our sacred faith. For compliance in these matters depends primarily on our Majesty's conscience. And what should be noted is that until today, the beginning of 1542, not only such a noble benefit of showing the road to salvation to these infidels has not been accomplished, but so much harm has been done with the bad example of the Christians, and prelated, and persons of doctrine . . .) Relación del Licenciado Martel de Santoyo (Lisson Cháves 99).

24. "C'est le même esprit tridentin que suivirent, en 1582, les pères du IIIème Concile provincial de Lima: 'El principal fin del cathecismo y doctrina cristiana es percibir los mysterios de nuestra fee al español en romance y al yndio también en su lengua, pues de otra suerte, por muy bien que recite las cosas de Dios, con todo eso se quedará sin fruto en su entendimiento como lo dice el mismo apóstol. . . . Cada uno de los obispos dispute y señale en su diócesis examinadores que examinen a los que han de ser curas de yndios y de la suficiencia que tienen así en éstas como en la lengua de los yndios . . . para los que han de ser curas le aprendan [le catéchisme et la doctrine chrétienne] y entiendan y enseñen por él en la lengua de los yndios'" (It is the same Tridentive spirit that the priests of the III Provincial Council of Lima followed in 1582: 'The main aim of Catholicism and Christian doctrine is to teach the mysteries of our faith to the Spaniard in romance and to the Indian in his language, because otherwise, no matter how ell he recites the things of God, all that will be fruitless in their understanding as the same apostle says. . . . Each one of the bishops should name and select in his diocese examiners to examine those who will be priests to the Indians and in the knowledge they have in this language as well as in the Indian's language . . . so that those who will be clerics will learn it [the cathechism and Christian doctrine] and understand and teach through it in the language of the Indians) (Milhou 38).

25. "Les pères du Concile [du Letran] insistaient sur l'importance de l'instruction et de la prédication en langue vulgaire. . . . Ils inaugurait ainsi une politique qui devait s'épanouir au Concile de Trente . . ." (The priests of the Council [of Letran] insisted on the importance of the instruction and preaching in vulgar languages . . . Thus they inaugurated a politics that should flourish in the Council of Trent . . .) (Milhou 36).

26. He was also quoted by Milhou (24) in French.

27. Quoted by Milhou (29).

28. " . . . even though Southern Peruvian Quechua was the administrative language of an expansionist state, before the European invasion, it never became hegemonic, nor was it ever standardized, even in the territory immediately surrounding the Inca capital" (Mannheim 2).

29. "Y para que más fácilmente conozcan el error en que han bivido y conoscido, abracen nuestra sancta fe se ha hecho arte para hablar su lengua con industria, para que se entiendan los unos y los otros. En lo qual no ha trabajado poco el reverendo padre fray Domingo de sancto Thomás de la orden de señor sancto Domingo" (An art has been made to speak their language with industry so they can more easily learn about the error in which they have lived and known, and embrace our holy faith, so that they will understand each other. The Reverend Priest Fryer Domingo de Sancto Tomas or the Order of Lord Saint Dominic has not avoided any travail in doing it) (Cieza 1984: 143).

30. Santo Tomás is probably the first Spaniard to call this language a "lengua general" in a printed book (Santo Tomás 6). He explains why he says it is "general": " . . . es lengua que se communicava y de que se usava y usa por todo el señorio de aquel gran señor llamado Guaynacapa que se estiende por espacio de mas de mil leguas en largo y mas de ciento en ancho. En toda la qual se usava generalmente della de todos los señores y principales de la tierra y de muy gran parte de la gente comun della" (. . . it is the language in which they communicated and was used and is used now in all the fiefdom of that great lord called Guaynacapac, which extended for over one thousand leagues in length, and more than one hundred in width. In all of it that language was generally used, and was a large part of the common people) (9).

31. " . . . la tradición oral y la lengua quechuas fueron objeto, de parte de la iglesia peruana colonial, de una minuciosa e inteligente empresa de manipulación" (. . . oral tradition and Quechua were the object, of a meticulous and intelligent manipulation enterprise by the Peruvian colonial church) (Itier 1993: 172).

32. The experience of Tagalog echoes that of Quechua, Aymara and Puquina: " . . . when Christian discourse was translated into the vernacular, its key terms retained their original forms. Tagalog, thus permeated by words that had no equivalents in the vernacular, was made to appear to have a source other than its native speakers. Conversion thereby translated Tagalog into a new language (Rafael 213).

33. " . . . y los respectivos programas con que Nebrija justificó su *Gramatica latina* (1481) y su *Gramatica castellana* (1492): la latinización de Castilla, el primero; la castellanización de los dominios del imperio, el segundo" (" . . . and the programs with which Nebrija justified his *Latin Grammar* (1481) and his *Spanish Grammar* (1492) were respectively: the latinization of Castile, and, the castilianization of the Empire's domains) (Mignolo 171).

34. Luis Jaime Cisneros had pointed out this fact in an article published in 1951, and quoted by Rodolfo Cerrón-Palomino in his "Estudio introductorio" to Santo Tomás's *Gramática.*

35. He writes in his Prologue to the King: " . . . luego comence a tractar de reduzir aquella lengua [general] a arte para que no solamente yo pudiesse en ella aprovechar en aquella nueva iglesia enseñando y predicando el Evangelio a los indios, pero otros muchos que, por la difficultad de aprenderla no emprendian tan apostolica obra, viendola ya en arte y que facilmente se podia saber, se animassen a ello y con facilidad la apren-

diessen, como se começo a hazer . . ." (" . . . then I started to try to reduce that [general] language to an art so that I would not be the only one that could teach and preach the Gospel to the Indians in that new church, but that many others who, because of the difficulty in learning it, did not start such an apostolic deed, but seeing it was already composed and that it could be so easily known, they would be encouraged to do so and would easily learn it, as they began to do . . .) (6).

36. " . . . quien supiere la grande y extrema necessidad que ay en aquellas provincias de la predicacion del Evangelio y quantos millares de animas se han ido y van al infierno por falta de conocimiento dél y de las cosas de nuestra sancta fe catholica por defecto de la lengua sin la qual no se les puede predicar, y quantos buenos religiosos y siervos de Dios ay alla y aca que se retraen desta sancta obra y temen poner el hombro a tan apostolica sementera como esta, temiendo la difficultad de la lengua y creyendo no poder salir con ella: quien esto considerare atenta y christianamente y entendiere que esto que yo hago en querer redduzir esta lengua a arte y querer presentar ante vuestros ojos la fructa no enteramente madura y parir este concepto imperfecto que de la lengua tengo concebido antes de llegar a madurez y perfection es por la gran necessidad que ay della y para dar alguna lumbre a los que ninguna tienen y mostrarles que no es difficultoso el aprenderla y a animar a los que por falta de la lengua estan covardes en la predicacion del Evangelio . . ." (. . . those who knew of the great and extreme necessity there is in those provinces of the preaching of the Gospel and how many thousands of souls have gone and will go to Hell for lack of knowledge of it and of the things of our holy Catholic faith for not knowing the language without which preaching cannot be done, and how many good religious men and God's servants there are here and there who refrain from that sacred work and are afraid to put the shoulder to such an apostolic sown land as this is, fearing the language's difficulty and believing they cannot learn it; he who will consider this attentively and christianly and understand that my work in wishing to reduce this language into an art and wanting to present before your eyes the fruit not entirely ripe and bringing forth this imperfect concept that I have of that language before it reaches maturity and perfection, is because of the great need there is of it and to give some light to those that have none and show them that it is not difficult to learn it and to encourage those who for lack of language feel cowardice in the preaching of the Gospel . . .) (14–15).

Works Cited

Adnès, Michel. "Le don de la syntaxe." *Langues et Cultures en Amérique espagnole coloniale*. Paris: Presses de la Sorbonne Nouvelle, 1993. 47–72.

Ares Queija, Berta. "Relación del licenciado Michael de la Torre (Quito, 1574): Lengua, cultura y evangelización." *Cuadernos para la Historia de la Evangelización en América Latina* (CHELA) (Cuzco, 1988): 129–42.

Castañeda-Delgado, Paulino. "La Iglesia y la Corona ante la nueva realidad lingüística en Indias." *I Simposio de Filología Iberoamericana.* Zaragoza: Libros Pórtico, 1990. 29–41.

Castro de Trelles, Lucila. "Edición, estudio preliminar y notas." *Relación de la religión y ritos del Perú hecha por los padres agustinos.* Lima: Fondo Editorial PUC, 1992. ix-xci.

Cerrón-Palomino, Rodolfo. "Estudio Introductorio y Notas." *Grammatica o arte de la lengua general de los indios de los reynos del Peru* (1560). Cuzco: Ed. CERA Bartolomé de las Casas, 1995.

Cervantes, Fernando. *The Devil in the New World. The Impact of Diabolism in New Spain.* New Haven and London: Yale UP, 1994.

Cieza de León, Pedro. *Crónica del Perú. Primera Parte,* Introd. F. Pease, Notes M. Maticorena. Lima: PUC, 1984.

————. *Crónica del Perú. Tercera Parte,* Ed. Prolg and Notes by F. Cantù, Second ed. Lima: PUC, 1989.

De Certeau, Michel. *L'ecriture de l'histoire.* Paris: Gallimard, 1975.

Díaz del Castillo, Bernal. *Historia verdadera de la conquista de la Nueva España I* (1632). Introd. y notas de J. Ramírez Cabañas, 17ª ed. México: Porrúa, 1998.

Duverger, Christian. *La conversión de los indios de la Nueva España con el texto de los Coloquios de los Doce de Bernardino de Sahagún* (1564). Victoria G. de Vela, trad. Ecuador: Ed. ABYA-YALA, 1990.

Fennelly, Beth. "Fruits We'll Never Taste," originally printed in the *Michigan Quarterly Review,* reprinted in *Utne Reader,* No. 110 (March-April 2002): 64–70.

Fossa, Lydia. *Narrativas problemáticas: Los Inkas bajo la pluma española.* Lima: Instituto de Estudios Peruanos, In Press.

Garrido Aranda, Antonio. *Moriscos e indios. Precedentes hispánicos de la evangelización en México.* México: UNAM, 1980.

Guaman Poma de Ayala, Felipe. *Nueva coronica y buen gobierno* [1615?], Edición y prólogo F. Pease G.Y., Vocabulario y traducciones de J. Szeminski. Lima: Ed. Fondo de Cultura Económica, 1993.

Husson, Jean-Philippe. "Contresens, malentendus, quiproquos: ce qu'il advint du quechua lorsqu'on en fit une langue d'évangélisation." *I Simposio de Filología Iberoamericana.* Zaragoza: Ed. Libros Pórtico, 1990. 257–75.

Itier, César. "La littérature quechua d'évangelisation (XVIe et XVIIe siècles) comme source ethnolinguistique." *Amérindia. Revue d'ethno linguistique amérindienne,* Vol 19/20 (Paris, SELAF, 1995): 321–30.

————. "Estudio y comentario lingüístico." *Relacion de antiguedades deste reyno del Piru* by Joan de Santa Cruz Pachacuti Yamqui Salcamaygua. Cuzco: IFEA-CBC, 1993. 129–78.

Lisson Cháves, Emilio (Ed.). *La Iglesia de España en el Perú.* Sevilla, 1943.

Mannheim, Bruce. *The Language of the Inka since the European Invasion.* Austin: University of Texas Press, 1991.

Mignolo, Walter D. "Teorías renacentistas de la escritura y la colonización de las lenguas nativas." *I Simposio de filología iberoamericana* (Zaragoza, 1990): 171–99.

Milhou, Alain. "Les politiques de la langue à l'époque moderne." *Langues et Cultures en Amérique espagnole coloniale.* Paris: Presses de la Sorbonne Nouvelle, 1993. 15–40.

Morales Padrón, Francisco. *Teoría y Leyes de la Conquista.* Madrid: Ed. Cultura Hispánica, Centro Iberoamericano de Cooperación, 1979.

Pérez Fernández, Isacio. *Bartolomé de las Casas en el Perú. El espíritu lascasiano en la primera evangelización del imperio incaico. 1531–1573.* Cuzco: CERA Bartolome de las Casas, 1986.

Rafael, Vicente L. *Contracting Colonialism. Translation and Christian Conversion in Tagalog Society Under Early Spanish Rule.* Durham: Duke University Press, 1993.

Saint-Lu, André. "Langue, évangelisation et culture chez Las Casas." *Langues et Cultures en Amérique espagnole coloniale.* Paris: Presses de la Sorbonne Nouvelle, 1993. 41–46.

San Pedro, Juan (Fray). *Relación de la religión y ritos del Perú hecha por los padres agustinos.* "Edición, estudio preliminar y notas" by Lucila Castro de Trelles. Lima: Fondo Editorial PUC, 1992.

Santa Cruz Pachacuti Yamqui, Juan. *Relacion de antiguedades deste reino del Perú,* edición índice analítico y glosario de Carlos Araníbar. Lima: FCE, 1995.

Santo Tomás, Domingo de. *Lexicon o vocabulario de la lengua general del Perú.* [1560a] Valladolid. Fernández de Córdova, Ed. Lima: Fac, UNMSM, 1951.

———. *Gramática o arte de la lengua general de los indios de los reynos del Peru.* [1560b] Introd. y notas, R. Cerrón-Palomino. Cuzco: Ed. Centro Bartolomé de las Casas, 1995.

Solano, Francisco de. "Aprendizaje y difusión del español entre indios (1492/1820)." *Langues et cultures en Amérique espagnole coloniale.* Paris: Presses de la Sorbonne Nouvelle, 1993. 291–321.

Vitoria, Francisco de. *Relaciones de Indios y del derecho de la guerra con trozos referentes de la potestad civil.* Marques de Olivart, trans. Madrid: Espasa Calpe, 1928.

◆ **2**

The Pre-Columbian Past as a Project:
Miguel León-Portilla and Hispanism

Ignacio M. Sánchez-Prado

And the problem is that man, perplexed, does not succeed in grasping the indigenous being. His image becomes faint, his being is oscillating and blurry; mystery beats behind his pupils and, in every bend of his world, hidden, the enigmatic, double-faced sign of his profile appears.
—Luis Villoro. *Los grandes momentos del indigenismo en México* (110)

Defining the state of the Nahuatl literature studies prior to the 1950s is simple: they were nonexistent. In his classical essay "Visión de Anáhuac," for instance, Alfonso Reyes regrets that the system of the poetry of the ancient Mexicans was lost and that the only thing remaining is a group of fragments recorded by the Spanish, fragments that, in Reyes's opinion, do not give account of the poetry as an activity in Pre-Columbian times (13). Even as late as the 1940s, in his landmark history of Latin American literature *Literary Currents in Hispanic America,* Pedro Henríquez Ureña completely omitted any mention of Pre-Columbian literature and began his account with the Conquest. These two examples, coming from some of the most prominent advocates of Latin American culture, are only random illustrations of the enormous ignorance scholars had of ancient indigenous culture. This ignorance, needless to say, is even more overwhelming when one considers that many of those scholars claimed the indigenous past as a fundamental part of "our identity." The situation today is quite different, as we find that the discipline has grown enormously in the past fifty years, in which, starting almost from scratch, it constructed and institutionalized something we might call "Pre-Columbian knowledge." The primary figure responsible for this shift is Miguel León-Portilla.

Based on the seminal works of Ángel María Garibay, León-Portilla has written a considerable number of books and essays which provides the foundations for the study of the scarce and complex textualities that compose the corpus known as "Nahuatl literature." His contributions range from the paleography of manuscripts to the construction of a theoretical apparatus used to approach the form, content, and context of the "texts." He is also one of the founders of the most important academic institution in the field (the Seminar on Nahuatl Culture at the National University of Mexico, created in 1957) and of the most important publication in the field (*Estudios de cultura náhuatl,* a 32 year-old journal published by the Seminar). Moreover, León-Portilla is recognized as one of the most outspoken advocates for indigenous causes, which has earned him membership in and awards from many important institutions in Mexico and abroad. In short, the core of the discipline is centered on the work of this man and the critical school he has founded.[1]

In the following pages, I will analyze the Hispanist and nationalist foundations of Nahuatl literary studies as represented in León-Portilla's work. This articulation revolves around three approaches to the Nahuatl question: The recovery of Fray Bernardino de Sahagún's methodology, the modern appropriations of Bartolomé de las Casas's advocacy of Indian causes (including its consequences in the constitution of a national discourse in Mexico and in the use of Pre-Columbian culture in contemporary identity politics), and the role of Spanish language in the construction of the relationship between the national project and the specific agendas of the *indígenas,* addressing particularly the role of the Spanish language as *lingua franca* amongst the different ethnic groups. These three topics, I believe, fairly represent the essential problems established both at the conceptual and ideological levels of León-Portilla's project and the way in which this project reflects on the objects of study and ideological agendas surrounding Nahuatl literature.

The first half of the twentieth century in Mexico can be characterized as a very active ground for discussing the nature of both national and Latin American identities. From the fertile intellectual activity of the *"Ateneo de la Juventud"* to the somewhat inane discussions on the nature of national literature, the culture of the Mexican Revolution and its aftermath produced considerable national awareness, and the intellectual need to define the "imagined community" at the foundation of the new Mexican State.[2] The relationship between *indigenismo* and Hispanic heritage was one of the key issues in this discussion, since the ideology of *mestizaje* started to occupy a preponderant place in the construction of national narrative. Thus, to properly discuss the role León-Portilla has played in the construction and consolidation of Mexican *indigenismo,* the Hispanist and Americanist bases of his work must be taken into consideration. One of the most important discussions within the field of cultural production in Mexico and Latin America was precisely the way in which the region should reconcile its Hispanic heritage with its claims of authenticity. This is why both Reyes and Henríquez Ureña wrote a considerable number of pages about Spanish culture. For instance, Alfonso Reyes devoted an important part of his critical work to reading many of the authors within the Peninsular tradition as a form of reappropriation of Hispanic heritage in the constitution of an American specificity.[3] In addition, many of the cultural foundations in Mexico were due to Spanish exiles, whose work was key in the creation of the country's cultural institutions.

León-Portilla's work with Spanish culture is based on his recovery of the missionary work performed by the Franciscan order during the sixteenth Century. The main source of his investigation is the corpus of Fray Bernardino de Sahagún's work, particularly the so-called *Códice Florentino,* a manuscript in which Sahagún recovered many indigenous practices by presenting them in three columns: one on pictographic writing, reproducing the Nahuatl writing system, one in transcriptions of Nahuatl language into the Western alphabet, and a Spanish translation of the corpus. In other words, the primary reference for studying the whole corpus of Nahuatl literature is a series of texts produced by a sixteenth century Spanish scholar. León-Portilla regards himself as continuing Sahagún's work, a position with important consequences in his textual approaches (Hernández de León-Portilla 74–75).

To illustrate this situation, the anthology of Nahuatl literature he compiled for Biblioteca Ayacucho (*Literatura del México Antiguo*) offers a good example. Some sections of the book include direct quotes from Sahagún's *Códice* without any differentiation from the texts attributed to Nahuatl writers. In other words, the book implicitly considers Sahagún's work as not only part of the corpus of Nahuatl literature in general, but also as a representative text to be incorporated in a collection conceived to establish a canon of Nahuatl texts in the context of Latin American Literature.[4] Also, the organization of the anthology, which, at a glance, seems to follow a taxonomy based on the concepts of *cuicatl* and *tlahtolli,* profits from a perception of "Pre-Columbian culture" constructed by Sahagún. If one reads Sahagún's most accessible work, the *Historia general de las cosas de la Nueva España,* it is clear that the chapter division used by León-Portilla follows a taxonomy similar to the one provided by Sahagún's accounts.[5] This apparently non-critical approach to Sahagún, present in most of León-Portilla's earliest work (which implies a denial of the mediations inherent in both the writing process and ethnographic system developed by the Franciscan friar),[6] not only proceeds from the lack of other sources, but also indicates a re-evaluation of Sahagún's humanist work, and with it, a reconsideration of the Spanish cultural approach to the Indians beyond the negative conceptions of early colonial strategies toward approaching the Other.

The rescue of Sahagún's work implies a point of view regarding the process of the Conquest, which does not necessarily adhere to the colonialist idea of the "Discovery," but still has positive connotations towards the notion of "cultural encounter." In other words, rescuing Sahagún's strategies, such as the question-naires given to "informants"[7] or the use of Western referents to describe indige-nous cultural practices,[8] as a possibility of reconstructing an "authentic" Pre-Columbian culture permits for a different perspective on the clash of cultures in which the Spanish Renaissance's "high values" incarnated by the Franciscan intellectuals can be regarded as a repositioning of the Spanish approach to the Indians, one that goes beyond the one-dimensional vision of the Conquest as an act of pure violence. Nonetheless, we must not forget that Sahagún's work, as Luis Villoro has noted, lies in a paradox: it allowed the indigenous Other to enter the realm of "universal" mankind while, at the same time, it became an instrument for his/her subalternization: "In that time, historical discourse will reflect the uncanny consciousness of the one who faces a dual world. Thus, the apparent incoherency in all the theoretical judgements and practical attitudes of those who lived within that consciousness. Love and protection towards the Indian come before rejection and condemnation; the respect towards their free-dom becomes the worst slavery" (109, my translation). I will discuss some of these ideological implications when I address the question of the relation-ship between Nahuatl scholarship and indigenous advocacy. Villoro's remarks on Sahagún allow us to see the fundamental operations lying behind León-Portilla's use of the Franciscan's sources. The paradox pointed out by Villoro (a paradox that in Villoro's argument underlies any indigenist discourse) is, to some extent, implicitly denied by León-Portilla. For instance, in his book on Sahagún, León-Portilla seeks to recover his work in terms of his biography, through a detailed analysis of his humanistic formation, his articulation with Renaissance projects and the effect this had on his work. This biographic/philo-logic approach, nonetheless, lacks precisely the factor that enables Villoro's remarks: an ideological critique of Sahagún. Here, of course, I am not implying that such lack is intentional, but that the fact that León-Portilla never really at-tempts this ideological critique of his sources raises a series of problems, both methodological and ideological.

In terms of methodology, one of the most common critiques towards León-Portilla's work is the reluctance he shows in some of his translations to distin-guish between the Nahuatl text and the mediations and interpolations introduced by the Spanish friars. This is probably one of the most polemic issues regarding León-Portilla's approach to Pre-Hispanic culture. Amos Segala, throughout his book *Literatura Nahuatl,* questions the authenticity of the Pre-Columbian corpus defined by Garibay and León-Portilla by stating that the manuscripts used as sources are basically testimonies of Spanish colonial and epistemological intervention and that they do not offer evidence of being a reliable source for establishing a rigorously Pre-Columbian "literary" production.[9] However, the approach towards Sahagún's work by León-Portilla and others carries very different academic presumptions depending on their position on the relations between Indians and Spanish friars.

There are basically three ideological approaches to this question. The first is the one implied in León-Portilla's work; he attempts to locate an essential Pre-Columbian culture in Sahagún's work. As we have seen before, that is why he devoted a book, *Bernardino de Sahagún: Pionero de la antropología,* to re-create Sahagún's life and give him legitimacy as one of the founders of ethnography as a discipline. The entire book seems a defense of Sahagún's admiration of Indian culture as a primary motivation for his work, which also becomes a defense of his objectivity.[10] Even though the book addresses the Franciscan ideals and projects (such as the attempt to construct a "pure" society as opposed to the corrupt civilization of Europe), it never questions the validity of methods such as the questionnaires Sahagún used to interview his sources. In *El destino de la palabra,* the book in which, after more than three decades of work, León-Portilla recognizes the violence of the alphabetical recreations of indigenous orality (*"transvase"* is the word he uses), he continues to defend the critical value of Sahagún's work as source (58). The basic problem is that questioning the validity of Sahagún's work, the primary source of most of the Nahuatl texts, would undermine both the possibility of having a Pre-Columbian literature to recover in the first place, and the methods through which Garibay, León-Portilla and their disciples (such as Patrick Johansson or Ascensión Hernández) have studied the texts. Moreover, when León-Portilla claims himself as a follower of Sahagún, he transfers the validity of applying a humanistic approach towards the Indian other to his own project. In other words, the methodological appropriation of Sahagún's work signifies an ideological appropriation: the legitimization of classical humanism as a form of understanding the Pre-Columbian heritage as a "culture" in the same sense of other Western cultures. That is why, for instance, both Garibay and León-Portilla apply Western notions such as "verse" or "philosophy" to the Pre-Columbian corpus.[11]

Even in approaches that adopt a very radical methodology, such as Bierhorst's translation of the *Cantares mexicanos,* the possibility of recovering an authentic indigenous text is not out of the question. Bierhorst's main thesis is that texts do not have a direct interpretation since they are written in a symbolic language whose logic can only be found within the texts themselves. The book goes even further by presenting a connection between these texts and the ghost songs of the ancient North American natives. This hypothesis is very bold and polemic but still accepts the possibility of finding an "authentic" Pre-Columbian culture in the texts. The difference is that while León-Portilla believes in the possibility of understanding culture through Western linguistic paradigms, Bierhorst sustains the unattainability of those texts in terms of Western epistemology.

León-Portilla's positions have been questioned both openly and implicitly by two other approaches to the sources. One of these approaches goes to the other extreme and denies that the texts may have any relation whatsoever with an "authentic" Pre-Columbian culture and understands the operations of Sahagún and the other friars as the construction of a colonial discourse which imposes European values and ideas on the newly conquered people. One very significant illustration of this position is Mignolo and Ebacher's article on the *huehuetlahtollis,* the texts inherited by Pre-Columbian wisemen. These texts serve as the foundations of some of the core concepts in León-Portilla's system, since he considers them to be examples of the Nahuatl philosophy and one of the most important evidences of the existence of a Nahuatl wisdom. Mignolo and Ebacher criticize Garibay's, and, implicitly, León-Portilla's approach to Pre-Columbian literature because it "doesn't problematize the fact that oral discursive genre had been fixed alphabetically and then comparatively interpreted with discursive genres of the Greek-Latin tradition" (21, my translation). Moreover, they sustain that the process of "alphabetization in a colonial situation implies transformation" and that when one transcribes the *huehuetlahtollis* into an alphabetical writing, they enter "a process of transformation, a process that had its beginnings in that first inventory and rigorous organization of the indigenous languages in Nebrija's style" (23, my translation). All of this means that "discursive pieces from colonized cultures become part of the colonizer's culture" (27, my translation). In other words, Mignolo and Ebacher believe that the "colonial semiosis" produced in the transfer of oral discourses into the alphabetical writing makes them part of the colonizing process, which leads to the impossibility of considering them a source of authentic Pre-Columbian culture.

The other position is based on the idea that Sahagún's works are some form of "in-between." Louise M. Burkhart's book, *The Slippery Earth,* for instance, is based on the idea that Sahagún's texts are more productive when considered as testimonies of the contact rather than recoveries of an authentic indigenous culture (5). Nonetheless, this hypothesis does not exclude any of the previous approaches, constructing a critical position that does not adopt the standpoint of the colonizer nor of the colonized, but instead problematizes both positions. In this sense, Burkhart's book rediscovers Sahagún's work as a process of epistemological encounter rather than as a method for approaching the indigenous texts, thus denying the idea of an "authentic" Pre-Columbian discourse attainable through these texts.

It is evident that Mignolo, Bierhorst and Burkhart's approaches undermine a considerable number of León-Portilla's presuppositions. Regarding León-Portilla's appropriation of Sahagún, these two positions raise a series of problems not directly addressed by León-Portilla. First, they deny, or at least doubt, the possibility of a Western scholar successfully approaching the Pre-Columbian textualities, because the sources are questionable and such an approach always implies a violence against the original texts. Second, if Sahagún's work is not based on rescuing indigenous culture as such, but on the purely colonial motivation of "knowing the Other" as a form of domination, then the ideological claims of recovering the Pre-Columbian past (which I will discuss next) are contradictory to methods that appropriate them for a colonizing project. For example, the invitation that the *Seminario de Cultura Náhuatl* has extended to indigenous intellectuals and the use of contemporary indigenous testimonies and records to state the authenticity of the sources[12] (two strategies clearly based on Sahagún's educational projects and his use of informants[13]), can be understood as the exercise of disciplinary cooptation of indigenous culture. Finally, since Sahagún provides, from León-Portilla's point of view, most of the sources, translations and transcriptions, questioning his method means leaving the discipline with far fewer reliable sources. That would leave the discipline with the sole possibility of studying the cultural contact and acknowledging, against itself, that Pre-Columbian culture is ultimately unnattainable.

Concluding that León-Portilla's usage of Hispanic heritage to study indigenous texts is nothing more than a form of cultural appropriation of the Pre-Columbian texts for a Western project or a naive use of problematic textualities would be easy, but a second Hispanist articulation makes this reading questionable. If Sahagún represents a form of approaching the Pre-Columbian Other from a methodological point of view based on the epistemological instruments of Renaissance humanism, the archetype of the Western humanist advocating for the cause of the Indians is Bartolomé de las Casas. As one of the humanists that came to the New World, Las Casas is a symbol of the struggles for Human Rights and emancipation of the indigenous peoples even today. Through an approach to the indigenous question based on the idea of an equivalence of worth between the Nahuatl culture and the classic Western cultures,[14] León-Portilla has found a structural base for political agencies regarding the indigenous question in the continent as his recovery of indigenous culture has allowed a formulation of it beyond the notions of the superiority of Western culture as an argument for colonization. His book, *La flecha en el blanco,* for instance, is a historical account of the alliance between an indigenous leader named Francisco Tenamaztle and Las Casas in the defense of the rights of the Indians in front of a court of law in Valladolid in 1555. This book has special significance if one considers that it was published one year after the Zapatista uprising, in which the question of the indigenous people became a central part of the debate of the Mexican transition.[15] Another good example of León-Portilla's political concerns in relation to the indigenous question may be found in a small book, *Pueblos originarios y globalización,* where he discusses the articulation of the Indians in current international contexts, defending their position as the original inhabitants of the American lands. As Bartolomé de las Casas did, León-Portilla defends the Indians' Human Rights against the violence exercised by Western misunderstanding and imposition. In this case, *Pueblos originarios y globalización,* published in 1997, uses the argument of the *indígenas* original rights considering that they were the original inhabitants of the continent, thus stating the legitimacy of their rights *vis-a-vis* Western culture. Here, León-Portilla's work is one of the basic foundations of such a claim since the existence of an organized culture in American lands prior to the arrival of the Spanish is one of the fundamental ideas to understand the Conquest not only as an encounter of cultures but also as a process of political oppression that has lasted more than five centuries. Therefore, questioning the possibility of reaching an "authentic" Pre-Columbian culture through the sources used by León-Portilla has consequences beyond purely heuristic considerations, since this possibility seems necessary to sustain the political agency for the *indígenas* implied in his political positions, precisely because such culture works as a testimony of a civilization lost by colonial violence, civilization in which the claims of "origin" by many indigenous groups today are rooted. Also, the validation of both Sahagún as scholar and Las Casas as advocate sustains the idea of Western intellectuals, such as León-Portilla, acting as legitimate mediators between cultures.

In this sense, it is important to point out León-Portilla's claims for the culture and rights of the Mexican *indígenas,* preceded the Zapatista by decades cause and that his advocacy, however strenghtened by the uprising in Chiapas, has its origins in the very first of his works. If León-Portilla claims the appreciation of Pre-Columbian heritage in *La filosofía náhuatl,* the anthologies published under the titles *Visión de los vencidos* and *El reverso de la conquista* are real political statements on reclaiming the "other side of history." Both, especially the former, contributed a great deal to the dissemination of León-Portilla's work around the world. These works have been translated into a number of languages and have impacted various debates on Third World literatures and postcolonial representations. It is important to note that *Visión de los vencidos* and *Reverso de la conquista* are anthologies heavily grounded in the Sahaguntian method discussed previously because they basically translate texts recovered by the different *Códices* produced by the Franciscan efforts in Tlaltelolco and, in the case of *Reverso,* by similar sources in both the Mayan and the Inca worlds. Nonetheless, their successful inscription in the political agendas of the 1960s postcolonial and third world-ist academic movements is not so much due to its accuracy of representing the other, but to its presentation as the recovery of a silenced voice. In other words, the importance of these books rests not so much on their rigor in recovering the indigenous textualities, but on the very gesture of recovering those textualities and presenting them as voices silenced by the colonial process.

This is clear when one reads one of the more enthusiastic approaches to the "vision of the vanquished" from Third World agendas in the Western academy: Jorge Klor de Alva's introduction to *Visión de los Vencidos* addressed an academic audience located in the United States. Klor de Alva states four basic functions of León-Portilla's works in the international context. First, the documents collected in the books are inscribed in an agenda of the so-called Third World by addressing concerns regarding the revision of colonial histories in postcolonial societies, an inscription that has allowed the book to be hailed in unlikely contexts, such as Roque Dalton's reading of *La visión de los vencidos* as an inspiration to Latin American revolutionaries. Second, these new textualities provide instruments for the formation of Mexican identity on both sides of the border. In other words, Klor de Alva's statement implies that the "vision of the vanquished" has not only served to revalue Mexican heritage but also as a form of cultural empowerment and agency within the Mexican-American community. Third, León-Portilla's books, whose later editions included testimonies from the Seventeenth to the Twentieth centuries, are also part of the discussions of multiculturalism in contemporary Western society and have been used, for example, in U.S. classrooms for discussions about racial, ethnic, and multicultural issues. Finally, the manner in which the texts are presented to the Western reader conveys a skillful construction and readability that allows them to speak eloquently against the "triumphalist Spanish interpretations" of the Conquest (Klor de Alva 101–104).

Even though this reading does not refer directly to Las Casas, Klor de Alva's remarks constitute one of the most interesting examples of the consequences of the "lascasian" adscription of León-Portilla's work. Probably the most eloquent argument in Klor's interpretation lies in the idea of recovering and re-reading Pre-Columbian textuality as a form of constructing effective political agency in today's causes. If Las Casas provides inspiration by defending the Indian as part of humankind,[16] the validation of the subalternized voice of the Indian as part of the identity constructed by current political and social movements (such as the anti-imperialist struggles in Central America or the emergence of a Mexican-American consciousness, as Klor de Alva points out) carries a defense of such subaltern groups through the recovery of elements in which those groups dialogue directly with the colonizer.[17] In other words, Klor de Alva's reading of León-Portilla is symptomatic of the agendas implied throughout the Mexican scholar's work: the importance of recovering Pre-Columbian cultures not as a form of building a foundational myth for the liberal state,[18] but as a strategy of empowerment for which contemporary *indígenas* might claim their political rights.

If *Visión de los vencidos* clearly responds to the attempt to recover political and epistemological instances from the silenced discourse of Pre-Columbian Indians, the consequences far exceed that because the topics involved in this project of lascasian nature are not limited to this postcolonial appropriation. One has to remember that the defense of the indigenous people and the recovery of their cultural origins within a national state constructed and sustained by a *criollo/mestizo* ideology after the Mexican Revolution allowed the use of the Pre-Columbian imaginary in the different discourses that has sustained the revolutionary regime's ideology. From the idealization of the Indian and his culture in works such as Ermilo Abreu Gómez's *Canek* to the use of supposedly indigenous traits as a form of defining, and sometimes criticising the "Mexican self" (i.e., Samuel Ramos's *Perfil del hombre y la cultura en México*) and reaching one of its more paradigmatic points in José Vasconcelos's work, a large intellectual tradition of recovery of the Pre-Columbian past as icon of the agendas of the revolutionary regime has led to a reading of León-Portilla's work as one of the bases for the constitution of a national ideology. As such, León-Portilla's recovery and defense of indigenous culture acquires a paradoxical form of political empowerment that goes beyond the defense of the cause itself, for the recognition of Pre-Columbian origins allows a prescriptive construction of notions of national identity through its usage by different instances of the political hegemony.

Thus, despite the implications discussed in Klor de Alva's account, it is undeniable that León-Portilla's *indigenismo* is rooted in a national context that problematizes it as a form of approaching the Other. In 1950 before the publication of the first works of Garibay and León-Portilla, a key book appeared on the Mexican cultural horizon: Luis Villoro's *Los grandes momentos del indigenismo en México*. The focus of Villoro's book is an intense critique of indigenist approaches throughout Mexico's history, stating that it has been, amongst other things, the construction of a false consciousness supported by an approach to the Indian based in a set of preconceptions that distort his reality (8–9). Furthermore, Villoro considers that all the *indigenismo* prior to his book is founded on the need that the *mestizaje* ideology had to co-opt the Indian in order to justify its claims as the sole ideology capable of exercising an agency for the construction of a nation (216–17).[19] Finally, Villoro understands the possibility of proposing *indigenismo* as a movement that destabilizes Mexican identity and functions as a strategy of self-reflection in which Mexico discovers the contradictions within its national being (275).[20]

Reading León-Portilla through some of Villoro's insights reveals one of the most interesting paradoxes of the political articulation of his work. As we have discussed, León-Portilla's sources are the texts that lie precisely in the foundational point of *indigenismo* understood in Villoro's book as an epistemology that concurrently seeks a defense of the Indian through the external understanding of his culture while silencing the specificities of that voice through the process of its incorporation into a larger discourse (from universal mankind to Mexican nation). León-Portilla's work has implied, in some cases, an overcoming of this paradox, particularly in his latest works. Nonetheless, León-Portilla's institutional adscriptions have resulted in some lines of interpretation where the scholarship on Nahuatl literature and culture is understood as part of a Mexican national discourse rather than the basis for agencies of indigenous autonomy or specificity.

It is undeniable that León-Portilla openly sympathizes with the contemporary claims of indigenous autonomy, despite the fact that some of his disciples, such as Patrick Johansson, state the process of transculturation of indigenous cultures as an inevitable reality and question the fact of imposing a standard of autonomy to that ongoing process (Johansson, "MLP y el mundo indígena" 213–215).[21] Moreover, Mexican official discourse has claimed León-Portilla's work as part of the construction of Mexican nationality. Leaving aside León-Portilla's performance as an intellectual figure (which includes his efforts to institutionalize the study of Pre-Hispanic cultures within the context of the National University and his public functions in government agencies and as

Mexico's UNESCO representative), the Mexican State has used a monumental-izing interpretation of Nahuatl culture in order to claim the Pre-Columbian past as the origin of a Mexican nation lead by the Revolutionary regime and in the middle of a struggle for the recognition of its historical role in the world. This claim has pre-empted León-Portilla's approach, shown by the tribute organized by the government of the Mexican state of Jalisco in 1989. The historian José María Muriá, for example, considers that the most important contribution of León-Portilla is the legitimating of Mexican history as a chapter of universal history (7). Another historian, Guillermo García Oropeza speaks of León-Por-tilla as the agent who has been "the guide of Telemacus's return to the origin" (15, my translation). Furthermore, in his speech, the governor of Jalisco ad-dressed León-Portilla by saying: "And you, sir, have given an unmistakable example that Mexico also has a place to occupy in the concert of the universe" ("Palabras del gobernador" 22, my translation). Behind the hyperboles, the rhetoric and the entire performativity of the political act lies an attempt to co-opt the Pre-Columbian discourse as a form to create what Renan has called the "mythical origins of the nation."[22] This, of course, generates one of the deepest paradoxes in León-Portilla's work. On the one hand, his attempt to recover Pre-Columbian culture is founded on the idea of reclaiming the voice silenced by the colonial process as a form of resistance from the indigenous groups. Yet the other, its institutional inscriptions provoke the use of this very same recovery in the construction of legitimacy for the national identity promoted by the state, an identity that is based on the monumentalization of the Pre-Columbian past in a national discourse that subalternizes indigenous groups.

Interestingly enough, León-Portilla's work allows for this second ap-proach, since it has provided, along with the "scientific" methods of contem-porary archeology, a consistent narrative of Pre-Columbian culture distanced at some points from current indigenous practices. If archeology provides an enormous patrimony of physical monuments dated carefully by a number of methods, León-Portilla and Garibay's research certainly presents a coherent cultural system to go along with it. In many works, both proposed chronologies based on the historical accounts (known basically as the *Anales*) recollected both by Sahagún's informants and the Indian nobles educated at the school of Santa Cruz de Tlaltelolco. However, this historical method is not always free of controversy. One of the most polemic issues is the notion of authorship. In a series of works, included in his book *Quince poetas del mundo náhuatl,* he has established a series of authors of some of the most important poems in the corpus. The method of establishing this authorship is extensively discussed throughout León-Portilla's work, but it is based on two primary strategies: the fact that the names are usually identified as the poetic voice of the texts (in other words, that the poems are in first person and usually that first person is one of the alleged poets) and that the historical records give evidence of the historical existence of those figures. Nonetheless, this method does not necessarily resist the criticism articulated by scholars such as Bierhorst, Segala, or Burkhart, in the sense that most of those alleged authors are actually emperors and that it does not seem unlikely to think that poets identified them as the poetic voice for a number of possible reasons, including the pledge of allegiance towards them or the legitimating of the emperors as power figures. Hence, the actual authors of the poems might not have been the emperors, but someone within their subjects that used the persona of the emperor as poetic voice in order to pay tribute. In any case, the assumption of authorship does serve the purpose of creating a series of cultural heroes to add to the Mexican national pantheon.

An extreme case in the construction of authorship is José Luis Martínez's *Nezahualcóyotl: Vida y obra.* This book, published as a commemoration of the 500th anniversary of Nezahualcóyotl's death and currently part of the curriculum in Mexican schools at all levels, consists of a narrative recreation of the Aztec emperor's life, allegedly based on historical documents and a compilation of poems attributed to him. The book's fictional rhetoric is a clear example of the pedagogical uses of the Aztec figures in the reproduction and idealization of Pre-Columbian sources of national identity. It is also clear that the book is part of a trend that poses Nezahualcóyotl as an icon of Mexican nationality.[23] What is possible to observe here is that a book like this is possible due to the theoretical foundations León-Portilla has given to the notion of authorship. Even though it is methodologically questionable, Martinez's book proves that the constitution of individual figures in the context of Pre-Columbian studies provides a necessary fiction in order to create a place for the Indians in the country's official history. Thus, we can conclude that León-Portilla's work has successfully represented a wide range of ideological articulations, and the debate on the indigenous question, both in terms of claims of autonomy and national appropriation, is far from over.[24]

A final articulation of León-Portilla in the paradigm of Hispanism is his recovery of Spanish language in the context of contemporary indigenous claims.[25] In his speech after his entry into the Mexican Language Academy, León-Portilla addressed the *mestizaje* of the Spanish language as a positive factor, since it paralleled the racial *mestizaje* on which the nation is founded ("Los maestros prehispánicos" 3). This first development of the concept of Spanish language as a fundamental part of the ideal of incorporating the indigenous peoples into the national paradigm is clearly inscribed in the nationalistic ideology characteristic of the *indigenismo*. Therefore, León-Portilla's earliest discussion of Spanish language as part of the constitution of an indigenous agency within the nation's discursive limits was presented within the context of his incorporation into the very Academy that represents the normative aspect of the "national language" and as an introduction to a lecture that centered on recovering the value of the "ancient voice." In this presentation, León-Portilla seeks a connection that may reconcile the revaluation of Pre-Columbian culture with the hegemonic conception of Mexican nationality. The relationship he establishes between language and cultural processes is quite interesting since linguistic claims are a fundamental part of contemporary indigenous struggles.

The overwhelming growth of indigenous movements in Mexico, mainly expressed in the work of anthropologists such as Guillermo Bonfil Batalla and in the claims of the Zapatistas, has provoked a change in the perception of *mestizaje* within León-Portilla's work. Probably the most important claim that has been recovered is the right of cultures to exist within a pluralistic society that recognizes each group's right to its own culture (Bonfil Batalla 229–45). León-Portilla, who has openly sympathized with contemporary indigenous struggles, in 1997 offered a new approach to his posture regarding the Spanish language as a fundamental part of the political processes of the *indígenas* in Mexico. In *Pueblos originarios y globalización,* he defends the Spanish language as the *lingua franca* among the different ethnic groups of the country (44–45). Interestingly enough, in the same essay, León-Portilla explicitly states that this usage of the Spanish language is not exclusive of the plurality of cultures and languages existent within Mexico because its use as common ground in discussion between cultures does not contradict or challenge their right of existence or cultural specificity (57).

This posture distances itself from the triumphant exaltation of the linguistic and cultural *mestizaje* León-Portilla endorsed in 1962, but it still represents an implicit ideological problem. One of the first questions one can raise to such a posture surrounds the implications of considering Spanish as the *lingua franca*. The need for using the "national language" in such function operates at two levels. First, since Spanish is the official governmental language and constantly used for political negotiation, the knowledge and use of Spanish by communities is an indispensable tool for the advancement of political agendas, such as the creation of laws and the everyday relations with the state. However, the adoption of Spanish by communities implies that bilingualism is also indispensable because the indigenous languages are unable to offer effective communication with a state system where Spanish is not merely the hegemonic language, but the only language valid for political interaction. Thus, bilingualism, when adopted only because of an imposed political necessity, may be regarded as one of the factors that obstructs cultural autonomy since it is based precisely on the subalternization of alternate linguistic systems which are unable to convey a political agency in the context of the relations with the hegemonic powers.[26]

Finally, it is necessary to emphasize another factor concerning the Spanish language in its relationship with Nahuatl scholarship: most "knowledge" produced about Nahuatl literature and culture is channeled through Spanish and addressed primarily to Spanish-reading audiences. In terms of specific textual strategies, this means that the approach that León-Portilla has to the texts sometimes follows the intention of constructing legibility for the Spanish-language reader. For instance, in his recent translation of the *Nican mopohua*, a Nahuatl text that narrates the legend of the Virgin of Guadalupe, León-Portilla states that the purpose of his translation is to reach a version that allows the reader to perceive the "spirituality" presented in the text (15). In other words, the priority of the translation is to translate an experience from one cultural horizon to a very different one. Furthermore, the fact that the scholarship on Nahuatl literature is primarly addressed to a Spanish-speaking audience is conflictual with the claims of cultural continuity because readers who actually profit from this scholarship are not necessarily the *indígenas* claiming cultural autonomy, but Spanish-speaking readers who, in most cases, have perceived in the idea of Pre-Columbian culture as part of a wider Mexican culture. Thus, establishing a connection with the wide Spanish-speaking audience falls into Villoro's criticism of *indigenismo,* since in the end there is still an attempt to identify the national self with the indigenous other. The possibility of a recovery of these texts in the context of contemporary indigenous cultures is an urgent item in the agenda of Nahuatl literature's criticism.

After considering these three examples of the Hispanist articulation of the study of Nahuatl literature (the recovery of Sixteenth Century scholarship as the authoritative source for the Pre-Columbian studies discipline, the reference to Las Casas as a form of articulating political agendas around the discipline and the problem of language politics within a corpus of texts where this problem carries both methodological and political consequences), it is clear that both the methodological and the ideological foundations of León-Portilla's work carry a re-evaluation of approaches and concerns inherited by the Spanish humanism of the sixteenth century. These concerns are recovered through their articulation with contemporary ideological concerns regarding both the need of a Mexican and Latin American national/regional narrative and the claims of contemporary indigenous groups. The sometimes paradoxical way in which those factors interact constitutes the ideological core of the discipline. Therefore, the work that León-Portilla has developed throughout nearly five decades is inscribed, in its foundations, in a different form of Hispanism. His Hispanism is not so much about the struggles between Peninsular and Latin American Spanish or the colonial impositions of the Spanish language but a revision of a legacy that implies the identification with the Peninsular sources of Mexican and Latin American culture as a strategy to recover the pertinence of the Pre-Columbian as a source of our Latin American imagined community. This Hispanism participates in a careful revision of the colonial legacy against deterministic and Manichean approaches to it. It seeks to constitute a postcolonial agenda not by fully rejecting any intervention of Spanish culture, but by carefully reconsidering some of its contributions as a valuable political instrument to be reappropriated in the context of contemporary claims. Within contemporary Hispanism, León-Portilla's work has been a powerful reminder that the struggles five centuries ago occupied the Spanish humanists against the violent logics of coloniality and that the need to reconcile our Spanish heritage and language with the claims of contemporary indigenous peoples is far from over. Moreover, León-Portilla's legacy requires new approaches where the different humanist ideological paradoxes are interpreted and considered beyond simplistic interpretations that understand Spanish humanism as fundamentally colonial. New understandings of these colonial foundations, through a reading in which they appear as a source of productive paradoxes that have constituted many of the region's cultural problems, may contribute to one of the most urgent debates in Latin America today: the relationship between Western and indigenous cultures in a political context where understanding the *indígena* as an unattainable Other or as part of a larger national discourse seems less viable.

Notes

1. A clear example of this is the tribute *In Iihiyo, in Itlahtol* in which many of the most important scholars on current Pre-Columbian studies name León-Portilla as a primary source and as the founder of the discipline. The book includes both biographical accounts and theoretical discussions of his work.
2. For an account of most of the intellectual discussions and their political and institutional origins, see Pedro Ángel Palou's *Escribir en México durante los años locos.*
3. A study of this has been conducted by Héctor Perea in his book *España en la obra de Alfonso Reyes,* which includes an anthology of Reyes's work on Spanish culture and its relations to the foundation of an American cultural specificity.
4. The sections I refer to are primarily the ones devoted to the religious rituals and to the feasts. See León-Portilla, *Literatura del México antiguo,* 48–87 and 238–83.

5. The *Historia general de las cosas de la Nueva España* follows a taxonomy which divides the Nahuas' world through a scholastic model that goes from the "heavenly matters," (that is, the Gods) to the "earthly" ones (feasts, and so on). Some of Sahagún's classifications stand just as presented by the friar in León-Portilla's anthology.
6. See the articles by Mignolo and Mignolo and Ebacher.
7. This method consisted in designing detailed questionnaires in order to obtain information from indigenous noblemen about the different cultural practices among the Nahuas.
8. This has been noted and analyzed by Todorov, 229–54.
9. After the publication of the Spanish translation of Segala's book, León-Portilla published a review ("Una nueva aportación") in which he argued that Segala's criticisms were not valid because the Italian scholar did not speak Náhuatl, thus lacking the basic methodological tools to make such a criticism. This gave way to a controversy, in which Segala accused León-Portilla of turning Náhuatl literature into a "coto privado" (a private preserve) (Segala "La literatura náhuatl"), to which León-Portilla produced yet another response ("A modo de comentario"). Since this controversy is more related to academic politics than to the concerns of the present work, I will not give a detailed account of it.
10. In contrast, Todorov accepts Sahagún's strive for objectivity (235), but also recognizes his interference in the constitution of the corpus.
11. Garibay, in his *Panorama literario de los pueblos nahuas,* applies the classical distinction between epic, lyric, and didactic discourses to Nahuatl poetry, while León-Portilla's distinction between *cuicatl* and *tlahtolli,* collected in the book *El destino de la palabra,* is analogous to the Western distinction between poetry and prose. One must not forget that Garibay, far from being devoted only to Pre-Columbian textualities, was also one of the most important editors and translators of Greek and Latin literature in Mexico.
12. For the former, see Silva Galeana. For the latter, see León-Portilla, *El destino de la palabra* (63).
13. The invitation of indigenous intellectuals to the Seminar has the enormous merit of re-incorporating them into the debates of Pre-Columbian culture, yet still can be read as a recovery of the idea of the indigenous informant that provides "authentic" information to western scholars. This can also be noted by the method in which contemporary documents are used to establish the authenticity of sources, just like Sahagún used the recounts of Ixtlixóchitl or Tezozómoc in the Colegio de Tlaltelólco, without considering the fact that such documents were already under the influence of Spanish culture.
14. See, for example, the introduction to his first book, *La filosofía náhuatl,* where he claims the existence of a Nahuatl philosophical thought equivalent to Greek production (5). This statement, of course, is aligned with similar statements by Alfonso Reyes, whose studies on the classical culture are part of the claim of the existence of an American philosophy. See also Dussel's debate with Appel.
15. The introduction of the *indígenas* as part of the political agenda was due to the

Zapatistas. This new centrality has allowed intellectuals aligned with indigenous causes such as Carlos Montemayor or León-Portilla himself to direct their work towards more concrete political causes.

16. For this, the reference is again *La flecha en el blanco.*

17. Just to mention an example, one can see how this claim operates in a project such as Gloria Anzaldúa's. In *Borderlands/La frontera,* Anzaldúa constantly refers to the Nahuatl roots of Chicano culture, to the extent of using some Nahuatl terms as part of her linguistic performance. The book includes a poetry section named "Ehécatl" after the Náhuatl god of the Wind, in which she appeals to many symbols of the Pre-Columbian imaginary. This approach, along with movements such as Aztlán, show the potential of Pre-Columbian scholarship as a foundation for political agendas within the context of identity and subaltern politics.

18. As Luis Villoro criticized. See Villoro, 113–209.

19. Villoro: "The indigenous also appear as a reality in which I can recognize myself, without disregarding the fact that it is different from me. It is like the surface of a pound, sometimes dark, sometimes clear, that always allows me to find the outline of my own figure" (294, my translation). It has to be noted that the first person used here by Villoro does not convey his own opinions but poses itself in the perspective of some authors studied in his book.

20. Despite being more than fifty years old, Villoro's book remains the most insightful and provocative approach to the politics of *indigenismo* in the Mexican context, with notions and observations that can be applied even to contemporary approaches to the indigenous question all over the continent. However, it is evident that much has happened in the last fifty years regarding the articulation of the Pre-Columbian cultures in the Mexican national narrative. For an accessible account of this process in the years following Villoro's book, see Florescano, *El nuevo pasado mexicano,* 15–28.

21. It is worth mentioning that there has been an ongoing tendency of claiming continuity between the Pre-Columbian cultures and the contemporary indigenous people from distinct points of view. The seminal work is Guillermo Bonfil Batalla's *México profundo,* which claims recognition of the indigenous culture against the consistent denial it has suffered throughout Mexican history. James Lockhart wrote an extensive book, *The Nahuas after the Conquest,* in which he discusses the continuity and rearticulating of the Nahuatl culture during the Colonial period. Lockhart's analysis engages a wide spectrum of topics, from everyday life and the forms of government to the changes in cultural production. Finally, Enrique Florescano's most recent work, *Memoria indígena,* claims the indigenous practices of cultural and historical memory as a form of resistance towards the national constructions and the traditional historiography.

22. I take the idea from Renan's classic essay "What is a nation?" where he talks about the need for a national discourse to create mythological roots beyond a regular temporality to state the perennial existence of the nation.

23. This incorporation goes as far as including cities and streets named after him and

using his image on one of the denominations of the Mexican currency, where the one-hundred pesos bill includes a fragment of one of his most popular poems written in fine print.

24. For a study on how the Mexican state has appropriated the Pre-Columbian past, Luis Villoro is once again an authoritative source. A broader study on the role of the ethnic question in the construction of the modern national state is another book by Enrique Florescano, *Etnia, estado y nación.* Another interesting text, that sums up the articulation of the Pre-Columbian, the Hispanic and the "universal" in the context of Mexican identity is a compilation of classical works assembled by León-Portilla under the title *Raíces indígenas, presencia hispánica.* The book recollects texts from some of the landmark thinkers of national identity, such as Octavio Paz, Alfonso Reyes, Ignacio Bernal, and Carlos Fuentes. León-Portilla, in a speech later published under the title *México: De su historia, penuries y esperanzas,* identifies himself with the celebratory discourse, by claiming that "thanks to the Mesoamericans we can affirm that Mexico has been, through the millenniums, a land of books, in which schools existed and culture flourished" (21, my translation).

25. A related topic that I will not address for reasons of space is the role that the Spanish language played in the colonization of the Pre-Columbian culture. This topic is widely analyzed by Walter Mignolo in his book *The Darker Side of Renaissance,* where he discusses, among other things, the role of Nebrija's linguistic project in colonization and the diverse roles that the Spanish friars played in this process.

26. In spite of these political tensions, some approaches to this question have attempted a conciliatory view of the relationship between Spanish and the indigenous languages. Pilar Máynez, for instance, has analyzed something in León-Portilla's work she considers a form of "linguistic *indigenismo*" in which Pre-Columbian culture acquires agency through the incorporation of Nahuatl terms into the Spanish language ("El indigenismo lingüístico" 412). This approach seems more related to the defense of a *mestizaje* project within the field of Pre-Columbian studies, which as we have seen lies at the bottom in some of León-Portilla's works, especially the earliest ones. However, this consideration of *indigenismo* no longer appears to be at the center of León-Portilla's discussions as his views have shifted toward an understanding of the problem from the cultural autonomy perspective.

Works Cited

Abreu Gómez, Ermilo. *Canek.* Mexico: Plaza y Janés, 2000.

Anzaldúa, Gloria. *Borderlands/La Frontera.* San Francisco: Aunt Lute Books, 1991.

Bierhorst, John. *Cantares Mexicanos: Songs of the Aztecs.* Stanford: Stanford University Press, 1985.

Bonfil Batalla, Guillermo. *México profundo: Una civilización negada.* Mexico City: Grijalbo, 1994.

Burkhart, Louise M. *The Slippery Earth.* Tucson: University of Arizona Press, 1989.

Dussel, Enrique. "A Nahuatl Interpretation of the Conquest: From the 'Parousia' of the Gods to the 'Invasión.'" *Latin American Identity and the Constructions of Difference.* Ed. Amaryll Chanadi. Minneapolis: University of Minnesota Press, 1994. 104–29. (Hispanic Issues, vol. 10).

Florescano, Enrique. *El nuevo pasado mexicano.* Mexico: Cal y arena, 1991.

———. *Etnia, estado y nación.* Mexico: Aguilar, 1998.

———. *Memoria indígena.* Mexico: Taurus, 1999.

Gamio, Manuel. *Forjando patria.* Mexico: Porrúa, 1916.

García Oropeza, Guillermo. "Homenaje a Miguel León Portilla." *Homenaje.* 13–19.

Garibay K. Ángel Ma. *Historia de la literatura náhuatl.* 2 vols. Mexico: Porrúa, 1954.

———. *Panorama literario de los pueblos nahuas.* Sepan Cuantos 22. Mexico: Porrúa, 1997.

Henríquez Ureña, Pedro. *Literary Currents in Hispanic America.* Cambridge: Harvard University Press, 1945.

———. *Obra crítica.* Mexico; Fondo de Cultura Económica, 1960.

Hernández de León-Portilla, Ascensión. "Presencia y aliento de la obra de fray Bernardino de Sahagún." *In Iihiyo.* 67–85.

Homenaje a Miguel León-Portilla. Guadalajara: Gobierno del Estado de Jalisco, 1990.

In Iihiyo, in Itlahol: Su aliento, su palabra. Homenaje a Miguel León-Portilla. Mexico City: Universidad Nacional Autónoma de México/El Colegio Nacional/Instituto Nacional Antropología e Historia, 1992.

Johansson K., Patrick. "Miguel León-Portilla y el mundo indígena." *In Iihiyo.* 205–20.

———. *La palabra de los aztecas.* Mexico: Trillas, 1993.

———. *Voces distantes de los aztecas.* Mexico; Fernández Editores, 1994.

———. *Ritos mortuorios nahuas precolombinos.* Puebla: Secretaria de Cultura Puebla, 2002.

Klor de Alva, J. Jorge. "The Vision of the Vanquished." *In Iihiyo.* 101–10.

León-Portilla, Miguel. *Visión de los vencidos.* Biblioteca del estudiante universitario 81. Mexico: Universidad Nacional Autónoma de México, 1959.

———. *Los maestros prehispánicos de la palabra: Discurso de ingreso a la Academia Mexicana de la Lengua.* Mexico: Cuadernos Americanos, 1962.

———. *El reverso de la Conquista.* Mexico: Joaquín Mortiz, 1964.

———. *Literatura del México antiguo.* Biblioteca Ayacucho 28. Caracas: Ayacucho, 1978.

———. *Pre-Columbian Literatures of México.* Trans. Grace Lobanov and Miguel León-Portilla. Norman: University of Oklahoma Press, 1979.

———. *Toltecáyotl. Aspectos de cultura náhuatl.* Mexico City: Fondo de Cultura Económica, 1980.

———. "¿Una nueva aportación sobre la literatura náhuatl?" *Estudios de cultura náhuatl* 21 (1991): 293–308.

————. *América Latina: Múltiples culturas, pluralidad de lenguas.* Mexico: El Colegio Nacional, 1992.

————. "A modo de comentario." *Cahiers du Monde Hispanique et Luso-Brasilien/Caravelle* 59 (1992): 221–23.

————. *Quince poetas del mundo náhuatl.* Mexico: Diana, 1994.

————. *La flecha en el blanco.* Mexico: Diana, 1995.

————. *México: De su historia, penurias y esperanzas.* Mexico: El Colegio Nacional, 1995b.

————. *El destino de la palabra.* Mexico City: Fondo de Cultura Económica/El Colegio Nacional, 1996.

————. *La filosofía náhuatl.* Reviewed Edition. Mexico: Universidad Nacional Autónoma de México, 1997.

————. *Pueblos originarios y globalización.* Mexico: El Colegio Nacional, 1997b.

————. *Bernardino de Sahagún. Pionero de la antropología.* Mexico: Universidad Nacional Autónoma de México/El Colegio Nacional, 1999.

————. *Tonantzin Guadalupe.* Mexico City: Fondo de Cultura Económica, 2000.

León-Portilla, Miguel, ed. *Raíces indígenas, presencia hispánica.* Mexico: El Colegio Nacional, 1993.

Lockhart, James. *The Nahuas after the Conquest.* Stanford: Stanford UP, 1992.

Martínez, José Luis. *Nezahualcóyotl: Vida y obra.* Mexico City: Fondo de Cultura Económica, 1972.

Máynez, Pilar. "Las traducciones de textos nahuas recogidos por Sahagún." *In Iihiyo.* 113–23.

————. "El indigenismo lingüístico en la obra de Miguel León-Portilla." *Estudios de Cultura Náhuatl* 24 (1994): 411–18.

Mignolo, Walter. "Signs and their Transmission: The Question of the Book in the New World." *Writing without Words.* Eds. Elizabeth Hill Boon and Walter D. Mignolo. Durham: Duke University Press, 1994b. 220–70.

————. *The Darker Side of Renaissance.* Ann Arbor: University of Michigan Press, 1995.

————. *Local Histories/Global Designs.* Princeton: Princeton University Press, 2000.

Mignolo, Walter D and Coleen Ebacher. "Alfabetización y literatura: Los *huehuetlatolli* como ejemplo de la semiosis colonial." *Conquista y contraconquista.* Eds. Julio Ortega y José Amor Vázquez. Providence/Mexico City: Brown University/El Colegio de México, 1994. 17–31.

Muriá, José María. "En homenaje de León-Portilla." *Homenaje.* 7–12.

"Palabras del Doctor Miguel León-Portilla." *Homenaje.* 23–30.

"Palabras del gobernador del Estado de Jalisco, Licenciado Guillermo Cosío Vidaurri." *Homenaje.* 21–22.

Palou, Pedro Ángel. *Escribir en México durante los años locos.* Puebla: Benemérita Universidad Autónoma de Puebla, 2001.

Perea, Héctor. *España en la obra de Alfonso Reyes.* Mexico: Fondo de Cultura Económica, 1990.

Renan, Ernest. "What is a Nation." *Nation and Narration.* Ed. Homi Bhabha. London: Routledge, 2000. 8–22.

Ramos, Samuel. *El perfil de la cultura y el hombre en México.* Mexico: El Colegio Nacional/Espasa Calpe, 2000.

Reyes, Alfonso. *Última Tule y otros ensayos.* Biblioteca Ayacucho 163. Caracas: Ayacucho, 1993.

Sahagún, Fray Bernardino de. *Códice Florentino.* México: Secretaría de Gobernación, 1979.

———. *Historia general de las cosas de la nueva España.* 2 vols. Madrid: Alianza, 1988.

Segala, Amos. *Literatura náhuatl: Fuentes, identidades, representaciones.* Trans. Mónica Mansour. México: Consejo Nacional para la Cultura y las Artes, 1990.

———. "La literatura náhuatl: Un coto privado?" *Cahiers du Monde Hispanique et Luso-Brasilien/Caravelle* 59 (1992): 209–19.

Silva Galeana, Librado. "El seminario de cultura náhuatl." *In Iihiyo.* 265–75.

Todorov, Tzvetan. *La conquista de América. El problema del otro.* Trans. Flora Botton Burlá. Mexico: Siglo XXI, 1998.

Villoro, Luis. *Los grandes momentos del indigenismo en México.* Mexico City: El Colegio de México/El Colegio Nacional/Fondo de Cultura Económica, 1996.

3

"La hora ha llegado"
Hispanism, Pan-Americanism, and the Hope
of Spanish/American Glory (1938–1948)[1]

Sebastiaan Faber

How does one justify writing fiction and poetry—or, for that matter, literary criticism—in a time of international crisis? What legitimacy does creating and studying literature have when the newspapers are full of war and death? North-American Hispanists and Spanish-speaking intellectuals facing these questions in the 1930s and '40s had a confident, double answer to that dilemma. In the first place, as scholars and writers, they saw themselves as a powerful force for peace. After all, they were guardians of Culture, which they conceived of as a privileged realm of essential "spiritual values" not only transcending economics and politics, but also national borders. As representatives par excellence of this realm, they viewed themselves as major players in world history. In 1935 and 1937, for instance, hundreds of Western intellectuals concerned with the rise of fascism gathered in Paris and Valencia to join forces "In Defense of Culture"; and when in 1938 almost a hundred professors of Latin American literature united in Mexico City to found the "Instituto Internacional de Literatura Iberoamericana" (IILI), they did so under the slogan *"A la fraternidad por la cultura"* (toward fraternity through culture).

In the first case, "culture" was directly linked to antifascism, functioning as an umbrella concept that allowed for an alliance between the liberal bourgeois intelligentsia and the more radical leftist sectors associated with the Socialist and Communist parties—a phenomenon closely connected with the Popular Front strategy ratified in the summer of 1935 by the Communist International. The fraternity invoked in the second case, on the other hand, did not primarily refer to antifascism, nor to the universal brotherhood of man, but rather to the brotherhood of Spanish and English-speaking Americans. To be sure, the members of the newly founded IILI believed that studying literature was in itself a practice conducing to peace and progress; they also believed that this was especially true for the literature of the Americas. Two years after the Institute's foundation, while the Second World War was raging through Europe, the IILI's journal, the *Revista Iberoamericana,* optimistically predicted a great future for the American continent: "¿Quiénes habrán de recoger el tesoro de la cultura occidental para salvarlo y glorificarlo?" the editors asked, and their answer could not have been more confident: "¡La Hora de América ha llegado!" ("Hora" 13) (Who will recover the treasure of Western culture in order to safeguard and glorify it? . . . The Time of the Americas has come!). If culture was constructed in spiritual terms as a privileged space of peace and progress, then, for the members of the IILI, this space had its precise geographical equivalent in the Americas. The *Revista*'s editors were sure that "América ha de aceptar su augusto destino singular: realizar para siempre el ensueño de las edades y hacer posible el reino del Espíritu entre los pueblos" (The Americas will accept their singular, magnificent destiny: to realize for eternity the dream of all ages, and allow for the reign of the Spirit to rule among all peoples) ("Hora" 13–14). In other words, they saw culture both as a transcendental tool of peace and understanding, and as a *specific* source of pride and glory for their nation, their language, or, in this case, their continent. As we will see in the following, Popular Frontist intellectuals celebrated culture in much the same way as a positive force in both global and regional terms, as both a source of universal values and concrete, local prestige. Underlying both cases is an unresolved tension between a universalist, humanist, Enlightenment conception of culture, and a Romantic, essentialist, or exceptionalist one.

In what follows, we will identify this tension as one of the main problems underlying the concept of Hispanism. The general purpose of this essay, however, is to discuss the ideological dimensions of Hispanism in the light of the transformations it underwent between 1938 and 1948, the turbulent decade preceding the outbreak of the Cold War. In these years, Hispanism was redefined by three major historical and political events in a crucial way: the Spanish Civil War (1936–1939) and its aftermath of intellectual exile; Roosevelt's Good Neighbor Policy and the accompanying revival of U.S.-sponsored

Pan-Americanism; and the Second World War, which damaged Europe's power and prestige, seemingly leaving the Americas as the only hope for humankind. Three important journals founded during this period will serve to illustrate these redefinitions: the *Revista Iberoamericana,* already mentioned, *España Peregrina,* and *Romance.*[2]

The ideological underpinnings of Hispanism are complex, contradictory, and not always politically sound, as has been argued by several critics in recent debates on the topic.[3] From these debates, four areas have emerged as especially problematic. Most notable is perhaps the tension between Hispanism as a *transnational* concept spanning the entire former Spanish empire, and its role in bolstering—or negating—different *national* identities. The academic practice of Hispanism, it turns out, has been closely connected with different cultural nationalisms, and with exceptionalist readings of different national histories and national "missions" or "destinies." This is especially true for the cases of Spain, Germany, and the United States.[4] A second area of controversy is the definition of *"Hispanic culture,"* that is, Hispanism's purported object of study. This definition has proven doubly problematic. On one hand, different Hispanisms have alternatively privileged or excluded Peninsular, Latin American, or U.S. Latino phenomena as belonging to the realm of the "Hispanic." On the other hand, the notion of "culture" has privileged or excluded culture in its high, folk, or mass manifestations. A third area of debate has centered around the relationship between Hispanism and *politics.* At stake here are Hispanism's explicit ties with political parties, programs, ideals, and interventions; the field's own implicit political dimensions or foundations; and the role and status of the Hispanist qua intellectual or scholar in relation to his or her object of study. Finally, since its very inception, Hispanism has been significantly shaped by preoccupations with the *status and prestige* of the field itself, as well as its object of study; a sense of injustice, of not having received the appreciation it deserves, seems never to have been completely absent. It is in this debate that we should situate the problematic relationship of Hispanism with "theory," the question whether Hispanism is "behind" or "ahead" of other disciplines, and whether it can or should adopt "foreign" disciplinary paradigms or, rather, generate its own.[5]

This essay will confirm the major arguments made in recent debates around Hispanism and show that many of the issues at stake now were in fact already being discussed—though not resolved—sixty years ago, sometimes in quite similar terms. My approach here is rather critical, and from what follows one might well conclude that Hispanism, as a term and a disciplinary paradigm, has long outlived its validity and legitimacy—or, for that matter, its usefulness. Incidentally, this is also the view of Sir Raymond Carr, the distinguished historian of modern Spain, who expressly refuses to see himself as a Hispanist. In fact, as he confessed to Santos Juliá in *El País,* he outright despises the term. It makes it seem, he says, "como si un historiador de España tuviera que tener dotes psicológicas, casi espirituales, para penetrar en el alma de España. . . ." (as if a historian of Spain would need special psychological, almost spiritual talents to penetrate Spain's soul . . .). Carr, in other words, disapproves of the term Hispanism because it is rooted in Spanish cultural nationalism: He rejects its essentialist connotations implying the existence of a national soul or character and, more importantly, the corresponding exceptionalist reading of Spain and its history—an interpretation which Carr and his followers have always forcefully rejected (Juliá).

But, one might wonder, would Raymond Carr normally be considered a Hispanist? Perhaps not in the realm of the U.S. academy, where the term Hispanism seems to have been monopolized by literary scholars, particularly those in Peninsular studies.[6] We should not forget, however, that one of the traditional meanings of "Hispanism" refers, indeed, to a multidisciplinary field of study that covers literature, culture, and history. The problem is, of course, that this is not by far the term's only definition. In fact, the concept is so vague that this would in itself constitute sufficient reason to argue against its usage. Is Hispanism, for instance, limited to Spain, or does it also include Latin America? Does it primarily focus on literature, or rather on history and culture? Is it necessary for a Hispanist to be a Hispano*phile* as well? And if so, does that imply a love and interest for Spain, for Spanish America, or just for the Spanish language? Are scholars of Catalan or Quechua also considered Hispanists? And perhaps the most important question: Is Hispanism founded on the very premise that the former Spanish empire still forms a tightly-knit cultural unity? In other words, is Hispanism the same as, or closely related to, *Pan*-Hispanism?

It is important to keep in mind that this terminological confusion stems partly from cross-linguistic contamination between Spanish and English. *Hispanismo* and Hispanism do not necessarily mean exactly the same thing, and neither do *hispanista* and Hispanist. According to the *Diccionario Salvat,* for instance, a *hispanismo* is in the first place a "giro o modo de hablar propio y privativo de la lengua española" or a "vocablo o giro de esta lengua empleada en otro" (turn of phrase or way of speaking typical of, and restricted to, the Spanish language . . . word or turn of phrase from this language used in another language)—the Spanish equivalent, in other words, of a Gallicism or Anglicism. Salvat only lists as its last meaning of *hispanismo* the "afición al estudio de lengua y literatura españolas y de las cosas de España" (fondness for the study of the Spanish language and literature and other things pertaining to Spain) (note the amateur status implied by the word "afición": Hispanists are "fans" of Spain; Spain is their hobby, perhaps their passion). The definition given by the Spanish Real Academia is very similar. It defines *hispanismo* as, again, an "afición," but a slightly more expansive one which includes "las lenguas, literaturas o cultura *hispánicas.*" A *hispanista* is a person "que profesa el estudio de lenguas, literaturas o cultura hispánicas, o está versada en él" (the Hispanic languages, literatures, or culture . . . who is a professional student of Hispanic languages, literatures, or culture, or who is versed in them)—that is, someone who has turned the aforementioned *afición* into a profession. According to Webster, a "Hispanism" is "a characteristic feature of Spanish ocurring in another language"; but the term is also used to denote "a movement to reassert the cultural unity of Spain and Latin America"—as a synonym, in other words, for Pan-Hispanism. A Hispanist, in turn, is "a scholar specially informed in Spanish or Portuguese language, literature, or civilization."[7] These conflicting definitions indicate that, apart from the telling hesitation between hobby and profession, the most indistinct aspect of the term is geographical. It is especially unclear whether and how Hispanism as a field, and the Hispanist as its professional representative, include the overseas members of the former empire. The fact that, in Webster's definition, Portugal is mentioned while Latin America is not, is an indication of this point. This is also true of the Spanish definitions quoted here: Even though the Real Academia is politically correct enough to speak in the plural of Hispanic *languages* and *literatures,* it oddly refuses to recognize the existence of more than one Hispanic *culture.*

In historical and ideological terms, Hispanism as a field of study is, indeed, closely related to Hispanism as a movement that proclaims the cultural unity of the Spanish-speaking world. And in spite of what the Spanish dictionaries say, *hispanismo* was in fact one of the names that this movement adopted in nineteenth- and twentieth-century Spain, although it was also known as *hispanoamericanismo, panhispanismo,* and *iberoamericanismo.* Peninsular *hispanismo* has emerged in many different guises, with political orientations ranging from outright reactionary to relatively liberal. In the context of Latin America, of course, *hispanismo* takes on an even more explicitly political charge as the opposite to *indigenismo,* signaling a literary, cultural, or historical privileging of the Spanish heritage over the indigenous one (it is in this sense that José María Arguedas is an *indigenista* and Alfonso Reyes a *hispanista*). Nor should it be forgotten that, in Latin America, *hispanismo* is an opposite of sorts to Pan-Americanism. While the latter movement believes that Spanish America is, above all, American and that its destiny is tied up with the United States and Canada, *hispanistas* maintain that it should strengthen its cultural, political, and economic bonds with Spain. Finally, both Pan-Hispanism and Pan-American-ism compete with the more narrowly defined, and more explicitly anti-imperi-alist, Latin Americanism or *americanismo* of Bolívar, Martí, and others, who deny the claims to Latin America of both the old empire (Spain) and the new one (United States), but do argue in favor of a transnational cultural and politi-cal unity of all Latin-American nations.[8]

As defined by Fredrick Pike, hispanismo is based on "the conviction that through the course of history Spaniards have developed a life style and culture, a set of characteristics, of traditions, and value judgements that render them distinct from all other peoples" (1). Hispanistas furthermore assume that the Spaniards, through the conquest of the New World, transmitted these traits to the indigenous populations, mestizos, and Africans that populated their colo-nies. Hispanismo manifested itself in different ways throughout the nineteenth century; and in fact, as Van Aken points out, liberal Spanish hispanistas were essential in the formation of the anti-yankee disposition of Latin-American anti-imperialism (59–71). Nevertheless, it was not until the the turn of the century—in reaction to the definitive liquidation of the Spanish empire—that hispanismo lived a veritable renaissance in both Spain and Spanish America. Precisely around this time, when the possibility of a political reunification of the Spanish-speaking world had disappeared—and when Hispanic intellectuals on both sides of the Atlantic were made sharply aware of the underdevelopment of their nations in comparison to their northern neighbors—many intellectuals expressed the desire of *spiritual* bonds across the former empire. These senti-ments were especially strong in Spain, where the definitive collapse of the po-litical empire was even positively interpreted as a necessary condition for such a spiritual union. Spanish American intellectuals such as José Enrique Rodó, meanwhile, tended to shun Madrid and eye Paris instead, in a celebration of their *latinidad* rather than their *hispanidad.*

Within Peninsular hispanismo there were, in fact, widely divergent ideas about the form this spiritual unity of the Spanish-speaking world should adopt and, consequently, about the degree and kind of leadership Spain would have to exercise over its former colonies. Whereas the right-wing Catholic version of hispanismo depicted Spain in its traditional role of the guiding, imperial *madre patria,* the lay, liberal, and republican hispanistas envisioned a relationship on a more egalitarian basis. The conservative strain would, over time, develop into the infamous doctrine of Hispanidad, whose emphasis on hierarchy, tradition, and empire would form the ideological backbone of the Spanish Falange and, later, of Francoism. However, to the left of the liberal strain there evolved a more truly progressive brand of hispanismo. Instead of the hierarchichal social structures of the right-wing version, this celebrated republicanism, democracy, and social justice as the political expressions par excellence of Hispanic "humanist" spirituality. This kind of hispanismo was embraced by the intellectuals of the Spanish Second Republic (1931–1939) and their sympathizers on the other side of the Atlantic, who received the Spaniards with open arms once, after the defeat of the Republic, the latter found themselves exiled there.

Mexico City, Cradle of Culture (1938–1948)

Mexico City, especially, was an authentic haven for European refugees, and as such it was the undisputed cultural center of the Spanish-speaking world between 1938 and 1948. These years were of crucial importance to the cultural and political relations between Spain, Latin America, and the U.S., and therefore to Hispanism in both its meanings: as a field of study and as the belief in the cultural unity of the Spanish-speaking world. As indicated previously, three historical developments made this possible: first, the Spanish Civil War, which focused the Americas' attention on Spain and then confronted it with the influx of tens of thousands of exiled Spaniards, among whom were hundreds of intellectuals; secondly, the revival, in both the United States and Latin America, of the Pan-American movement which, supported since 1933 by Roosevelt's Good Neighbor Policy, gave an important impulse to Latin American studies in North American academia (Fagg 52); and third, World War II, which seemed to confirm the demise of Europe as the world's cultural leader, ceding the scepter to the Americas. To illustrate the redefinitions and transformations of Hispanism in the context of these developments, I will focus on three journals founded in Mexico City between 1938 and 1940: the *Revista Iberoamericana,* first published in 1938 by a group of North American and Mexican professors of literature as the journal of the recently created Instituto Internacional de Literatura Iberoamericana (IILI); *Romance,* founded in 1940 by a group of young Spanish intellectuals, many of whom had also written during the Civil War in *Hora de España,* and published until late 1941; and *España Peregrina* (1940–41), directed by exiled Spaniards Juan Larrea and José Bergamín, and the official organ of the "Junta de Cultura Española."

It is important to note from the outset that these were three very different enterprises. The *Revista Iberoamericana* was conceived of as a professional journal bringing together scholars of Latin American literature in the U.S. and Latin America, which primarily hoped to promote intellectual understanding and exchange between the two Americas. *Romance,* in contrast, was created as an expressly Pan-Hispanic project of *difusión cultural,* serving to bring the Spanish, Latin American and, more in general, the entire Western cultural heritage to the Spanish-speaking masses. As such, its goals and premises were as much political as cultural; *Romance*'s project was in fact closely connected to the "cultural front" which, in many parts of the West, had accompanied the Popular Frontist alliance between Communists, Socialists, and bourgeois democracy and which hoped, among other things, to overcome or abolish the separation between "high" and "popular" culture. *España Peregrina*'s principal concern was, in a way, more limited. It strove to help preserve and continue what it defined as "authentic Spanish culture"—that is, the culture of the Spanish Republic—in the harsh circumstances of exile and in the face of fascist censorship and repression. Nevertheless, we shall see that the journal defined this enterprise with a very specific view of Spanish America in mind. Together with publishing companies such as Bergamín's *Séneca*, *España Peregrina* constituted one of the Republicans' important early attempts to meet Franco's reactionary canon with a cultural counteroffensive from exile.[9]

In spite of these differences, however, the three journals also shared a number of important traits that makes a comparison among them all the more interesting. First, even though all were founded in Mexico, Mexican intellectuals played only a minor part, if any, in them. Second, all three possessed what one could call transnational or continental ambitions, aiming at an audience reaching far beyond Mexico. Third, all three demonstrated an extreme awareness of the historical moment, marked most importantly by the rise of fascism, the Spanish Civil War, and, especially after 1940, the apparent decadence of Europe. Moreover, all three seemed to derive a paradoxical sense of hope from the bloody chaos paralyzing the Old World. The moment is seen as one of transition, as the beginning of a new era in which America—either its Anglo-Saxon or Spanish-speaking part, or both—will lead the world towards greater peace and justice. In the fourth place, all three journals are dense with an idealistic rhetoric that barely manages to conceal the contradictory premises on which they were founded—contradictions which, I would argue, continue to haunt Hispanism to this day. Next, I will briefly describe the scope, focus, and content of these journals, with the aim of determining their significance for Hispanism in terms of the four "problem areas" identified at the beginning of this essay: the tension between Hispanism as a transnational field and its use to bolster different forms of cultural nationalism; the precarious definition of its object of study ("Hispanic culture"); the explicit and implicit politics underlying it; and the importance of concerns of status and prestige.

The *Revista Iberoamericana*

In August of 1938, a group of 96 scholars of Latin American literature met in Mexico City, where they founded the "Instituto Internacional de Literatura Iberoamericana" and an accompanying journal, the *Revista Iberoamericana*. Again, the first issue to address is terminological—a seemingly perpetual curse of our field. Why, one might wonder, do these scholars speak of "literatura *iberoamericana*" and not "latinoamericana" or "hispanoamericana"? The answer is less obvious than it seems, since in reality the adjective *iberoamericano* is as vague, confusing, and politically polyvalent as "Hispanism." As Rojas Mix explains, the terms "Iberoamérica" and "iberoamericano" began to appear in Spain towards the end of the nineteenth century and were increasingly common in the beginning of the twentieth in political and diplomatic circles, as well as scientific and academic ones (197–98). In the Spanish context, *Iberoamérica* was used to signify a large cultural unity including the entire Iberian Peninsula (including Portugal) and the whole of Latin America (including Brazil). The term was also thought to be more accurate or appropriate than *Latinoamérica,* propagated since the mid-nineteenth century by the French, because it more clearly identified the continent's Iberian roots (Berger, *Under* 15; Avelar, "Toward a Genealogy").[10] In Latin America, in turn, the notion of *iberoamericanismo* was used throughout the 1920s as a variant of *hispanismo,* that is, to signify the cultural attitude emphasizing Latin-America's bonds with Spain, an attitude radically opposed to the Pan-Americanism propagated since the nineteenth century by the United States.[11]

Be that as it may, for the founders of the IILI, "Iberoamérica" was clearly meant to include Brazil but not Spain, and the bilingual sections of the journal show that "Iberoamérica" was thought of as the normal Spanish equivalent of the English "Latin America."[12] Spain and Portugal were, in fact, emphatically excluded from the journal's scope.[13] However, while the United States was, naturally, not thought of as belonging to "Iberoamérica," the journal did include articles on North American literature and culture.[14] The *Revista Iberoamericana,* in short, was much more "American" than "Iberian." This impression is confirmed by the documents accompanying the creation of the *Revista* and the Instituto. Both were initially founded to accomplish three principal goals: to establish the study of Latin American literature as an autonomous academic field, independent in terms of status and prestige from that of Peninsular literature; to improve contact and communication among scholars of Latin American literature; and, perhaps most importantly, to work toward the intellectual rapprochement of the U.S. and Latin America, based on the premise that they shared a common "continental" destiny.[15]

Given the location and historical moment of its founding, one would suppose the creation of the Instituto and the *Revista* to be closely linked to the Spanish Civil War—which in 1938 was still in full swing and on everyone's mind, especially in Latin America (Schuler 57–60)—and the arrival of the first exiled intellectuals from Spain in both Mexico and the United States. The way in which the IILI presents itself today, in 2004, confirms this impression. On the IILI's Pittsburgh website, for instance, it is stated that the Instituto "fue fundado en 1938 en la Ciudad de México a instancias de personalidades tales como Pedro Henríquez Ureña y Alfonso Reyes como un intento de reafirmación de la unidad hispánica en tiempos de la Guerra Civil Española" (was founded in 1938 in Mexico City at the initiative of well-known individuals such as Pedro Henríquez Ureña and Alfonso Reyes in an attempt to reaffirm Hispanic unity at the time of the Spanish Civil War). This information, however, which is based on a version of the Instituto's foundation as it was established in the 1980s by the *Revista*'s long-time director Alfredo Roggiano, does not seem entirely accurate.[16] For one, there is no evidence that the role played by Reyes and Henríquez Ureña in the foundation of the Instituto was anything more than tangential.[17] More importantly, none of the scholars initially involved in the enterprise seem to have been driven by the kind of Pan-Hispanist ideals mentioned by Roggiano. They did not want to reaffirm the unity of the Spanish-speaking world—quite to the contrary. While both the Instituto and the *Revista* recognized the importance of the Spanish heritage to Latin American culture, both were, from the outset, heavily pronounced in favor of Pan-Americanism. The editorial of the journal's first issue leaves little doubt in this respect. The first paragraph, to be sure, exalts the "unidad espiritual" of "América," and could perhaps, given the ambivalence of the latter term, be interpreted as specifically celebrating Latin American unity:

> Cargado de portento es el fenómeno que durante estos diez últimos años se ha producido en la atmósfera cultural de América: este lento despertar de la conciencia a la realidad de su unidad espiritual. Mientras mejor van logrando las diversas nacionalidades acentuar los rasgos de sus características diferencias, más al descubierto queda el asiento común sobre el cual ellas descansan. ("Editorial" 7)

> (Full of wonder is the phenomenon that has been unfolding over the past ten years in the cultural sphere of the Americas: this slow awakening to the awareness of the reality of its spiritual unity. The better its diverse nationalities are able to accentu-

ate their different traits, the more obvious the common foundation on which they rest will become.)

The second paragraph makes clear, however, that "América" and its "continental destiny" are expressly meant to include the United States as well:

> Es una fuerza interior, a modo de marea, que genera ideas, o interpretaciones, o acontecimientos. No se organizan conferencias panamericanas para exaltar la marea. Antes por el contrario, son ellas plenitudes sintomáticas que acusan la presencia de un continental destino: sufren, no engendran el influjo. ("Editorial" 7)[18]

> (It as an interior force, like a tidal wave, that generates ideas, or interpretations, or events. Pan-American conferences are not organized to exalt the tidal wave. To the contrary: they are symptomatic peaks that betray the presence of a continental destiny: they are the product of this influence, not its cause.)

The Instituto's "hard core" was formed by a group of scholars working in the United States, of both American and Latin American background, together with two professors from the Mexican National University. The IILI was led by Manuel Pedro González, Edwin K. Mapes, Julio Jiménez Rueda, John A. Crow, and John E. Englekirk, with Federico de Onís as one of the *vocales;* the *Revista*'s editors were Roberto Brenes Mesén, Carlos García-Prada, Sturgis E. Leavitt, Francisco Monterde, and Arturo Torres-Rioseco.[19] Among these were some of the most authoritative spokesmen on Latin-American culture and literature in the U.S.: García Prada had published a translated anthology of Darío with MacMillan as early as 1928; Torres-Ríoseco and Leavitt, both members of the Harvard Council on Hispano-American Studies, had compiled a series of bibliographies of Spanish American literature in the 1930s with Harvard University Press; and Crow published the first edition of his best-selling college reader *Spanish American Life* in 1941, followed in 1946 by his much more ambitious *The Epic of Latin America.*

The content of the *Revista* was equally free of references to Pan-Hispanic unity. Corresponding to the journal's stated goals, it specifically aimed to present Latin America as an autonomous cultural space and continually emphasized the need and desirability of close contact and improved understanding between the United States and Latin America. While the *Revista* paid regular attention to North American literature in its own right, with introductory texts on Robert Frost, Walt Whitman, and others,[20] Spanish Peninsular literature was conspicuously absent from the *Revista*'s pages—except, that is, when it was viewed in function of Latin America. In the fourth issue, to be sure, Englekirk published a long article on the Generation of 1898, but it exclusively focused on its ties with and interest in Latin America. Similarly, when Crow wrote about García Lorca in the second issue, it was about his presence and reception in the Americas.[21]

In fact, the importance of the *Revista* for U.S. Hispanism lies precisely in its explicit rejection of the idea that Latin-American literature should be seen, as it had been until then, as a mere appendix to Peninsular literature. More than a century after the political independence of Latin America, the foundation of the IILI represents the coming of age of Latin American literature as a field of study in its own right. As such, its significance cannot be overestimated. However, this did not mean that the tension between cultural nationalism and Hispanism as a transnational scholarly practice was resolved. On the contrary, the emancipation of Latin-American literature and culture from the former colonizer was legitimized through a familiar Romantic, "Americanist" or telluric mythology of *Blut und Boden*. "El suelo americano," the editors wrote, "nutre un nuevo espíritu que lucha por manifestarse en formas propias de cultura original" (The soil of the Americas . . . is feeding a new spirit that is struggling to manifest itself in forms that are characteristic of an original culture) ("El Segundo" 262). Similarly, in the second issue, Torres-Rioseco published a series of "Consideraciones acerca del pensamiento hispanoamericano" (Reflections on Spanish-American Thought), in which he argued that, after centuries of letting itself be defined by foreigners, it was about time that Latin America started defining itself:

> Nosotros . . . hemos sido los conejos de India . . . ¡Y qué no han dicho de nosotros los turistas de todos los tiempos! . . . ¡[C]uánta falsedad, cuánta falta de comprensión y de sentido americano! ¿Cuál de estos turistas miró cara a cara al indio, vio su alma angustiada y perdida en el cruce de cien caminos, descendió hasta lo más profundo de su tragedia? . . . Sólo ahora empezamos a sospechar que bien pudiéramos nosotros mismos meternos en nuestro yo y explicar luego al mundo lo que tenemos, pensamos y queremos . . . Ya nos cansamos pues de ser espectáculo . . . ("Consideraciones" 277–78)

> (We . . . have been the guinea pigs . . . And what haven't the tourists of all times said of us! . . . Such an amount of falsity, such a lack of comprehension and of American sense! Which one of these tourists has looked the Indian in the face, seen his anguished soul, lost on the crossroads of a hundred paths, or descended to the bottom of his tragedy? . . . Only now are we beginning to suspect that it might well be us who can penetrate our own self and then explain to the world what we have, think, and want . . . In short, we are tired of being a spectacle . . .)

It is significant however, that the false, "foreign" view of the Americas that Torres-Rioseco rejects, is that of Europe. The author specifically criticizes "el dogmatismo de un Spengler" (the dogmatism of someone like Spengler) and "el malabarismo verbal de un Ortega y Gasset" (the verbal juggling acts of someone like Ortega y Gasset) (279). On the other hand, he welcomes North American philosophy as a necessary corrective to the inherent flaws of Latin-American thought:

> Debemos buscar la solución de [estas preguntas] con un criterio esencialmente realista, forma de sistema que yo creo típicamente americana,. . . . Frente a nuestra actitud de misticismo contemplativo están el pragmatismo de James y la *Weltanschauung* del profesor Dewey. Acaso nuestro caótico misticismo se pueda orientar por caminos seguros y sólidamente construidos. (279)[22]

> (We have to find the solution to these questions with an essentially realistic criterion, a kind of system that I believe to be typically American. . . . Opposite our attitude of contemplative mysticism stands James's pragmatism and the *Weltanschauung* of Professor Dewey. Perhaps our chaotic mysticism can find its way along roads that are safe and solidly built.)

The IILI, then, did not cast off the cultural-nationalist heritage of Hispanism. While disconnecting the destiny of Latin America from that of Spain and its "universal mission," it substituted it with an pan-nationalist connection to the United States, with similar invocations of cultural uniqueness, shared destiny, and future glory. If, as Mariscal has shown, traditional U.S. Hispanism used Spain's proverbial "backwardness" as a "spent" cultural force to bolster U.S. exceptionalist expansionism (3), the IILI represents an attempt to link Latin American literature to this, now "continental" destiny.

How did the IILI conceive "Hispanic culture," the second problem area defined previously? As said, the Instituto was explicitly founded as an organization for university professors, and, naturally, this professional focus had implications for both the definition of Latin-American literature as an object of study and the relationship of the Instituto's members to it. For the members of the Instituto, "culture" should function as a conduit for continental "fraternity" and was neatly defined as an object of the professional *academic* gaze: It was an object that could be clearly demarcated; divided up into currents, tendencies, and "generations"; and described through careful analyses and exhaustive bibliographies. Moreover, texts could be measured in terms of both literary quality and cultural authenticity.[23] Throughout the *Revista,* there is an unmistakable awareness that its contributors are in effect laying the foundation of a whole new field of study; hence, the importance given to the publication of textbooks, anthologies, and new series of Latin American literature.[24]

The IILI's professional, academic-literary focus also implied that it presented itself as politially neutral. Its members started from the premise that politics were not a major part of its institutional concerns. The editors declare as much in their first editorial:

> La creación de este Instituto comporta onerosa responsabilidad . . . [Los hombres a quienes ella se confió . . .] no han jurado pleitesía a escuela o agrupación alguna. Les ha asociado una comunidad de visión, un grande amor por las Letras de América, una misma aspiración de independencia intelectual y una misma elevada comprensión de cuanto implica la unidad espiritual de todas nuestras nacionalidades. ("Editorial" 8)

> (The foundation of this Institute carries with it an onerous responsibility. . . . [The men in whose care the Institute was placed . . .] have not sworn allegiance to any school or group. What has brought them together is a common vision, a great love of American Letters, a shared aspiration to intellectual independence and a shared lofty understanding of what is implied by the spiritual unity of all our nationalities.)

Politics, then, were deemed less important than the members' shared love of literature, desire for cultural independence, and belief in a common continental identity. Implictly, of course, the IILI was impregnated with politics of several different kinds, of which its Pan-Americanism is most obvious. Indeed, what did it mean to be Pan-Americanist in the 1930s and 1940s? In the first place, it implied a lack of fear or apprehension about United States expansionism—a form, so to speak, of anti-anti-imperialism, or at least a U.S.-friendly form of anti-imperialism.[25] Pan-Americanism, after all, is built on the premise that the interests of the United States and those of Latin America are not at odds, but are essentially the same.[26] As said, this automatically excluded the idea, propagated since the turn of the century by Martí, Rodó and countless others, that the U.S. could be a threat to Latin American culture and autonomy. The editors of the *Revista* dismissed these concerns as a manifestation of a harmful inferiority complex on the part of the Latin Americans, and a sign of a shameful lack of interest in U.S. culture among the Latin American intelligentsia.[27] In the second place, being Pan-Americanist in the 1930s and 1940s meant being anti-fascist, that is, opposed to the infiltration of Germany and Italy in Latin America. This threat was real, and it was a principal concern in Roosevelt's policy toward Latin America, both before and after the entry of the United States into the war (Berger, *Under* 48; Fagg 59). Thirdly, Pan-Americanism was associated with a commitment to "democracy" that already implied a certain degree of anti-Communism (but that, paradoxically, also allowed for the emergence in Latin America of U.S.-friendly dictatorships [Berger, *Under* 48–49]). One of the three editorial texts of the second issue, written by Brenes Mesén a propos of the death of Lugones, is not only apologetic of Lugones' reactionary turn,[28] but also explicitly identifies the Soviet Union with the Axis powers: "¿Quién, que no mire las apariencias tan sólo," (Whoever, looking beyond appearances) Brenes writes, "no descubre el casi perfecto paralelismo entre las formas totalitarias de gobierno de Rusia, y de Alemania y de Italia [?]" (fails to discover the almost perfect parallels between the totalitarian forms of government of Russia, Germany, and Italy?) (11–12). Written in November of 1938, the date Brenes Mesén signed this text, this statement implies a radical political stance. At the height of Popular Frontism and the Spanish Civil War, it was difficult to be both anti-Communist and in full support of the Spanish Republic—or, for that matter, to adhere to the revolutionary regime of Mexican president Lázaro Cárdenas, which, apart from the U.S.S.R., was the only government openly to stand by the Republic, and which in Mexico itself had implemented a "socialist education," and nationalized the oil industry in March of that year (Krauze 448–49, 474).[29]

In fact, contrary to Roggiano's version of events, if the Spanish Civil War is present at all in the discourse of the *Revista,* it is as a rather uncomfortable *absence.* At the first Congress, to be sure, the Instituto's members had adopted a vaguely formulated motion expressing their "más sincera simpatía por los países en que la libertad de pensamiento y el ejercicio de la cátedra merecen el respeto de los Gobiernos, cualesquiera que sea la posición filosófica o política de quienes ejercen la docencia," (sincerest sympathy for those countries in which the freedom of thought and scholarly practice are respected by the Government, regardless of the teachers' philosophical or political position) and rejected "la actitud de aquellos Gobiernos e instituciones que han perseguido o separado de sus cátedras, a hombres cuya única falta ha consistido en pensar y obrar con libertad" (the attitude of those Governments and institutions that have persecuted men whose only fault was to think and act in liberty, or removed them from their professorships) ("Acta" 241–42). While this motion could be interpreted as referring to Spain, the explicit references to the Spanish Civil War in the first years of the *Revista's* existence can be counted on the fingers of one hand.[30]

One could say, of course, that the war was a political event that, as such, had nothing to do with literature as a professional field of study. Yet the whole anti-fascist movement had been constructed, precisely, on the *identification* of anti-fascist politics with culture. As explained previously, the journal's Pan-Americanism was also anti-fascist and, as such, could be seen as a version of this identification; at the same time, however, it obviously was a *rival* version to the Popular Frontist alliance between bourgeois liberals and radical leftists of which the Spanish Republic was the most tangible embodiment. This partly explains why the first issues of the *Revista* contain so few references to the Spanish Civil War. It also helps explain the almost total absence of exiled Spanish intellectuals among the journal's contributors. To be sure, Spanish scholar Federico de Onís was among the Instituto's founding *vocales,* but he had been in the U.S. since the 1920s. However, in 1939, Manuel Pedro González wrote a letter to a group of liberal Spanish intellectuals, inviting them to contribute to the *Revista,* but the response was rather tepid: Pedro Salinas contributed twice; Juan Ramón Jiménez and Américo Castro only once.[31] Otherwise, the only exiled intellectual contributing with any kind of regularity was Enrique Díez-Canedo.

In light of the journal's ideological foundations and Pan-Americanist aims, this absence is only logical. In addition, it is important to point out that the Spaniards generally had little knowledge and interest in Latin American literature. In spite of their liberal or progressive credentials, their attitude vis-à-vis Latin America was in fact rather problematic and quite oblivious of Latin American sensibilities (Rehrmann 544–56). This is all too clear from Castro's article, in which the historian cannot help but complain about the "aberration" of Latin American nationalists who claim the indigenous cultural heritage as their own: "Hay que decir a México . . . que en tanto no sienta de veras que a Hernán Cortés debe el haber salido de la sanguinaria e inerte vida precortesiana, México carecerá del esencial equilibrio que tanto necesita" (One has to say to Mexico . . . that, as long as it does not truly feel that its escape from the bloodiness and inertia of Pre-Colombian life is due to Hernán Cortés, Mexico will lack the essential equilibrium that it so badly needs) ("Sobre" 33–34).[32] Secondly, many of the exiled Spaniards were committed to a Popular-Frontist abolition of the distinction between high and popular culture, as well as between culture and politics. This, of course, went against the Instituto's ideal of a "pure" and professionalized field of literary studies. Finally, many were Communists or philo-Communists and, for good reasons, highly suspicious of the United States, which was not only the mecca of capitalism, but had also failed to support the Republic throughout the Civil War.

I would like to close the discussion of the ILII with some comments on the last of Hispanism's four "problem areas": the issue of status and prestige. As we have seen, this was a central concern of the Instituto's founders. Their very goal was to improve the status and prestige of Latin American culture in the U.S.—but also that of U.S. culture in Latin America. The journal's lemma proclaimed that it aspired "a constituir, gradualmente, una vital representación de los grandes valores espirituales de la creciente cultura iberoamericana" (to gradually constitute a vital representation of the great spiritual values of our growing Ibero-American culture). Similarly, when assuming the Instituto's presidency in 1938, Manuel Pedro González declared that its creation obeyed to "una gran fe en las posibilidades y en los destinos de América, y de una clara conciencia de sus valores éticos e intelectuales" (a great faith in the possibilities and destinies of the Americas, and a clear awareness of its ethical and intellectual values), and to "[u]n generoso ideal de fraternidad continental y un fuerte anhelo de enriquecer y propagar nuestra cultura" (a generous ideal of continental fraternity and a strong desire to enrich and propagate our culture) ("Palabras" 229). In the third issue, the editors wrote that "la obra de cultura continental . . . , hasta el presente oscurecida e ignorada, debe brillar como merece y ha de difundirse sin trabas ni miedos de ninguna índole" (the works of our continental culture . . . , which until now have been obscured and ignored, deserve to shine, and should be spread without obstacles or fears of any kind) ("*La Revista*" 15–16). For the members of the Instituto, in other words, the study of Latin American literature was naturally connected with something of a public relations campaign on behalf of Latin American culture as a whole.

Given the time and circumstances of its creation, the fact that the founders of the IILI were proud and convinced Pan-Americanists is not at all surprising.[33] As Mark T. Berger has shown, the state-sponsored Pan-Americanism of the Roosevelt administration was instrumental to the coming of age of U.S.-Latin American studies between the Wars, and by the early 1940s "Pan Americanism had become central to the dominant professional discourses on Latin America" in the United States ("Greater" 45; *Under* 16). In the framework of Roosevelt's Good Neighbor Policy, initiated in the early 1930s, the United States had modified its attitude toward Latin America, moving from an arrogant "Anglo-Saxonism" that viewed Latin cultures as intrinsically inferior, toward a discourse of mutual respect and understanding, emphasizing the "commonality of the hemispheric experience in contrast to other parts of the world" (Berger, "Greater" 55). At the same time, partly in response to the increase in fascist propaganda efforts, the U.S. government realized that it could use cultural relations to secure its position of power in Latin America. With this purpose in mind, in August 1940 Roosevelt created the Office for Coordination of Commercial and Cultural Relations Between the American Republics, soon renamed the Office of the Coordinator of Inter-American Affairs (CIAA). Headed by Nelson Rockefeller, this office closely cooperated with the State Department's Division of Cultural Relations "to channel US economic and cultural influence throughout the hemisphere" (Berger, *Under* 50; Fagg 61–62). In reality, Berger argues, the Good Neighbor discourse of mutual appreciation and respect was little more than an excuse to use "cultural relations as a conduit for the transmission of North American influence"—a foreshadowing of sorts of the "cultural Cold War" of the 1940s, '50s, and '60s: "For the first time, under Roosevelt, the State Department explicitly pursued international cultural understanding as a component in its foreign policy agenda" (*Under* 50–51). Needless to say, the goals formulated by the IILI almost literally coincided with those of the Roosevelt government, and, for that matter, with many other academic efforts of the late 1930s and early 1940s.[34] Several of the Instituto's founders were, in fact, connected with the Pan American movement.[35]

España Peregrina

At around the same time that the IILI was founded, five distinguished Spanish intellectuals arrived in Mexico City to become the first inhabitants of La Casa de España en México. The Casa was created for the purpose of housing Spanish intellectuals whose work had become impossible in a Spain torn by civil war.[36] If Alfonso Reyes was only tangentially involved with the IILI, it was he, together with Daniel Cosío Villegas, who were key figures in the creation of the Casa, as well as its first directors. The project was almost entirely financed by the Mexican government, and by the end of 1939 it had fifty members working in thirty different academic and artistic fields. La Casa de España—which in 1940 was renamed as El Colegio de México, which still today remains one of Latin America's most prestigious graduate institutions—stands as a symbol both of President Cárdenas' solidarity with the Spanish Republic, and of the Spaniards' lasting impact on Mexican society. Once the Republican defeat appeared unavoidable, the same sense of solidarity would prompt Cárdenas to open Mexico's doors to an unlimited number of Spanish refugees. In total, between 15,000 and 30,000 Spaniards took advantage of this offer, and so a good part of Spain's intellectual elite ended up in Mexico City, where they immediately displayed impressive, almost feverish, cultural activity. Not only did they help strengthen Mexico's cultural institutions, ranging from the Fondo de Cultura Económica to the National University, but they also created their own schools, publishing companies, and journals.

One of the first of the exile journals was *España Peregrina,* founded in 1940 by Juan Larrea and José Bergamín as the official journal of the Junta de Cultura Española. The Junta had been created by a group of intellectuals in early 1939 as an organization of "creators or maintainers" of "authentic" Spanish culture, that specifically aimed at avoiding the dispersal of the exiled Republican intelligentsia, and encouraged the foundation of institutions fostering the "creación, expresión y conservación de la cultura española." The journal, made by and for intellectuals, had a circulation of around 1000 copies, was generally some 50 pages in lenght, and was sold in Mexico for the price of one peso (Caudet, *Cultura* 68n). Every issue opened with an editorial article that addressed topics directly related to the situation, significance, and responsibilities of the exiled intellectuals. The rest of the journal was filled with essays on culture and history, literary criticism, and poetry. Although a combination of personal conflicts and financial problems would cause it to collapse after only nine issues, the foundation of *España Peregrina* was an important event: In the same way that the Casa de España lived on as El Colegio de México, *España Peregrina* resurrected soon after its disappearance in the shape of *Cuadernos Americanos*.

Even though the Junta de Cultura Española was specifically concerned with the preservation of Peninsular culture in the face of exile and fascist repression, *España Peregrina* from the outset saw its cause in connection with the glorious future of Spanish America. This is already clear in the opening statement of *España Peregrina*'s very first issue, in which the editors address the "nations of Spanish America" as follows:

> [N]os dirigimos a vosotros, pueblos de América, incorporados materialmente a la universalidad por el esfuerzo creador de España. Bajo el signo de un Nuevo Mundo a ella nacisteis y en ella habéis ido creciendo desprendidos de Europa. La época universal que abre en la historia el holocausto de la Madre España, señala sin duda el tiempo de vuestra madurez en que habéis de desarrollar lo que os es peculiar y definitivo, la esencia de Nuevo Mundo que continentalmente os diferencia y caracteriza. Entre vosotros nos hallamos movidos por un mismo designio histórico, consagrados a una empresa similar de mundo nuevo. . . . Llevamos un mismo camino. ¡Ojalá nos hermanemos en una sola marcha! ("España Peregrina" 6)

> (We address ourselves to you, people of the Americas, who were materially incorporated into universality by the creative effort of Spain. You were born to universality under the sign of a New World, and in it, detached from Europe, you have been growing up. The universal time period opened up in history by the holocaust of Mother Spain no doubt signals the moment of your adulthood, in which you will develop that which characterizes and defines you: the New World essence that continentally differentiates and identifies you. Among all of you, we find ourselves being moved by the same historic plan, dedicated to a similar new-world enter-

prise. . . . We are going in the same direction. Hopefully we can join in one single march!)

From this text, whose tone and attitude are representative of the journal as a whole, the editors' Pan-Hispanist aspirations are unmistakable. But it is also clear that these aspirations are ultimately rooted in Spanish cultural nationalism: If the former colonies are bound for a great future, it is thanks to the "creative effort" of Spain, which had unselfishly insisted on spreading its "spiritual values" across the New World. This idea is indeed central to the journal's editorials and a good number of its articles. Together, these formulate a particular interpretation of the Spanish nation and its history, an interpretation most clearly articulated by Juan Larrea, the main intellectual force behind *España Peregrina* (Bary 120). In a series of essays published either as editorials or under his own name, Larrea tried to prove that the exiled intellectuals had been chosen as the privileged instruments of Providence.[37] In Larrea's view, no doubt inspired by Spengler, Europe was collapsing under the weight of its own civilization. Its cultural and moral decay had been exemplified, first, by the "betrayal" of the Spanish Republic on the part of the great Western democracies and, second, by the outbreak of the Second World War. But according to Larrea, the "death" of the Republic and the sacrifice of the Spanish people, however tragic, inaugurated a new phase in history in which the cultural hegemony of Europe would be replaced by that of the Americas.

At first glance, Larrea's editorials share an important motive with those of the *Revista Iberoamericana,* in that both see Spanish America as the redeemer of mankind. Where the the two diverge, however, is in the role attributed to Spain, and particularly the Republican exiles, in this historical transition. For Larrea, the exiles were nothing less than crucial. As the "soul" of the deceased Republic, they were destined to carry Europe's, and particularly Spain's, spiritual essence across the Atlantic towards the promised land of the future. If the resurrection of a new, higher form of civilization was possible on the American continent—or, in Larrea's terms, "el continente del espíritu"—it was in large part due to the Spaniards. For Larrea, the historic role of the sacrificial Spanish *pueblo*—a collective incarnation of the Christ figure of which the exiles were in turn the sublimation—was to facilitate access to "ese mundo de civilización verdadera" (that world of true civilization) by being "su precursor efectivo e indispensable" (its effective and indispensible precursor) ("Introducción" 23). In the end, then, Larrea's "Americanism," is little more than an adapted version of hispanismo. The main idea underlying it is the familiar claim that Spain, or the former Spanish empire, represents a particular way of life characterized by a set of spiritual values, without which the world would not be able to survive ("Por un orden" 147; "Entereza" 244).

How did the editors of *España Peregrina* conceive of "Hispanic culture"? It is clear that they saw it as a dynamic phenomenon, strongly rooted in Spain, but capable of growth and transformation. In the predominant intellectual discourse of the Spanish Republic, of which the Junta de Cultura was quite representative, culture was seen as a universal tool of emancipation, but also as the essence or "soul" of a nation and its people, in this case, Spain. The fact that intellectuals were seen as its representatives par excellence—its "creators and maintainers"—points to a fundamental paradox that in fact underlies the whole of Popular Frontism: While idealizing the *pueblo* as the source of authentic culture and national identity, Popular Frontist intellectuals were not willing to give up their position of cultural power. As a result, they remained caught in a form of paternalism.

Due in part to this ambiguous conception of Hispanic culture, its relationship to politics as conceived by the Spaniards is also ambivalent. On one hand, the members of the Junta believed that, as guardians of "authentic" national culture, intellectuals had an important mission to fulfill, and this also implied taking a political stand—in this case, against Francoism. As Eugenio Ímaz, the Junta's secretary, wrote: "Nosotros los intelectuales . . . no creemos que el mundo está ahí . . . para que lo vayamos contemplando con delectación o con asco . . . No hay escape. . . . Hay que tomar una postura, . . ." (We intellectuals . . . do not believe that the world exists . . . for us to contemplate it with delight or disgust . . . There is no escape . . . One has to take a stand . . .) (17). At the same time, however, the editors declared, like those of the *Revista,* that the cause of culture really transcended party politics. Finally, much like the members of the IILI, the editors of *España Peregrina* saw their cause and "mission" as bound up with the status and prestige of Hispanic culture as a whole. And yet, while, in the eyes of the Instituto, Spanish America should emancipate itself *from* Spain, and would redeem the world *in spite of* its historical connection with Spain, for the editors of *España Peregrina* Spanish America redeemed both itself and the world *because* of its essential link with the Peninsula.

Romance

Romance: Revista Popular Hispanoamericana, was as shortlived as *España Peregrina*—it only published 24 issues between February 1940 and May 1941—but no less important. The journal, of 24 pages on large newspaper format, generally appeared every two weeks and was sold for 30 centavos (Santonja 59). The first issue had a print run of 100,000, which was for the most part distributed freely across the whole of Spanish America in an attempt to attract subscriptions. All of the editors were Spanish, and most of them had belonged to the group that during the war had published *Hora de España*.[38] In format and content, the journal resembled *La Gaceta Literaria,* published in the 1920s in Madrid, and, in addition to several editorial sections dedicated to political and intellectual issues related to Spanish Civil War exile, the topics covered were quite diverse.[39]

The journal's title expressed its two main goals: to join Spanish and Spanish American intellectual forces and to make "culture" accessible to a large popular audience. In their mission statement, the editors declared that they had chosen to name their journal *Romance* because the *romance*—the traditional medieval ballad form—was not only a "medio de expresión maravilloso de los sentimientos populares españoles, crónica viva de la historia de la nacionalidad española" (marvellous means of expression of Spanish popular sentiment, a living chronicle of the history of the Spanish nation), but also the most important expression of "the popular soul" of Latin America.[40]

Like *España Peregrina,* then, *Romance* was premised on a unitary concept of Hispanic culture as covering the whole of the Spanish-speaking world, with a Pan-Hispanic folk tradition as its strongest bond. The editorials of *Romance,* too, celebrated the "spiritual" unity of Spaniards and Latin Americans. The journal itself was presented under aegis of this unity and seen as its confirmation. Much like in *España Peregrina,* culture was perceived as both rooted in, and directed towards, the *pueblo.* Thus, the intellectuals of *Romance* ended up proclaiming their desire to emancipate the popular classes by administering to them a culture whose origins were also assumed to be popular—a culture with which, we must assume, the *pueblo* itself had somehow lost touch. In other words, the project suffered from the paternalist attitude adopted by many of the Republican intelligentsia, idealizing the people as a premodern, innocent entity that embodies national identity but is in need of intellectual guidance.

These representations of culture and the folk are of course suffused with nostalgia—a nostalgia that, in the case of *Romance,* was closely associated with its progressive, anti-capitalist politics, but that also allowed for an idealization of Spanish America *because* of its perceived backwardness with respect to Western Europe. Much like Larrea in *España Peregrina,* the editors of *Romance* believed they were living the apocalypse of European civilization and the emergence of a utopian America which would be the cradle of peace, democracy, and social justice. The peoples of Spanish America, *Romance* stated, tienen la suerte . . . de que son aún PUEBLOS, es decir, comunidad de hombres en los que la vida mecánica y fácil no ha secado las más puras fuentes de la inspiración, del poder y la creación. . . . Un pueblo tiene ante sí espléndido porvenir cuando aún conserva un alma pura. ("Sobre la unidad" 7)

(are lucky enough . . . to still be FOLK, that is, a community of human beings whose purest sources of inspiration, power, and creation have not yet been dried up by an easy, mechanical way of life. . . . A nation that still preserves a pure soul has a splendid future ahead of it.)

Thanks to having preserved this "purity of soul," Spanish America was in the unique position to remind the rest of humanity of man's true function in the world. In *Romance*'s utopian reading, the Americas were represented as a "vivo e intacto caudal del espíritu," "sin horrendas cicatrices que lo deformen" (living, intact reservoir of spirituality; not disfigured by horrible scars) ("Voluntad y destino" 7; "Una paz" 7). Of course, for a Spaniard to claim that the American continent is free of scars is not only naive, but no doubt offensive to Latin American ears. In the end, *Romance*'s Pan-Hispanism was as naively Eurocentric as that of Juan Larrea's *España Peregrina*.

Despite the clear political basis of its project, *Romance,* like the *Revista Iberoamericana* and *España Peregrina,* proclaimed that its commitment to culture was fundamentally disinterested or "spiritual," transcending both economic and political concerns. The stress on disinterestedness also allowed the editors of *Romance* to counter the broad opposition within Mexican society to the Spanish refugees by sharply distinguishing the Spanish Republicans from the economic immigrants that had preceded them. While agreeing with the Spanish Americans that it would be unadvisable to open the continent's doors to "gentes de un chauvinismo estrecho o de una grosera mentalidad mercantilista, cuyo objeto principal fuese el enriquecimiento por cualquier medio" (people with a narrowly chauvinistic attitude or a gross, mercantilistic mentality, whose principal aim is to enrich themselves by whatever means), they emphatically declared that

los desterrados republicanos españoles no vienen a América a enriquecerse, sino a trabajar, a colaborar; odian tanto, y por las mismas razones que los americanos, a esa España negra y nefasta, cruel, contra la que han luchado de 1936 a 1939 como hace más de un siglo lucharon los americanos. El mismo hecho de haber sostenido en unas condiciones de inferioridad militar absoluta sus convicciones frente a la demogogia del fascismo, acredita a estos españoles . . . de gentes nobles y de gran espíritu. ("Más emigrados" 7)

(the Spanish Republican exiles are not coming to Spanish America to become wealthy, but to work, to cooperate; they share the Spanish Americans' hate of that black, ill-fated, and cruel Spain against which they fought from 1936 to 1939, as the Spanish Americans did more than a century ago, and they hate it for the same reasons.)

Politically, *Romance* presented itself as a journal "Sin carácter de grupo ni de tendencia, pero claramente partidaria de un aspecto esencial de la cultura: su popularización . . ." (Not characterized by any particular group or tendency, but clearly in favor of one essential aspect of culture: its popularization . . .) ("Propósito"). "No ha entrado ni entra en los propósitos de *'ROMANCE,'*" (What not figures among the aims of *Romance* is) a later editorial states,

recoger, de manera directa, en sus páginas, los fenómenos políticos que se producen en forma de lucha o polémica, entre otras razones, porque la razón misma de su existencia está circunscrita a registrar, en el terreno estrictamente cultural, lo que esos mismo fenómenos u otros de carácter distinto determinan en las actividades del espíritu. ("El ejemplo" 7)

(to comment directly in its pages on the political phenomena that present themselves in the shape of struggles or polemics, among other reasons, because *Romance*'s very raison d'être is limited to register, in the terrain of the stricly cultural, the effect of those phenomena, or other phenomena, on the activities of the spirit.)

However, the journal was more interested in political and economic matters than its editors would admit. First, the fact that the whole editorial team consisted of Spaniards seemed at odds with its Pan-Hispanist rhetoric. As editor Sánchez Barbudo wrote in hindsight, "cometimos . . . el gran error de permitir, aunque ello no fuera en verdad una decisión deliberada, que todos los miembros de la redacción de *Romance* fueran refugiados españoles, lo cual además de grosero era sin duda inconsistente con nuestro proclamado deseo de colaborar íntimamente con los mexicanos" (we made . . . the grave mistake—although it was not really a deliberate decision—of allowing *Romance*'s entire editorial staff to be composed of Spanish refugees. This was not only rude, but also, undoubtedly, inconsistent with our proclaimed desire to closely collaborate with the Mexicans) ("Introducción"). Moreover, the editorial team was mostly composed of Communists and philo-Communists, thus excluding the more moderate sectors of the Republican intelligentsia. Finally, *Romance*'s spiritual quest was funded by the publishing company "Edición y Distribución Ibero-Americana de Publicaciones" (EDIAPSA), a quite materially and commercially-minded enterprise which contradicted the very claim that the Spaniards had not come to America to become rich. Founded with Mexican capital by the Spanish editor Rafael Giménez Siles, a Republican exile himself, EDIAPSA soon became an important publishing house with continental ambitions, modeled on the Compañía Ibero-Americana de Publicaciones (CIAP), which had published *La Gaceta Literaria* in the 1920s (Caudet, *Romance* 21–32). According to Caudet, Giménez Siles had intended that *Romance* from the outset would function primarily as the company's promotional vehicle (*Exilio* 120). Still, EDIAPSA itself preferred to represent its interests in different terms; in one of the issues, for instance, there appeared a report on the company in which its project was conveniently recast in a non-commercial discourse: Its goal, the article stated, was to serve the cause of the spirit, and respond to the "profundo anhelo de unión espiritual que existe arraigado en los pueblos americanos" (profound desire for spiritual unity that is deeply rooted among the American peoples) ("La difusión" 14). Nevertheless, these contradictions between spiritual ideals and commercial practice were too much for the enterprise to bear. After the eleventh issue, two of the editors left the board, followed five issues later by all the original founders, including the journal's director, Communist poet Juan Rejano. In a declaration published in *El Nacional,* the editors declared themselves "moralmente incompatibles" with Giménez Siles, announcing the foundation of a new journal, "libre en absoluto de compromisos de empresa, hecha . . . sin propósito alguno de lucro, por redactores y colaboradores dispuestos a renunciar a toda recompensa material mientras sea preciso" (absolutely free of entrepreneurial commitments, produced . . . without any aim for profit, by editors and contributors willing to give up, if necessary, all material reward). This new journal would continue "el significado espiritual y la pureza moral que siempre hemos defendido" (the spiritual significance and moral purity that we have always defended) (quoted in Caudet, *Exilio* 140n).

Although the journal's more immediate goal was to foster the sales and prestige of its publishing company, it was also, as *España Peregrina* and the *Revista Iberoamericana,* conceived as a public relations campaign to boost the prestige of Hispanic culture. Its editors not only signaled the dawn of a renewed spiritual unity of the Spanish-speaking world, but explicitly linked it to its global emancipation. Hispanic culture, they stated, had not yet been able "en el mundo, alcanzar el respecto debido" (to garner from the world the respect it is due) but it nevertheless carried promise of a glorious future ("Sobre la unidad" 7).

Conclusion: Hispanisms and Its Alternatives

From the first section of this essay it is clear that the concept of Hispanism suffers from two main problems. First, it seems to deny Latin America any real form of cultural specificity. Second, it is unclear whether it denotes an academic discipline or a combination of disciplines (including literature, history, and culture), a hobby or passion of sorts (*"afición"*), an enlightened state of mind (Carr's special talent to penetrate the nation's soul), or a political and cultural program in favor of reuniting the Spanish-speaking world and securing for it the cultural prestige to which it feels entitled—a program with a certain counterhegemonic quality about it (mainly because of its purported opposition to Anglo-Saxon modernity), but ultimately stemming from an exceptionalist reading of Spanish history. These problems are closely related to a series of issues that have been raised in recent discussions on Hispanism as an academic field of study, particularly in the United States. In addition to the four problem areas discussed in the course of this article, critics have mentioned the insularity of Hispanism; its methodological and disciplinary conservatism; and its uneasy relation to cultural studies, theory, and politics (Mariscal 4, 20; Avelar, "Clandestine" 54–55). In the North American academy, the concept of Hispanism is also put into question by the different agendas and mutual competition between its Peninsular and Latin-American branches, which has led critics to wonder whether it is still possible, or even desirable, to maintain the concept of Hispanism as a "strategic alliance" between the two (Resina 118–22).

The developments of Hispanism in the 1930s and 1940s, three instances of which have been discussed here, might help explain what is seen as today's "crisis" of the discipline. For one, they shed more light on the friction or split between Peninsular and Latin-American literary studies (Avelar, "Clandestine" 57n). Both branches, to be sure, received an important boost in the late 1930s and early 1940s—one from Pan-Americanism; the other from the arrival of the Spanish Republican exile scholars in the U.S. But the history of the IILI shows that the study of Latin American literature and culture has, so to speak, a much more "organic" relation to the North American academy, in that it sprouted from truly North American concerns and interests. Peninsular studies, on the other hand, have never really moved beyond their status of imported discipline, gradually declining in status as Spain stopped being regarded as a world power.

I would argue that the three institutional histories sketched in this essay shed some light on the current debates on Hispanism in other ways, as well. With a little bit of imagination, one can conceive the *Revista Iberoamericana, España Peregrina,* and *Romance* as representing three alternative Hispanisms, each attempting to overcome one or more of the field's flaws. While none of the three truly succeed in liberating themselves of Hispanism's ideological baggage, they do make some important steps toward a liberation of sorts. The *Revista Iberoamericana* is the only one of the three to explicitly distance itself from the imperial underpinnings of Hispanism by rejecting the premise that Latin American literature can only be understood in terms of the Iberian Peninsula. The IILI also lays the basis of Latin American Hispanism as a rigorous, professional academic discipline, albeit still shaped according to the philological model. *España Peregrina,* in turn, views culture as a crucial tool for large-scale political struggles—in this case, the struggle against fascism and for social emancipation and national liberation—in which the intellectual (either scholar or writer) is explicitly called upon to take a political stand. *Romance* is even more radical in this respect, arguing that it is the intellectual's duty to spread culture to a wider, popular audience, and that culture owes its existence, its life force, to its connection with the popular. Neither of the two, however, is willing to abandon the fetishized conception of culture as a "spiritual" realm rising above politics.

At the same time, it is clear that in their attempts to formulate and legitimize these alternatives, all three enterprises fall into different ideological traps. The most important of these is the fallacy of cultural nationalism, or rather, cultural pan-nationalism, which leads them to cloak their goals in a highly idealistic rhetoric that partly undoes the otherwise revolutionary dimensions of their proposals. While *España Peregrina* and *Romance* remain caught in a version of Euro-centric, Spanish exceptionalism ultimately motivated by a form of imperial nostalgia, the *Revista Iberoamericana* ends up trading one cultural pan-nationalism for another. Furthermore, in, all three cases the editors' grandiloquent rhetoric serves to gloss over their dependence on interests that they claim are outside of, or contrary to, their lofty aims—to wit, cultural politics and market forces. As we have seen, the *Revista Iberoamericana,* as a vehicle of a state-sponsored, academic Pan-Americanism, was much more political (i.e., pro-U.S., anti-Communist) than its founders were willing to admit. In the same way, the Spanish Civil War exiles were much more attached to the idea of the Spanish empire—albeit in cultural terms—than their otherwise quite progressive political orientation would seem to indicate. Their naive but paternalist idealization of Spanish America, moreover, can be interpreted as one more symptom of their Spain-centeredness. Finally, the editors of *Romance* were slow to realize their function as a vehicle for the essentially commercial enterprise of their corporate sponsor.

In different ways, all of these ideological slips make the case against the concept of Hispanism. Studying the cultures of Spain and Latin America within the framework of Hispanism is to open the door to a whole series of mystifications. One could in fact argue that, to a large extent, the concept of Hispanism itself is one big mystification. Revisiting our four "problem areas" will help clarify this point. As we have seen, in spite of Hispanism's transnational ambitions, it is simply too tied up with cultural nationalism. Raymond Carr was right to argue that the concept of Hispanism somehow presupposes that Spain, and by extension the whole of the Hispanic world, is endowed with a unitary "soul" that sets it apart from the rest of the globe, can only be "penetrated" by especially gifted specialists (i.e., Hispanists), and holds the promise of a glorious future. Like all forms of cultural nationalism, moreover, Hispanism's vindication of cultural difference vis-à-vis its external others (specifically the Anglo-Saxon North) ends up repressing or erasing most forms of internal otherness—an erasure of difference in the name of difference. Not only is Latin America denied its cultural specificity, but so are the continent's indigenous cultures and, within Spain, those of Catalonia, the Basque Country, and Galicia (Resina 118–19).

Hispanism encourages similar mystifications in the other three "problem areas." It mystifies the idea of "Hispanic culture" as, at the same time, quintessentially "popular" (i.e., pure, innocent, suffused with cultural identity), and exceptionally "spiritual"; similarly, it mystifies the relation of the Hispanist qua intellectual to that culture, celebrating the popular but refusing to recognize the *pueblo* as an agent in its own right. The concept of Hispanism also blinds its practitioners to the political underpinnings of their discipline, leaving the door wide open to stealthy political appropriations and mobilizations of various kinds; Hispanism is easily put at the service of different cultural imperialisms. Finally, the concept of Hispanism is inextricably tied up with the notion that Hispanic cultures have been systematically but unjustly excluded from the "universal" canons, and that it is therefore the Hispanist's mission to remedy that situation. Hispanism thus becomes synonymous with a publicity campaign in its own favor, turning the Hispanist almost automatically into a defender, promoter, or propagandist of his object of study or, worse, into a cultural diplomat of sorts. As Resina points out, from there it is but a small step for Hispanism to become mobilized by corporate interests, and not just of the publishing industry (86).

Perhaps, most importantly, the concept of Hispanism presupposes a commonality of interests and aims that is simply not there. The concerns, focuses, struggles of distinct social classes, ethnic groups, and other communities across the Iberian Peninsula and the American continent differ widely, and are, many times, even opposed to each other. The same can be said for the scholars studying those communities. The concept of Hispanism, in other words, should be rejected precisely because it *assimilates* a reality whose main characteristic is its heterogeneity—a heterogeneity that should not be effaced, but celebrated. Those of us who work in the field of Hispanic studies should be free to choose our political, cultural, and theoretical affiliations and alliances, and not be forced into the disciplinary, Hispanophilic straitjacket that the concept of Hispanism seems to presuppose. To be sure, often these alliances will naturally unite a section of Latin American studies with one working on the Peninsula—the historical and cultural bonds between the two of course are real, and much of their respective development can be fruitfully compared. But there is no need for these trans-Atlantic connections and cross-fertilizations to be legitimized with the invocations of "spiritual unity," "common soul," or other lofty, Pan-Hispanist rhetoric.

It is high time, in short, that Hispanic studies emancipates itself from its Romantic, cultural-nationalist heritage. This does not mean that all of the Hispanist tradition should be rejected; on the contrary, much can be salvaged, among other things its interdisciplinary, "holistic" approach to history and culture, its embrace of culture in both its high and popular forms, and its sense of commitment to its object of study.[41] In this sense, one could argue that developments in Spanish and Latin American cultural studies are paving the way back to the committed multidisciplinarity of traditional Hispanism, though this time without its claims to cultural uniqueness, superiority, and corresponding future glory. To be sure, cultural studies are not immune to the ideological traps of Hispanism, most notably its populism, paternalism, and market-driven institutionalization (Avelar, "Clandestine" 50). But I would argue that it *is* much more likely to encourage a truly critical scholarly practice.

Notes

1. The first sections of this essay are part of a larger project on the influence of Pan-Americanism on the study of Latin American literature in the United States. I would like to thank Mabel Moraña, Erika Braga, Keith McDuffie, and John Beverley for their generous help. The sections on Spanish Civil War exile are derived from my book *Exile and Cultural Hegemony*. (All translations are mine).

2. The analysis I offer here of the field's transformations in the 1940s is part of the "inward turn" in Hispanism, a trend in which Hispanists themselves, inspired by Foucault and cultural studies, take a critical look at the institutional history and ideological underpinnings of their own discipline. These kinds of institutional histories are, as Danny Anderson points out, "one of the genres available for work in cultural studies as scholars shift attention from the literary text as the sole object of study and turn toward analyses of the conditions and positions from which Hispanists create knowledge" (9).

3. The most important contributions to this debate on Hispanism have been by Alonso, Anderson, Avelar, Beverley, Mariscal, McGaha, Moreiras, Read, Resina, and Round.

4. Resina and Mariscal have not only shown, for instance, how Hispanism helped strengthen a Castile-centric image of the Spanish nation at the expense of other Peninsular cultures, but also how "the study of Spanish literature in the United States helped crystallize the national identity by projecting an antithesis," serving as a counterweight to an exceptionalist and triumphalist celebration of North America: "From the beginning Anglo-America associated Spanish culture with the decadence of the Spanish empire. The latter's downturn—due to essential characteristics which the scholar could trace in its literature—providentially coincided with America's growth. Thus [George] Ticknor elaborated the constrast between both cultures, supporting the idea of a God-ordained Spanish decline with clear implications for American expansionism" (Resina 115–16).

5. For Carlos Alonso, "resistance to theory has been an integral part of the Hispanic critical tradition." He argues, however, that "it has not surfaced *merely* as a reactionary response to the demand that Hispanic criticism be more responsive to theoretical speculation": "Spanish American intellectuals who argue for modernity—and hence theory—are always in an ambiguous rhetorical position vis-à-vis the discursive model of modernity that they advance as a desideratum. . . . The history of Hispanic literary criticism since the late eighteenth century . . . can . . . be understood as being generated by the simultaneous and contradictory action of two movements, towards and away from theory, towards and away from modernity" (147–48). See also Avelar, "Clandestine" 51–52.

6. Resina, for instance, in his otherwise excellent piece on the institutional histories of Hispanism in Germany, the U.S., and Spain, decides to use "the term 'Hispanism' to denote primarily the field of so-called Peninsular studies, leaving Latin American literary and cultural studies out of the picture" (87–88). While understandable from a practical point of view, this limitation unfortunately prevents him from a full discussion of Hispanism's ideological function as an academic form of Spain-centered cultural imperialism vis-à-vis Latin America.

7. Historically, the first term to appear in the dictionary of the Real Academia is *hispanismo* as "modo de hablar particular y privativo de la Lengua Española" (way of speaking that is particular and exlusive to the Spanish language) (1734 edition). *Hispanista* does not appear until 1914, when it is defined as "la persona versada en la lengua y literatura españolas" (a person versed in Spanish language and literature). In the 1914 dictionary, *hispanismo* is still only defined in linguistic terms. The 1936 edition is the first one to define *hispanismo* as "Afición al estudio de la lengua y literatura españolas y de las cosas de España" (interest in the study of the language and literature of Spain and things Spanish). The 1956 edition specifies that the title of *hispanista* is commonly used for foreigners ("los que no son españoles") (those that are not Spaniards), a qualification that is repeated in the 1970 edition, which still defines *hispanista* as "persona versada en lengua y cultura españolas" (a person versed in Spanish language

and culture), but is left out again starting in 1984, the first post-Franco edition, which is also the first to define a *hispanista* as someone "que profesa el estudio de lenguas, literatura o cultura hispánicas" (who professionally studies Hispanic languages, literature, or culture). According to the Oxford English Dictionary (2003), "Hispanism" as an alternative to "Hispanicism" ("a Spanish idiom or mode of expression"), was itself a Hispanicism (i.e., an import from Spanish into English) and first used by Salvador de Madariaga in 1949. "Hispanist" made its first appearance in the 1934 edition of Webster's dictionary, which defined it as "one versed in, or devoted to, the Spanish language or the study of Spanish." The OED's 1989 edition defines it as "a student of the literature, language, and civilization of Spain."

8. Pan-Hispanism, Latin-Americanism, and Pan-Latinism have many traits in common; most importantly, they all tend to invoke their culture's "spirituality" as an essential trait setting it apart from the "materialist" Anglo-Saxon cultures of Northern Europe and North America.

9. Among the first books published in 1940 by Séneca were García Lorca's *Poeta en Nueva York* and Antonio Machado's *Obras*.

10. In 1927, Guillermo de Torre published a controversial piece in *La Gaceta Literaria,* entitled "Madrid, meridiano intelectual de Hispanoamérica" (Madrid, intellectual meridian of Hispano-America) in which he wrote: "evitamos escribir el falso e injustificado nombre de América Latina. Nombre advenedizo que, unas veces por atolondramiento, y otras, por un desliz reprobable—haciendo juego a intereses que son antagónicos a los nuestros—, ha llegado incluso a filtrarse en España. . . . No hay, a nuestro juicio, otros nombres lícitos y justificados para designar globalmente—de un modo exacto que selle los tres factores fundamentales: el primitivo origen étnico, la identidad lingüística y su más genuino carácter espiritual—a las jóvenes Repúblicas de habla española, que los de Iberoamérica, Hispanoamérica o América española" (we avoid using the false and unjustified term "Latin America." It is a parvenu term that has even managed to filter into Spain, at times due to silliness, and at other times due to a reprehensible mistake, serving interests that are opposed to ours. . . . In our opinion, there are no other licit and justified terms to refer in general to the young Spanish-speaking Republics—and in a precise way that points out three fundamental factors: their primitive ethnic origin, their linguistic identity and their most genuine spiritual character—than those of Ibero-America, Hispano-America, or Spanish America) (1).

11. It is in this sense that José Carlos Mariátegui uses it in his 1925 essay "El íberoamericanismo y pan-americanismo" (26–30).

12. Nevertheless, there is some degree of vacillation in the journal's official discourse. Thus, the editorial statement of the first issue speaks of the "First Congress of Professors of *Iberoamerican* Literature," while the *Revista* is presented as offering "the only complete panorama of *Latin American* literature in existence today" ("Members"; my emphasis). The section on "Condiciones de venta" reads: "Consciente el Instituto de los escasos recursos económicos de que tantos las bibliotecas como la mayoría de los profesores en *Hispanoamérica* disponen, así como de la general despreciación de la moneda nacional en los países hermanos, . . . ha decidido reducir en un 50%

la cuota de los socios tanto como el precio de subscripción a la *Revista*. Esperamos que nuestros colegas *latinoamericanos* sabrán apreciar la altruista intención del Instituto y que colaborarán de manera activa y eficaz en la noble tarea en que estamos empeñados. Es ésta una labor que sólo a *Hispanoamérica* beneficia y en particular a sus hombres de letras" (The Institute, aware of the scarce financial resources of both libraries and professors in *Hispano-America*, as well as the general depreciation of the national currencies in our brother countries, . . . has decided to reduce the membership fee, as well as the *Revista*'s subscription rate, by 50%. We hope that our *Latin-American* colleagues will appreciate the Institute's altruistic intentions and that they will contribute actively and efficiently to the noble task to which we are committed. It is a job that is solely beneficial to *Hispano-America*, and particularly to its men of letters) ("Condiciones"; my emphasis).

13. When the distinguished Spanish Republican historian Rafael Altamira, exiled in Paris, founded his own Iberoamerican Institute, the editors of the *Revista Iberoamericana* wrote: "En Europa, con asiento en París, se ha creado el Instituto Internacional de Estudios Iberoamericanos, bajo la presidencia de Rafael Altamira. Se propone el estudio científico de los problemas sociológicos, políticos, económicos, jurídicos e históricos de España, Portugal y los países de origen hispanoportugués en América. . . . /Hay, como se ve, una profunda diferencia entre el Instituto presidido por el señor Altamira y el que se organizó en la ciudad de México en agosto de 1938. . . . Trata el primero de establecer y dilucidar los problemas que atañen a la Sociología, la Política, la Economía, la Legislación de España, Portugal y los países de origen ibérico en América. Aspira el segundo a reflejar en las páginas de su *Revista Iberoamericana* la conciencia actual de los pueblos de América que escriben en español o portugués" (In Europe the International Institute of Ibero-American Studies has been created, based in Paris, under the presidency of Rafael Altamira. Its objective is the scientific study of the sociological, political, economic, judicial, and historical problems of Spain, Portugal, and the countries of Hispanic-Portuguese origin on the American continent. . . . /A profound difference is apparent between the Institute that is presided over by Mr. Altamira and the one organized in Mexico City in August of 1938 . . . The first Institute attempts to determine and throw light on the problems concerning the sociology, politics, economy, and legislation of Spain, Portugal and the countries of Iberian origin in the Americas. The second Institute aspires to reflect in the pages of its *Revista Iberoamericana* the current awareness of those American nations that write in Spanish or Portuguese) ("Editorial" 258).

14. The journal's editorial note to potential contributors explicitly mentions the possibility of articles "sobre un autor o tema norteamericano" (about a North American author or topic) ("A los autores" 235–36).

15. The editorial introduction in the first issue of the *Revista* states: "In brief, the purpose of the *Instituto* is to broaden and intensify cultural relations between the Americas. To this end it has provided for the publication of a journal of some 250 pages, the *Revista Iberoamericana*, which constitutes the only complete panorama of Latin American literature in existence today. . . . Other activities of the *Instituto* are: the maintenance of

a standing committee to promote and direct the exchange of professors, men of letters and science, artists, and students between the Americas; the printing and distribution of books and articles on Iberoamerican culture; encouraging the creation of chairs of Iberoamerican Literature in the United States, and chairs of North American literature in Latin American Universities" ("Members").

16. In an interview with Sonia Mora, Roggiano said: "[El Instituto s]urgió de una conversación entre Pedro Henríquez Ureña y Alfonso Reyes, como necesidad, en tiempos de la Guerra Civil española, de mantener o re-establecer (los dos términos son aplicables) la unidad hispánica, en ese momento más que amenazada" ([The Institute] emerged from a conversation between Pedro Henríquez Ureña and Alfonso Reyes, as a need, at the time of the Spanish Civil War, to maintain or re-establish (both terms are applicable) the unity of the Hispanic world, which at that moment was more than threatened) (Mora 711). When addressing the participants of the IILI's 23rd Congress, in Madrid in 1984, Roggiano said that the Instituto "se estableció en 1938, durante la guerra fratricida más cruenta del mundo hispánico, como un corolario que se proponía corregir ese horror . . . de la desmembración . . . de la familia hispánica" (was established in 1938, during the bloodiest fratricidal war the Hispanic world has known, as a corrolary aiming to repair that horror . . . of the Hispanic family's . . . dismemberment) (15).

17. The only time they are mentioned is in a list of writers to whom the Instituto is sending a "mensaje de simpatía" (message of sympathy) at the time of its first Congress in 1938 ("Acta" 241).

18. Nevertheless, within the same editorial text there is some curious slippage between "América," "América Hispana," and "Iberoamérica": "Este Instituto se propone coordinar y revelar el sentido de la obra literaria de *América* mediante la elaboración del conjunto de la historia de las ideas que han prevalecido en el Continente . . . [El Instituto] está formado por los catedráticos de Literatura *Iberoamericana,* así en los Estados Unidos, donde hay más de cien de ellos, como en la *América Hispana,* en donde, además buscamos la colaboración de los escritores y el apoyo de quienes aman estas cosas del espíritu en *América.*/La creación de este Instituto comporta onerosa responsabilidad . . . [Los hombres a quienes ella se confió . . .] no han jurado pleitesía a escuela o agrupación alguna. Les ha asociado una comunidad de visión, un grande amor por las Letras de *América,* una misma aspiración de independencia intelectual y una misma elevada comprensión de cuanto implica la unidad espiritual de todas nuestras nacionalidades./[En las páginas de la *Revista*] se tratará de registrar . . . la obra literaria que con tanta hermosura se va desenvolviendo en las naciones de *Iberoamérica*" (This Institute intends to coordinate and reveal the significance of the literature of the *Americas* by assembling the whole of the history of ideas that have prevailed on our continent . . . [The Institute] consists of professors of *Ibero-American* literature, both in the United States, where there are more than a hundred of them, and in *Hispanic America,* where, moreover, we seek the collaboration of writers and the support of all those who love these things of the spirit in the *Americas.*/The foundation of this Institute carries with it an onerous responsibility. . . . [The men in whose care the Institute

was placed . . .] have not sworn allegiance to any school or group. What has brought them together is a common vision, a great love of *American* Letters, a shared aspiration to intellectual independence and a shared lofty understanding of what is implied by the spiritual unity of all our nationalities./[In the *Revista*'s pages] we will try to register . . . the literature that is unfolding with so much beauty among the nations of *Ibero-America*) ("Editorial" 8–9).

19. González and Crow were affiliated with the University of California-Los Angeles; Mapes with Iowa State; Englekirk with the University of New Mexico; De Onís with Columbia; Brenes Mesén with Northwestern; Leavitt with the University of North Carolina; García Prada with the University of Washington; Torres Ríoseco with University of California-Berkeley; and Jiménez Rueda and Monterde with the National University of Mexico.

20. Starting in 1941, Alfredo Ortiz-Vargas published a series of "Perfiles angloamericanos" on Archibald MacLeish, Edna St. Vicent Millary, Edgar Lee Masters, Eugene O'Neill, Robert Frost, Carl Sandburg, and Robinson Jeffers. Other contributors wrote articles on Stephen Crane, Henry David Thoreau, and Florence Hall.

21. "[N]uestro poeta ofreció a la huérfana América Hispana algo que no ha podido ofrecer . . . ningún otro escritor español de nuestros días: esa luminosa fragua de concentración lírica y dramática que es la herencia popular de España. Este 'regreso a la sangre' hubo de conmover a los hijos del Nuevo Mundo, separados durante tan largo tiempo del tronco que nutre el fruto tradicional . . . Hispanoamérica, debido a su fuerte fondo andaluz, se moría de hambre por este manjar y extendió las manos ávidas hacia el duro vástago de la raza que le había dado nuevo ser . . . / . . . En conclusión, es curioso notar que esta es la primera vez en la historia de las influencias literarias entre España e Hispanoamérica, en que la vieja madre patria ha expresado sus valores en términos de una *juventud* tan rebosante. Así la península volvió a conquistar este nuevo mundo literario con la misma energía cabal de los conquistadores, . . ." (Our poet offered the orphan Hispanic America something that no other Spanish writer of our time . . . has been able to offer: that luminous forge of lyrical and dramatic concentration constituted by the popular legacy of Spain. This "return to the blood" was bound to move the children of the New World, who had for so long been separated from the trunk that feeds the fruit of tradition . . . Hispano-America, due to its strong Andalusian background, was starving for this feast, and avidly extended its hands toward this robust child of the *raza* who had breathed new life into it . . . / . . . In conclusion, it is curious to note that this is the first time in the history of the literary influences between Spain and Hispano-America that the old Mother Country has expressed its values in terms of such a boundless youth) (307–308, 317–18).

22. Curiously, this celebration of North-American pragmatist philosophy is combined in the same article with a rejection of global capitalism: "Desde luego, . . . Bolivia no es sino una colonia del capitalismo internacional. Esta es la tragedia de América, tragedia provocada por los grandes capitanes de la industria mundial. Ellos nos observan, nos sonríen, nos adulan, para luego despojarnos de nuestras más queridas posesiones . . ." (Of course, . . . Bolivia is nothing but a colony of international capitalism. This is the

tragedy of the Americas, a tragedy provoked by the great captains of global industry. They observe us, they smile at us, they flatter us, only to strip us of our most beloved possessions . . .) ("Consideraciones" 284).

23. In an article on new tendencies in the Latin American novel, for instance, Torres-Rioseco wrote: "Creo que en estos treinta y nueve años del siglo presente el sentido americanista de nuestra literatura nos ha dado una alta representación en las letras universales y debemos mantener este tono de sinceridad, pero al mismo tiempo se nos impone, como necesidad absoluta, la variedad temática y la diferenciación estilística" (I believe that during these first thirty-nine years of this century, the Americanist consciousness of our literature has given us a high representation in universal letters, and we should maintain this tone of sincerity; but at the same time we are confronted with the absolute necessity of thematic variety and stylistic differentiation). For Torres-Rioseco, Jorge Icaza's novel *Cholos* was "genuinamente americana" (genuinely American) but it also suffered from a "flojedad en la forma" (weakness of form) and a "confusión de propósitos" (confusion of intentions) ("Nuevas" 92–94). The reviewer of Gerardo Gallegos' novel *Embrujo y desembrujo de Haití* similarly characterized it as "un libro de pura sangre americana" (book of pure American blood) that "traduce alientos verdaderos del genio de América" (expresses true spirit of the American character). The novel's connection with *Uncle Tom's Cabin* was for this reviewer "un intensísimo hilo de vida a lomos del cual se levanta un mundo: el del totalitario sentimiento de América" (an extremely intense slice of life in whose wake a world emerges: the world of a totalizing feeling of Americanness) (Magdaleno 145–46).

24. As one of the first editorials states: "Este Instituto se propone coordinar y revelar el sentido de la obra literaria de América mediante la elaboración del conjunto de la historia de las ideas que han prevalecido en el Continente . . . Señalando las lagunas podrá sugerir la obra por hacer: bio-bibliografías, estudio de las bibliotecas particulares, monografías . . . ediciones de obras dignas de sobrevivir . . ." (This Institute intends to coordinate and reveal the significance of the literature of the *Americas* by assembling the whole of the history of ideas that have prevailed on our continent . . . Pointing out the gaps will suggest what work remains to be done: bio-bibliographies, the study of private libraries, monographs . . . editions of works that are worthy of survival . . .) ("Editorial" 8).

25. In an open letter written in August of 1939 to six Spanish liberal intellectuals, IILI director Manuel P. González states that Latin America "Ha de vivir . . . alerta y ha de forjar vigilante su propio destino" (Has to be . . . alert and has to be vigilant in the forging of its own destiny) adding that "[e]n esta misma pugna con que se la disputan varios imperialismos solapados, encontrará probablemente nuestra América su propia defensa . . . El peligro real consistiría en entregarse confiada a uno solo; pero creo que vamos rebasando ya esta estapa y este riesgo" ([i]n this same struggle in which several overlapping imperialisms are fighting over it, our America will probably find the means of its own defense . . . The real danger would be for our America to surrender itself to only one of those imperialisms; but I believe that we are already overcoming that phase and that risk) (*Letter* 21).

26. As Berger points out, in the 1930s and 1940s "the Pan-American system served primarily as a means by which the U.S. could maintain its hegemony in the Western hemisphere" (*Under* 50).

27. "Las Américas no pueden seguir desconociéndose mutuamente . . . El suelo americano nutre un nuevo espíritu que lucha por manifestarse en formas propias de cultura original. Es preciso fortalecer ese espíritu, que nos ofrece vida más rica en contenido humano y un ascenso libre y gallardo de fuerza y plenitud. . . . En Estados Unidos existe un grande interés por la joven cultura de los países iberoamericanos. . . . Este plausible interés . . . no ha sido plenamente correspondido por los estudiosos del Sur. En las universidades iberoamericanas no se dictan cursos ni de historia, ni de geografía, ni de economía, ni de literatura norteamericanas. Los pueblos del Sur desconocen casi por completo la cultura del Norte en sus aspectos más nobles. Allá se contentan con temer, o con recelar . . . como si todos se hallasen bajo la funesta acción de un complejo de inferioridad que niega o destruye, sin aspirar a construir. Esta situación debe modificarse. A la amistad respetuosa y a la cooperación fecunda sólo iremos los americanos por el conocimiento mutuo. El Instituto . . . quiere que tal conocimiento sea una realidad viva, eficaz, creadora, integrante . . . /En los Estados Unidos, los agentes oficiales de los países de muy antiguo prestigio, tales como Inglaterra, Francia, Alemania e Italia, gastan ahora sumas enormes de dinero por hacer conocer sus respectivas culturas, y dotan de libros y obras artísticas las bibliotecas y museos de las numerosas universidades norteamericanas, y les conceden los altos honores especiales a los profesores que en ellas dedican la vida a la enseñanza. . . . /Sólo los países iberoamericanos han permanecido indiferentes, o llenos de pueriles y absurdas sospechas, ante la labor de difusión que de su cultura hacen los hispanistas de Norteamérica . . . /Los países del Nuevo Mundo quieren conocerse mutuamente, y comprenderse, porque quieren hacer germinar y fructificar las semillas ya sembradas de una cultura propia, continental" (The Americas cannot go on not knowing each other . . . The American soil is feeding a new spirit that struggles to manifest itself in its own forms of an original culture. It is necessary to strengthen that spirit, which offers us a life richer in human content, and a free, gallant rise of force and plenitude. . . . In the United States, there exists a lively interest in the young culture of the Ibero-American countries. . . . This commendable interest has not been corresponded by the scholarly community of the South. At Ibero-American universities, no courses are taught about North American history, geography, economy, or literature. The peoples of the South are almost completely ignorant of the noblest aspects of Northern culture. In the South, people are content just to feel fear or distrust . . . as if they all were under the ill-fated influence of an inferiority complex that either negates or destroys, but that does not aspire to construct anything. This situation needs to change. Only by knowing each other can we Americans move toward a respectful friendship and fruitful cooperation. The Institute . . . wants such mutual knowledge to be a living, efficient, creative, integrating reality . . . /In the United States, the official representatives of countries of ancient prestige, such as England, France, Germany and Italy, spend enormous sums of money in order to foment the knowledge about their respective

cultures, they donate books and works of art to the libraries and museums of the many universities of North America, and they bestow high honors on the North American professors who dedicate their lives to teaching./Only the countries of Ibero-America have remained indifferent, or filled with childish and absurd suspicion, with respect to the spreading of knowledge about their culture by North American Hispanists . . . /The countries of the New World wish to know each other, and understand each other, because they want the seeds of their own, continental culture, which have already been sown, to sprout and bear fruit) ("El segundo congreso" 261–65).

28. "Lugones no ha cesado de ser la gloriosa enseña de Almirante de las letras de América. . . . [É]1 sabe que si la justicia alza en su mano izquierda la balanza, con su derecha empuña la espada. Y pues que las democracias no han sabido ni querido establecer una paz de justicia y de derecho humanizado, puede que haya llegado la 'hora de la espada.' . . . Pero no ven, quienes ven en su actitud de la 'hora de la espada' un retroceso ideológico" (Lugones has not ceased to be the glorious Admiral standard of American letters. . . . [H]e knows that Justice, while sustaining the balance in her left hand, with her right hand grasps the sword. And given that the democracies have been unable and unwilling to establish a peace characterized by justice and humanized law, it is possible that the "time of the sword" has come. . . . But those who see [Lugones'] stance of the "time of the sword" as an ideological step back, are blind) (10–11).

29. In this respect, it is important to remember that, in the 1930s and 1940s, the Mexican National University was a bulwark of conservatism, and that the relationship between the university and the revolutionary regime during these years was a difficult one (Guevara Niebla 176; Krauze 585).

30. The few mentions of the Spanish Civil War are, however, all sympathetic to the Republic. Crow opens his article on García Lorca with the statement that the poet "fue fusilado en Granada . . . por los falangistas de Franco" (was executed in Granada . . . by Franco's *falangistas*) (307). Pérez Domenech uses a review of Germán Arciniégas' *Los comuneros* to point out the Pan-Hispanic affinities between the struggle of "comuneros" and that of the Republic: "Este hondo sentimiento de la dignidad y de la independencia es una virtud imprescriptible y sin latitudes en la hispanidad: es quizás el vínculo más recio y fértil que abraza a este manojo de repúblicas altivas con la república española, asaetada hoy por las mayores infamias" (This profound sense of dignity and independence is among the peoples of the Hispanic world a widespread and spontaneous virtue: perhaps it is the sturdiest and most fertile bond that unites this bunch of haughty republics with the Spanish republic, which today is the target of the most criminal attacks). (Pérez Doménech 207). In 1943, Jerónimo Mallo, defining himself "[c]omo escritor español que ha vivido en su patria hasta que España dejo de ser un pueblo libre, como hispanoamericano que en México encontró una segunda patria y como profesor que en Estados Unidos enseña disciplinas relacionadas con su lengua nativa" (as a Spanish writer who lived in his fatherland until Spain ceased to be a free nation, as a Hispano-American who in Mexico found a second fatherland, and as a professor who in the United States teaches subjects related to his native tongue)

argued that Pan-Americanism and Pan-Hispanism were not incompatible, while at the same time rejecting the anti-yankee propaganda of Francoist *Hispanidad* (369–76).

31. In his letter, directed to Amado Alonso, Américo Castro, Enrique Díez-Canedo, T. Navarro Tomás, Federico de Onís, and Pedro Salinas, González emphasized that Latin American literature coming into its own did not imply "antagonismo ni mucho menos divorcio entre la cultura peninsular y la que en América se gesta": "En mi concepto, cuanto más evolucionemos en América hacia una cultura propia, que sea expresión auténtica de nuestra naturaleza, de nuestro paisaje y de nuestra idiosincrasia americana, y a la vez reflejo de nuestra madurez espiritual, más cerca nos encontraremos de la corriente más valiosa que España ha producido: la popular" (any antagonism, nor any separation between the culture of the Iberian Peninsula and the culture being born in the Americas, to the contrary: In my view, the more we in America evolve toward our own culture—a culture which is the authentic expression of our character, our landscape and our American idiosyncrasy, while at the same time a reflection of our spiritual maturity—the closer we will be to the most valuable current that Spain has produced: the popular) (Letter 18).

32. In December of 1940, when accepting his professorship at Princeton, Castro held an inaugural speech on "The Meaning of Spanish Civilization," in which, among other things, he presented a highly idealized interpretation of the Conquest. In the Americas, Castro said, Spain had spent three centuries expending "the best part of herself in a creative effort": "Mexico, Peru, Colombia, the Antilles were not colonies, but were, rather, expansions of the national territory that were enriched with rare artistic and ideal generosity." The Spanish colonizers were not acting out of self-interest, but "on behalf of the Pope for the purpose of christianizing the Indians," only exploiting the gold and silver mines "because precious metals were needed for the furtherance of religious, moral and vital ideals." "In Mexico and other Spanish American countries," Castro said, "there are numerous monuments representing this tendency toward harmony. . . . The Spaniards, however, destroyed the 'teocalis,' because in them the Mexicans performed their ritualistic human sacrifices. . . . Some historians still say that the Spaniards destroyed Mexican civilization. But the Mexicans did not know the wheel and the domestic use of light when the Conquistadors arrived" (*Meaning* 25–27).

33. The history of the *Revista Iberoamericana* can be divided in three main periods: pre-Roggiano (1938–1955), Roggiano (1955–1991), and post-Roggiano (1991-present). As far as I have been able to determine, only the first period (1938–55) can be characterized as predominantly Pan-Americanist. When Roggiano took over *Revista* in 1955, Pan-Americanism was replaced with more Pan-Hispanist tendencies, which were intensified in the 1970s and 1980s. In 1975 and 1984, the Instituto celebrated its conference in Spain, and on the latter occasion, Roggiano reverted to familiar Pan-Hispanist commonplaces: "España nos descubrió, nos propuso un camino para un ser en el mundo, y nunca dejó de seguir descubriéndonos, . . . Y, lo que importa en [las] relaciones literarias de España y América . . . no es sólo lo que España dio de sí—que

fue lo mejor que tuvo—sino (y sobre todo) lo que nos enseñó a poseer, a descubrir y a valorar como nuestro propio ser, desde sus mismas raíces, en las que perdura España; porque lo hispánico—su esencia única y distintiva—nunca se nos quitó del todo, como tampoco España nos conquistó total y definitivamente. . . . Si es verdad que Cortés arrojó las naves al mar para quedarse en la nueva tierra descubierta, lo fue acaso para que aquí arraigaran los dioses de la confraternidad humana, y se unieran las razas y los pueblos para hablar una lengua común y rezar a un Dios universal en procura de un ideal de Eternidad. . . . España, lo hispánico, ahora con todos sus cachorros vivos allende del océano—'sangre de Hispania fecunda, inclitas razas ubérrimas'—está aún viva, 'aún reza a Jesucristo,' y habla mejor que nunca el español. ¿Relaciones de España e Iberoamérica? No. Algo más, unidad de todo lo hispánico en un ideal de los ideales que nos asegure la fe en el hombre y su salvación . . ." (It was Spain who discovered us, proposed a road for us to be in the world, and never stopped discovering us . . . And the important thing in the literary relations between Spain and the Americas . . . is not only what Spain gave of itself—and it gave us the best it had—but (and above all) what it taught us to possess, to discover, and to value as our own being, starting with our very roots, in which Spain lives on, because the Hispanic—its unique and distinctive essence—is something that we never completely lost, in the same way that Spain never totally and finally conquered us . . . If it is true that Cortés threw his ships into the ocean to stay in this newly discovered land, perhaps he did this so that the gods of human brotherhood would take root here, and so that races and peoples would unite and speak a common language and pray to a universal God in pursuit of an ideal of Eternity. . . . Spain, the Hispanic, with all of its cubs living across the ocean—"blood of fecund Hispania, illustrious fertile races"—is still alive, "still prays to Jesus Chirst," and speaks its Spanish better than ever. Relations between Spain and Ibero-America? No. Something more: the unity of all things Hispanic in an ideal of ideals that assures us faith in man and his salvation . . .) (13–15).

34. In August of 1939, a group of scholars at the University of Florida at Gainesville founded the *Revista Interamericana: Revista dedicada al estudio de la cultura iberoamericana,* which presented itself as "un alba de la era nueva en este gran movimiento Panamericano" (a dawn of the new era in this great Pan American movement) (Ramírez 1). The journal was sponsored by the University of Florida's "Institute of Inter-American Affairs," whose aims were, among other things: "to foster international good will between the Americas, . . . to promote the teaching of Western Hemisphere languages and civilizations in schools, colleges, and universities, . . . [and] to promote an inter-play of cultural ideals" ("Institute" 2). The overlaps with the *Revista Iberoamericana,* both in content and stated goals, are evident.

35. In 1942, the Pan-American Union published two articles by Manuel Pedro González; both Jiménez Rueda and Onís partipated in a 1942 conference in Texas on "Cultural bases of hemispheric understanding"; and Englekirk participated in a Conference on Education Problems in the Southwest sponsored in part by the CIAA. Furthermore, Américo Castro's article mentioned above, first published in the *Revista,* was reprinted

in the first issue of the Pan American Union's periodical *Viewpoints*. In the 1950s, the Union, which by then had already turned into the Organization of American States, published an index for the *Revista* and the Instituto's conference proceedings, covering the years 1939–1950.

36. This first group consisted of philosopher of Law Luis Recaséns Siches; poet León Felipe; painter, poet and critic José Moreno Villa; philosopher José Gaos; and historian and lawyer José María Ots Capdequí.

37. These were later compiled in *Rendición de Espíritu* (1943).

38. From February through December 1940, the editorial board, presided over by poet Juan Rejano (1903–1976), consisted of painter Miguel Prieto, poet and prose-writer José Herrera Petere, philospher Adolfo Sánchez Vázquez, poet Lorenzo Varela, and Antonio Sánchez Barbudo (editor of *Hora de España* and co-founder of *El Hijo Pródigo* in Mexico). In addition, *Romance* boasted a prestigious "Consejo de colaboración" which, with the exception of Enrique Díez-Canedo, consisted wholly of prominent Spanish-American writers: Enrique González Martínez, Martín Luis Guzmán, Pedro Henríquez Ureña, Juan Marinello, Rómulo Gallegos, and Pablo Neruda.

39. The first three issues, for instance, carried articles on José Clemente Orozco, Goethe, Tolstoi, Goya, Shaw, Wilde, Valle-Inclán, Gracián, Picasso, Racine, Hieronymus Bosch, and Antonio Machado, and also articles on film and science. González Boixo estimates that roughly a third of the journal was dedicated to Spanish America, one third to Spain, and other third to other cultural fields (757).

40. In his letter to six Spanish liberals, Manuel Pedro González had also referred to the *romance* as one the principal elements binding Spanish and Latin American culture together (*Letter* 18).

41. According to Anderson, cultural studies can be defined by for main characteristics: "First, work in cultural studies questions disciplinary boundaries. Second, such scholarship displaces 'literary' texts as the traditional or sole objects of study and opens the way to academic consideration of other cultural expressions. Third, a cultural studies approach contends that all forms of cultural production have a political dimension, . . . And fourth, cultural studies makes a claim for political participation, for solidarity with excluded or oppressed groups . . ." (5–6).

Works Cited

"A los autores iberoamericanos." *Revista Iberoamericana* I.1 (1939): 235–37.

"Acta de la Sesión Plenaria Extraordinaria del Primer Congreso Internacional de la Enseñanza de la Literatura Iberoamericana, efectuada el lunes 22 de agosto de 1938." *Revista Iberoamericana* I.1 (1939): 239–42.

Alonso, Carlos J. "Cultural Studies and Hispanism: Been There, Done That." *Siglo XX/ Twentieth Century* 14.1–2 (1996): 137–51.

Anderson, Danny J. "Cultural Studies and Hispanisms." *Siglo XX/Twentieth Century* 14.1–2 (1996): 5–13.

"Institute of Inter-American Affairs." *Revista Interamericana* 1.1 (1939): 2.

Avelar, Idelber. "Toward a Genealogy of Latin Americanism." Online. Internet. 23 September 2001.

———. "The Clandestine Ménage à Trois of Cultural Studies, Spanish, and Critical Theory." *Profession 1999*. 49–58.

Bary, David. *Larrea: poesía y transfiguración*. Barcelona: Planeta, 1976.

Berger, Mark T. *Under Northern Eyes: Latin American Studies and U.S. Hegemony in the Americas 1898–1990*. Bloomington: Indiana University Press, 1995.

———. "A Greater America? Pan Americanism and the Professional Study of Latin America, 1890–1990." *Beyond the Ideal: Pan Americanism in Inter-American Affairs*. Ed. David Sheinin. Westport, Conn: Greenwood Press, 2000. 45–56.

Beverley, John, Diana Goffredo, Vicente Lecuna. "A Little Azúcar. Una conversación sobre estudios culturales." *Siglo XX/Twentieth Century* 14.1–2 (1996): 15–35.

Brenes Mesén, Roberto. "Leopoldo Lugones." *Revista Iberoamericana* I.1 (1939): 10–12.

Castro, Américo. *The Meaning of Spanish Civilization. The Inaugural Lecture of Américo Castro, Emory L. Ford Professor of Spanish in Princeton University*. Princeton, N.J: Princeton University, 1941.

———. "Sobre la relación entre ambas Américas." *Revista Iberoamericana* 2.3 (1940): 25–34.

Caudet, Francisco. *Cultura y exilio: la revista "España peregrina" (1940)*. Valencia: Fernando Torres, 1976.

———. *El exilio español en México: las revistas literarias (1939–1971)*. Madrid: Fundación Banco Exterior, 1992.

"Condiciones de venta y circulación de la revista." *Revista Iberoamericana* I.1 (1939): 2.

Crow, John A. "Federico García Lorca en Hispanoamérica." *Revista Iberoamericana* 1.2 (1939): 307–19.

De Torre, Guillermo. "Madrid meridiano intelectual de Hispanoamérica." *La Gaceta Literaria* 1.8 (1927): 1.

"Editorial." *Revista Iberoamericana* I.1 (1939): 7–9.

"Editorial." *Revista Iberoamericana* I.2 (1939): 257–59.

"El ejemplo de Chile." *Romance* 1.13 (1940): 7.

"El segundo congreso internacional de catedráticos de la literatura iberoamericana." Editorial. *Revista Iberoamericana* 1.2 (1939): 260–62.

"Entereza española." Editorial. *España Peregrina* 1.6 (1940): 243–45.

"España Peregrina." Editorial. *España Peregrina* 1.1 (1940): 3–6.

Faber, Sebastiaan. *Exile and Cultural Hegemony: Spanish Intellectuals in Mexico, 1939–1975*. Nashville: Vanderbilt University Press, 2002.

Fagg, John E. *Pan Americanism*. Malabar: Krieger, 1982.

González, Manuel Pedro. "Palabras del Presidente, en la toma de posesión de la Directiva del Instituto." *Revista Iberoamericana* I.1 (1939): 229–31.

————. Letter to Amado Alonso, Américo Castro, Enrique Díez-Canedo, T. Navarro Tomás, Federico de Onís, and Pedro Salinas. *Revista Iberoamericana* 2.3 (1940): 17–23.

González Boixo, José Carlos. "La identidad España-América en la revista *Romance* (1940–41)." *Las relaciones literarias entre España e Iberoamérica. XXIII Congreso del Instituto Internacional de Literatura Iberoamericana. Madrid, 25–29 de junio de 1984.* 753–56.

Guevara Niebla, Gilberto. "La cultura mexicana moderna y el exilio español." *Cincuenta años de exilio español en México.* Tlaxcala: Universidad Autónoma de Tlaxcala, 1991. 173–94.

Imaz, Eugenio. "Discurso in partibus." *España Peregrina* 1.2 (1940): 15–18.

Juliá, Santos. *Raymond Carr: 'El historiador debe rechazar la visión de España como un país excepcional.'* 21 April 2001 <http://www.elpais.es/suplementos/babelia/20010421/b12.html> (23 April 2001). Babelia.

Krauze, Enrique. *Mexico: Biography of Power: A History of Modern Mexico, 1810–1996.* Trans. Hank Heifetz. New York: Harper Collins, 1997.

"La difusión de la cultura en América. E.D.I.A.P.S.A. a los seis meses de comenzar su labor. *Romance* 1.13 (1940): 14–15.

"*La Revista iberoamericana* y la hora presente." Editorial. *Revista Iberoamericana* 2.3 (1940): 15–23.

Larrea, Juan. "Introducción a un mundo nuevo." *España Peregrina* 1.1 (1940): 21–26.

Magdaleno, Mauricio. "Tres libros de esencia americana." *Revista Iberoamericana* 2.3 (1940): 145–60.

Mallo, Jerónimo. "Hispanismo y panamericanismo en la dirección cultural de Hispanoamérica." *Revista Iberoamericana* 6.12 (1943): 369–76.

Mariátegui, José Carlos. *Temas de nuestra América.* Lima: Biblioteca Amauta, 1970.

Mariscal, George. "An Introduction to the Ideology of Hispanism in the US and Britain." *Conflicts of Discourse: Spanish Literature in the Golden Age.* Ed. Peter W. Evans. Manchester: Manchester University Press, 1990. 1–25.

"Más emigrados españoles a América." Editorial. *Romance* 1.12 (1940): 7.

McGaha, Michael. "Whatever Happened to Hispanism?" *Journal of Hispanic Philology* 14.3 (1990): 225–30.

"Members and Subscribers." *Revista Iberoamericana* I.1 (1939): 1.

Mora, Sonia M. "Encuentro con Alfredo Roggiano." *Hispania* 73 (1990): 711–13.

Moreiras, Alberto. "Neohispanismo y política de la cultura." *Journal of Hispanic Research* 2 (1993–1994): 407–16.

Pérez-Doménech, J. "Un libro americano para toda la Hispanidad. Glosa en tres pausas a *Los comuneros,* de Germán Arciniegas." *Revista Iberoamericana* I.1 (1939): 205–208.

Pike, Fredrick B. *Hispanismo, 1898–1936: Spanish Liberals and Conservatives and Their Relations with Spanish America.* London: University of Notre Dame Press, 1971.

"Por un orden consciente." Editorial. *España Peregrina* 1.4 (1940): 147–49.

Ramírez, Manuel D. "Artículo de fondo." *Revista Interamericana* 1.1 (1939): 1–2.

Read, Malcolm K. *Language, Text, Subject: A Critique of Hispanism.* West Lafayette, IN: Purdue University Press, 1992.

Rehrmann, Norbert. *Lateinamerika aus spanischer Sicht: Exilliteratur und Panhispanismus zwischen Realität und Fiktion (1936–1975).* Frankfurt am Main: Vervuert, 1996.

Resina, Joan Ramon. "Hispanism and Its Discontents." *Siglo XX/Twentieth Century* 14.1–2 (1996): 85–135.

Roggiano, Alfredo. "Discurso inaugural." *Las relaciones literarias entre España e Iberoamérica. XXIII Congreso del Instituto Internacional de Literatura Iberoamericana. Madrid, 25–29 de junio de 1984.* Madrid: ICI, 1987. 13–15.

Rojas Mix, Miguel. *Los cien nombres de América. Eso que descubrió Colón.* Barcelona: Lumen, 1991.

Round, Nicholas G. "The Politics of Hispanism Reconstrued." *Journal of Hispanic Research* 1 (1992–93): 134–47.

Sánchez Barbudo, Antonio. Introduction. *Romance.* Repr. Glashütten im Taunus: Detlev Auvermann, 1974.

Santonja, Gonzalo. *Al otro lado del mar. Bergamín y la editorial Séneca (México, 1939–1949).* Madrid: Círculo de Lectores, 1997.

Schuler, Friedrich E. *Mexico Between Hitler and Roosevelt: Mexican Foreign Relations in the Age of Lázaro Cárdenas, 1934–1940.* Albuquerque: University of New Mexico Press, 1998.

"Sobre la unidad espiritual de los pueblos de América." Editorial. *Romance* 1.4 (1940): 7.

Torres-Rioseco, Arturo. "Consideraciones acerca del pensamiento hispanoamericano." *Revista Iberoamericana* 1.2 (1939): 277–86.

"Una paz efectiva." Editorial. *Romance* 1.6 (1940): 7.

Van Aken, Mark J. *Pan-Hispanism; Its Origin and Development to 1866.* Berkeley: University of California Press, 1959.

"Voluntad y destino de los pueblos americanos." *Romance* 1.8 (1940): 7.

Part II
Consolidation and Transformations of Hispanism:
Ideological Paradigms

4

Rapping on the Cast(i)le Gates: Nationalism and Culture-Planning in Contemporary Spain

Thomas Harrington

On December 18, 2001, two members of Spain's ruling conservative party, María San Gil, a city councilor from the Basque Country and national party official, and Josep Piqué, the Catalan-born Minister of Foreign Affairs, presented their much awaited *ponencia* on "Patriotismo Constitucional" to the press in Madrid.[1] As the pre- and post-presentation spin generated by the *Partido Popular* made quite clear, the proposal, which was ostensibly rooted in Habermas' notion of Constitutional Patriotism, was designed with the outsized pretension of closing the debate on how best to guarantee comity between the state's various nationalistically-defined political communities.

That debate had begun (in a formal sense at least) 24 years earlier (in August 1977), when a commission of seven newly-elected members of parliament (Miquel Roca, Jordi Solé-Tura, Manuel Fraga, Miguel Herrero de Miñon, Gabriel Cisneros, José Pedro Pérez-Llorca, and Gregorio Peces-Barba) came together in the hope of crafting Spain's first democratic constitution since the Second Republic (1931–1939). The draft that emerged from their meetings in the fall of 1977, which would form the kernel of the Constitution which was ratified by popular sovereignty in December of 1978, sought to steer a middle path between Spain's deeply rooted, and highly antinomic centralizing and decentralizing legacies. Aware of the dangers of tilting too strongly to one side or the other on this contentious issue, which had wreaked havoc on Spanish political and civic life for over a century, they sought refuge in calculated vagueness:

> La Constitución se fundamenta en la indisoluble unidad de la nación española, patria común e indivisible de todos los españoles, y reconoce y garantiza el derecho a la autonomía de las nacionalidades y regiones que la integran y la solidaridad entre todas ellas. ("Constitución" s.n.)

> (The constitution is rooted in the undisolvable unity of the Spanish nation, common and indivisible fatherland of all Spaniards. It also recognizes and guarantees the right of autonomy for all of the nationalities and regions contained therein as well as bonds of solidarity between them). (My translation)

Aware of the key role that language and cultural symbols have in mediating juridical abstractions the authors went on to state that:

> El castellano es la lengua española oficial del Estado. Todos los españoles tienen el deber de conocerla y el derecho a usarla. Las demás lenguas españolas serán también oficiales en las respectivas Comunidades Autónomas de acuerdo con sus Estatutos. La riqueza de las distintas modalidades lingüísticas de España es un patrimonio cultural que será objeto de especial respeto y protección. La bandera de España está formada por tres franjas horizontales, roja, amarilla y roja, siendo la amarilla de doble anchura que cada una de las rojas. Los estatutos podrán reconocer banderas y enseñas propias de las Comunidades Autónomas. Estas se utilizarán junto a la bandera de España en sus edificios públicos y en sus actos oficiales. ("Constitución" s.n.)

> (Castilian is the official Spanish language of the State. All Spaniards have the obligation to know it and the right to use it. The other Spanish languages will also be official in particular Autonomous Communities in accordance with their Statutes. The richness of the distinct linguistic modalities of Spain is a cultural inheritance that will be given special respect and protection. The Spanish flag is formed by three horizontally positioned fields whose colors are red, yellow, and red, with the yellow field being twice as wide as each of the red ones. The statutes allow for the recognition of the Autonomous Communities's own flags or standards. These will be used along with the Spanish flag at public buildings and in official ceremonies). (My translation.)

These ambiguous passages from the Constitution's "Preliminary Title" were designed to express the new polity's core presumptions, along with Title VIII, devoted to questions of its territorial organization, paved the way for the creation and ratification, between December 1979 and April 1981, of statutes of autonomy for Catalonia, the Basque Country, and Galicia. In the first two of these three "Autonomous Communities," historistically-defined nationalist parties (*Convergència i Unió* in Catalonia, the *Partido Nacionalista Vasco* in the Basque Country) quickly accended to political power because they were committed to maximizing local control over economic and political resources. Since then, neither party has relinquished its control of their respective autonomous parliaments. In contrast, the Galician autonomous government has always been controlled by parties or by coalitions whose missions are state-wide in profile and thus considerably less energetic in terms of their autonomist demands.

In this context, we can speak of the period between 1980 and the present as one in which both Catalan and Basque nationalists sought (with Galicians essentially riding on their coattails) to establish through political thrust and parry the full parameters of the vaguely defined prerogatives accorded them in the Constitution of 1978. The transfers of power in each case have been considerable, and include, among many other things, autonomic control over education and health care, and in the particular realm of the Basque country, the right to levy taxes. However, during much of the latter half of this twenty-year period, a time during which the spell of exhilaration and calculated forgetting (*el pacto de olvido*) which made the Spanish transition possible began to wear off, the long-term sustainability and desirability of this largely *ad hoc* and highly opportunistic arrangement has been frequently questioned by important centralists as well as a significant number of their nationalist counterparts on the so-called periphery.

The "solution" to this dilemma proposed by Piqué, San Gil, and the Aznar government is basically to say that "enough is enough," that is, that there was no further need for devolution of powers from the center to the periphery. But rather than propose a change in the Constitution aimed at rigorously and straightforwardly codifying the current level of decentralization, they instead sought to establish the essential inviolability of that purposely vague 1978 text, and in so doing, to suddenly reverse their party's own tradition of open scorn for many of its decentralizing provisions. They sought to justify this abrupt about-face by invoking Habermas' progressive ideas on reconciling voluntaristic and organicist notions of identity within a single polity.

What they failed to talk about, however, was the intense campaign that the same *Partido Popular* (PP) had waged to re-deploy the historically-charged signs and symbols of Castilian cultural hegemony since coming to office in 1996, and with more intensity still, since achieving an absolute parliamentary majority in May 2000. Perhaps more importantly, they blithely ignored the fact that Habermas' idea of constitutional citizenship presumes, indeed absolutely depends upon, a pitiless examination of the past, especially of the abuses committed in the name of nationalisms constructed on the basis of a shared linguistic, ethnic or racial traits. There is no acknowledgement anywhere in the PP proposals on Spain's future shape concerning the Castilian center's fairly constant, albeit always unsuccessful, attempts to cripple and/or eradicate the "other" linguistic cultures of the state during the past. Indeed, there are few lexical resources even available for articulating such a point of view.[2]

I believe that an awareness of this "silence" maintained by the Madrid-centered establishment is one of the keys to developing an overall understanding of the complex and highly problematic interactions between movements of national identity in Spain not only today, but during the entire contemporary era. In the pages that follow, I hope to show that each of the four primary movements of national identity within the Spanish state (Castilian, Basque, Galician, and Catalan) have been deeply and fundamentally imbued with the logic of historicist essentialism. In the so-called 'peripheral' nations of the state, this fact may have been strategically obscured from time to time, but never widely denied. Within the Castilianist discourse of identity, however, a similarly frank appraisal of this reality has never truly emerged. This ongoing denial, which has been frequently camouflaged by the language of state prerogative and the type of pseudo-progressivism recently invoked by the Aznar government, has served to virtually guarantee that brinksmanship rather than reasoned negotiation be the *leitmotiv* of Spain's ongoing search for more cohesive, representative (and hence enduring) social and political institutions.

When we speak of national identity issues, there is a tendency among many observers to fixate primarily on juridical questions such as those that I have briefly touched on thus far. However, if there is one thing that has become increasingly clear over the last two decades of study on the genesis and evolution of nationality issues,[3] it is that such political constructs, and the debates that attend to them, are located, more often than not, on the trailing edge of social change. The leading edge of that process is what Even-Zohar has termed "culture planning." For the Israeli theorist, culture planning is "regular activity in the history of collective entities of any size, be they 'family,' 'clan,' 'tribe,' 'community,' or 'nation'" ("Culture Planning" s.n.) whose principle goal is the creation of a repertoire of options aimed at channeling the human energies of the collective toward a sense of both internal cohesion and differentiation from such other groups.

> What is generally meant by 'cohesion' is a state where a widely spread sense of solidarity, or togetherness, exists among a group of people, which consequently does not require acts enforced by sheer physical power. The basic, key concept to such cohesion is readiness, or proneness. Readiness (proneness) is a mental disposition which propels people to act in many ways which otherwise may be contrary to their 'natural inclinations.' For example, going to war ready to be killed in fighting against some other group would be the ultimate case, amply repeated throughout human history. To create a large network of readiness (proneness) on a fair number of issues is something that, although vital for any society, cannot be taken for granted by that society. ("Culture Repertoire" 395–96)

A key presumption here is that the aforementioned types of communities are not, and should not be characterized as, "natural" or "spontaneously created" entities. Rather, they are the end result of a process of conscious organization marked by both "native invention" and the strategically motivated importation of tropes, texts, ideas, and cultural models from non-native cultural systems. Another premise is that the literate, or perhaps more accurately today, "semiotically savvy" elites, working in variously explicit degrees of complicity with the collective's (or would-be collective's) economic and political power brokers, play a preponderantly important role in these efforts.[4] Such an approach obviously dispenses with the largely romantic—but still widely propagated—construct of the individually powerful cultural producer and focuses instead on the broader issue of how his or her "inspiration" is stimulated and/or mediated by a carefully created and vigorously maintained set of institutional structures.

For Even-Zohar, late medieval Spain is the locus of a key quantitative transformation in the history of such activities. It was there that proponents of culture planning, whose history he considers to be coterminous with the trajectory of organized societies dating back to Sumer and perhaps beyond, first successfully imparted "socio-cultural cohesion to a large population which had long been divided" ("The Role" 26). In other words, the Castilian monarchy led the world in taking techniques of strategic textual manipulation beyond a limited circle of adepts to a plurality of a much larger and broader scheme of social organization. This proselytizing ambition is perhaps most succinctly adduced in Nebrija's *Prólogo a la Gramática de la lengua castellana* (1492). The grammarian makes absolutely clear that he sees standardized Castilian writing as an absolutely indispensable—if not *the* indispensable—pre-condition for the execution of an extremely wide-ranging Castilian political project. In this way, he added the "nation" to the list of entities that could be fortified by a well-run campaign of culture planning.

However, it should be pointed out that the concept of the "nation" in Nebrija was not the neatly parsed and heavily glossed construct of today's political theorists and philosophers. Rather, throughout his short but remarkable treatise on culture planning, he regularly conflates his concept of the Castilian "nation" with that of the Castilian "empire." Thus, to be a possessor of Castilian was for him not simply to be *different from,* but also *superior to,* the "other," a category which not only included "los enemigos de nuestra fe" (the enemies of our faith) but also "los vizcainos, navarros, franceses, italianos, y todos los otros que tienen algún trato y conversación en España" [the Bizcayans, Navarrrese, French, Italians, and all the others who have any type of dealings or conversation in Spain." (Nebrija s.n.] (My translation). Indeed, he sees the linguistic subjugation of the other Christian peoples of the peninsula as the crowning element in a centuries-long campaign for peace:

[Castilian] tuvo su niñez en el tiempo de los juezes y Reies de Castilla y de León, y començó a mostrar sus fuerças en tiempo del mui esclarecido y digno de toda la eternidad el Rei don Alonso el Sabio, por cuio mandado se escrivieron las *Siete Partidas, la General Istoria,* y fueron trasladados muchos libros de latin y aravigo en nuestra lengua castellana. La cual. se estendió después hasta Aragón y Navarra y de allí a Italia, siguiendo la compañía de los infantes que embiamos a imperar en aquellos Reinos. I assí creció hasta la monarchía y paz de que gozamos, primera mente por la bondad y providencia divina; después por la industria, trabajo y diligencia de vuestra real majestad. En la fortuna y buena dicha de la cual, los miembros y pedaços de España, que estavan por muchas partes derramados, se reduxeron y aiuntaron en un cuerpo y unidad de Reino. (Nebrija s.n.)

([Castilian] had its childhood in the time of the magistrates and Kings of Castile and León, and began to show its strength in the age of the very illustrious and eternally praiseworthy King Alfonso, the Wise, under whose orders were written the *Seven Divisions, The General History,* and translated into our Castilian language many Latin and Arabic books. Our language later was spread to Aragón and Navarra, and from there, to Italy, following the presence of the princes that we sent to rule in those kingdoms. It grew from that time right up to the monarchy and peace that we now enjoy, firstly because of goodness and divine Providence and thereafter through the industry, work and diligence of your Royal Highness. *Thanks to his fortune and good luck,* the limbs and pieces of Spain, which had been scattered across many realms, were subdued and joined together in one body and a *single royal unity.* (My translation)

In keeping with its late-medieval provenance, Nebrija's vision of the Castilian nation was also heavily inscribed with religious imperatives. However, its messianic tone—evidenced perhaps most clearly in the parallels he draws in the prologue between the historic missions of Jews and Castilians—would appear to be extraordinary even by the standards of that age. For him, the great triumph of the Hebrews was that of establishing a written language supple enough to transmit the well-ordered laws of God into a humanly accessible form. He subsequently makes clear later that he sees Castilian, and those that speak it, as his era's intermediaries between the province of transcendent logic and "muchos pueblos bárbaros y naciones de peregrinas lenguas" (Nebrija s.n.) (many uncivilized peoples and nations of odd languages) (Nebrija s.n.) (My translation).

That Nebrija and the Castilian elite for which he spoke had stumbled upon a winning geopolitical formula was made abundantly clear over the ensuing two centuries. The bundled combination of linguistic fundamentalism, religious fervor and hegemonic ambition, fueled the creation of the largest empire that the world had ever seen. There can be no doubt that the Castilian emphasis on linguistic standardization and explicit cultural hierarchies greatly facilitated the task of extending and managing the vast and far-flung empire.

So impressive was the success of this Castilianist model of culture planning that other European polities began imitating its most salient features, especially its obsession with linguistic homogeneity, and from there, bureaucratic cohesion. Perhaps owing to their lack of first-hand contact with the memory and tradition of the Reconquest, however, few of the imitators could match its extremely high level of overtly bellicose religiosity. Further diluting the religious content of the Castilian culture planning model as applied in other European polities was the need for leaders in many of those places to enter into dialogue with the ideas of the Protestant Reformation, which had as one of its prime thrusts the drastic diminution of the role of the Church in public life and governmental affairs. This is not to say that the desire for religious transcendence disappeared for the nationalist culture planning efforts in those places. Rather, simply that it began to be subsumed by new *social* and *metaphysical* constructs.

Emblematic in the first regard was the ever-more centralized and secularized France of Louis XIV (1638–1715), where the Catholic Church, while still important, saw its prerogatives increasingly subjugated to the "reason" of the state. By the time of the French Revolution, some 75 years after the disappearance of the Sun King, things had advanced to the point where many Frenchman no longer viewed an overt connection with the almighty as an indispensable trope for the maintenance of social cohesion. Representative of the second tendency was late eighteenth-century Prussia. There, Herder, clearly troubled by the potential cultural effects of the universalizing pretensions of the French *philosophes* and their revolutionary descendants, basically reiterated Nebrija's belief in the transcendent origin and power of language. However, whereas the Spaniard had viewed the church-state conglomerate of Isabel and her successors as the prime guarantors of this continuing flow of vital civilizing energy, the German placed his trust in the decidedly non-sectarian vehicle known as "nature." Only by maintaining active and conscious contact with the land, the prime sources of a people's vital and social rhythms, one could expect to maintain the "timeless" character and cohesiveness of the individual nation.

Few people or social organisms possessed enough tenacity and ego strength to presciently engage in the ongoing revision of a core social concept that they themselves engendered. And so it was with the Castilian-centered Spanish monarchy which remained remarkably blind to these apparent "upgrades" in the nationalist pedagogy program it had pioneered at the end of the fifteenth century. True, the ascension of the Bourbons to the Spanish throne in 1715 brought with it a brisk dose of French-style juridical centralism. However, it was not accompanied, as it was north of the Pyrenees, by a concomitant rise in the production of secular creeds of universal social organization. A similar pattern of administrative reform with only tepid advances in new theories of national identity was evident during the reign of Carlos III. The growing gap between the two principal strains of nationalism (contractual vs. metaphysical) came to a head in the Spanish case upon the arrival of Napoleonic troops to the Peninsula in 1808. Though the liberal Constitution of Cádiz was certainly a noteworthy component of the famous patriotic backlash of the Spaniards to the French invasion, the strain of thought it represented was, as subsequent events showed, quite far from ever being hegemonic within the early nineteenth-century Spanish and/or Castilianist discourse of national identity. Indeed, when we contemplate the semantics of the widely employed traditionalist epithet of *afrancesado,* with its implication that those who embrace liberalism (and reject the social structure of the Old Regime) somehow become apostates of the national community, we can see just how much influence the overtly religious culture planning model enunciated by Nebrija, and subsequently enacted by the educating clergy and state bureaucrats, continued to have three centuries after its inception.

The period between the restoration of Bourbon absolutism in 1814 and the outbreak of the Glorious Revolution in 1868 is often portrayed as an ongoing oscillation between extremely liberal and traditionalist concepts of the nation. While this is in some sense true, it can lead to certain misleading assumptions.

The first, eagerly and understandably promoted by contemporary progressives, is that there was a rough equivalence between the strength and predominance of liberal and traditionalist elites during this period. It is perhaps more accurately viewed as a long stretch of relative political, social, and cultural conservatism punctuated by brief but intense periods of progressivist predominance (1820–1823, 1835–1837, 1854–1856). The existence of Carlism meant that the entire Spanish spectrum of cultural, and from there, political options was located much farther to the right than it was in France and other European nations. For example, none of the intermittent progressivist projects mentioned previously (and not even the grandfather of them all, the Constitution of Cádiz) ever seriously considered an abrogation of the long-standing relationship between church and state. As a result, the bundled discursive relationship between faith (with its strong undercurrent of monistic logic) and national identity developed in the time of Nebrija was never seriously challenged. Another common misconception, perhaps induced by a tendency to use the Second Republic (1931–1939) as a prism through which to view the entire history of the Spanish left, is that this so-called liberalism of the mid-nineteenth century was notably more sympathetic than mainline Bourbon absolutism to the non-Castilian cultures of the peninsula. In fact, if anything the administrative reforms of this "versión muy conservadora del liberalismo" (very conservative version of the liberalism) (Tusell 45)—the institution of the provincial system, the founding of the *Guardia Civil,* and the *Ley de Moyano* among many others—greatly strengthened the bureaucratic hand of those who were seeking to impose the notion that Spanish identity was essentially and fundamentally Castilian in nature.

The first notable alteration in Castilianism's rigidly exclusivistic cultural logic came during the *Sexenio Revolucionario* (1868–1874) when Prim's leadership coalition offered Dom Fernando, father of Luis I of Portugal, the possibility of acceding to the Spanish throne, a move that would have led inexorably to the (re) creation of a multilingual kingdom. However, Fernando refused the offer owing, among other things, to his doubts about the ability of the Castilian political class to guarantee the cultural integrity of Portugal under such an arrangement. The monarchy was eventually reconstituted in unitary terms under Amadeo I. However, when he resigned in early 1873, the First Republic was established, and with it, the beginning of an even more radical and far-reaching break with the Castilianism's dominant set of cultural assumptions.

The Federalism that would dominate the short-lived Republic (which until 1870 or so had existed as a splinter tendency of the mid-century "liberalism" outlined previously) was, as one would expect, inherently hostile to the designs of centralism. This does not mean, however, that it was necessarily sympathetic to the historistically determined identities of Spain's non-Castilian cultures. Indeed, if there was one thing that appears to have doomed the First Republic to a short life, it was its general negligence in the realm of culture planning, that is, its leaders' naive proudhonian belief that a population's sincere desire to form both local and supra-local polities was enough to guarantee the coherence and survival of the very same entities. This extreme faith in the voluntaristic capacities of the citizenry meant that the "management of memory"—be it the well-codified cultural repertoire of the center or the incipient cultural repertoires of the periphery—was largely ignored. In this context then we can speak of the First Republic as a time within which the circulation of the time-tested repertoire of monistically-inspired tropes of national identity was not replaced, but rather momentarily suspended.

A recognition of this culture-planning failure inspired Almirall's *particularisme,* the first modern iteration of the family of socio-political theory we refer today as Catalanism. Originally attracted to public life by the ideas of Pi i Margall, the prime ideologist of the failed Federal Republic, Almirall understood instinctively that his mentor's vision was doomed to future failure if it did not take into account the important role of historically inscribed linguistic and cultural artifacts, (as well as the autochthonous the institutions necessary for reproducing and distributing them) in the creation of enduring political allegiances. In 1879, for example he founded *El diari català,* the first daily newspaper ever written in the language of that region. Through this and other initiatives, he sought to effect a fusion of the dominant features (minus the marked centralism) of the French nationalistic tradition (universalism, egalitarianism) and Romantically inflected German historicism with its emphasis on the enduring power of language and local customs.

Yet if the disruption of the Castilianist discourse during the First Republic was for Almirall a useful, if flawed, incitement to a potentially wide-ranging redefinition of the Spanish state, it was for Cánovas, the prime architect of the political order of the Restoration, a frightening anathema. In his *Discurso sobre la nación* (1882), for example, he resurrects all of the key elements of the hierarchical, imperialistic, and religiously imbued concept of Castilian identity that had enabled both Spain's meteoric rise and its agonizingly slow fall, going so far at one point to characterize the less widely extended linguistic codes of a nation as the "plantas parásitas" (Cánovas s.n.) (parasitic plants) (Cánovas s.n.) (my translation) in the nation's otherwise ordered and fundamentally united linguistic ecosystem. For all his embrace of principles forged in the past, however, Cánovas avoided his conservative predecessors' tendencies toward intellectual insularity and olympian disdain of modern progress. For example, he was acutely aware of the latest developments in nationality theory such as Renan's "What is a Nation?" And rather than simply ignore that famous talk delivered to great effect in Paris six months before his own, he forcefully refutes it. Through this speech and hundreds of others like it, the fearsome wordsmith greatly updated and expanded Spanish traditionalism's dialectical toolbox. In doing so, he was implicitly recognizing the increasing importance of urban intellectuals (like himself) and their institutions (like the Ateneo of Madrid where he gave the speech) in the creation and maintenance of any future consensus on the issue of national identity.

Cánovas's efforts to effect a rhetorical facelift of Castilian traditionalism in the political arena were paralleled by those of Menéndez y Pelayo (a fellow Conservative member of parliament) in philology, the new "science" of culture whose genesis and development is intimately linked to the rise of a largely hermetic, hegemonic, and temporally infinite concept of German nationalism during the early and mid-nineteenth century. In keeping with the comparative nature of the German model of philology pioneered by thinkers such as Friedrich Schlegel and Franz Bopp, Menéndez Pelayo demonstrated a sincere interest in all of the linguistic traditions of the Peninsula. However, (and here again we see his kinship with his German disciplinary forebearers), he was, nonetheless, possessed of belief in the existence of a clearly hierarchical relationship between them. Similarly, as a devout Catholic, he was strongly imbued with Spanish traditionalism's long-standing belief in a link between this Castilian-forged unity and the Church. In short, the prodigious labor of Menéndez y Pelayo was to become the cornerstone of a whole new and revitalized Castilianist culture planning project. In terms of its core postulates, it differed surprisingly little from the embraced enunciated four hundred years before by Nebrija. However, its ostensibly "scientific" and "dialogic" nature appealed greatly to a growing urban intellectual class that wished to expunge its long-standing sense of inferiority versus the cultures of Northern Europe. In this sense, the cultural project of Menénedez Pelayo and that of his political correlate, Cánovas, might be compared with those of the sixteenth-century Jesuits and the twentieth-century members of *Opus Dei*. In all three movements, the leadership recognized a need to modernize both the theory and practice of Spanish intellectual and civic life. However, none was willing to dispense with any of their fundamental socio-religious convictions to make this happen.

The success of this philologically-fueled revival of the Castilianist repertoire of cultural options was not lost upon the generation of Catalanists that followed Almirall and began to come of age during the late 1880s and early 1890s. Like the neo-traditionalists of Castile, Prat de la Riba, Cambó, Puig i Cadafalch, and Torras i Bages were conservative and Catholic, and, consequently naturally given to monistic and hierarchical conceptualizations of national and social identity. Not surprisingly, they tended to view with suspicion Almirall's social progressivism and disposition (however theoretical) to multipolar, pan-Iberian solutions to the nationalities problem. It was thus not long before they began creating an explicitly historicist apology for the singularity of what they saw as *their* one and only true nation: Catalonia. The first great public demonstration of this newly politicized organicist vision of the Catalan nation was the famous political manifesto of *La Unió Catalanista, Les Bases de Manresa* (1892). Arguably more important in the long-run, however, were initiatives such as the *Cercle Artistic Sant Lluc,* an artists collective run under the theoretical tutelage of Torras which sought to give expression to what they viewed as the "essential," *spiritually-inspired* elements of Catalan identity, and in this way, counteract *modernisme's* "foreign" brand of secular cosmopolitanism. It would be this brand of Catalanism that would be politically ascendant from 1888 onward.[5]

The first formulations of Basque national identity, generated by Sabino Arana during the same decade, grew out of a similar social and religious environment. The major difference in the Basque case was the movement's much higher degree of distrust toward both universalizing modernity and the Castilian center, the latter of which it saw (quite mistakenly) as being wholly dominated by the former. This stridency can be traced, in great measure, to the effects of the long-standing Carlist movement in that part of Spain, and more specifically still, the family of Arana. Unlike the conservative Catalan bourgeoisie which had been enticed into a certain complicity with the Castilian center through the granting of relatively new mercantile privileges in the Caribbean, the rightward extreme of the Basque social spectrum had been pursued by Castilianist armies during the same period. Further differentiating the two movements was the fact the emergent ideological and cultural praxis of *La Unió Catalanista* had been forged in active, and often quite personal dialogue, with both Almirall's group and the "worldly bohemians" of *modernisme,* interchanges made possible by "bridge" institutions and figures such as *El Ateneo, El Centre Català* Maragall, Ramón Casas, Joaquim Casas-Carbó, Masso i Torrents, and Donènech i Montaner. No such comparable intramural dialogue was present in the incipient Basque movement of national identity.

Like his Castilian and Catalan counterparts, Sabino saw language as the central force in the creation of national solidarity. However, unlike them, he had an extremely limited repertoire of autochthonous linguistic artifacts at his disposal. One reason for this was the relatively advanced state of castilianization in society. Another was that in those areas where the Basque language was spoken, it was far less standardized than either Castilian or Catalan in their particular realms. Finally, and perhaps most decisively, its written manifestations were relatively few, owing to the tradition of granting bards (*bertsolaris*) rather than scribes the central role in the preservation of the shared cultural patrimony. Though such oral records often have great intrinsic value, they generally fail to generate the same level of socio-semiotic cohesion that written texts can provide.[6] In order to fill this evident *lacuna* in an otherwise classically historicist apology of the nation, the early Basque nationalists recurred, much like Irish nationalists caught in the same bind at the same time, to the promotion of traditional sports as a banner of communal cohesion. Of far more transcendence in the long run, however, was Sabino's embrace of an expressly racial understanding of Basque exceptionalism. For Arana, Basques were a noble race whose prime goal must be that of cleansing themselves of the genetic and social contamination suffered during the previous centuries of Castilian subjugation. Needless to say, he does not address how such a view is compatible with the centuries-long history of apparently willing Basque collaboration in Castilianist enterprises, nor the fact that his much-cherished Catholic faith was undoubtedly transmitted to his countrymen through the good offices of yesteryear's version of the *maketo*.

During the 1880s and 1890s, *Galeguismo* lagged well behind these two movements of national identity in political impact. As was the case with their counterparts in other areas of the peninsula during this time (with the possible exception of the remaining core of Pi i Margall-inspired federalists in Catalonia), the logic of discourse was fundamentally historicist in nature, placing a great deal of emphasis on the importance of building upon the linguistic renaissance set in motion by the poets of the *Rexurdimento* (Rosalía, Pondal, and Curros Enriquez) from the mid-1860s onward. However, neither of the two great theoretical figures of the movement, Manuel Murguía nor Alfredo Brañas regularly wrote, or demanded that their supporters regularly write, in the autochthonous code of the region. Perhaps for this reason, they, like early Basque nationalists, showed an uncommon interest in the example of Ireland. But the British colony was not the only source of "fraternal referents" for their nascent cultural repertoire. Portugal and Catalonia are also primary sources for the tropes, symbols, phrases, and discursive strategies used to justify the historic singularity of their people. Particularly striking in terms of its reliance on conservative Catalanism is Brañas' *El Regionalismo* (1889), which is often presented as the movement's first great systematic declaration of principles.

The American defeat of the Spanish in 1898 had the effect of placing proponents of the hegemonic Castilianist discourse of the Restoration, with its hardwired imperial logic, on the defensive. Quick to seize on this opening were the Catalanists under the direction of the still quite youthful Enric Prat de la Riba. As mentioned earlier, heavy involvement in the Caribbean market during the latter half of the nineteenth century had served to moderate the autonomous demands of many among Catalonia's conservative bourgeoisie; moreover, they were willing to maintain their allegiance to the central government as long as it continued to safeguard their exploitation of this key market. With this benefit now gone, they began to channel their energies increasingly toward the *institu-tionalization* of the culture planning concepts that they and their more progressive Catalanist rivals from the *particularist* and *modernista* camps had been espousing for more than a decade. Notable among numerous happenings in this initial explosion of culture planning activities, was the founding or initiation of *La Veu de Catalunya* (1899) and the Barcelona Football Club (1899), *La Lliga Regionalista* (1901), September 11th commemorations (1901), *Estudis Universitaris Catalans* (1903), and the *Palau de la Música Catalana* (1905).

These activities took a quantum leap forward after the November 1905 sacking by Spanish army officers of the building that housed *Cu-cut,* a satirical Catalan language journal, and *La Veu de Catalunya.*[7] In addition to the founding of *Solidaritat Catalana* in March of that year, 1906 saw the publication of Prat de la Riba's famed catechism of national identity, *La nacionalitat Catalana,* the organization of the first *Congrés Internacional de la Llengua Catalana,* the founding of the *Museu de Belles Arts* and Eugeni d'Ors's debut as the "glosador" Xènius in the pages of *La Veu de Catalunya.* This last event was of transcendent importance as d'Ors would utilize his platform in the nationalist paper as well as his keen cosmopolitan sense of taste to greatly fill out and then order the canon of nationalist signs and symbols. Along the way, he would also renovate Catalan prose stylistics, transforming a heretofore archaic and poetically-oriented language into a supple tool for everyday communication. The intense wave of culture planning continued in 1907 with the creation of the *Junta de Museus de Barcelona, La Biblioteca de Catalunya,* and the *Institut d'Estudis Catalans.* This last institution created a beachhead for Catalan in world scholarly and scientific linguistic codes and would later underwrite Pompeu Fabra's effort to normalize the spelling and grammar of Catalan.

With this extraordinary burst of energy, Catalan nationalism had, in effect, leap-frogged centralist efforts in the realm of nationalist pedagogy. The irritation felt by those who identified with the Castilianist project of national identity can be seen in the peevish articles written by Unamuno[8] on his 1906 trip to Barcelona and Ortega's disparaging comments on Prat, Cambó, and the core legitimacy of the entire Catalanist movement.[9]

The Castilianist counterattack was not long in materializing. In January 1907, the *Junta para Ampliación de Estudios* (JAE) was founded by Royal decree. It later gave life to the *Residencia de Estudiantes* (1910), the *Centro de Estudios Históricos* (1910), and the *Instituto Nacional de Ciencias Físico-Naturales* (1910). Core members of these institutions later played important roles in the *Liga de Educación Política Española* (1914) and its official organ, *España* (1915).

In his study of the impact of these important cultural institutions, Inman Fox has gone to great pains to stress their "liberal" orientation; that is, their drive to serve as a counterweight against the hermetic traditionalism of the nineteenth century Spanish right. In their important analysis of the history of the *JAE*, Laporta, Miguel et al, take a similar line, highlighting the institution's close links with Giner and the *Institución Libre de Enseñanza*. On one level, there can be no denying this set of interlocking institutions did affect an important break with the traditionalist cultural project in terms of its open embrace of the scientific method, European culture, and, in the case of the more politically-minded, democratic processes. Nor can their links to the progressivism of Krausist circles be understated. Finally, it can be assumed that most, if not all, of the brilliant constellation of thinkers involved (i.e., Menéndez Pidal, Ramón y Cajal, Azcárate, Altamira, Ortega, Castro) clearly had an image of themselves as transforming liberals.

Yet, if there is one thing that the twentieth-century history of ideas (and more immediately our own recent academic history of political correctness) has shown with great clarity, it is that reformist movements also often contain "black boxes," areas of inquiry (usually quite close to home psychologically) into which their leading cultural actors cannot, or will not, extend the critical acuity that marks their theorizing in other realms. For all of their efforts to deconstruct and rectify the long-standing Spanish tradition of obscurantism, xenophobia, social hierarchy, and hostility to science, the thinkers of this newly founded set of cultural institutions did virtually nothing to problematize the "naturalness" of the unitary and Castilian-centered conception of Spanish nationalist life. In fact, they did quite a bit to reify the assumptions inherited from the traditionalist discourse first articulated by Nebrija.

Nowhere is this tendency more evident than in the work of the *Revista de Filología Española,* the marquee publication of the *Centro de Estudios Históricos.* The research agenda of this publication shows an uncommon interest in demonstrating the essential "timelessness" of the Castilian "character" as evidenced in its language and literature, and from there, the center's anointed role as the prime organizer of Iberian life. The key figure at the *Revista* was

Menéndez Pidal, the great chronicler of the Spanish epic and erstwhile disciple of Menéndez y Pelayo. Though he would suggest, in contravention to the hierarchical ideals of his mentor, that *El Cid,* and the Castilian *Romancero* demonstrated the existence of strongly democratic tendencies within "el pueblo español," he in no way sought to challenge or to deconstruct "the people's" proclivity toward religiously-inspired warfare. Indeed, that aim was viewed by him to be one of the defining features of *lo nacional.* In other words, Menéndez Pidal's vision of the past put a very slight liberal patina on a very old story. Those reading his scholarly articles and/or the famous *Clásicos Castellanos* series produced for the broader public by his co-researchers and disciples would receive very few messages disabusing them of the belief that, should the need arise, the center and its "people" were entitled to use institutional coercion against those they viewed as denying their set of historically ratified prerogatives.

Despite this Castilianist counter-offensive, the Catalanist culture planning drive continued unabated during the second decade of the twentieth century. It was during this period that Eugeni d'Ors solidified the esthetic and moral canons of *Noucentisme* and Prat de la Riba leveraged the scarce resources of the *Mancomunitat,* inaugurated after a protracted political battle in 1914, to further multiply the number of institutions dedicated to widening the repertoire of Catalan cultural options. The evident success of the *Lliga's* in this realm, as well as Prat's famous call for the creation of *l'Espanya Gran* in 1916, emboldened those with similarly structured discourses in the Basque provinces and Galicia.[10] In the first case, this was translated into a re-doubled emphasis, especially within the branch of the movement linked to one of the late Arana's more trusted collaborators, Engracio Aranzadi, to the creation of autochthonous cultural artifacts. Aranzadi's efforts culminated with the publication in 1918 of his "breviary" of national identity, *La nación vasca.* In Galicia, the Catalan example, along with the notions of a re-born Portuguese identity (a cultural commerce largely catalyzed by the writings of the Catalan Iberianist Ignasi Ribera i Rovira) gave birth to that region's first overtly nationalist (as opposed to regionalist) movement.[11]

Like the dominant discourses of national identity in all of the other areas of the peninsula, the Galician discourse of identity was profoundly marked by both the logic of Herderian nationalism and a frank admittance of religion's key role in the maintenance of social cohesion. Its foremost theorist and cultural impresario was Vicente Risco who, quite consciously following the examples of Prat de la Riba and Aranzadi, as well as their Portuguese correlate Teixeira de Pascoaes, sought to capture the "essence" of his people in a single "popular"

essay: *Teoria do nacionalismo galego* (May 1920).[12] If there was a salient difference between this text and the models that had preceded it, it was on the level
of mimesis. Like Brañas and Murguía before him, Risco was much more heavily indebted than his non-Galician counterparts to the vocabulary and tropes of
nationalist activists in other places.

A very short time after the publication of *Teoria do nacionalismo galego,*
Ortega began publishing a series of articles in *El sol* that would later come to be
known as *España invertebrada.* As a man who took pride in his ability to be "a
la altura de los tiempos," we can assume that as he sat down to write the series
he was deeply aware of the growing consolidation of the cultural repertoires
of national identity on the so-called periphery of the peninsula. Adding to his
concern was the ongoing Irish struggle for independence, Wilson's calls for
the right to national self-determination (issued in January 1918), and closer to
home, the apparent radicalization of Catalanism following the defeat of Cambó's bid for a statute of autonomy the year before. As has been noted, Ortega
had been for a number of years a harsh critic of historicist nationalisms who
was deeply implicated in generating a supposedly new "liberal" justification
of the Spanish state. After three years in which he had somewhat drifted away
from the public forum to attend to the more intimate concerns showcased in *El
espectador,* Ortega clearly sought to make a resounding statement on Spain's
"nationalities problem."

True to his widely professed liberal sympathies, he began by making a
convincing case (using the example of the Roman Empire) for the superiority of voluntaristic (as opposed to ethnic, territorial, or linguistic) conceptions
of national identity. However, when he expanded his analysis to the particular
realm of Spanish history, his liberal *sang-froid* unexpectedly starts to boil, forcing him to emit openly historicist justifications of past Castilian comportment.
Just as the "black box" of reflexive Castilianism had led Menéndez Pidal to
sustain—in apparent contradiction of the truth—that the Castilians were unique
among the peninsular peoples in having had the grandeur of vision necessary
for generating epic poems, Ortega sustains that "sólo cabezas castellanas tienen
órganos adecuados para percibir el gran problema de la España integral" (only
Castilian minds have the necessary organs to perceive the great problem of integral Spain) (61).[13] Moreover, this special leadership talent is, he tells his reader,
not a function of human factors but rather a "quid divinum" (55). So much for
the Renanian ideal of a public space and governed by earthly prerogative free
from *a priori* notions of ethnic privilege!

Although Ortega and the vast majority of those involved in the Castilanist
culture planning thrust begun in 1907 were deeply opposed to the Primo de

Rivera dictatorship, it can be argued that their brand of "sanitized traditional-ism" and/or "black box liberalism" provided the regime with a certain degree of intellectual justification. When we exclude the admittedly large and important issue of civil liberties, the two projects saw pretty much eye-to-eye on the need to pursue technological and economic progress, "clean up" corrupt government, and re-establish the unquestioned protagonism of Castile in peninsular affairs. In a sense, Primo accomplished with his loyal divisions and his calculated court-ing of the monied elite what that army of historians and philologists had wished to do with their pens: consign the so-called "peripheral" movements of national identity to a place of clear marginalization and institutional bankruptcy.

This forceful rollback of the culture planning initiatives of the socially con-servative nationalist parties in Catalonia, Galicia, and the Basque Country only speeded up the radical turn that had begun among them in the wake Cambó's failure in Madrid. Emblematic in this regard is the trajectory of Francesc Macià. A career officer in the engineering corps of the Spanish army who had first been elected to Parliament in 1907 as a part of *Solidaritat Catalana,* Macià, like the majority of his fellow *solidaris,* possessed an outlook that was essen-tially ameliorative in nature; ultimately he believed that in time Madrid would have no choice but to cede to the reality of a culturally distinct Catalonia and a bipolar conception of the state. After several years in Madrid, however, he became increasingly convinced that this outlook was naive, as it did not take into account the visceral anti-Catalanism of the majority of the Castile-based political and cultural elite. Eventually, he became openly separatist in orienta-tion, founding *Estat Català* in 1922, an event which would lead, in turn, to his wildly unsuccessful attempt to foment an armed insurrection at Prats de Molló in the Pyrenees in 1926. A similar shift took place in 1922 in the Basque coun-try when the so-called *grupo aberriano* of Gallastegui established hegemony over Aranzadi's more accidentalist faction of the movement. With the onset of the Primo dictatorship, important operations of these new more strident groups were carried out in exile.[14] In Galicia culture planning activities of the type that had defined the decade of the teens continued apace. This can probably be ex-plained by the fact that the link between such activities and real political change had always been much more tenuous there than in Catalonia or the Basque Country. Thus, the regime allowed initiatives like the *Seminario de Estudos Ga-legos* to proceed with minimal interference. But even still, the movement suf-fered schisms. For instance, the more militant *Irmandade Nazionalista Galega* (ING) split off from the *Irmandades de Fala* in 1922.

For those on the periphery, the centralist intolerance under Primo and Berenguer merely proved what they had always feared, and what a close reading of the contemporary history Iberian discourse of national identity makes crystal clear: Castilianists perennially reserve for themselves the prerogative to use institutionalized violence when they feel that their hegemony is called into question by one or more of their peninsular others. As the numerous civil conflicts of the nineteenth century indicate, the general tendency had been to maintain the pressure on the so-called "periphery" until such time as the "threat" is deemed to be extinguished, or to put it in culturalist terms, until such time as the centralist repertoire of signs and symbols successfully displaces those repertoires generated by groups on the periphery. However, the sudden flight of Alfonso XIII in April 1931, unexpectedly truncated this exercise in "forced forgetting." Yet the short length of the dictatorship was not the only problem. Throughout his years in control, Primo had consistently harassed and denigrated the Madrid-based intellectual class. They had responded by denying the regime their valued services in the realm of culture planning. Thus, the dictator found himself in the awkward role of having nothing much to offer the periphery (in terms of compelling myths of collective identity) in exchange for their forced abandonment of cherished autonomous institutions.

With the declaration of the Republic, the situation became cruelly reversed. As we have seen, the latent threat of violence, or at the very least, the right to invoke some supernatural prerogative in relations with peninsular "others," had always formed part of even the most progressive versions of the Castilianist discourse of identity. Now, due to their acrimonious "divorce" from Primo and the power structure he represented, the liberal intellectuals of Madrid who had charged themselves with the duty of creating a new framework for intrapeninsular cohesion no longer had that vaunted tool at their disposal. In effect, they were in the difficult position of having to quickly and radically re-invent a centuries-old discursive model along completely non-coercive lines. Their failure to effectively do so is not surprising. Owing to this reality, the center was now at the mercy of the now more cohesive culture planning models of the periphery. That Catalonia remained part of the Spanish state in the spring of 1931, for example, has much more to do with Macià's sense of calculated restraint than the inherent powers of the center. When the *Cortes* finally did grant the re-established *Generalitat* a Statute of Autonomy in 1932 (stripped of the peninsula-wide federalizing provisions with which it had originally been proposed), it was approved over the objections of Castilianist intellectual lions such as Unamuno and Ortega. The narrowness of the "enlightened" Castilianist vision can further be seen in the Azaña government's harshly negative reaction to the *Galeuzca* pact of August 1933, in which leaders of all of the major Catalan, Basque, and Galician nationalist parties agreed to cooperate in promoting the regular exchange of cultural artifacts between the three nations. Far from seeing this as a new and credible way to perhaps begin reshaping the nation from the periphery, the "liberal" Republican government attacked it stridently in the press.

In many ways, the pact was the high point of attempts to fundamentally reconfigure the parameters of the Spanish repertoire of cultural options. It was also the beginning of the end of the tradition of pseudo-cosmopolitan Castilianism begun by Cánovas and practiced through the Primo de Rivera dictatorship. In November of 1933, the coalition formed around Gil Robles' CEDA movement assumed power. This change, in turn, encouraged the re-emergence of the type of reactionary and frankly anti-modern Castilianism practiced intermittently in the early 1800s, and more assiduously still, in the sixteenth and seventeenth centuries. In the eyes of military leaders and most of the Catholic right, the mere existence, however tenuous, of composite visions of national identity such as those that were uneasily tolerated by the Republican center-left, proved that the liberal political class had lost whatever *bona fides* it might have had in its *sacred* role as guarantors of national cohesion. Though both Basque and Galician statutes of autonomy were proposed (with the Galician one actually gaining a preliminary plebiscitary approval at home) during the pre-war Popular Front government, it was already clear to most that the moment to peacefully implement a radical re-alignment of the relations between Spain's major culture-nations had already come and gone.

As had been widely demonstrated, the Francoist culture-planning efforts were rooted, from quite early onward, in a frank revival of Spain's pre-modern repertoire of nationalist signs and symbols. Like the arrows held tightly in the talon of the Falangist eagle, causes of the Army, Church, and the Castilian language were re-bundled and proffered as a cultural package that would enable a new Imperial crusade like the one that had first expelled the infidels from the peninsula, and later made possible the "civilization" of the overseas territories. "Háblame en cristiano," the widely utilized insult/response used by Francoist troops with those using or known to favor the use of one of the non-Castilian languages, reveals quite succinctly the contours of its logic. When we consider the frequent insinuations concerning the "Jewishness" of the Catalans, and the habitual canards about the devious dealings of protestant Great Britain and Masonic cells, Francoism's Tridentine and even pre-Tridentine logic becomes more apparent. It was a desire to inculcate the population with this very particular Castilianist view of the peninsular past, that animated the production of the famous wave of historicist films produced by directors such as Juan de Orduña, Rafael Gil, and Saenz de Heredia in the late 1940s and early 1950s.

As mentioned earlier, Cambó's failure to gain a statute of autonomy in 1918–1919, combined with rightist oppression of the Primo years, engendered a change of orientation in all of the peripheral discourses on identity. There is a tendency, especially when we look at the Catalan case and Barcelona's famously "red" comportment during the Civil War, to characterize these transformations in terms of a simple migration from the left to the right side of the political spectrum. While it is certainly true that the causes of nationhood and egalitarianism came together in Catalonia, and to a lesser extent, Galicia, in the period 1931–1937, it would be a grave error to overstate the case. For all of their apparent ideological transformations in the public arena, the discursive architecture of the nationalist discourses of the Macià s and Castelaos remained heavily indebted to the logic of historicism, with its emphasis on the pre-eminent role of language, place, and the work of lettered elites in the creation of social cohesion. This, of course, served as a built-in brake on their long-term ability to truly adopt universal notions of social justice. Moreover, with a few notable exceptions, the source of leadership in these now seemingly leftist movements of national identity was what it had always been: the comfortable urban upper-middle class which had a long record of cooperation with clerical authority. While these contradictions were either downplayed or papered over in Catalonia and Galicia during the Republic, the same could not be said of *Euzkadi*. There, the strongly historicist and confessional cast of the PNV (Partido Nacionalista Vasco) caused it to clash repeatedly with its supposed republican "allies" within the country.

It is important to bear all this in mind when we look at the evolution of the major Iberian discourses of national identity over the last half-century. According to a vision that is still widely circulated today, the clash of national culture planning projects during this period went something like this. From 1939 to the early 1950s, Franco utilized the cinematic, journalistic, and literary resources at his disposal (not to mention those having to do with the employ of state violence) to expunge and/or simply overwhelm with religiously-imbued Castilianisms any remaining signs of Catalan, Basque, and Galician identity. As he did so, the non-Castilian leaders and artistic producers kept the flame of their national cultures alive in exile. As good Republicans, these exiled patriots felt a strong affinity toward egalitarian politics and a generalized aversion toward confessionally-informed social thought. As the 1950s wore on, it became clear to the Franco regime that some entente with instrumental modernity was necessary. The first step in this process was the entry of the so-called "technocrats" of *Opus Dei* into the government. It was followed, in the early sixties, with the country's decision to make tourism one of the prime engines of its economic development. As a result of these changes, Spaniards born after 1940 began to fall increasingly into step with the dominant social-democratic views of Spain's European counterparts. As the regime's ideological vehemence declined in the mid-sixties, numerous exiles returned home. In dialogues with them, and with their new trans-pyrenaean interlocutors, the post-war generation began re-connecting with its country's "lost" history of progressive politics and cultural diversity. It was out of this ferment that recovery of the Catalan, Basque, and Galician cultural systems arose during the 1960s, 1970s and 1980s.

While such a vision holds some truth, it pays short shrift to the important role played by home-based, *religiously-informed* nationalist organizations in this renaissance. This was especially the case in Catalonia, the place which, in one form or another, had always served as vanguard of nationalist mobilization of the Iberian periphery. While figures like Tarradellas ambled through solitary and often humiliatingly inconsequential exiles, Jordi Pujol and other Catholic nationalists like him were busy reconstructing the basis of the Catalan identity through their participation and leadership in groups such as the brotherhood of *La Mare de Déu de Montserrat, Crist Catalunya,* and the *Grup Torras i Bages.* In these organizations, the example of Prat de la Riba was valued much more highly than that of Company's or even Macià, and Marxist forms of analysis were generally shunned. In Galicia, the process of nationalist regeneration followed a similar route with the catholically-inflected Galaxia Group, led by Ramón Piñeiro, García Sabell, and Carballo Calero, gradually reviving the goals and works of the largely conservative *Xeneración Nós* of Risco. In the Basque Country, the model of analysis outlined above conforms somewhat better to reality. There, the PNV of the post-war was hobbled, just as it had been at the turn-of-the-century, by an inability to generate and place into wide circulation among the intellectual class (never mind the general public) a compeling repertoire of unquestionably "native" cultural materials. This culture planning failure was one of the prime reasons why a younger generation of impatient activists felt the need to break from the PNV and found ETA in 1959, filling this "cultural gap," as it were, with armed violence heavily informed by Marxism and anti-colonial theory. However, when we look a little closer, we can see that for all its apparent interest in non-confessional and ostensibly left-leaning ideologies, ETA and its present political arm, EH, have discourses that are heavily indebted to highly mystical notions of communal identity. In many ways, the constructs of *abertzale* sacrifice and martyrdom are as close as one gets in the so-called Western world to the militant religious fervor found in some branches of Islam.

The seemingly natural symbiosis between historistic and religiously imbued politics and nationalism has been made readily manifest in the years since the ratification of the 1978 Constitution. In the months previous to the inaugural autonomous elections in Catalonia (March 1980), it was widely believed that one of the major leftist groups (PSC-PSOE or the PSUC) would gain a leading plurality of the votes. To the surprise of many, it was Pujol's coalition (CiU) with its strong, and largely complex-free, relationship to the culture planning repertoire engendered by Prat de la Riba, d'Ors, Cambó, and others at the outset of the twentieth century that carried the day. A similar process can be seen in the Basque Country. In the 1980 autonomous elections there, the PNV, linked like Pujol's coalition to confessional social thought and early twentieth-century culture planning repertoires, quickly reasserted its hegemony (unbroken until today) within both the nationalist camp and the country as a whole. The story has been pretty much the same in Galicia, except for the fact the long domi-nant right-wing party is a "sucursal" of the state-wide PP. But even this is very much in keeping with the early twentieth-century history of Galeguismo, within which claims for self-rule were always much less strident than in Catalonia or the Basque Country owing to: a) the relative weakness of the urban bourgeoisie, and b) the continuing grip of a Madrid-oriented *caciquista* regime over public life in many rural areas.

Owing to both its own experience as a persecuted party under Franco as well as its acute awareness of the need to engender a workable civic consensus after years of one-party rule, the PSOE adopted a largely "hands-off" policy to-ward both Castilianist culture planning and the movements of national identity in Catalonia, Galicia, and the Basque Country during its long stay in office. In its reluctance to use centralist power for blatantly centralist ends, it can be com-pared to the Republican government of the period 1932–1934. However, it was also like that government in terms of its general refusal to work pro-actively towards the development of a more fully articulated and truly multi-polar model of intra-state cultural relations.

During its firm term in office, a time when its working majority depended on support from Pujol's CiU, the Aznar government more or less continued with the line established by the Socialists. But even while maintaining this os-tensibly non-committal posture in the realm of day-to-day tactics, it was deeply engaged in a culture planning effort aimed at reigniting the dormant flames of Castilianism. One key element of this campaign was the rehabilitation of the historical legacy of Cánovas del Castillo and the politics of the Restoration. This was accomplished through a barrage of government-backed commemora-tions, studies, and reissues of his work. In this way, the PP prepared the ground not only for a re-legitimation of his peculiar brand of governance by an elitist minority, but the return of his pseudo-dialogic approach to the problem of dealing with progressivism and Castile's peninsular others.

Another was the creation of the *La Fundación San Millán de la Cogolla*, dedicated to "investigar, documentar y difundir los orígenes de la Lengua Castellana y la utilización de las nuevas tecnologías para la difusión y actualización del castellano en el mundo" ("Origen y constitución" s.n.) (research, document and disseminate the origins of the Castilian Language as well as the use of new technologies for updating and spreading Castilian throughout the world) ("Origen y constitución" s.n.) (My translation). San Millan, located in Old Castile is, of course, the site of the Monasteries of Suso and Yuso which, according to the late-nineteenth and twentieth- century philological school, was the "cuna de la lengua española" (cradle of the Spanish language) owing to its link with *Glosas emilianenses* and later on, the poetry of Berceo. The monasteries possess the added symbolic advantages of having been definitively put out of business by the *desamortización* of Mendizábal in 1835. Thus, in creating the foundation in 1998, the Aznar government was not only creating an institutional bulwark for Castilianism, destined in time to become the "atalaya de nuestra cultura" ("Origen y constitución" s.n.) (watchtower of our culture) (My translation) but also righting what in traditionalist eyes was one of lay progressivism's most egregious assaults on the church's rightful place in Spanish society. In the ensuing years, it has become a launching ground for all types of centralist culture planning initiatives. In July 2000, the government finally released its long-awaited white paper on the teaching of humanities with its call for a "vertebration" of the national educational system; nevertheless, it did so at the newly renovated monasteries. It has also played host to events such as the *Encuentro de Embajadores Iberoamericanos, Reunión de las Academias de la Lengua Española,* an *Exposición Pictórica en Homenaje a la Lengua Española y a San Millán de la Cogolla, Presentación oficial de la nueva edición de la Ortografía de la Lengua Española.* At this last event, the then Minister of Culture Mariano Rajoy said:

> España no es una potencia económica ni industrial, pero sí una colosal potencia cultural gracias al castellano, que hablan en el mundo unos 400 millones de personas . . . España es inexplicable sin su proyección hacia América y a esa cultura común hispánica debemos hoy nuestro lugar en el mundo ("Presentación oficial" s.n.)

> (Spain is not an economic or industrial power but rather a giant cultural power thanks to the Castilian language, which is spoken by over 400 million people in the

world . . . Spain cannot be explained without taking into account its drive toward America. It is thanks to this common Hispanic culture that we occupy the place we do in today's world). (My translation)

Could the drive to re-bundle the fundamental building blocks of the centuries-old tradition of Castilanism (language, faith, tradition, and a "universal" imperial mission) be any clearer?

In *El bucle melancólico,* the Basque writer and former member of ETA, Jon Juaristi, suggests that the self-pitying hermeticism of the contemporary Basque discourse of identity has virtually guaranteed the failure of substantial and constructive dialogue between its adherents and those of the peninsula's other nationalist projects. Similarly in Catalonia, intellectuals such as Alejo Vidal-Quadras from the centralist right and Josep Ramoneda from the Catalanist left have long railed against what they see as conservative Catalanism's inherent inability to engender a meaningful ecumenical dialogue leading to the construction of a truly plural Spain. In Galicia, figures such as Alfredo Conde and Marcial Gondar Portasany have criticized *Galeguismo's* tendency to greatly overplay its hand on the issue of linguistic uniformity. Implied in all of these criticisms is a belief that the discursive structure of historicist nationalisms— which as we have seen have been the dominant strains of nationalist thought in the Iberian periphery during the contemporary era—carry within them a need for exclusivity, and from there, a tendency toward institutional coercion, that is fundamentally antithetical to the construction of a functioning multi-national polity. These criticisms, especially those of Juaristi and his countryman Mikel Azurmendi, have been enthusiastically received and re-circulated by the current conservative government in Madrid. Yet, while they celebrate these "deconstructions" of the peripheral culture planning projects, they do nothing to encourage a similar analysis of Castilianism's ample tradition of historicistically-justified exclusivity.

In the wake of the Piqué and San Gil's *ponencia,* Aznar himself has stressed that the time has come for Spaniards to live "sin prejuicios, ataduras ni cuentas pendientes con la historia" (Huesca s.n.) (without prejudice, ties, or unresolved historical business) (Huesca s.n.) (My translation). These are certainly strange words from a man whose administration has shown such a keen interest in Cánovas, *Academias de la Lengua,* the Monasteries at San Millán de la Cogolla, and the "vertebrated" teaching of history in public schools. What he really means, of course, is that non-Castilian Spaniards should dispense with *their* "unhealthy" obsession with the past and cede to the "natural fact" of Castilian historical supremacy. In doing so, he is tapping into a deep well of Castilian exceptionalism which has been institutionalized to the point of being imperceptible to many who uphold its main aims. Yet while it may be inperceptible to him and his core group of support, the reality of Castilianism's hegemonic logic will never disappear for most on the periphery. He is, of course, free to engage in the politics of the *trágala*. But before employing the sword that is concealed behind the colorful *muleta* of his *Patriotismo Constitucional,* perhaps he should reflect a bit more on the scant level of lasting success achieved by his ideological forebearers. If Cánovas and Primo, whose regimes had far more repressive machinery at their disposal, could not eradicate the "unnatural" reality of the so-called peripheral movements of national identity, why should he expect to be able do so now? Would it not be easier for everyone involved if the Neo-Castilianists of today would simply admit, and base any and all negotiations over the future of Spain's civil society, on the unassailable fact that today's Spain contains not just three, but four major, historistically-defined movements of national identity?

Notes

1.   In this context, *ponencias* are reports commissioned by the leadership of the party for the purpose of framing discussion at its annual convention. They might be compared to the so-called "planks" within political platform of a party in the U.S. The annual convention of the PP took place in Madrid from January 26–28, 2002.

2.   The critical discourse attendant to nationality issues in Spain has, in its Spanish-language iteration, long included the use of terms such as *catalanismo, galleguismo, bizcaiatarrismo* and even *vasquismo* (although "el nacionalismo vasco" is now much more common than these last two terms employed by Ortega and Unamuno respectively). However, the term *castellanismo* has never really achieved the status of a common linguistic currency. I believe this omission is quite telling. In an attempt to spur a leveling of the semantic playing field, I will use the term Castilianism throughout the remainder of the paper.

3.   Until the mid-eighties, there was still a relatively high level of critical unconsciousness among most scholars whose work centered on nationalist discourses. One either tended to accept and thus "work within" the *prima facie* claims of essentialists concerning the spontaneity and "timelessness" of nationalist belief systems or to simply dismiss such discourses as pesky and illogical vestiges of a soon-to-be-extinguished system of social meaning. It was a situation that, in many ways, mirrored the tendency in literary studies to either accept the canonicity (another metaphor for "timelessness") of certain works on the basis of previous critical pronouncements or to reject the whole system of relative literary value as nothing more than a feeble and fundamentally self-interested bourgeois imposition. Thanks to Bourdieu and others like him who have

concentrated on the broader dynamics of the economy of symbolic goods, and the far from disinterested role that intellectuals and intellectual institutions play within it, many literary scholars have distanced themselves from such facile posturing and have begun to examine the full range of processes through which "taste" is generated. Benedict Anderson is, of course, the most frequently cited exponent of such "critical reflexivity" in the realm of nationality studies. However, scholars from the Tel Aviv and Leuven schools, trained in literary and translation studies, have taken the Cornell historian's fecund intuitions to a much higher level of specificity and rigor. The reason would appear to be clear. While historians and political scientists often possess ample tools for macro-theorizing, they often lack the level of linguistic competence, global cultural experience, and attention to textual nuance that is common among scholars of literature. When we consider the importance of intersystemic "cultural commerce" and the need to push intra-cultural "hot buttons" on the successful creation and maintenance of such schemes of identity, we can see that these abilities are of absolutely crucial interpretive importance.

4. Applying these postulates to present circumstances in the U.S. (albeit in admittedly crude and reductionist fashion) it might be argued, for example, that the outpouring of patriotic fervor following the events of September 11th, far from being a spontaneously occurrence or the result of a profound appreciation for the qualities of President George Bush or Secretary of Defense Donald Rumsfeld, was the logical result of a culture planning entente forged in the 1980s and 1990s between the small and increasingly interrelated concentrated group of major audiovisual producers and an evermore unilateralist and militarized political establishment. Aware that the so-called Vietnam Syndrome was a direct result of the fact that many Americans were "too intimate" with the gruesome carnage of war and the moral grayness of neo-colonialist adventurism, the national security establishment (greatly strengthened by new funding for conservative Washington think-tanks) desperately hoped for a new repertoire of morally unambiguous story lines that minimized or caricaturized armed conflict's human toll and portrayed political deliberation as an unnecessary drag on "decisive" and "heroic" action. Hollywood, increasingly aware that introspection and moral angst of *The Deer Hunter* vintage simply did not sell as well as manichaeanism, readily obliged in providing such "uplifting" and cartoonishly simplistic images and plots. The massive implantation of this newly established repertoire of tropes and symbols (with its systematic degradation of the non-U.S. "others") has been fundamental to generating the apparently overwhelming "proneness" for the type of foreign policy the U.S. is pursuing post-September 11. In short, if we were really serious about explaining our current way of acting in the world, we would be far less interested in the insider gossip concerning the ascendancy within the Bush Adminstration of Condoleeza Rice or Colin Powell and far more interested in how people like Jerry Bruckheimer, Menachem Golans, Rush Limbaugh, Roger Ailes, Arnold Schwartzenegger, and Chuck Norris substantially re-engineered many Americans' perception of the core terms of engagement between "us" and the world outside our borders.

5. See Castellanos, 25–35.

6. See Even-Zohar "Repertoire," 389–92.
7. Despite fervent Catalan cries for justice, the central government not only exonerated the rioters, but passed a statute, *La Ley de Jurisdicciones* (March, 23 1906) that insured that army officials would be exempt from prosecution should they engage in similar activities in the future.
8. See Unamuno, "Solidaridad" and Dendle.
9. See Ortega, "Pidiendo" and "Diputado."
10. However, in making his famous call for a multipolar form of Iberian unity, the leader of the Lliga was, in fact, co-opting ideas that had long been popular among Catalanists such as Ribera-Rovira, Casas-Carbó and Joan Maragall who tended to identify not so much with *noucentisme* and its implied orthodoxies, but rather with the Republican and/or *modernista* branches of the movement.
11. See Harrington, "Risco."
12. See Harrington, "Risco."
13. See Fox, 105.
14. For more on this phenomenon, see Harrington, "Agents."

Works Cited

Almanach des noucentistes. Barcelona: Horta, 1911.

Almirall, Valentí. *Lo Catalanisme*. Barcelona: Edicions 62, 1979.

Anderson, Benedict. *Imagined Communities: Reflections on the Origin and Spread of Nationalism*. London: Verso New Left Books, 1983.

Arana Goiri, Sabino de. *La patria de los vascos: antología de escritos políticos*. San Sebastian: R&B Ediciones: Haranburu Editor, 1995.

Aranzadi Etxeberria, Engracio de. *Ereintza: Siembra del nacionalismo vasco 1894–1912*. San Sebastian: Editorial Auãmendi Argitaldaria, 1980.

———. *La nación vasca*. Bilbao: Viuda. e Hijos de Grijelm0,1918.

Azurmendi, Mikel. "Etnicidad y violencia." *Claves de la razón práctica* 43 (junio 1994) 28–41.

———. *La herida patriótica*. Madrid: Taurus, 1998.

Brañas, Alfredo. *El regionalismo*. Barcelona, 1889. Facscimile version. La Coruña: La Voz de Galicia, 1982.

Cánovas del Castillo, Antonio. *Discurso sobre la nación: inauguración del curso del Ateneo de Madrid, noviembre de 1882*. <http://cervantesvirtual.com/servlet/SirveObras/34867048416151047256 0102/p0000001.htm> Biblioteca virtual Miguel de Cervantes.

Castellanos, Jordi. "Gaudí, arquitecte de Déu." *Intel.lectuals, cultura i poder: entre el modernisme i el noucentisme*. Barcelona: La Magrana, 1998. 9–71.

Carner-Ribalta, Josep. *De Balaguer a Nova York passant per Moscou i Prats de Molló*. Paris: Edicions Catalanes de Paris, 1972.

Castro, Rosalía de. *Poesías*. Vigo: Patronato de Rosalía de Castro, 1973.

"Constitución Española" *Congreso de Diputados* <http://www.congreso.es /funciones/ constitucion/indice.htm>

Curros Enriquez, Manuel. *Aires da minha terra e outros poemas.* Vigo: Galaxia, 1985.

Dendle, Brian. "Unamuno en Barcelona: Una entrevista desconocida de 1906." *Cuadernos de Investigación Filológica* (Logroño) XV (1989) 159–62.

Even-Zohar, Itamar 1994. *Culture Planning and the Market: Making and Maintaining Socio-Semiotic Entities* <http://www.tau.ac.il/~itamarez/papers/plan_clt.html>

———. "Culture Repertoire and the Wealth of Collective Entities." In *Under Construction: Links for the Site of Literary Theory. Essays in Honour of Hendrik Van Gorp.* Ed. De Geest, Dirk et al. Leuven: Leuven UP. 389–403.

———. "The Making of Culture Repertoire and the Role of Transfer." *Target* 9 (2), 1997. 373–81.

———. "The Role of Literature in the Making of the Nations of Europe: A Socio-Semiotic Examination." *Applied Semiotics/Sémiotique appliquée* (AS/SA) 1, 20–30.

Fabregat, Ramon, ed. *Macià, la seva actuació a l'estranger.* Mèxic: Edicions Catalanes de Mèxic, 1952.

Fox, E. Inman. *La invención de España: nacionalismo liberal e identidad nacional.* Madrid: Cátedra, 1997.

Gondar Portasany, Marcial. *Crítica da razón galega.* Coruña: A nosa terra, 1994.

Habermas, Jurgen. *The Inclusion of the Other.* Cambridge: MIT Press, 1998.

———. *The Postnational Constellation: Political Essays* translated, edited and with an introduction by Max Pensky. Cambridge: Polity Press, 2001.

Harrington, Thomas S. "Agents of an Intersystem: Contributions of the Cuba-Based Diaspora to the Construction of the Nation in Galicia and Catalonia." *Catalan Review* (in press).

———. "Catalanism in the Portuguese Mirror: Skirmishes Between "Unitarians" and "Pluralists" for Control of the Movement (1900–1925)." *Revista de Estudios Hispánicos* 35(2001) 257–80.

———. "Invenciones de Españas." *Claves de Razón Práctica* 82 (mayo de 1998): 50–51.

———. "Laying the Foundations for an Integrated and Multi-polar Approach to the Study and Teaching of Peninsular Culture: Labanyi and Graham's *Spanish Cultural Studies: An Introduction. Siglo XX/Twentieth Century* 14, 1–2 (1996): 181–92.

———. "Literatura e nación." *Grial* 134 (1997): 379–92.

———. "Los hispanistas de EE.UU., el 'Boletín' y la vieja España." *Suplemento de Arte e Ideas.* La Vanguardia (Barcelona) 11 febrero 2000.

———. "Risco and Portugal: Contacts Previous to the Institutional Consolidation of Galician Nationalism" *Galician Review* (in press).

Huesca, José. *Aznar condena la exaltación de la diferencia.* 5 February 2002, <http://www. lavanguardia.es> (5 February 2002). *La Vanguardia Digital.*

Jardí, Enric. *Francesc Macià.* Barcelona: Edicions 62, 1991.

Juaristi, Jon. *El bucle melancólico: historias de nacionalistas vascos.* Madrid: Espasa Calpe, 1997.

————. *Sacra Némesis: nuevas historias de nacionalistas vascos.* Madrid: Espasa, 1999.

Laporta, José, Alfonso Ruiz Miguel, Virgilio Zapatero, and Javier Solana. "Los orígenes culturales de la Junta para Ampliación de Estudios" *Arbor,* CXXVI.493 (1987) 17–87.

"Les bases per la constitució regional catalana" (Les bases de Manresa) in González Casanova, J.A. *Federalisme i autonomía a Catalunya 1868–1938.* Barcelona: Curial, 1974. 536–39.

Máiz, Ramon. *Alfredo Brañas: O ideario de rexionalismo católico tradicionalista.* Vigo: Galaxia, 1983.

Menéndez y Pelayo, Marcelino. *Estudios de crítica literaria.* Madrid: Sucesores de Rivadeneyra, 1893.

————. *Historia de las ideas estéticas en España.* Madrid: Hernando, 1928.

————. *La conciencia española.* Recopilación de Antonio Tovar. Madrid: Ediciones y Publicaciones Españolas, 1948.

Murguía, Manuel. *Los Precursores.* Buenos Aires: Emecé Editores, 1944.

————. *Política y Sociedad en Galicia.* prólogo de Castelão. Madrid: Akal, 1974.

Nebrija, Antonio. "Prólogo a la gramática de la lengua castellana" in *Proyecto ensayo hispánico.* Ed. José-luis Gómez-Mártinez <http://ensayo.rom.uga.edu/ antologia/XV/ nebrija>

"Origen y constitución, La fundación, fines" *Fundacion San Millán de la Cogolla.* <http:// www.fsanmillan.org/marc02.htm>

Ortega y Gasset, José. "España invertebrada" *Obras Completas* III. Madrid: Revista de Occidente, 1947–1983. 35–128.

————. "Pidiendo una biblioteca" (1908) *Obras Completas* I. Madrid: Revista de Occidente, 1947–83. 81–84.

————. "Diputado por la cultura" (1910) *Obras Completas* X. Madrid: Revista de Occidente, 1947–83. 145–146.

Pascoaes, Teixeira de. *Arte de Ser Portugues.* Obras de Texeira de Pascoaes/10 Lisboa: Assirio e Alvim, 1991.

————. "O Génio Português na sua expressão Filosofica Poetica e Religiosa." *A Saudade e o Saudosismo.* Obras de Texeira de Pascoaes/7 Compilação e fixação do texto e notas de Pinharanda Gomes Lisboa: Assirio e Alvim, 1988. 67–95.

Pi i Margall, Francisco. *Las Nacionalidades.* Introducción por Jordi Solé-Tura. Madrid: Centro de Estudios Constitucionales, 1986.

Pondal, Eduardo. *Poesias.* A Coruña: Xuntanza editorial, 1990.

Prat de la Riba. Enric. *La nacionalitat catalana i Compendi de la doctrina catalanista.* Edició a cura de Jordi Casassas i Ymbert en Biblioteca dels Clàssics del Nacionalisme Català, 30. Barcelona: La Magrana, 1993.

"Presentación oficial de la nueva edición de la Ortografía de la Lengua Española." *Fundación San Millán de la Cogolla.* < http://www.fsanmillan.org/marc04.htm>

Ramoneda, Josep. "Final de etapa." *El País Digital* 2 octubre, 1998 <http://elpais.es>

Renan, Ernest. "What is a Nation?" trans. Alfred E. Zimmern in Zimmern, Alfred E. ed. *Modern Political Doctrines.* New York: Oxford University Press, 1939. 186–205.

Resina, Joan Ramón. "Hispanism and its Discontents." *Siglo XX/Twentieth Century* (1996): 85–129.

Risco, Vicente.*Teoría nacionalista.* Acercamento biográfico e bibliografía por Fernando Salgado, edición e limiar de Teoria Nacionalista de Francisco Bobillo. Vol. 1 de las *Obras Completas.* Madrid: Akal Editor, 1981.

Torras i Bages, Josep. *La Tradició Catalana.* Barcelona: Editorial Selecta, 1966.

Tusell, Javier. "El fin del antiguo régimen: Fernando VII" in Tusell, Javier, Carlos Martínez Shaw and José-Luis Martín, eds. *Historia de España: Edad Contemporánea.* Madrid: Taurus, 2001. 17–45.

Unamuno, Miguel de. "Solidaridad Española" *Obras Completas VII.* Madrid: Afrodisio Aguado, 1958. 729–55.

Vidal-Quadras, Aleix. *Cuestión de fondo.* Barcelona: Montesinos, 1993.

5

Beyond Castro and Maravall:
Interpellation, Mimesis, and the Hegemony
of Spanish Culture

Anthony J. Cascardi

With certain notable exceptions, Hispanism in the twentieth century labored under the reputation that it was a backwater of literary and cultural studies. For reasons that seem at once very old and very new, Spanish studies outside of Spain long seemed to lag at some significant pace "behind" that of cognate fields. If there is reason to hedge this broad-based claim, it is not so much because the picture inside Spain was so very different but because some of the relevant perspectives were. While it may seem too familiar a historical truth to bear repeating, the development of Hispanism in the twentieth century was burdened by two rather ponderous weights. One was the legacy of Franco, the last major dictator of the World War II era to remain in power in Western Europe, and the other was Spain's ongoing attachment to the "problem" of its own past. But *that* attachment was at least as old as Quevedo, who was already writing about Spain's decline at the height of the Golden Age. And yet Quevedo was as given to exaggerated boasting about the prestige of Spanish culture as he was to talking about Spain's decline. In either case, his literary posture was bound up with ideas about Spain's cultural hegemony, whether in the form of hyperbolic praise, as in his claims about the antiquity of the Spanish language relative to all other modern tongues, or in the form of elegiac lament about the demise of

Spain's cultural dominion, as in the famous sonnet "Miré los muros de la patria mía."

Quevedo's contradictory stance is remarkable, but its divided vision is not atypical. Even in the twentieth century, Spanish writers and intellectuals sought to reinforce images of Spain's cultural hegemony by strenuously defending against notions of decline. Often that defense took the form of efforts to separate and preserve a core of things purely "Spanish" from those not. Vigorous attempts to resolve the "problem of Spain" often masked a much deeper traditionalism whose key points of reference were the Middle Ages and the Golden Age. Little wonder that Menéndez Pidal devoted massive efforts to a historical reconstruction of the Spain of the Cid, that writers of the Generation of '27 mounted a literary campaign to "return" to the poetry of the baroque, or that both Miguel de Unamuno and José Ortega y Gasset produced major philosophical works oriented around *Don Quijote.* But attempts to fortify an essential Spanish identity could not easily come to terms with the cultural and ethnic contradictions of what Spanish "national" culture was comprised nor could they adequately represent the many regional interests that remained in contention despite the political unification of the country. Likewise, the task of articulating the relationship between Spanish cultural nationalism, the politics of Absolutism, and the Spanish imperial project remained on the margins, even while it was often said that the twentieth-century "crisis of Spain" was precipitated by the loss of Spain's last remaining colonies. It is more or less well known that the formation of a Spanish "national identity" was staked on the political suppression of the differences among the various cultures, languages, races, religions, and histories that came together on the Iberian peninsula. The elevation of the interests that centered in Castile and in Christianity into a national ideology was a crucial part of this process.

While these issues reach back at least to the time of the *Reyes Católicos,* the reactions against them are as current as Basque separatism and the resurgence of Catalan as a regional language on the Spanish side of the Pyrenees. Yet in part because the writing of cultural history is typically given to the "victors," scant attention has been paid to many of these questions in mainstream Spanish studies. This is not altogether surprising. The Franco regime hardly provided a climate in which the critique of ideology and empire could flourish. In spite of the influx of exiled Spanish intellectuals to the United States during and after the Spanish Civil War, Hispanism in the U.S. remained too far removed from the political stakes of these issues and too enmeshed in the practices of close reading and textual scholarship for them to have had much of an impact. To be sure, the close reading of a sonnet by Garcilaso or the disentanglement of

Góngora's intricate syntax are endeavors without which the broader social and political interpretations of literature would be impossible. But reading that is blind to history is as far from the truth about literature as is a kind of criticism that regards texts as nothing more than bearers of reigning ideologies. There must be some way to locate productive discrepancies and contradictions even within an ideological framework as apparently homogeneous as that of Spain at the height of its empire.

This is not to say that the complex and conflictive nature of Spanish culture went completely unnoticed in Spanish studies. On the contrary, Américo Castro was responsible for crafting an approach to Spanish history whose core insight centered around the convergence and conflict of three district racial/religious groups on the Iberian peninsula (Christians, Moors, and Jews). Since the fundamentals of the Castro thesis are well known there is scant need to recapitulate them here. But I would point out that underlying Castro's views was the notion that Spanish history was shaped not just by the presence of these three groups but by the fact that the pattern of their interactions was based on the principles of caste, not class. Viewed in purely structural terms, caste societies are relatively fixed. They encourage sedimented differences for what may be obvious reasons: to the extent that one's affiliation with a particular caste is racially determined, movement from one caste to another is virtually impossible to achieve in any legitimate sense. A society of castes can function well only if the differences among the various groups comprising it are imagined as clear and distinct. Moreover, those differences are conceived to be constitutive of the social order itself. In societies based on divisions of caste, ideology gains power via the representation of social relations as if they were natural phenomena.

Scholars whose work has yet to be incorporated into Spanish studies, such as Franz Fanon, have demonstrated how race can be linked to physiognomy in ways that bind the physical to the imaginary; but the fact remains that when it comes to the differences between Christian and Jew the "essence" of race cannot itself be seen.[1] The criteria for making such caste distinctions in Spain were invisible. There was thus a potential for Spanish society to be haunted by fantasmatic worries that were generated by the desire to seek certainty about the uncertifiable. As is manifestly evident both in the workings of the Spanish Inquisition and in the "honor plays" of the Golden Age, the impossible pursuit of unattainable certainties generated a collective psychology of suspicion and fear that the analysis of caste in purely structural terms could not fully explain. As accounted for by Castro, the quality of this fear was "existential"; and yet one can hardly overlook the fact that the "existential" content of such experience was dependent upon the structural conditions in which subjects came to exist.[2]

I will return to some of these matters in connection with the more recent debates over the questions of subject formation, social structures, and discursive practices. For now I wish simply to note that Castro's thesis about the primacy of caste led him to a view of Spanish history that attributed existential qualities to the collective subject of Spanish history. Consider the following remarks from the introduction of one of the first translations of any of Castro's major works into English (*The Spaniards*), in which he argues for the primacy of the personal dimension of national history over and above all others: "This new title, *The Spaniards*, indicates that I wish to accentuate and emphasize the personal, rather than the structural, nature of this history. It is not sufficient merely to narrate and evaluate what was done by the Spaniards. It is imperative especially to determine the identity of a great people. The *ser* (being) and the *hacer* (doing) of the Spaniards refer to their very mode of existence" (v). Consider, likewise, Castro's account of what it means for a work like *Don Quijote* to be a quintessentially "Spanish" book. Castro writes:

> It is difficult to understand the peculiarity of this book [*Don Quijote*] without first making comprehensible the human reality represented by the word *Spaniard*. As I have tried to explain, it is not a matter of naively establishing a relation of identity between men and the land on which they dwell. What is authentically Spanish originated and was formed as a consequence of the intercrossing of Christian, Moorish, and Jewish people on the Iberian Peninsula. But in addition to being Spanish, the *Quijote* was produced at a particular time in Spanish history—the beginning of the seventeenth century. That is to say, it was produced in the wake of certain human situations . . . The themes and literary forms (ways of seeing and expressing what was passing through human lives) that prior literature could offer were filled with Muslim, Hebrew, Stoic (Petrarch), Neoplatonic (Marsilio Ficino), and other resonances. All this, however, did not simply pour over Cervantes as a rain of culture, but was reflected and refracted by the Spanish situation of 1600 and above all by Miguel de Cervantes, as a self that had to find its place in the Madrid of 1600. Only an authentic biography could clarify this situation. (*Idea* 127)

The question that Hispanists had long left unanswered was what allowed for the formation of the collective "we" that Castro counts as the only legitimate "subject" of history. Castro was himself well aware of the question: "algún lector tal vez se pregunte por el papel del individuo, del 'yo,' dentro del 'nosotros' de las historias. . . . Bastaría ahora con apuntar que el 'yo' y su obra historiable adquieren sentido al ser enfocados y entendidos desde el punto de vista del 'nosotros' en que existen" (some reader may perhaps wonder about the role of the individual, of the 'I' within the 'we' of history and histories. . . . It should be sufficient for now to point out that the 'I' and its historiable work acquire meaning by being brought into focus and understood from the point of view of the 'we' in which they exist) ("El 'nosotros'" 274).[3] And yet his best responses were more or less reiterations of the question itself, albeit cast in the language of expressivist historicism whose roots lie in Ortega and Dilthey:

> el "nosotros" adquiere dimensión histórica, digna de historia, como un proyecto de vida colectiva, como un hacer dirigido hacia ciertas metas, como un proceso en el cual es inseparable *el hacer* y *el hacerse* de quienes van infundiendo realidad de vida—de vida nuestra—al construir ciudades, naciones, formas de pensar, de creer, de embellecer. El fenómeno cultural es inseparable del propósito de la situación de vida colectiva expresados o latentes en él. (263)

> (the "we" acquires a historical dimension, one worthy of history, as a project of collective life and as a process of doing directed toward certain goals, as a process in which the "making" and the "becoming" of those who are in the process of infusing the reality of life, our life—building cities, nations, ways of thinking and belief, forms of beauty—are inseparable. The phenomenon of culture is inseparable from the purpose of collective life expressed or latent in it.)

By personalizing collective history, by phrasing it in vitalistic terms, and by identifying the racial-religious underpinnings of Spanish society with the principles of caste, Castro's work tended to foreclose the possibility of linking Spanish history to that of the rest of Western Europe. But even more revealing is the fact that Castro regarded the racial uniqueness of Spain as a fact that was invisible to the Spaniards who were living it. If there is any hint in Castro's work that the social structure of caste secreted an ideology, it is because the reality of caste was both ever-present and repressed: "What we forget is that the Spaniards were—and are—Islamic-Hebraic-Asiatic as much as they were—and are—Christian-European. This is a reality, however much Spaniards would prefer to be unaware of it. It is a reality that I have found both agreeable and truth-revealing, but that others have found repellant" (*Idea* 112).

Critics of Castro opposed his work on many grounds, but Castro's most significant adversaries may not in the end have been those who explicitly resisted his interpretation of the role of the Jews and Jewish *conversos* in Spanish history (e.g., Claudio Sánchez-Albornoz, author of the avowedly anti-Castro book *España, un enigma histórico,* 1956), but social historians of a younger generation like José Antonio Maravall, whose work stands much closer to the perspectives of Weberian sociology and the history of *mentalités*. Maravall is only a literary critic in a very limited fashion, but with the publication of *La cul-*

tura del barroco in 1975 (English translation, 1986) and the appearance of *La literatura picaresca desde la historia social* in 1986, Maravall's work became of increasing importance for North American Hispanists interested in understanding the dynamics of literary history in relation to social structures, particularly in his work on the baroque, Maravall attempted to view culture as a whole without privileging the aesthetic field, in this case by relating considerations about baroque art and literature, the strategies of war, urban society, and mass culture, to a vision of state power centered on the role of Spanish Absolutism.

One of the significant advantages of this approach was that it removed literature and the arts from the isolation in which textualist scholarship had kept them. In most of Maravall's work, the boundaries between literature and the non-literary domains of culture are treated as flexible and fluid. He thus provided the opportunity for subsequent critics to investigate some of the links between the formation of a national identity and the development of an autonomous literary sphere within that social whole.[4] But one striking limitation of this work was that aesthetic designations (e.g., "baroque") served mainly as umbrella terms for historical phenomena that could not easily be imagined as associated on other grounds. Maravall revived the notion of historical periods and did so in a way that placed literature among the many different discourses of a given cultural epoch.[5] And yet Maravall remained relatively unable to explain the structuring elements that shaped or limited a particular cultural period, such as the baroque. For example, he proposed that

> it's not that baroque painting, the baroque economy, the baroque art of war, [and so on] don't resemble one another . . . but rather, given the fact that they develop in the same circumstances, under the same conditions, answering the same vital needs, responding to the modifying influence of all the other factors, each one of them finds itself thus transformed, and comes to depend on the epoch as a whole. . . . These are the terms in which one can ascribe the definitive character of a period—in this case its character as baroque—to theology, painting, the art of war, physics, to an economy in crisis, monetary upheaval, the uncertainty of credit, and economic wars, along with which came the growing control of agricultural property by the nobility and an increase in poverty among the masses; these factors created a feeling of uncertainty and instability in personal and social life, which was dominated by repressive forces that in turn shaped baroque man and that allow us to call him by this name. (28–29, my translation)

Maravall's invocation of the category of "baroque man" resonates all too deeply with notions of transcendental subjectivity. It is bound to seem vapid unless one supplants it with an account of the ways in which institutions, discourses, and practices enable concrete subjects to exist. Louis Althusser's argument about the role of interpellation and of "Ideological State Apparatuses" in the process of subject-formation is very much to the point in this regard, and yet Althusser's work has rarely been incorporated into peninsular Spanish studies.[6] One of the key questions that Althusser posed bears directly on Maravall's description of the "culture of the baroque": how can so many different social "institutions" of society be knitted together? What enables religious institutions, the family, literature and the arts, and the political system (all of which Althusser calls "Ideological State Apparatuses") to function in a unified fashion? And how do these in turn enable the formation of concrete subjects? (110–111).

I will comment on how answering Althusser's questions can contribute to Hispanism, and also on how Spanish Golden Age and Colonial studies might help nuance Althusser's views. But first I will point out that despite its limitations, Maravall's work was important for Hispanists interested in thinking about the embeddedness of literature in social and historical circumstances in part because it did not hinge upon the kind of personalized interpretations of racial and religious categories that pervaded Castro's work. If some of Maravall's writings, such as his *magnum opus* on the picaresque, seem to invest too heavily in a kind of social analysis that takes literature into account primarily for its documentary value (Maravall calls it "testimonio"), his views on historical change, on the political context of much of the literature of Spain's "hegemonic" period, and on the culture of Spanish Absolutism, all left an important mark on a branch of literary studies that was just beginning to think about its place among the debates about literary subjectivity and social/historical structures.[7] Indeed, Maravall's perspectives helped some American Hispanists gain access to issues about the ways in which historical and political structures condition literary production—issues concerning state power, ideology, the institutional mechanisms of social control, and the circulation of social power.[8]

In spite of the fact that Maravall's work helped create these openings, it suffered from a number of drawbacks. If Castro tended to predicate subjectivity of the structures of history, Maravall's focus on institutions and ideas tended to efface subjectivity at the concrete level. Maravall makes it difficult to see how the manner in which individual subjects inhabit social or political structures might in fact alter the constitution of those same structures. The link between individual subjects and the collective subject of Spain (the historical "we") remained somewhat obscure in Maravall's work, in part because the social whole, of which literature is a part, is so comprehensively defined; concrete subjects seem, as a result, transformed into types. Literature, for its part, "no es retrato, más sí testimonio en el que se refleja una imagen mental de la sociedad. . . . Nos traslada el conjunto de creencias, de valoraciones, de aspiraciones, de pretensiones que se reconocían en el mundo social y aquellas atrevidas negaciones de las mismas en las que se estimaba desmoronarse gravemente el sistema establecido" (is not a portrait but rather a testimonial in which a mental image of a society is reflected. . . . It brings us the conjuncture of beliefs, values, aspirations, and of pretensions which were recognized in the social world as well as the daring negations of those same things, in which the established order was deemed to be crumbling) (*Literatura* 13). To be sure, Maravall's longstanding interest in Spanish Absolutism—which dates back to his 1944 work on the political thought of the seveteenth century—opened the door for a consideration of the repressive nature of culture in the Golden Age and of the instabilities within that same culture. This is equally so of his work on the picaresque, on Golden Age theater, and on the culture of the baroque. The baroque, for instance, is not just a cultural phenomenon of the masses but of a controlled society ("una sociedad dirigida"). Perhaps more importantly, the picaresque registered tensions among social groups within the social whole. *La literatura picaresca desde la historia social* provides an unusually detailed map of these currents and counter-currents, but the theoretical salience of the work can be epitomized in a phrase: "Las versiones de la literatura venían a definir y a dar expresión a los temores que, según la estimación de los conformistas, se provocaban en la esfera de relaciones entre individuos de estratos diferentes; por tanto, en alguna medida, lo que aquellos estaban significando en la vida cotidiana" (Literary versions came to define and to give expresion to fears that, according to the opinion of conformists, were provoked in the sphere of relations among individuals of different social strata; and therefore, to some degree, what they were meaning in their daily life) (13).

How, then, does Maravall read the "individualism" of the *pícaro?* His answer is given in no uncertain terms:

Se me ha preguntado alguna vez cómo se puede afirmar una vinculación tan decisiva al estado de una sociedad por parte de un género narrativo basado en una forma de redacción autobiográfica que resulta tan significativa de aquél, ya que en una autobiografía la originalidad del yo individual asume todo protagonismo. Siempre, sin embargo, es un ente social el yo y ese 'ego' picaresco lo es superlativamente y esto se potencia si pensamos que, a diferencia de los protagonistas anteriores, el pícaro posee personalidad, aunque sin embargo, carezca todavía de propia intimidad. El pícaro es, fundamentalmente, una respuesta a la sociedad de la que surge y a la que se enfrenta, condicionada, mejor dicho, contorsionada en su caso, por la presión asfixiante del entorno colectivo y de los instrumentos de poder que operan en éste. (772)

(I have sometimes been asked how such a decisive link to the state of a society can be affirmed on the part of a narrative genre based on an autobiographical form of writing that turns out to be so laden with meaning about it, since in an autobiography the orginality of the individual "I" takes on the complete protagonist role. The "I" is nonetheless always a social entity and that picaresque "ego" is such par excellence; this empowers it if we believe that, unlike previous protagonists, the picaro has a personality, although he may nonetheless lack any interiority of its own. The picaro is, fundamentally, an answer to the society from which it emerges and which it confronts—conditioned, better said in this case, distorted, by the soffocating pressure of its collective surroundings and by the instruments of power operating there)

Whatever the picaresque novel may do to oppose the hegemonic culture surrounding it does not diminish the fact that Maravall regards it as rooted in the desire to give expression to the newly revealed category of "individuality": "La autobiografía no es un documento 'íntimo' de confesiones, que nos permita conocer la evolución de un pecador hacia su irremediable pérdida; sí es un claro testimonio de interés hacia una individualidad, lo que siempre supone ponerla de relieve, destacarla" (Autobiography is not an 'intimate' confessional document which allows us to know the evolution of a sinner toward his irredeemable perdition; it is indeed a clear statement of interest in individuality, which of course presupposes bringing it into relief, making it stand out) (298). It has sometimes been thought that one of the tasks facing Hispanism is to allow the historical expressivism of Castro and the socio-economic analyses of Maravall to engage one another more fully than they have done so far. But examples such as this suggest that the distance between the two perspectives may not be as great as was sometimes supposed. Indeed, Maravall operates within the framework of a historical expressivism, sometimes linked to the history of "mentalities," that can be just as powerful as Castro's, and equally attached to the pre-eminence of the subject as a center of value and experience: "Cualquiera que sea su valor moral tradicional, tiene el valor irrepetible y en ciertos aspectos supremo de ser un individuo centro de experiencias. Por ello es, si se quiere, una visión antropológica que deriva de la moral del egocéntrico, de la preeminencia, a todos los respectos, del yo" (Whatever its traditional moral value might be, it has the unique and in some ways supreme value of being an individual center of experiences. Therefore it is, if you will, an anthropological vision that derives from a moral egocentrism, that of the preeminence, at all costs, of the 'I') (298).

Given the fact that both Castro and Maravall leave the question of subject-formation unaddressed, a step beyond their work would require a renewed engagement with the contemporary debates over subjects and structures. One goal of such an effort would be to discover the points of articulation between collective entities of an ideal sort—the national/historical "we"—and the individuals who support or oppose them. How is a collective identity or national image-ideal inscribed in the individual, and how is the individual in turn capable of challenging that process of inscription? Louis Althusser's notion of interpellation can help explain some of these things; nevertheless it is up to Hispanists to explore the possibility that Althusser's notions should be revised in light of the circumstances of Imperial Spain. The Althusserian notions of ideology and interpellation may help explain how subjects—Imperial/Peninsular and Colonial alike—were fashioned through their interaction with various cultural institutions and "Ideological State Apparatuses." However, facts such as the existence of a colonial culture that mirrored and distorted its Peninsular counterpart also direct our attention back to those moments in Golden Age culture where the unifying force of ideology was far less seamless than the Althusserian notion of interpellation might allow. Indeed, the culture that emerged under Spanish Absolutism on the Iberian peninsula itself turns out to be less the perfect mirror of state ideologies than is sometimes supposed. One suggestion open for Hispanists to pursue as they work beyond the perspectives of Castro and Maravall is this: subject-formation in Imperial Spain occurred as part of a fractured mimesis, which is to say that the mirror-like mold of social production was broken or otherwise transformed in the course of its re-production.

The concept of mirroring in relation to subject-formation can hardly dispense with Lacan's discussion of the "mirror stage" in the process of development. In relation to social production, however, the mirror paradigm was most famously invoked by Jean Baudrillard in 1973. However, his well-known work entitled *Le Miroir de la production* was meant to break the spell of the Marxist notion of production rather than to replace it by the paradigm of mirroring.[9] When, in a very different context, and at a much more recent moment, Carlos Fuentes invoked the mirroring relationship between Spain and the New World, it was with reference to the ways in which mirrors can reflect existing images and generate different ones (11). The preponderance of Fuentes' examples are indigenous and register the role of mirrors in the culture and cosmology of the Aztecs. Yet the indigenous fascination with mirrors remains in an inescapable dialogue with its peninsular counterpart. Fuentes notes the mirrors of polished black slate found buried at El Tajín as well as others in the circular temple of the Toltec pyramid at Teotihuacán, but mirrors are virtually unavoidable in some of the central examples of the peninsular baroque—in Velásquez' "Las Meninas," in Cervantes (the "Knight of the Mirrors") and in Saavedra Fajardo's *Emblemas morales,* to mention but a few. Indeed, Hispanists have yet to take full stock of the ways in which peninsular modes of subject-formation were themselves rooted in a process of cultural (re)production that involved the fracturing of mirrored images.

Some examples may help support the rationale for working past the perspectives of Castro and Maravall, through Althusser, toward a model of fractured mimesis in Imperial Spain. The first is drawn from the well-known beginning of the *Lazarillo de Tormes,* in which Lazarillo presents himself as a subject who has been created through what can indeed be recognized as the process of interpellation. Lazarillo is "hailed" as a subject in advance of fully becoming one, and the process of this "hailing" is also what defines him as a concrete individual; it makes that concrete existence possible. As Althusser remarks in explaining interpellation,

> we all have friends who, when they knock on our door and we ask, through the door, the question "Who's there?," answer (since it's obvious) "It's me." And we recognize that "it is him," or "her." We open the door, and it's true, it really was she who was there. . . . In this preliminary remark and these concrete illustrations, I wish only to point out that you and I are *always-already* subjects, and as such constantly practise the rituals of ideological recognition, which guarantee for us that we are indeed concrete, individual, distinguishable and (naturally) irreplaceable subjects. . . . *All ideology hails or interpellates concrete individuals as concrete subjects,* by the functioning of the category of the subject. (130–31)

At the beginning of the text, Lazarillo speaks in a manner that suggests how the rhetoric of self-assertion can provide a very effective cover for the ideological work of interpellation. On one hand, there is the bold public address made by a figure who is in other respects quite abject: (3). "Yo por bien tengo que cosas tan señaladas, y por ventura nunca oídas ni vistas, vengan a noticia de muchos, y no se entierren en la sepultura del olvido; pues podría ser que alguno que las lea halle algo que le agrade y, a los que no ahondaren tanto, los deleite" (I think it's right that such important events, which may perhaps never have been seen or heard, should come to the attention of many and not be buried in the grave of oblivion; since it might appear that someone who might read them might find pleasure and that those who don't delve too deeply into them might find delight) (3). Indeed, it has sometimes been claimed that the protagonist of this picaresque novel transforms the act of addressing a guardian of the "ideological" structures of society into a declaration of his autonomy from those very same structures. Maravall's views of the "individualism" of the picaresque suggest this much, as does Castro's argument that all the characters in the book *except* Lazarillo are types—"*a* blind man, *a* squire, *a* friar, etc., all of them externally known and deprived of an inner life."[10] But rather than credit Lázaro with the achievement of autonomous subjectivity, it would be more accurate to say that this picaresque subject is produced by the process of interpellation. Indeed, the opening of the *Lazarillo* lays bare the mechanisms that make interpellation possible in its most classic form. Lazarillo does not say "Me llamo Lazarillo de Tormes . . ." but rather "A mí llaman Lazarillo de Tormes . . ." Furthermore, the condition of his existence is constituted by what "Vuestra Merced" calls for from him, i.e., an account of the "caso."

To be sure, interpellation works. There is no creation of the individual (Lazarillo) without the pre-existence of the master-signifier (V. M.), the figure who holds the ideological framework in place. For Althusser, this figure is typically a member of the "ruling class," and considering him as such certainly adds depth to Maravall's sociological reading of the picaresque. It allows us to shift from the more literal ways in which social differences are portrayed, to the ways in which social power takes root in the relational "space" between one subject-position and another, and on terms that neither may be able to control independently. This may, in turn, provide the ideological support for the apparent "sympathy" that Lazarillo expresses for the impoverished squire, who sacrifices his private "self" in order to maintain his "public" image before the abject pícaro. Says Lazarillo, "tanta lástima haya Dios de mí como yo había dél, porque sentí lo que sentía" (37). While Althusser would lead us to believe that power typically rests with those who are empowered to speak, the *Lazarillo* suggests something more complex: that power shows up principally by means of its effects, and in this case it is refracted through a mirror that also distorts it. Moreover, the tale of the *caso* turns out to sting the one who requested that it be told. This is the reason Lázaro decides to tell in its complete form—not just amply, as V.M. requests, but from the very beginning (*ab ovo*), indeed, from a moment that seems to pre-date the "beginning":[11]

> Suplico a vuestra merced reciba el pobre servicio de mano de quien lo hiciera más rico, si su poder y deseo conformaran. Y pues vuestra merced escribe se le escriba y relate el caso muy por extenso, parecióme no tomarle por el medio, sino del principio, porque se tenga entera noticia de mi persona, y también porque consideren los que heredaron nobles estados cuán poco se les debe, pues fortuna fue con ellos parcial, y cuánto más hicieron los que, siéndoles contraria, con fuerza y maña remando, salieron a buen puerto. (4)

> (I beg Your Grace to receive this little gift from the hand of one who would have made it richer if his desire and his abilities had coincided. Since Your Grace writes that I should write and tell him about the matter extensively, it seemed to be best not to begin in the middle but rather from the beginning, so that he might have full

knowledge of who I am; and also so that people of highborn status may consider how little of that is owing to them, since fortune was favorable to them, and how much more worthy are those who have come to land in a happy port by dint of hard work and wits, in spite of ill fortune.)

The possibility of a distortion in the mirroring process of cultural reproduction exists only because cultural production takes place on the symbolic
plane. The subject's "ascent" into culture (which in the *Lazarillo* is figured as a
death-like "descent") occurs as the world of material needs is transformed into
the domain of symbolic desires. To be sure, Lazarillo confronts the problem of
physical survival, and at one level the *Lazarillo* appears to be "all about" the
need to meet the body's basic requirements of food, shelter, etc. Moreover, as
the episode with the squire so clearly suggests, the point at stake in this book
is hardly survival in the "natural" world. What Lazarillo learns is how to survive as a subject, how to continue his existence in the symbolic domain. (His
question is roughly the same as Hamlet's: to be or not to be, though not as a
"natural" being, but as a subject). Culture is not produced "naturally," but occurs only through a symbolic process that permits the fracturing of the mold
through which its reproduction takes place. Althusser writes that there is no
prospect for transforming culture other than by the efforts of those few teachers
who might choose to resist it, but the learning process visible in the *Lazarillo*
suggests a different possibility: the "learning" that reproduces society's means
for reproducing itself involves a process in which the subject reflects critically
upon the mirror of its production. This, I would argue, is the source of the biting
irony that is mixed into the prideful tone of Lázaro's letter to V.M. It signals the
moment at which the reflection of a hegemonic discourse becomes something
counter-hegemonic.

For Américo Castro, however, the mixture of bitter irony and pride—located in the exaggerated humility with which Lázaro describes his text ("el
pobre servicio")—is a symptom of conflictive national emotions and a sign of
the "problem of Spain." It takes root in what he describes as "a feeling consubstantial with the very existence of the Spanish people, especially since the
fifteenth century: they were what they were, and, at the same time, many were
not pleased with their way of existing. This feeling should be called anguish—
'tragic sense of life,' as Unamuno says." It is no coincidence that the *Lazarillo*
concludes with the evocation of a proud moment in national/imperial history,
that is, of the time when "our victorious Emperor entered this great city of
Toledo and held the Cortes here, and there was much rejoicing." As clearly as
anything in the text, this reference aligns the author's ironic double vision of

Spanish culture with a critical reflection on Spain as an imperial power. Even though Castro's existentializing may be dubious, he was far from wrong to have reminded us that "that day was long past in 1554, when, as a writer as excellent as he was daring, exposed to the public view a false and illusory picture of Spanish life, on which a fading but still respectable *hidalguía* cast a melancholy light. Positive artistic values emerged, as in other outstanding Spanish creations, from anguish and uncertainty" ("Introduction" xii).

The second example is drawn from the figure who is both the most "canonical" of all Spanish authors and the best-known among non-Hispanists: Cervantes. Indeed, among Golden Age figures only Velásquez has a comparable stature. Both Velásquez and Cervantes are often cited for the way in which their work epitomizes the greatness of Spanish culture while also quintessentializing the fleetingness, the evanescence, of Spain's time of cultural glory. In them, there seems to be both limitless pride in Spain's cultural prowess and an awareness of Spain's debility. Both Castro and Maravall have ways of dealing with this ambivalence in the case of Cervantes, Castro by linking the historic-existential conditions surrounding Cervantes as a writer to the projection of a problematic selfhood in the *Quixote,* and Maravall by refracting the issues through Cervantes' critical response to the utopian visions that were associated with the romances of chivalry, the pastoral novel, and works of non-fiction such as Antonio de Guevara's *Menosprecio de corte y alabanza de aldea.*[12] Althusser's notion of interpellation might well be of assistance in determining how concrete subjects were formed in relation to such utopian visions, but something else is needed in order to grasp the contradictory nature of the subjectivity that was so formed, i.e., the way in which images of greatness or prestige, or the nostalgia for a more perfect age, created a consciousness that was divided both with and against the hegemonic culture surrounding it.

Consider what seems to be the blank slate that Cervantes seems to give his self-fashioned character, Don Quixote. Out of the vagueness of historical records emerges the profile of a character who seems to have the power to name the essential things of the world around him. Interpellation, the naming that forms subjects in advance, seems to be blocked or undone. And yet the reader remains well aware of the Althusserian truth that "authentic" self-creation of the naming subject occurs only in relation to models that pre-exist him. They set the condition of possibility for his existence, call him into being. Moreover, it would seem that there is no bridge between heroic self-assertion that is capable of bearing the standard of national pride and the dull reality of imitation in which the mirror of praise reflects the image of a fading past. Consider as well Cervantes' mix of unbridled praise for the Spanish imperial mission—and his own participation in it—with a wry sense of the slipperiness of the historical self-assertion that the task of empire required. The boasts about his own role in the battle of Lepanto in the Prologue to the *Novelas ejemplares* are unmistakably encomiastic, perhaps excessively so. Indeed, this rhetoric of inflated praise is reflected back in a mirror that seems to deform the hegemonic force of the imperial power it appears to support. Cervantes adheres to a relatively conventional linguistic form of address in describing himself ("Llámase comúnmente Miguel de Cervantes Saavedra"), but this self-description is passed through a filter that magnifies it to the point of hyperbole:

> Fue soldado muchos años, y cinco y medio cautivo. . . . Perdió en la batalla naval de Lepanto la mano izquierda de un arcabuzazo, herida que, aunque parece fea, él la tiene por hermosa, por haberla cobrado en la más memorable y alta occasión que vieron los pasados siglos, ni esperan ver los venideros, militando debajo de las vencedoras banderas del hijo del rayo de la guerra, Carlo Quinto, de felice memoria. (63)

> (He was a soldier for many years, and for five and a half a captive. . . . In the naval battle of Lepanto he lost his left hand from a gunshot, a wound that, although it may seem ugly, he holds to be beautiful for having earned it on the highest and most memorable occasion that has been seen by past centuries or that future ages might hope to see, fighting under the victorious flags of the son of the lightning bolt of war, Charles V, of happy memory.)

In passages such as this, Cervantes makes it clear that the mechanisms by which culture is (re)produced are discursive just as they are institutional. Indeed, Cervantes helps us see that virtually all of what Althusser describes as "Ideological State Apparatuses" function discursively. Furthermore, going beyond Althusser, he also demonstrates that those same discourses may undermine or reverse themselves in the process of shaping the subjects who "must" conform to them. Discourse does not just "hail" subjects, but, as in the case of this encomiastic rhetoric, it weakens the reigning ideology by forming aggrandized images. Reading Cervantes' hyperbolic praise of imperial deeds in the light of *Don Quixote*—the first Part of which had been published some eight years before the preface to the *Novelas ejemplares*—it seems that the very same language that reinforces the cultural hegemony of Spain's imperial power ends up undermining its intended effects. This is especially clear as one tracks the reflection of the "glories" of the historical battle of Lepanto through the Captive's story in *Don Quijote,* Part I. Set aside, for the moment, the fact that Cervantes never devoted any major narrative work to an account of the battle he claims was the most glorious military moment of all time, the famous battle passes swiftly by in the episode of the Captive.[13] Indeed, one of the most noteworthy traits of the account of Lepanto as it appears in *Don Quijote* I, 39, is that it is riddled with clichés. The presentation of this supreme moment of national pride is not only concise but also reductive and formulaic: "*aquel día,* que fue para la cristiandad tan dichoso, porque en él se desengañó el mundo y todas las naciones del error en que estaban, creyendo que los turcos eran invencibles por la mar, en *aquel día,* digo" (*that day,* which was so fortunate for Christianity because on it the world and all its nations were disabused of the error in which they stood in believing that the Turks were invincible by sea, on *that day,* I say) (477). Mary Gaylord writes of

> la cualidad formuláica, de frase hecha, que ostenta el homenaje en miniatura que Cervantes dedica al magno encuentro. Podríamos preguntarnos por qué no se esforzara el 'raro inventor' a fin de representar de una manera más original aquel día de días. No es ésta, sin embargo, la única marca de reductividad que lleva este segmento del relato. Para evocar una batalla inmensa en la que perecieron muchos miles de hombres, el personaje narrador señala una sola acción, su propio salto atrevido; y saca de su propio destino oximorónico, el *cautiverio en la victoria,* la figura emblemática que estructura el resto de su historia. (27–28)

> (the formulaic quality, the cliché nature, which displays in miniature the homage that Cervantes accords the great encounter. We might wonder why the 'rare inventor' does not make an effort to represent this day of days in a more original way. But this is not, nonetheless, the only mark of reductivism that this segment of the story carries. To evoke an immense battle in which many thousands of men perished, the narrator points out a single action, his own brave leap, and from his own oxymoronic fate, that of captivity in victory, he makes the emblematic figure that structures the rest of the story.)

The internal rifts that Castro reads as existentialized reflections of historical anxiety in Cervantes' prose are thus better seen as signs of a split subject: one who is divided *for and against* empire, *for and against* the Spanish past, *for and against* heroic self-assertion, *for and against* the national-cultural project. Moreover, this splitting in turn registers something that Althusser failed to theorize about the process of subject formation, i.e., the fracturing of hegemonic demands that occurs as the subject responds to them.

The notion that the Spanish Golden Age subject may have been divided in contradictory ways has been countenanced by only a relatively few Hispanists, George Mariscal and Malcolm Read among them.[14] Few have transferred this model of contradictory subjectivity from the peninsular field to the colonial context or have considered the way in which colonial discourses were shaped by fractures and splits already existing within the "hegemonic" culture of Imperial Spain. It is of course well known that colonial authors often re-made many of the European cultural models and materials given to them, in the way, for instance, that Sor Juana Inés de la Cruz re-fashioned Góngora's sonnet on the evanescence of beauty in her sonnet "Este que ves, engaño colorido." But the formation of a colonial subject that evolves, in its height, as "baroque," depends upon something that more closely resembles the mechanisms of fractured mimesis just described.

Consider in this light a final example from the colonial context in which the question of "mirroring" in relation to the hegemonic culture of the Spanish peninsula comes into the foreground: the triumphal arches erected to honor the arrival of the recently appointed Viceroy to New Spain, the Marqués de la Laguna. Both Sor Juana Inés de la Cruz and Carlos Sigüenza y Góngora wrote texts for the occasion, each describing not only the arch they had designed but each also in honor of the Viceroy. Sor Juana's text is allegorical (the "Neptuno alegórico") while Sigüenza's (the "Theatro de virtudes políticas") is dominated by an unusual syncretism. In it, Sigüenza illustrates the Christian virtues and celebrates the Viceroy in a most incongruous way—by referring to the twelve Aztec rulers. The text of the "Theatro" is largely taken up with attempts to explain the connections between these rulers and New Spain. For this reason, the "Theatro de virtudes" has been seen as part of Sigüenza's attempt to establish an identity for the *criollo* inhabitants of New Spain by locating their origins in an ancient Mexican "empire." This is certainly true. However, Sigüenza attempted to link the Indians with the ancient civilizations of the Hebrews and the Romans through a series of tropes that stretch the basis of historical plausibility beyond the limits of belief (one recalls Quevedo's claim that the linguistic roots of Spanish reaching back to Hebrew). Anthony Pagden interprets Sigüenza's text as follows:

> This elaborate, at times highly unstable, edifice of synecdoche, analogy, and allusion linked the Indians with the Old World of the Hebrews and the Romans (and even at a later point with the ancient Egyptians). By so doing, it offered the *criollo* an association with an indigenous classical antiquity, a continuity between their present and the Indian past which . . . bypassed the Indian present; and it reinforced the idea that Cortés himself had tried to establish: that the Spanish conquerors were the Indians' legitimate and natural rulers. (96)

Two points need to be added to this account. The first is that there is a glaring mis-alignment in the "Theatro de virtudes" between the manifest purpose of the triumphal arch (to honor the King's "double," the Viceroy) and Sigüenza's effort to construct a legitimizing vision of *criollo* identity. The second is that in writing a text about this arch, Sigüenza was taking up a familiar continental tradition of designing and/or describing ceremonial arches and other similar monuments. Sigüenza notes that, by his day, the tradition of building triumphal arches in the New World was already well established. In the "Theatro," he says that Mexico City, "with inexpressible magnificence, has erected such triumphal arches or facades since December 22, 1528—the day the first Audiencia that came to govern the lands was welcomed—until the present time" (13). Cervantes himself made a noteworthy contribution to this tradition in his burlesque sonnet on the catafalque of Philip II ("Voto a Dios"). What Cervantes and Sigüenza share, beyond their common inheritance of a celebratory and encomiastic tradition rooted in the circumstances of empire, is a sensibility for the ways in which that tradition could undermine itself, generate its apparent opposite, or topple from its own weight, even as it appeared to offer "mirrors" designed to reflect and magnify the character-qualities of imperial heads of state. And yet Sigüenza's promise to sing the praises of the Viceroy ushers in a project to legitimize *criollo* identity. How much would this swerve have been apparent to the Viceroy or his delegates? To what degree would the fact that Sigüenza's encomium undermines itself have been visible to the addressee of the arch and its descriptive text?

This is not the place to embark on an exegesis of Sigüenza's "Theatro." Suffice it to say that behind the exorbitant syncretism that characterizes Sigüenza's work, there also lies the European tradition of offering written "mirrors" for princes and magistrates, a tradition in which mirrors were thought as presenting the *ideal* image of the figure reproduced in it. Indeed, the word *espejo* carried the sense of "example, exemplar" as well as "mirror" (Cervantes, in "El celoso Extremeño," describes his story as an "*ejemplo y espejo* de lo poco que hay que fiar de llaves, tornos y paredes cuando queda la voluntad libre").[15] In the tradition informing Sigüenza's effort, there are also examples in which the mirror reflecting the King was presented as fractured. A case in point is of Saavedra Fajardo's "emblems" in the *Emblemas morales* showing the image of a lion reflected in a broken mirror. The text of the emblem reads "siempre el mismo," thus re-constructing an idealized image of unity above and beyond the splitting of the subject.[16] The production of this unity is a "distortion" (and also, inevitably, an ideological one) as great as any other. But it serves a purpose. It allows the subject to preserve an integrated image of itself in the most fragmented of circumstances, even if only in order to enable articulation to take place. Although it occurs on a very different social plane, this is what allows

Lázaro to articulate his life as a whole and present it to V.M. Likewise, it may be what has allowed critics to feel justified in making ethical claims about Don Quixote's commitment to the ideals of virtue and justice, in spite of the unpredictable, quixotic nature to his actions. It is what permits the Viceroy to accept Sigüenza's legitimation of *criollo* identity as praise of himself, and it is likewise an element in the construction of "Spain" as an imaginary entity that remains intact in spite of the historical contradictions of which it is comprised.

To see such ideas and ideals of integrity emerge out of the fracturing that happens in the course of cultural (re)production returns us full circle to the question of Hispanism's relationship to the cultural materials with which it deals. The "problem of Spain" has long been associated with existential contradictions, with the failure of Spain to fit the models of bourgeois capitalism, or with Spain's reluctance to embrace modern science and the Enlightenment. National pride, the defense of cultural hegemony, and the encomiastic treatment of the deeds of empire all seem to cut two ways, and each serves as a reminder of the "decline of Spain" just as it offers testimony of Spain's glorious Golden Age. Critics have espoused both these views and have likewise attempted to construct narratives reconciling them. My suggestion here is that Hispanists might move beyond these efforts by taking the materials of Imperial and colonial Spanish culture as diagnostic resources for their own efforts to shape a unified image of Spanish culture. The existential historicism of Castro and the socio-economic analyses of Maravall can be supplemented by Althusserian models of subject-formation, and these in turn can benefit from an awareness of the process of fractured mimesis in the production and re-production of Spanish/colonial identities. However, the success of any such endeavor will require us to remain alert to the ways in which Spanish culture may run in advance of where Hispanism as a discipline has arrived, offering insights that have yet to be fully incorporated into Spanish cultural studies on a theoretical plane.

Notes

1. Fanon, *Black Skin, White Masks*. See especially pp. 115–16: "The Jew can be unknown in his Jewishness . . . He is a white man, and, apart from some rather debatable characteristics, he can sometimes go unnoticed . . . But in my case everything takes on a *new* guise. I am given no chance, I am overdetermined from without. I am the slave not of the 'idea' that others have of me but of my own appearance."
2. I believe that it would be better to say that this psychology registers two linked facts:

on the one hand, the force of the subject's attachment to the social system, and on the other, the way in which the social structure is inscribed in the subject.

3. Regarding the formation of a unitary collective subject, Castro writes: "La conquista de las tierras musulmanas fue para los futuros españoles empresa tan lenta y compleja como la forja de un 'nosotros,' de un nombre que auténticamente los incluyera en una unidad de conciencia colectiva" (270). "Los nombres de los 'nosotros' de dimensión historiable son aberturas hacia perspectivas problemáticas del vivir humano. Recordemos la situación de los catalanes, los vascos y los gallegos en España; la de los irlandeses, galeses y escoses en el Reino Unido; la de los bretones, alsacianos y catalanes en Francia" (The conquest of Muslim lands was for future Spaniards as slow and as complex a task as forging a 'we,' with a name that would authentically include them within a collective unity of conscience. The names of the 'we' that are of a historiable dimension are openings toward problematic perspectives on human life. Let's recall the situation of the Catalans, the Basques, and the Galicians in Spain; that of the Irish, the Welsh, and the Scots in the United Kingdom; that of the Bretons, the Alsatians, and the Catalans in France) (p. 272).

4. See, for example, Nicholas Spadaccini and Wlad Godzich, eds. *Literature Among Discourses.*

5. See also Maravall's essay "From the Renaissance to the Baroque: The Diphasic Schema of a Social Crisis," 3–40.

6. Among the few who have recognized his work are, Juan Carlos Rodríguez, professor of Spanish literature at the University of Granada, and Malcolm Read, at SUNY Stony Brook.

7. *La Literatura,* 13.

8. See Spadaccini and Godzich, *Literature Among Discourses* and the English language edition of *La cultura del barroco: The Culture of the Baroque.*

9. The phrase "mirror of production" belongs to Jean Baudrillard (*Le miroir de la production*). However, his book of that title concentrates on a critique of the Marxist paradigm of production rather than on the development of an alternative model based on mimesis.

10. See Castro, "Introduction" to the *Lazarillo* (ix).

11. As Francisco Rico very astutely pointed out, the opening of the book is written as if Lazarillo is already in full possession of the insights he gains only through the "experience" achieved at the culmination of the text. The growth-chart of the character is not one of linear progress from innocence to maturity, or from a naive moral optimism to a resolute cynicism, but rather a circle in which the very condition of moral optimism is overwritten by Lázaro's insights into the "illusions" of ideology. See *La novela picaresca y el punto de vista.*

12. See Maravall, *Utopía y contrautopía en el "Quijote."*

13. See Gaylord, "El Lepanto intercalado de *Don Quijote*," especially pages 27–28.

14. See Mariscal, *Contradictory Subjects* and Read, *Transitional Discourses.*

15. Cf. Cicero's notion, widespread among Golden Age authors, that comedy was a "mirror of human life."
16. My remarks on the relevance of the Saavedra Fajardo emblem to Sigüenza's text are directly indebted to the work in progress of Anna More, in a dissertation on Sigüenza and creole identity.

Works Cited

Althusser, Louis. "Ideology and Ideological State Apparatuses." In Salvoj Zizek, *Mapping Ideology*. London: Verso, 1994.

Baudrillard, Jean. *Le miroir de la production; ou, L'illusion critique du matérialsime historique*. Tournai: Casterman, 1973.

Castro, Américo. *The Spaniards*. Trans. Willard King and Selma Margaretten. Berkeley: University of California Press, 1971.

———. *An Idea of History: Selected Essays of Américo Castro*. Trans. and ed. Stephen Gilman and Edmund L. King. Columbus: Ohio State University Press, 1977.

———. "El 'nosotros' de las historias" *Revista de Occidente* 2nd Ser. 11, no. 15 June, 1964.

Cervantes Saavedra, Miguel de. *Novelas ejemplares*. Ed. Juan Batista Avalle-Arce. Madrid: Castalia, 1982.

———. *El ingenioso hidalgo Don Quijote de la Mancha* I. Ed. Luis Murillo. Madrid: Castalia, 1986.

Fanon, Franz. *Black Skin, White Mask,* trans. Charles Lam Markmann. New York: Grove Press, 1967.

Fuentes, Carlos. *The Buried Mirror: Reflections on Spain and the New World.* New York: Houghton Mifflin/Mariner Books, 1999.

Gaylord, Mary. "El lepanto intercalado de *Don Quijote*" in *Volver a Cervantes: Actas del IV Congreso Internacional de la Asociación de Hispanistas*. Palma: Universitat de les Illes Balears, 2001.

Lazarillo de Tormes [1948], Ed. Everett Hesse and Harry Williams. Madison: University Wisconsin Press, 1961.

Maravall, José Antonio. *La Cultura del barroco*. Barcelona: Editorial Ariel, 1998.

———. *La Literatura picaresca desde la historia social*. Madrid: Taurus, 1986.

———. "From Renaissance to the Baroque: The Diphasic Schema of a Social Crisis" in Spadaccini and Godzich. *Literature Among Discourses: The Spanish Golden Age*. Minneapolis: University of Minnesota Press, 1986.

———. *The Culture of the Baroque,* trans. Terry Cochran. Minneapolis: University of Minnesota Press, 1986.

———. *Utopia y contrautopía en el "Quijote."* Santiago de Compostela: Editorial Pico Sacro, 1976.

Mariscal, George. *Contradictory Subjects: Quevedo, Cervantes, and Seventeenth Century Spanish Culture.* Ithaca: Cornell University Press, 1991.

Pagden, Anthony. *Spanish Imperialism and the Political Imagination.* New Haven: Yale University Press, 1990.

Read, Marvin K. *Transitional Discourses: Culture and Society in Early Modern Spain.* Ottawa: Ottawa Hispanic Studies/Doveouse Editions, 1998.

Rico, Francisco. *La novela picaresca y el punto de vista.* Barcelona: Seix Barral, 1969.

Sigüenza y Góngora, Carlos de. *Theatro de virtudes políticas que constituyen a un príncipe, advertidas en los monarchos antiguos de México imperial* in *Obras con una biografía.* ed. Francisco Pérez Salazar. México: Sociedad de Bibliófilos Mexicanos, 1928.

Spadaccini, Nicholas and Wlad Godzich, eds. *Literature Among Discourses: The Spanish Golden Age.* Minneapolis: University of Minnesota Press, 1986.

Zizek, Slavoj. *Mapping Ideology.* London: Verso, 1994.

◆ **6**

Whose Hispanism?
Cultural Trauma, Disciplined Memory,
and Symbolic Dominance

Joan Ramon Resina

The Cant of Universality

A crucial function of the humanistic disciplines is to foster and preserve cultural memory. The memory thus preserved depends not only on each discipline's criteria of relevance but also on the force exerted by the discipline itself—through its investments, tradition, and incorporated assumptions—on the selected materials, that is, on its record. Before anything else, disciplines are competitive spaces for the definition of social memory: they decide what will be transmitted as legitimate knowledge, and in the process they determine the value of symbolic assets according to the position of the latter in the disciplinary field. That is why disciplines are also fields of struggle for their own definition. The more redundant the definition, the more easily it will be accepted, although that does not mean it will necessarily impose itself. Hispanism, for example, can be defined without much disagreement—although without great consequence—as the academic game that sets the rules and arbitrates the practices that endow with value the cultural memory of and about Hispania.[1] This definition, however, merely displaces the field of struggles to the scholastic entity Hispania, a fallacious universal which in turn begs definition. The abstraction and intellectualizing drift of the term removes it from the sphere of everyday forces and values, which alone endow with meaning the events that come to pass within an institutional field of knowledge. In practice, though, Hispanism operates as if "the Hispanic World" represented a somewhat variegated but strictly monolingual territory on the modern, i.e., institutionally relevant, cultural cartography. By adopting such a spurious universal—a practice that, with regard to the Anglo-American academy, George Mariscal has dated in the nineteen thirties (9)—the discipline contributed to naturalize a cultural monopoly. It appropriated the cultural law of a successful particularity, one that attained its hegemony through the negation (and, in some cases, the annihilation) of other cultural norms. Subalternity, although cast as part of the eternal order of things, was the flip side of the cultural law that Hispanism furthers.

Historically, Hispanism has been an expansive idea. There is reason to think that it exists solely for this idea. From Nebrija's understanding of language as an instrument of subjection, to Miguel de Unamuno's "evangelio hispánico" (Spanish gospel) (Castro 1948, 640), to contemporary state-funded efforts to add Brazil and the United States to the roster of Spanish-speaking countries, Hispanism has always conceived itself as a proselytizing enterprise. Swinging ambiguously, like Christianity, between a redemptive role as "el rumor de los desheredados" (the murmur of the disinherited ones) and a dogmatic civilizing project, it has never been free from ulterior motives. As a consequence, it has never been able to found an autonomous scholastic field. An emanation of empire, Hispanism is the earliest instance of a postcolonial ideology engaged in promoting hegemonic ambitions by cultural means. The paramount role assigned to the Spanish language in this ideology has turned the field into a prime site for symbolic struggles: struggles against neighboring fields for academic space,[2] internecine struggles that reproduce the conflicted yet complicit self-assertion of former metropolis and former colonies,[3] and the looming struggles between Hispanism as a whole and the suppressed multiculturalism represented by the other indigenous languages of Spain and Latin America.

It is convenient, at the outset, to dispel an ambiguity from which Hispanism still profits. I refer to the discipline's claim to an universal and, so to speak, utopian point of view, a claim it puts forth while repressing the memory of its origin. Hispanism operates as if it were the natural outcome of a civilization process coalescing around a language deemed superior to the ones it came into contact with and thus foreordained to replace them on its ascension to Peninsular, continental, and some day cosmic preeminence.[4] "Castilla," wrote the illustrious philologist and President of the Real Academia de la Lengua, Ramón Menéndez Pidal, in 1950, "muestra un gusto acústico más certero, escogiendo desde muy temprano,

y con más decidida iniciativa, las formas más eufónicas de estos sonidos vocáli-
cos" (Castile evinces a finer acoustic taste, choosing from early on and with a
clearer determination the most euphonic sounds for these vowels) (486).[5] By virtue of its phonetic appeal and other advantageous features, says Menéndez Pidal,
Castilian earned the privilege to be called Spanish and to guide the evolution of
the language in its global dissemination. Playing up the notion of this language's
inherent charm, the current director of the Cervantes Institute, Jon Juaristi, has
asserted that Spanish expanded not through imposition but through seduction.
Thus, the drive for global hegemony is naturalized through the alleged self-evidence of the acquired positions, while concealing the internal logic of the field.
The mystification is accomplished through the players' purported removal from
the historical field of action to a timeless universal sphere. Never mind that this
sphere comes into existence through the players' success in the contingent space
they claim to have left behind.[6]

Repression of the field's social history, in turn, discourages the explicit
articulation of the conditions of participation in the game. The illusion of objectivity, though, persists only as long as the players' unquestioning adherence to
the institutional rites. Sooner or later, it collides with the existence of competing
memories, the most damaging of which, for the scholar's aloofness from the
worldly implications of her work, is the memory of the field's historical origins. Tapping on this memory soon reveals the field's determinations, the dis-
cipline-specific constraints that circumscribe Hispanism as a social subspace,
while enabling it to endlessly reconstruct social space through its power of
representation.

The order of representation specific to Hispanism, and, above all, the re-
flexes that constitute the practical ideology of this field, are ultimately invested
and authorized by a historical violence that has been codified and transvaluated
into humanistic tokens of the tradition's superior worth. This permanent symbolic struggle is practically confirmed even by those participants who adopt
a critical standpoint, as the field's existence does not depend on the sign of
its internal self-evaluations but on the perpetuation of its discourses. In fact,
the more critical and sophisticated the discourses are, the better they validate
the field, for the latter accrues relevance not from the value of the judgement
but from its ratifying effect. Whatever its sign (critical or apologetic), criticism
confirms its object and sanctions the field, endorsing its exclusions. Ultimately
guaranteed by the violence that lies at the root of the social, the field's hierarchy
of values and their regulated play constantly reproduce the power relations on
which the Hispanistic mode of knowledge is predicated.

Symbolic dominance works best when it denies its connection to social violence. Cultural agents are, therefore, encouraged to repress not only the link between cultural universality and violence but even the historical traces of the latter. For the dominated and the excluded, the possibility of reclaiming a space of their own within the field of legitimate culture depends on their ability to roll back the forces that make them invisible or, when that is not possible, reduce them to a dispensable anecdote. Only if the excluded succeed in neutralizing the strategies of concealment, can they emerge from the margins and gain access to the universal spaces of representation. Access is never the reward for cooperating with the rules of the field, since the forces enshrined in the logic of scholastic procedures do their utmost to deflect the demands of the dominated to participate on the same footing. They do so by blocking the bids of marginal players and, given the opportunity, by expelling them from the game.

In the case of Hispanism, it would be a mistake to account for this disciplinary disposition by retaining the notion of a field warped by the particularism of the Francoist era—although the latter's contribution to the *doxa* of the *fait accompli* should not be underestimated. Hispanism rose in the nineteenth century, together with the national philologies, as a compensatory strategy to offset Spain's staggering territorial losses in America. As José del Valle and Luis Gabriel-Stheeman point out, conferences and symposia, as well as "transatlantic" publications like *La Revista Española de Ambos Mundos* and *La Ilustración Española y Americana* were examples of many efforts made to create a sense of a common Hispanic civilization anchored in Spain but extended over the former colonies (6). These linguists offer as a minimal definition of Hispanism its belief in: "The existence of a unique Spanish culture, lifestyle, characteristics, traditions and values, *all of them embodied in its language;* the idea that Spanish American culture is nothing but Spanish culture transplanted to the New World; and the notion that Hispanic culture has an internal hierarchy in which Spain occupies a hegemonic position" (Their emphasis, [6]). This definition should be modulated to conform with Hispanism's gradual accommodation to a more fluid arrangement that includes Latin American complicity with Hispanic universality.

A candid, if quaint, definition of Hispanidad was offered by Alfredo Sánchez Bella, first director of the Instituto de Cultura Hispánica, the Francoist forerunner of the current Instituto Cervantes. He described it as:

> la proyección de la síntesis española lograda dentro de la Patria por una milenaria tarea, lanzada con ímpetu sostenido desde hace cinco siglos sobre la redondez de la tierra, esta Hispanidad se multiplica en partes al producirse su dispersión geográfica. No dispersión babélica, sí evangélica, apostólica. (94)

(the projection of the Spanish synthesis accomplished inside the fatherland through the work of a millennium, broadcast with unflagging force over the entire globe during the last five centuries, this Hispanicity multiplies everywhere through its geographical dispersion. Not a Babel-like dispersion but an evangelical, apostolic dispersion.)

Notice the care with which the meaning of "dispersión" is confined to the Catholicity of the Hispanic mission; the care with which any confusion of tongues is conjured in advance. "Dispersión" here is an euphemism for the ideological radiation which, emanating from a "millenarian" center, reaches global proportions. Nothing is scattered; everything is collected under one dispensation. Within the Iberian Peninsula, Hispanic culture is the patriotic "synthesis" that supersedes the diverse historical cultures, while outside, it is a "sustained impetus" projected through conquest, empire, and cultural community towards a goal that is coterminous with the Earth's limits. Reference to an apostolic mission neatly condenses the religious sense intended by the founding of Spain's national holiday, the Día de la Raza, on the anniversary of the "Discovery" (Serrano 314). Notwithstanding the holiday's ethnic signification, soon after its promulgation on June 16, 1918, officialdom emphasized discovery and empire as historical assets justifying the pursuit of Spain's insatiable ambitions.[7] Thus, the cover of *Raza española,* a journal founded in 1919, displayed a caravel emblazoned with the date October 12, 1492 and sailing between Hercules's pillars, to which the legend PLUS ULTRA is attached.

Emblems associating mission and empire were honored by the American upper classes, doubtless because they provided legitimacy for their own hegemony over the indigenous populations. In a section entitled "Ecos de la Fiesta de la Raza," (Echoes from the Race Holiday) the journal reported the celebration of Spain's new national holiday in various American countries. A society of Bolivian students sent "un saludo reverente" (a reverential greeting) to Spanish youth, represented, they said, by the University of Salamanca, "fecundo y magno sol que nunca se pone" (great and fertile sun that never sets). Invoking next the geniuses of Columbus and Cervantes, and thus the confluence of language and empire, the association of Bolivian students "levanta a la Providencia fervientes votos por la fusión de los ideales de gloria de España y América" (elevates fervent vows to Providence for the fusion of the ideals of glory of Spain and America [116]).

The journal's editor took the opportunity to stress the empire's civilizing mission. At a time when the writers of the Generation of '98 were scouring the Castilian landscape for the soul of Spain, the journal traced this soul to the venerable university, presenting the colonial adventure as the natural issue of Castilian learning.

> Raza Española recoge con fervorosa gratitud el reverente saludo de la hidalga juventud de Bolivia a su hermana la juventud española, representada en la gloriosa *Alma Máter* salmantina, donde se formaron aquellos hombres *de tantas almas,* soldados, legistas, teólogos y misioneros que llevaron a América, con la eterna luz del Evangelio, la floración magnífica del Renacimiento español. (116)

> (Raza Española accepts with fervent gratitude the reverential greeting that Bolivia's noble youth sends to its sister, the Spanish youth, represented by Salamanca's glorious Alma Mater, which educated those men of so many souls, soldiers, lawyers, theologians, and missionaries, who conveyed to America the magnificent flowering of the Spanish Renaissance together with the Gospel's eternal light.)

Regardless of the fantasy of a colonial army provided with university degrees, the editor was right to emphasize the connection between knowledge and power, for the empire still underlay Spanish self-representations and ideals.

> España ha podido perder, por culpas propias y por injusticias ajenas, la posesión material de aquel Imperio colonial, el más grande que ha tenido pueblo alguno en la vida de la Humanidad; pero ni la misma fuerza material ha sido suficiente ni podía serlo, a arrebatarla la representación moral ante el Mundo de aquellos pueblos descubiertos por el genio español, conquistados por el heroísmo de sus hijos, y colonizados por la fe y por la cultura de nuestro espíritu. (Bécker 1919, 13)

> (Spain may have lost, through its own fault and foreign injustices, the material possession of its former colonial Empire, the greatest that any people has ever had in human history. But material force has not been able, nor could it ever be, to deprive Spain of the moral representation before the World of the peoples that the Spanish genius discovered, the heroism of its sons conquered, and the faith and culture of our spirit colonized.)

From the missionary zeal pervading Spain's imperial project, Hispanism acquired a religious pitch and a sacred language. From the beginning, the core of the nationalistic religion was the Spanish language. Although the Spanish Cortes settled for the name *Día de la Raza,* there were proposals to make it a holiday of the Spanish language and even to call it "fiesta del Idioma" (language holiday) (Serrano 321). And so, in July 1918, Unamuno's idea of a language-based "evangelio hispánico" received official sanction with the institution of the national holiday. The religious model for this linguistic celebration was never too far from the surface. As Carlos Serrano remarks, "Colón había tenido el buen gusto de tocar tierra en América en una fecha que coincidía con las fiestas del Pilar, de marcado signo nacionalista en toda la historia española de los siglos XIX y XX" (Columbus had the good taste of landing in America on a date that coincided with the holiday of [the Virgin of] el Pilar, a date with acute nationalist signification throughout nineteenth and twentieth century Spanish history) (322). Thus, when a Spanish priest, writing for a Buenos Aires weekly, proposed to rename the national holiday Día de la Hispanidad, Ramiro de Maeztu commented approvingly in the first issue of *Acción Española:*

> Si el concepto de Cristiandad comprende y a la vez caracteriza a todos los pueblos cristianos, ¿por qué no ha de acuñarse otra palabra, como ésta de Hispanidad que comprenda también y caracterice a la totalidad de los pueblos hispánicos? (8)

> (If the concept of Christianity includes and also characterizes all Christian peoples, why should we not coin a new word, such as "Hispanicity," to include and characterize all Hispanic peoples?)

Not surprisingly, the first question to which this proposal led Maeztu was that of inclusion and exclusion; that is, the question about the definition of the field. More important, though, was the question concerning its law. Hispanidad was a globalizing force, second only to Christianity, which, being embedded in it, endowed it with universality:

> Al descubrir las rutas marítimas de Oriente y Occidente hizo la unidad física del mundo; al hacer prevalecer en Trento el dogma que asegura a todos los hombres la posibilidad de salvación, y por tanto de progreso, constituyó la unidad de medida necesaria para que pueda hablarse con fundamento de la unidad moral del género humano. Por consiguiente, la Hispanidad creó la Historia Universal, y no hay obra en el mundo, fuera del Cristianismo, comparable a la suya. (15)

> (By discovering the ocean routes to the East and the West, ["Hispanicity"] physically unified the world. By imposing in Trent the dogma that guaranteed the possibility of salvation, and thus of progress, for all men, it constituted the necessary yardstick for any reasonable talk about the moral unity of humanity. Consequently, "Hispanity" created Universal History, and there is no achievement in the world, except for Christianity, that can compare to it.)

Hispanidad's universality, and therewith the much vaunted universality of its language, are rooted in this double claim of being both the creator-spirit of the world system and the only system that guarantees historical salvation. Again this is Unamuno's Hispanic gospel. From this religious point of view, there is no civilization, no culture, and no modernity outside its Church. "El camino hacia la libertad transita por la hispanización" (the road to freedom runs through Hispanicization) wrote Manuel Alvar, a member of the Real Academia Española, in reference to the indigenous peoples of America in 1991 (qtd. del Valle and Gabriel-Stheeman 208); Mario Vargas Llosa, a fellow *académico,* agrees. That is why, when the post-Franco constitutional regime confirmed the 12th of October as Spain's national holiday, it stressed that, besides the "Discovery," the nation celebrates "el origen de una tradición cultural común a los pueblos de habla hispánica" (the origin of a cultural tradition common to all the Spanish-speaking peoples) (Royal Decree of 27 November 1981, qtd. In Serrano 327). Hispanidad is, according to this definition, the lowest common denominator ascribed to the manifold, disparate, even incompatible cultures coexisting in the Darwinian space of posthistorical Hispanism.

This phantom imperialism overarches modern Spanish history from Restoration to Restoration. No matter how virtual it may appear at times, it is the firmest ideological ground for Spanish nationalism, as Ortega y Gasset's project for national salvation eloquently reveals. For it is surely revelatory that precisely the Spanish thinker who is often credited with the clearest vision of European integration would offer a Hispanic "Transatlanticism" as the single most important goal for Spain's "vertebration." Arguing in 1921 that a nation can only exist as long as it engages in great historical adventures, he claimed that the only possible future for Spain lay in "la unificación espiritual de los pueblos de habla española" (the spiritual unification of the Spanish-speaking peoples) (*España invertebrada* 75, n.). Either Spain strove for that "international destiny," or it would face its dissolution. In other words, Spain could remedy its alleged political breakdown only by pursuing a policy of "spiritual" centralization supported by its former colonies. The link between imperialism and aggressive nationalism, between the response to an internal crisis of the state and the unimaginative recourse to regressive solutions could hardly be more eloquent.

True, Spain found itself once more isolated through its neutrality in World War I, and sought a scope for its ambitions in pan-Hispanism. Moreover, it sought, as Ortega's book shows, a means to re-center the state in its decaying imperial center, and, thus, in the time-worn imperial idea. As we have seen, the Cortes's institution of the national holiday two years earlier had the same significance. Since the war, the state had been in crisis, and the prospect of a military coup loomed large. It would materialize in 1923. In that context, patriotic exaltation apropos the old imperial glories cleared the way for an authoritarian settlement of internal tensions dressed as the resumption of Spain's world-historical mission.

Similar conditions surrounded the inauguration of the Instituto de Cultura Hispánica during the Quincentennial of the birth of Queen Isabel I of Castile on October 12, 1951. Spain was re-emerging from its isolation since the decline of the Axis powers in 1942, and the Francoist regime, eroded by the disastrous economic conditions of the forties, was critically unstable. At that time, the Hispanic community was the only international platform on which Spain could hope to play an influential role. By commemorating Castilian Queen Isabel in the presence of the Latin American diplomatic corps on the *Día de la Raza,* the regime visualized the affiliation of the Latin American nations to a Hispanic community gathered, like Isabel's yoke and arrows, in its genealogical center. With Franco also in attendance, Spain's minister of foreign affairs, Alberto Martín Artajo, spelled out the purpose of Hispanidad:

> Su misión es un obrar común en la ancha órbita internacional en función con los restantes grupos regionales, una acción conjunta de todo lo hispánico en el campo de la gran política mundial y universalista, una actitud colectiva ante problemas de interés universal. Y sus nexos, toda una red o trama de ideas, de sentimientos, de modos de concebir la vida. (141)

> (Its mission is to act in common in the wide international sphere in conjunction with the other regional groups, [to undertake] a common action of all things Hispanic in the area of the great world and universal politics, [and to have] a collective attitude before the problems of universal interest. And its links [will be] an entire web or mesh of ideas, feelings, and worldviews.)

Martín Artajo did not reveal who would establish the guidelines for common action, nor how the divergent interests would be reconciled with the universal interest that appeared self-evident to him. Nevertheless, the material translation of the ideal links in the web of ideas, feelings and *Weltanschauungen* invoked, would eventually transpire in the preferential investment opportunities demanded by Spain in the name of its "especial" relationship to Latin America. The claim of a "special" relation of this sort must have appeared odd, not to say absurd, from the American perspective. In the wake of a conflictive history and of Spain's failure to supply usable societal models for the newly independent republics, that relation could consist of little more than a common language and, potentially, a shared linguistic ideology. The dearth of influential models explains the anxiety that the possibility of linguistic fragmentation evoked among Spanish intellectuals (del Valle 96–97) and the heavy-handed policies of support (often amounting to bribery) to Latin American intellectuals and collectives in solemnly staged and media-amplified performances of Spanish leadership. In 1991, the *Príncipe de Asturias* prize, an award nominally bestowed by the Heir to the Spanish crown, was granted to Puerto Rico after its Governor declared Spanish the island's only official language.[8] Spain, smarting from an antithetical move by the state of California in the mid-1980s, saw itself vindicated and forgot the criticism (including that of King Juan Carlos in an official visit to the Western state) that it had poured on California for passing monolingual legislation.

Notwithstanding the ideal webs of feelings and viewpoints invoked by Martín Artajo, his concept of Hispanism was uninhibitedly imperialistic. If in 1918 Hispanidad had awoken hopes of an international realignment, now it was conceived as an instrument for Spain's intervention in the block politics of the Cold War. The Franco regime looked forward to the day when a Hispanic block would challenge the superpowers: "pero esas naciones nuestras bien unidas forman un conjunto tan poderoso, en todos los órdenes, que nuestro Mundo Hispánico podrá, con verdad, llamarse la más grande entre las grandes potencias del mañana" (but our nations, provided they are united, will form such a powerful coalition in every domain, that our Hispanic World will truly be the greatest among the great powers of the future" (Martín Artajo 144).

From the perspective of Hispanism's political articulations, it is possible to perceive not only the stakes but also, and more importantly, the motives behind its maneuvers in the global arena. The discipline feels it must come to terms with global pressures which spell the obsolescence of the national philologies. However, this recognition need not pave the way for cut-throat Realpolitik in the present-day academic environment. Hispanism is a long-term project with a substantial trajectory behind it, and while its symbolic arrangements and practical commitments can be modified, they are nowhere near disappearing. Temporary influences and crises come and go without upsetting the field's structural dispositions. One of these dispositions, the linguistic monism, must be revised if the discipline is to be loosened from its foundational imperialism and steered towards a more complex and encompassing framework for concrete sites of knowledge, which need not be coterminous with state cultures.

The Epistemic Unfit

It is remarkable how, as soon as new circumstances challenge the field, epistemocentric aloofness gives way to practical reactions.[9] On such occasions, competition, not only in the field but also for its definition, emerges as one of Hispanism's durable dispositions. Such reactions to a broad challenge reveal the *a priori* stakes. The implicit consensus among the players surfaces very quickly when called upon to protect or expand the common turf. Furthermore, such consensus needs to be reasserted periodically in spontaneous expressions of adherence to the norm, or, what amounts to the same thing, in the ritual expression of belligerence against heretics or outside competitors. Although generally unspoken, the underlying consensus provides disciplinary conventions with the self-evidence of orthodoxy.

There is no need to posit a totalitarian intervention in the cultural sphere in order to identify the source of certain imperatives; the rapport between scholastic reason and the internal homeostasis of the state can be documented along the history of the discipline in almost genealogical fashion.[10] I have referred to the doctrine of Hispanidad as promoted by the anti-Republican right and, later, by the Franco regime. Yet, before the Civil War, Spanish intellectuals embodying different degrees of liberalism were in agreement about the state's priorities regarding a unified, post-imperial state. Barely three months had passed since the proclamation of the Second Republic, when Américo Castro warned the new government: "Lo más urgente, Cataluña. Aún más apremiante que las huelgas y el orden público" (The most urgent problem, Catalonia. Even more urgent than strikes and public order) (1990, 229). In 1932, Ortega vigorously combated the project of Catalonia's Statute of Autonomy in the Cortes, warning that the slightest implication of shared sovereignty would quickly lead to a national catastrophe (*Discursos* 239). Like Unamuno, Ortega opposed official status for the Catalan language, insisting on the preservation in Catalonia of a monolingual university system in Spanish despite, or rather because of the fact that, as he himself declared, the vast majority of students there were Catalan-speaking (*Discursos* 276).[11]

Why did these figures, often revered as Spain's finest intellectuals, align themselves instinctively with a reactionary post-imperial ideology? We must conclude that the foundational figures of contemporary Hispanism never reflected about the empirical constraints on their points of view. Apparently, they remained ignorant of the extent to which their scientific truths were beholden to a particular conception of the state. In part, this is understandable: no one can jump over his own shadow. More remarkable is that contemporary exegetes often fail to perceive their object's long shadow and rebuff those who do, dismissing their views as "ideological." Never mind that such systemic reactions naively invert the meaning of ideology. Ideology does not refer to *explicit* political interventions in the sphere of culture. On the contrary, as Marx and Engels defined the term in *The German Ideology,* ideology is the expression of dominant relations in the realm of ideas. Precisely what Hispanism is about.

It is true, as Bourdieu remarks, that "[n]o one can forge weapons to be used against his opponents without having those weapons immediately used against him by them or by others" (119). What is surprising in the reversal of a critique is not the reversal itself, but the reinforcement of the illusion of objectivity resulting from the scholar's alignment with the dominant view. Such scholars may simply call the disciplinary *doxa* to the witness stand, sparing themselves the trouble of meeting the critique in its own ground. Furthermore, guardians of the orthodoxy can rely on the disciplinary mechanisms to work for them. A long decanting has finally solidified former surmises into unassailable beliefs that trigger automatic compliance and automatic rejection, imposing the discipline's common sense impersonally.

The critic of orthodoxy is always forced into personal positions, with the result that she ends up underscoring her isolation. Always potentially pilloried for her deviation, she must continuously restate the obvious truth of her peripheral position, lest those who strive to conceal their own inscription in the social order accuse her of bad faith. And so, at every turn, she runs the risk of being disqualified on account of her position. This practical weakness is, nevertheless, her theoretical strength, for although every viewpoint is grounded in particularity, as a rule only those who engage in controversy against the structure of the field face the truth that *all* positions are invested in the distribution of value throughout the discipline. From this, it can be inferred that marginal and discordant critics tend to escape scholastic idealism by presenting their moves, often out of necessity, as the antithesis of disinterested participation in an objective contest of faculties.

And yet, a skeptic could ask if the participation of disenchanted players does not prove the field's neutrality—prove, that is, the impersonal regulation of competing viewpoints. I would venture that the existence of venues for counter-disciplinary work is an indication of the field's capacity to readjust itself after every critique. Orthodox players need only misinterpret the challenge to institutional common sense in order to fall back upon the familiar order of things. Given this hardly encouraging observation, the fact that some players take uncomfortable elocutionary positions may seem paradoxical, and one may wonder about the psychological dispositions that incline them to do so. Players in marginal positions continuously experience the truth that intellectual discourse alone cannot alter, much less undo, the dispositions that are routinely incorporated by those newly initiated into the field. Such dispositions are all the more intractable in that they define the conditions of symbolic capitalization and, as a result, powerfully influence the making and unmaking of scholarly reputations.

In times of crisis, however, explicit breaks with a discipline's organizing principles have a chance of gaining some currency, particularly if those moves take into account the fact that the discipline's practices have no intrinsic necessity. What they have going for them is the far from negligible power of inertia. Scholastic practices have developed in the course of time and changed over time. An epistemic crisis is the surest sign that they have reached the point of obsolescence. A renovation of the rules of the game becomes possible if challengers succeed in exposing the contradiction between the discipline's epistemological pretense and its actual scope. However, the necessary negative work of the dialectic must be complemented with indications of a more positive nature. It behooves the critic of the institution to refine the instruments of incorporation of the structures of the world in which the discipline acts. A change of scope inevitably means a change of cognitive structures, and this, in turn, means a permutation of practical dispositions and intellectual tools. In short, a crisis-confronting critique entails a revision which, if thorough or radical enough, may lead to a complete overhaul and the appearance of a new disciplinary field.

Stated plainly, the most pressing question highlighted by the crisis of so-called "Peninsular" Hispanism (which signals, although this is hardly obvious yet, the crisis of Hispanism as a whole) is how to turn this discipline into a venue for the open, plural, and equitable coexistence of the various cultures that have developed and exist today within the territory of the Spanish state and America. In what follows, I concentrate on the Peninsular stage of the Hispanic ideology; nevertheless, the critique applies also to a Latin Americanism that often seems invested in the expansionist monism chartered by the erstwhile metropolis.

For the discipline to evolve into a framework for the in-depth, multicultural study of the geopolitical areas that it claims for itself, mere assertions of the goal's desirability, of its fairness and legitimacy will not suffice. It is indispensable to neutralize the disciplinary logic that leads most players to suppress fundamental parts of the history and cultures of the peoples of Spain. Attaining this goal will require more than goodwill and condescending nods of recognition towards the dominated "minorities." First of all, it will require an intrinsic expectation that players survey the entirety of the field and subject competitive viewpoints to the test of demonstration against *the sum of the available record,* as is procedurally standard for more rigorous disciplines. In the meantime, a preliminary approach could prove helpful: turning explanatory reason to bear on those who consider themselves socially authorized to do the explaining. This work, which has already produced some lucid studies showing how the social atmosphere inscribed itself in the "scientific" work of Spanish philologists, still needs to be extended to the more perilous terrain of contemporary practices.[12] Here, rather than in the easier option of retrospective unveiling, lies the true engagement with the field's logic, for it is in the contemporaneity of practices that propositions for change will be resisted or silenced by those who shun the consequences of reflexivity.

Unlike scientific disciplines, where struggles are mainly over methodological or theoretical dominance, Hispanism's bias turns its very object into a resistance to the discipline's ambition to establish universal principles of understanding. This condition is not noted here in order to bemoan it; in the final analysis, it is irreducible and shared by all humanistic disciplines. However, the bias must be recognized and held in plain view, lest it becomes a blind spot in the vision of the realities which the discipline claims to show to advantage. The persistence of this socially generated bias can be gauged by tracing the nationalistic footprint not just of the classic figures—Menéndez Pelayo, Menéndez Pidal, Unamuno, Ortega, Sánchez Albornoz, Madariaga, Castro—but also of authors whose sensibilities are too close to those of the field's current practitioners to be subjected to the same detached scrutiny.

It befits the researcher of Hispanic ideology to stand outside the dominant mode of explanation in order to elucidate what that mode does not explain. This epistemic move cannot be accomplished without breaking the ranks with even the more iconic "deviations"; breaking ranks, that is, with the unorthodox orthodoxies that govern the field. One way to perform this task is to question the validity of the traditional division between conservative and progressive figures in a linear conception of Spanish history which, like Hegel's adventures of the idea, presumes the gradual self-disclosure of a politically correct Spanishness. Still efficient during the long Transition, this analytical scheme is now superseded by the coming to the fore of issues that demand an entirely different approach. Furthermore, such a scheme cannot recognize itself for what it is, because it ignores the privilege that unifies conservatives and progressives as beneficiaries of the historical path towards universality; a path which, as Hegel knew, is teleologically guided by the state. To put it differently, the state's relative democratization has allowed the issue of the nationalities to re-emerge. As a result, the condescending expressions of understanding for diverse national rights uttered during the Transition have been put to the test by demands for effective cultural and political autonomy as well as for actual representation in the state's organisms and in those of the European Union. The urgency of these demands disrupts the coziness of established critical reputations which now must shape up in reference to a different paradigm.[13] At present, the decisive and divisive issue is no longer the clash between Church and secular state, between public and private ownership of the means of production, or between individual and society. The stakes now are for and against the democratic extension of the means of access to cultural universality to all statutorily recognized constituencies, a process that cannot be accomplished without simultaneously revoking the cultural extraterritoriality of dominated groups.

Memory *bien entendu*

In the emergent political paradigm, the relation between language and ideological position is becoming ever more conspicuous, to the point of affecting the perception of the past: the much invoked, feared, and belabored historical memory. Evidence that the representation of the past depends to a not negligible degree on the linguistic medium employed is, in my mind, a strong argument for the renovation of the field in the multicultural sense suggested before. It simply will not do to continue to ignore or suppress experiences that are recorded in alternative languages.

The discipline's monolingualism needs to be recognized not as an effect of Hispanism's ideology but as its main vehicle. The voiding of entire tracks of historical memory is one of its consequences. This can be seen in the thinness of the approaches to the cultures and experiences of Spain's non-Castilian peripheries, which are often subjected to formulaic patterns of understanding, if they come into purview at all. What would be scandalous in any other area of knowledge is here the norm: incidental comments or sweeping judgements with little or no substantiation, ignorance of the scholarship in the relevant languages, and a complete lack of interest in the cultural agents themselves. The result is the construction and circulation of a new *doxa* that differs from the old in paying lip service to cultural pluralism. New meets old, however, in presuming a cultural awareness that the critical practices belie.

One example of scholarly shallowness in selected areas might be the listlessness (or incapacity for critical reaction) which meets the erasure of the memory of cultural victimization.[14] Revisionist books like Juan Ramón Lodares's *El paraíso políglota* and instances of flat denial, like Juaristi's declaration cited previously, have gained some currency not only among the less educated but also among the guardians of the legitimate knowledge. This example refers to the tension between institutional location and historical dynamic, and to the relation between the state's monopoly on universality and the anthropological treatment of non-state cultures. In the last analysis, two broad antagonistic approaches can be discerned. On one side, an effort to keep history open and to understand the implications of cultural genocide for the scholarly present. On the other side, the desire to close it, suturing the wound as if the violence had never occurred. Nevertheless, such suturing is itself violent, for it can never be the result of an agreement between equal forces.

For those who opt for the second of these approaches, the war and the dictatorship produced victims but not perpetrators. Or, what amounts to the same thing, the matter is considered settled once and for all by the Transition. Peter Burke observes that history is not just written by the victors, but it is also forgotten by them (106). Is it then surprising that memory, the memory of cultural-specific aggression, is keener in the linguistic archives of the victims?[15] There is a subtle, but for that reason highly effective, relation between knowledge and the linguistic medium in which knowledge is legitimated. The fact that for the most part studies and documentation about the extent of Catalonia's victimization have appeared in Catalan indicates that language is not a neutral conveyor of information but a space for investments of memory, of intellectual dispositions, of affective inclinations, and pragmatic choices. Those investments may further or preclude the apprehension of the situation in which individual agents are implicated. If choosing the wrong linguistic medium prevents scholarly work from having the status of legitimate knowledge, those scholars who challenge the established model are disenfranchised, not because their theses are necessarily wrong or poorly argued, but because they do not accord with the operative model. In his classic study on the structure of epistemic paradigms, Thomas Kuhn showed that it is in the logic of an existing paradigm to ratify the margins and fend off intrusions in its scheme of intelligibility. Homeostasis, which Jean-François Lyotard considers the principle that governs the institution of knowledge (63), is *a fortiori* the social law to which the state owes its self-preservation. In both fields, the epistemic and the political, homeostasis works by silencing or attempting to silence those who challenge the rules of the game.

Strategies of Denial

Like other humanistic disciplines, Hispanism is limited methodologically by the culture it mediates. This makes it difficult to transcend or even question those limits from the inside. Between the official denier and the academic Hispanist who feels aloof from the cultural genocides perpetrated in the name of Hispanic culture, there is solidarity, a visceral attachment, as Bourdieu defines the *esprit de corps* (145). Hispanism, as an academic discipline, extends a concrete social body of Hispanic culture, into which Hispanists are inducted through professional rites of passage and from which they can detach themselves as if from their own skins.

The sociology of denial merits a study on itself. Without even broaching the subject, it is possible to surmise that deniers' main purpose is to deter the possibility of redress. Denial involves a form of symbolic power. Deniers double the pleasures of dominance with their ability to suppress the victim's memory and concentrate the accumulated historical violence in the maintenance of repression. The violence inherent in denial illuminates the otherwise unexplainable forfeiture of the rules of arbitrated reasoning. Flying in the face of academic standards for debate, deniers lightly deploy *ad hominem* assaults and pass sentences of academic death. Sometimes they fall into the paradox of denouncing their opponent's participation in the game *because* she complies with the game's legitimate procedures. Statements such as "it was an affront to bring up those citations," or "wasn't the dishonesty even worse when she spoke publicly?" betray the denier's annoyance at the adversary's recourse to the same privileged venues of elocution that he, the denier, enjoys. The bottom line in such denunciations is never methodological; quite simply, it amounts to the communication of a verdict.

Denial denies itself. If it cannot sweep the facts under the historical carpet, it will arrange them into a pattern and pretend they are part of the wool. History can be normalized by means of rhetoric. Turkey denies the genocide of Armenians with a foolproof argument: there is no Armenian nation. If only Turks died in the course of a Civil War, then, from the state's point of view, victims and butchers were all in the same boat. No need for remorse or apologies. Another strategy of denial consists in restricting the term "genocide" to a few instances of world-historical proportions such as the Holocaust or the Cambodian Kmer Rouge, and refusing to mobilize ethical judgement around less conspicuous cases. Yet another strategy consists in denial through quantitative arguments (it was not six million but *only* four, or three, or . . .) or by trivializing the attempt on a people's specificity if it falls short of wholesale physical extermination. Some people dispute that the deliberate destruction of a culture, a language, a religion, or the economic basis of a society ranks as a crime of genocidal proportions.[16] This form of denial ignores that the physical destruction of an ethnic group always aims at the destruction of a culture, that groups are targeted not on account of the individuals they consist of but of the cultures whose carriers those individuals are.

Those who deny the past often gloss over the facts by inverting the relation between the factors, no matter how senseless the resulting picture might be. Repeated often and loudly enough, any absurdity will end up gaining currency.[17] Another strategy is to replace the uncomfortable facts with more acceptable "place holders." This can be done, for instance, by portraying Spanish, the state's symbolic fetish, as the exilic idiom par excellence, as Paul Ilie did in a revealing article published during the Transition ("Exolalia"). Such a view not only conceals the facts of linguistic deterritorialization, but also inverts their logic by presenting the aggression against the peripheral nationalities as a historical incident. That incident is even produced *ex post facto* with the remark that "Indeed, the danger of minority consciousness to the dictatorship was recognized by Francoist ideologues immediately after the Civil War" (Ilie 231).

By speaking of a post-War "recognition" of the "danger" posed by the defeated and repressed nationalities to the Francoist State, Ilie disingenuously manipulates the facts. In reality, dictatorship was the "solution," or more exactly, the institutionalization of the violent response to the modest gains obtained by the "minority consciousness" under the Second Republic. Long before the Civil War, the ideologues of Hispanidad had "recognized" the danger posed by "minority consciousness" for their imperial idea. That idea, entrenched in the Spanish tradition, was deeply rooted in the institutions and widely shared by large sectors of the intelligentsia.[18] Hispanists, insofar as they let the history of cultural repression come into their purview, often treat it as a localized episode, neglecting its long-term effects in contemporary legislation, media propaganda, and judicial practices.

A related and, widely used, strategy consists in "symmetrically" apportioning the responsibility for symbolic aggression among different players, denouncing both the "centralist" logic (without, however, tracing its specific practices or representations) and the centrifugal "excesses" (assumed to be self-evident). Yet, on the historical ground the actual dynamic looks quite different. Not a vague centralism but Spanish nationalism, which could not be shed by *fiat*—and now camouflages itself behind an imported "constitutional patriotism"[19]— is at the root of the hegemonic consciousness. Forever reborn, like the imperial eagle from its ashes, this consciousness leaves no stone unturned in its search for ideological weapons.

For two decades, but with growing intensity over the last one, a reaction has set in against the efforts to produce a critical break with the traditional relation of domination. The hatred wells from the pages of national-journalism as well as from more "scholarly" sources, and, as in the 1930s, it numbs the public conscience against the deadliness of rhetorical passions. Against the tendency to recast intellectuals who were committed to the idea of a uniform Spain as liberals, it must be said that the aggression against the non-state cultures in the 1930s was fed by dispositions cultivated by generations of intellectuals, who contributed to the formation of what Carl L. Becker, following Alfred North Whitehead (57), called a climate of opinion. "Whether arguments command assent or not," said Becker, "depends less upon the logic that conveys them than upon the climate of opinion in which they are sustained" (5). In the climate of Hispanidad, the logic of pluralism and of historical right did not stand a chance.

Encounters in Heteronomous Space

Whence come the dispositions that intellectuals ratify? The importance of this question for understanding corporate rationalizations can hardly be exaggerated. Notwithstanding a widespread presupposition, the source of those dispositions does not lie in the psychology of individuals but in objective mechanisms. Bourdieu has called the sum of such mechanisms a habitus—a solidified set of responses which, being acquired historically by a society, are appropriated by individuals through their participation in institutional life. Turning his attention to the field of Hispanism, Rafael L. Ninyoles explains the political conformity of many Spanish literary scholars by focusing on their status as civil servants, *funcionarios*. According to Ninyoles, the psychological adjustment required of civil servants by the conditions of realization of their group-specific modality of self-fulfillment (including, especially, the requirement of geographic mobility) contributes to their alienation from the cultural and linguistic pluralism encountered in the discharge of their duties.

There is no recourse to mentalism in this diagnosis: "psychological adjustment" refers to the subjective adaptation to causes that lie deep in the social order. It is in this order, not in ethno-psychology, that the conceit of "being above" the particulars of life has its source. Thus, Ninyoles accounts more plausibly than Américo Castro for the tendency which the latter observed in many Spaniards to behave like the discharged civil servants ("funcionarios 'cesantes'") of an imperial establishment (1973, 385). What produces this particular kind of civil servant is not the unutilized balance of personal or collective energies, as Castro believed, but the persistence of imperialistic structures in the social order. That is to say, the abundance of functionaries and would-be functionaries seeking to spend the least amount of energy possible in a discharged imperial establishment. In this context, subjective traits and dispositions are better accounted for as a function of the state, as *funcionariado*. Individuals tend to adopt the viewpoint required by their actual or intended function within a system.

Given the prominence of the institutional component in their mindset, *funcionarios* often display a pretended higher, but in truth homogenizing perspective, on the conflicts of interest between the state's cultural components (Ninyoles, *Mare Espanya* 89). Although this tendency is shared by all civil servants, from the police officer to the judge, from the minister to the tax collector, Ninyoles considers professors of Spanish history and Spanish literature (Hispanists par excellence) the paradigmatic instances of the logic of state service. Unlike the minister, who regulates the affairs of the state, the policeman and the judge, who enforce that regulation, or the tax collector, who extracts from citizens the means to run the state, the literature professor does not deal with primary administrative mechanisms. She contributes, instead, to adjust the consciousness of citizens for the smooth operation of the other "services." Her task is to produce subjective consent through the diffusion of the cultural paradigm promoted by the state.

Notwithstanding the civil servant's ideological encapsulation, geographic mobility brings this person into contact with other habitus shaped by different historical legacies. Thus, geographic mobility, while promising the fulfillment of institutionally generated expectations, can also create a predicament for the civil servant who is stationed as an outsider in Catalonia or Euskadi. Inevitably, this person's conception of "Spanish" history or literature is challenged by the realities with which she comes into contact. A common response is for the civil servant to assign subaltern importance to the cultures of the places to which she is destined, a temptation as powerful as that of overvaluing the already acquired homogenizing perspective. As a result of the confrontation between previous investments and new experiences, the state's antagonism to plurality is often compounded by the aversion developed by many civil servants toward the, from their standpoint, refractory reality of the places in which they are stationed (*Mare Espanya* 90).

Crossing the ocean between Spanish and North American, Hispanism creates visible problems for the preceding analysis. How does civil service behavior reproduce itself, if at all, in an academic structure characterized by market-driven mobility rather than by the protocols of ascent on the bureaucratic rung-ladder? The difficulties for any comparison are compounded by the belief, still in force in the U.S. scholastic sphere, in rational communication rather than historical privilege as the *nomos* that regulates a university in permanent transformation. Nevertheless, it is precisely this difference that offers a clue to the constants in the North American scholastic system. As Bourdieu warns, symbolic violence imposes itself most expeditiously through the power exercised in rational communication. For it is through the use of rationalized force that the most effective submission is extorted, reinforcing the objective relations of domination with a rationality that sets those relations above the arbitrariness of ordinary discourse (Bourdieu 83).

The most basic trait that U.S. Hispanism shares with state Hispanism is the discipline's narrow linguistic foundation, which is exacerbated in the United States by the scholar's dependence on language instruction for her clientele. Although there is an inverse value relation between the discipline's linguistic base and its cultural superstructure, language training has always been Hispanism's primary legitimation. Extrinsic factors such as a favorable demography or the appearance of heritage students do not affect the discipline's epistemic merits (which is surely one reason why it has failed thus far to actualize the desired leap in status). Hispanism's main source of political clout exposes the field's fallacy, namely the sublimation of lobbying power into an alleged scholarly advance. Arguing from the numerical strength of a *potential* constituency may or may not be a democratic gesture (it not always is, as Spain's constant incantation of the *trescientos millones* of Castilian speakers as an "argument" for its hegemonic goals demonstrates), but it is a poor epistemic strategy. More problematically, the reliance on exclusively demographic factors linked to migration blurs the complexities of the cultural spaces that Hispanism purports to mediate, fatally undermining its claims to epistemic vigor.

This weakness is related to a second paradox under which the U.S. Hispanist labors. The situation often described as academic marginality amounts, more accurately, to a dead-end exercise in the transmission of decontextualized knowledge. This is truer of the U.S. Peninsularist than of the Latin Americanist. The former, to a greater extent than the latter, and for structural reasons that are as historically complex as they appear to be sociologically simple, finds herself in an area of knowledge with very little resonance in the field.[20] That means that the hierarchies of prestige that the field bemoans in relation to other fields are internal to it. Geopolitical regulation of academic priorities is objectified not only in the disparity among individual reputations when considered by area of expertise, but more seriously in the growing disparity of access to ordinary academic channels. It suffices to mention here the virtual disappearance of publication venues in the foremost academic presses, which over the past decade have been dropping Peninsular subjects from their catalogues. It should be a matter of concern for the field, as a whole, that its chronic deficit of resonance within the U.S. university is being gradually corrected only to the extent that this area of knowledge is nativized, that is to say, legitimated through its nationalization.

Despite the U.S. Hispanist's substantial elbowroom in designing the programs of study that shape scholastic thought and mold the field's future trustees, American Hispanism has until now failed to embody the multiculturalism and multilingualism of Spanish and Latin American societies. Notwithstanding its different ethos, based on a long tradition of academic freedom rather than centralized government planning, U.S. Hispanism overlaps considerably with its Spanish counterpart, even if it has decidedly moved away from the philological and historical methodologies that reign unabated in the Spanish university. Foremost among the factors contributing to the overlap are canonical criteria, which circumscribe research and instruction to a fairly predictable set of authors and interests enshrined in the foundations of the field.[21] Equally important are the material pressures brought to bear on the scholar who departs from the doxa. It follows that the maverick scholar, who breaks with the routines of symbolic production, is likely to experience a blockage of ordinary channels of diffusion and a freezing vacuum around her work. In the United States, more than in countries with a centralized educational system, professional goals and priorities are maintained through corporate self-regulation. Although a premium is placed on individual initiative and field renovation, the overall consensus is ensured through highly personalized hiring practices, manipulation of student interest, and diffuse censorship linked to the politics of publishing. While university presses are likely to appeal to the balance sheets, subsidized journals encode the field's value domain through editors' discretionary powers, often shielded by the alleged objectivity of anonymous referees against whom there is no appeal. Despite its commendable use of "checks and balances," refereed arbitration can also safeguard entrenched biases under the guise of impersonal procedures. Other influences on the direction of scholarship are motivational. Official and semi-official incentives channel research into certain directions and contexts, as do various forms of recognition that play on the scholar's vulnerability to adulation. This foible is rarely perceived as such, for, in principle, scholars believe themselves worthy of every distinction and do not question the source or ulterior implications of their privilege.

While U.S. Hispanism has developed variegated lines of research and, in some cases, marshaled considerable creativity and theoretical ingenuity, it remains tied to its foundational ideologies in its self-positioning as a globalizing (that is, an aggressively competitive) cultural force. Enticed by the ambiguous

182 JOAN RAMON RESINA

benefits to be culled from the dogma of its language's alleged universality, U.S. Hispanism is neglecting the intellectually more fertile investigation of the rich multiculturalism and multilingualism in the territories of what still passes for *the* Hispanic world.

Notes

1. The historical origin of the term is irrelevant. Whether it originated as a formalization of the activities of foreign hispanophiles or from a domestic pan-Hispanic ideology, the term now stands for an international network of conventions and interests that relies on its academic niche for its definition and continuity.
2. Hence, the turf wars, for instance, when faculty in English departments teach Hispanic texts.
3. Festering tensions exist between Latin Americanists and so-called Peninsularists vying for the balance within a field that oscillates between historical depth and geographic extension. The apex of absurdity, from the standpoint of the field's self-interest, is the restriction of one of the axes. In the past, the geographic axis was restricted through a merely symbolic inclusion of Latin American culture; at present, it is history that is being dilapidated by catering to a narrow-minded consumerism. In these skirmishes, however, the fundamental exclusions are left in place. In this sense, the skirmishes themselves are surface activity designed to conceal deep immobility.
4. No sarcasm is intended. The cosmic dimension is present in José Vasconcelos's vision of Hispanism's "ethnic mission" (25), the creation of a globalized race that will culminate Hispanism's world historical destiny. Vasconcelos makes it clear that this "universal era of Humanity" (52), marked by cultural and racial homogeneity, can only be achieved by the Iberian part of the American continent. He even foresees the day when, from Universópolis, the world capital on the banks of the Amazon River, airplanes and armies will make sorties to continue the old Hispanic task of incorporating far-off places into "la sabiduría" (wisdom) (35). Although he does not broach the question of what universal language will be used in this late-day civilizing crusade, it is plain that his cosmic race will speak one of the two Iberian languages spoken in South America, or a mixture of the two. Through its policy of promoting Spanish in Brazil without a symmetrical effort to turn Portuguese into a common language for Latin Americans, the Spanish government is trying to settle the question, left open by Vasconcelos, of what language shall convey the "buenas nuevas" (good news) of the universal synthesis of cultures.
5. The translation of quotations is mine unless otherwise indicated.
6. In Juaristi's case, it is the space of nostalgic nationalism. See his book, *El bucle melancólico.*
7. Although it was the raving delusion of a decadent imperial people, the editorial state-

ment in *Raza española*'s first issue hardly differed from recent statements by twenty-first century academicians and politicians: "a la geografía que trazó la espada sobre el haz de la Tierra, se impone otra geografía más fuerte [. . .] la geografía animada y dominadora de las lenguas, que contienen infuso el espíritu de las razas; así, en la actualidad son y lo serán más cada día dos grandes lenguas, dos grandes razas representada y unida cada cual por su lengua: la Raza española y la Raza inglesa, las que se disputan el dominio del mundo" (the geography drawn by the sword is now replaced by a stronger geography [. . .] the lively and commanding geography of the languages that are pervaded with the spirit of the human races. Today—and this will become even clearer in the future—there are two great languages, two great races, each represented and unified through its language, that struggle for world domination. These are the Spanish race and the English race) (De los Ríos 8–9).

8. The previous year, the General Assembly of the Asociación de Historia de la Lengua Española had unanimously approved a proposal of the Asociación de Lingüística y Filología de la América Latina to request the Spanish Ministry of Education and Culture to implement courses on "American Spanish" in all Spanish universities. Concurrently, the General Assembly defeated the proposal of the departments of Catalan, Galician, and Basque to offer courses in these languages throughout Spain. Some members of the Assembly, like the linguist Gregorio Salvador, considered the discussion of this matter in the assembly "intolerable" and "unacceptable" (Romero).

9. On epistemocentrism, see Bourdieu, especially the chapter "The Three Forms of Scholastic Fallacy" in *Pascalian Meditations*. I am indebted to this book throughout this essay.

10. See Resina, 1996.

11. "[Y] espero que nadie al oír esto, no ya diga pero ni siquiera piense: '¡ah!, si es superior el número de estudiantes que prefieren la lengua catalana, entonces, es justo que ésta prevalezca.' No; ése es precisamente el planteamiento de la cuestión que no podemos aceptar: el Estado español, que es el Poder prevaleciente, tiene una sola lengua, la española, y ésta es, por ineludible consecuencia, la que jurídicamente tiene que prevalecer" ("And I hope that upon hearing this, no one will not just say but even think: "if there are more students who prefer instruction in Catalan, then justice demands that this language should prevail." No; that is precisely the way of presenting the issue that we cannot accept. The Spanish State, which is the dominant Power, has only one language, Spanish, and this is, ineluctably, the language that must prevail by law") (*Discursos* 276).

12. The already mentioned book by José del Valle and Luis Gabriel-Stheeman, and Jacques Lezra's article "La mora encantada" come immediately to mind.

13. I adapt the idea of "paradigm" from Thomas Kuhn's analysis of the rules of scientific practice, where he defines a paradigm as a social constraint that obliges people to think in agreement with a dominant logic or mode of explanation.

14. This is not the place to substantiate this statement. Hard data abound, but the need to

provide it in the context of Hispanism is in itself a symptom of the state of affairs that I am denouncing.

15. Confinement of memory to an alternative code that is then declared non-essential amounts to shelving the uncomfortable issues. Thus, José María Aznar, in an interview with the Barcelona daily *La Vanguardia,* asserted that "no sé cómo estaba el catalán durante la época de Franco" (I don't know the situation of Catalan under Franco) (Strubell). Aznar's plea of ignorance was disingenuous. It is not just that any reasonably curious person would find ample documentation, but Aznar would have had privileged information. His father, Manuel Aznar Zubigaray, a personal friend of Franco, had directed the very same daily from 1960 to 1963. Franco's Council of Ministers had nominated him for the post.

16. For a denial of the inaugural violence of Hispanism, in tandem with a denial of the Holocaust, see the recent book by a Spanish state employee, Juan Luis Beceiro García, *La mentira histórica desvelada: ¿Genocidio en América? Ensayo sobre la acción de España en el Nuevo Mundo* (1994). This book received support from the regional government of Galicia through the purchase of copies for distribution in the region's public libraries and reading centers (Hermida). Perhaps not coincidentally, the book includes an epilogue by that government's president, Manuel Fraga Iribarne, a former minister in charge of state security under Franco.

17. Insisting that Spanish ought to be the language of instruction in Catalan schools (the very situation mandated by Franco), sociologist Amando de Miguel declared that schooling the children of immigrants in Catalan would amount to a "cultural genocide" ("De la Babel").

18. In his prologue to the 1983 edition of his first book, *Notas marruecas de un soldado* (1923), Ernesto Giménez Caballero asserted that, after reading the manuscript, Américo Castro, had congratulated him "effusively" (5). He also claimed that Unamuno had saluted him as a "national writer" and praised the book in the newspaper *El liberal,* as well as in Madrid's *Ateneo.* Further attention was given to it by Ramiro de Maeztu in *El Sol* and by Eugenio d'Ors in *Nuevo Mundo.*

19. Cf. Aizpeolea. For a discussion of the origins and plausibility of "constitutional patriotism" as a substitute for nationalism, see my article "Postnational Spain? Post-Spanish Spain?" And for the ideological continuity between Francoism and post-Francoism, see my "Nationalism and Anti-Nationalism. Semantic Games for the Definition of the Democratic State."

20. I have analyzed some of these reasons in "Hispanism and its Discontents."

21. Noting the large variation in the composition of graduate reading lists among departments of Spanish, Brown and Johnson conclude that this is bad news, since "our small canon may not serve the graduate students whose reading lists we have compared" (19). It may be that, in observing wide discrepancies in the titles of works incorporated as mandatory graduate reading, the authors of this survey do not sufficiently estimate the importance of the higher rate of coincidence by author. Thirty-nine Spanish authors and 24 Latin American ones (a total, therefore, of 63 authors appearing

75% of the time in all reading lists) is a high yield of coincidence when one takes into account the enormous possibilities for variation offered by the cultures involved. Nevertheless, the truly significant information is the one the survey keeps discreetly to itself. Variation in the lists is firmly checked by a fixed center of agreement on the language in which the works must have been written to count as required or even recommended Hispanic reading.

Works Cited

Aizpeolea, Luis R. "Partido Popular y PSOE pugnan por adueñarse del 'patriotismo constitucional.'" *El País Digital.* November 3, 2001.

Beceiro García, Juan Luis. *La mentira histórica desvelada: ¿Genocidio en América? Ensayo sobre la acción de España en el Nuevo Mundo.* Madrid: Ejearte, 1994.

Becker, Carl L. *The Heavenly City of the Eighteenth Century Philosophers.* New Haven: Yale University Press, 1932.

Bécker, Jerónimo. "La reconquista moral de América." *Raza Española.* 1 (1919): 13–19.

Bourdieu, Pierre. *Pascalian Meditations.* Trans. Richard Nice. Stanford, CA: Stanford University Press, 2000.

Burke, Peter. "History as Social Memory." *Memory: History, Culture and the Mind.* Ed. Thomas Butler. Oxford: Basil Blackwell, 1989: 97–113.

Cardó, Carles. *El gran refús.* Barcelona: Claret, 1994.

Castro, Américo. "El asunto catalán." *De la España que aún no conocía.* Vol. I. Barcelona: Prensas Universitarias, 1990: 229–33.

———. "De la insatisfacción a la magnificación." *Sobre el nombre y el quién de los españoles.* Madrid: Taurus, 1973: 379–85.

———. *España en su historia: Cristianos, moros y judíos.* Buenos Aires: Losada, 1948.

De los Ríos de Lampérez, Blanca. "Nuestra Raza." *Raza Española.* 1 (1919): 7–12.

De Miguel, Amando. "De la Babel a la Pentecostés." *ABC,* 1 October, 1993.

"Ecos de la Fiesta de la Raza." *Alma española.* 13–14 (1920): 107–16.

Giménez Caballero, Ernesto. *Notas marruecas de un soldado.* Barcelona: Planeta, 1983.

Hermida, Xosé. "Fraga patrocinó un libro que cuestiona que los nazis cometieran el holocausto." *El País Digital.* May 5, 2000.

Ilie, Paul. "Exolalia and Dictatorship: The Tongues of Hispanic Exile." In Hernán Vidal (ed.) *Fascismo y experiencia literaria: reflexiones para una recanonización.* Minneapolis: Institute for the Study of Ideologies and Literature, 1985: 222–52.

Juaristi, Jon. *El bucle melancólico: Historias de nacionalistas vascos.* Madrid: Espasa-Calpe, 1997.

Kuhn, Thomas S. *The Structure of Scientific Revolutions.* Second ed. Chicago: University of Chicago Press, 1970.

Lezra, Jacques. "'La mora encantada': Covarrubias in the soul of Spain." *Journal of Spanish Cultural Studies.* I, 1 (2000): 5–27.

Lodares, Juan Ramón. *El paraíso políglota: Historias de lenguas en la España moderna contadas sin prejuicios.* Madrid: Taurus, 2000.

Lyotard, Jean-François. *The Postmodern Condition: A Report on Knowledge.* Trans. Geoff Bennington and Brian Massumi. Minneapolis: University of Minnesota Press, 1984.

Maeztu, Ramiro de. "La Hispanidad." *Acción Española.* 1.1 (1931): 8–16.

Mariscal, George. "An Introduction to the Ideology of Hispanism in the US and Britain." In Peter W. Evans (ed.). *Conflicts of Discourse: Spanish Literature in the Golden Age.* Manchester: Manchester University Press, 1990: 1–25.

Martín Artajo, Alfredo. "Presente y futuro de la comunidad hispánica." *Presente y futuro de la Comunidad Hispánica.* Madrid: Ediciones Cultura Hispánica, 1951: 131–44.

Marx, Karl and Friedrich Engels. *The German Ideology. Collected Works.* Vol. 5. New York: International Publishers, 1976.

Menéndez Pidal, Ramón. *Orígenes del español: estado lingüístico de la Península Ibérica hasta elsiglo XI.* Madrid: Espasa Calpe, 1950.

Ninyoles, Rafael L. *Mare Espanya. Aproximació al nacionalisme espanyol.* Trans. Eduard J. Verger. Valencia: Tàndem, 1997.

Ortega y Gasset, José. *Discursos políticos.* Ed. Paulino Garagorri. Madrid: Alianza Editorial, 1974.

———. *España invertebrada.* Ed. Paulino Garagorri. Madrid: Alianza Editorial, 1988.

Resina, Joan Ramon. "Hispanism and Its Discontents." *Siglo XX/20th Century* 14. 1–2 (1996): 85–135.

———. "Nationalism and Anti-Nationalism. Semantic Games for the Definition of the Democratic State." *Revista de Estudios Hispánicos.* 37 (2003): 383–400.

———. "Postnational Spain? Post-Spanish Spain?" *Nations and Nationalism,* 8.3 (2002): 377–96.

Romero, Justo. "La pasión por la lengua." *El País,* March 12, 1990.

Sánchez Bella, Alfredo. "La Hispanidad y sus obras." *Presente y futuro de la Comunidad Hispánica.* Madrid: Ediciones Cultura Hispánica, 1951: 91–113.

Serrano, Carlos. *El nacimiento de Carmen: Símbolos, mitos y nación.* Madrid: Taurus, 1999.

Valle, José del. "Menéndez Pidal, national regeneration and the linguistic utopia." In José del Valle and Luis Gabriel-Stheeman (eds.), *The Battle over Spanish between 1800 and 2000.* London and New York: Routledge, 2002: 78–105.

Valle, José del and Luis Gabriel-Stheeman. "Nationalism, *hispanismo,* and monoglossic culture." In José del Valle and Luis Gabriel-Stheeman (eds.), *The Battle over Spanish between 1800 and 2000.* London and New York: Routledge, 2002: 1–13.

Vasconcelos, José. *La raza cósmica: Misión de la raza iberoamericana.* México: Espasa-Calpe Mexicana, 1948.

Whitehead, Alfred North. *Science and the Modern World.* New York: The Free Press, 1967.

Part III
Latin Americanism and Cultural Critique

Latin America in the U.S. Imaginary: Postcolonialism, Translation, and the Magic Realist Imperative

Sylvia Molloy

The programmatic categories of my title attempt to summarize a discomfort, an ideological blind spot in the construction of "Latin America" by the United States academy and by the public at large. Academically, I refer to the discomfort felt by many Latin American intellectuals when presented with a postcolonial "model" to which Latin America is expected to conform; a model whose terms have been formulated from, and in reference to, a "center" whose interventions, however well intentioned, continue to be seen as imperialistic and/or simplistic. This is a postcolonialism with which modern Latin American intellectuals and scholars have, at best, a mediated relation, one necessitating multiple reformulations and translations. Furthermore, this is a postcolonialism which very much depends on its site of enunciation, a postcolonialism that is constituted by shifting perspectives. In other words, it is a postcolonialism which, formulated "over here" (and by this I mean the U.S. academy), signifies one thing while "over there" (in Latin America, itself a site of multiple enunciations), it signifies something quite different; or, better said, signifies many different things.

As a Latin American studying in France back in the early sixties (I should say as an Argentine, therefore a Latin American: these things happen in two stages), I received a fairly traditional training in comparative literature. When the time came to write my dissertation, I gravitated towards an adviser and was practically assigned a dissertation topic: I was from Latin America, I would therefore write on the reception of Latin American literature in France, a project I remember my adviser describing as "immensely useful," although it was unclear who or what (myself, my reader, the discipline?) would benefit from my compilation, conclusions and, mainly, conjectures. I protested I knew very little Latin American literature, having been trained in French, and was curtly told: "Vous l'apprendrez" (you will learn). Even then, I knew that I was being assigned the role of the native informant, a role I have been asked to play more than once since then, a role many scholars from other countries working in the United States no doubt find familiar.

What certainly *was* "immensely useful" to me was to study certain preconceived French notions of what Latin American literature "should" be. In other words, I noted early on how, even as Latin American literature became available in France, it was already spoken for. Thus, for example, Jean Cassou, as early as 1900, regretted that Rubén Darío had opted for what he, Cassou, considered derivative symbolism, instead of writing about what he termed, with considerable geographical license, "ce dont nous rêvons, sa forêt et sa pampa natales" (Molloy, *Diffusion* 58). The writer who discredited these preconceptions was of course Borges, a figure that puzzled French critics to no end because *he did not fit*. "Ne cherchons pas en lui un 'écrivain argentin'— bien qu'il aime et évoque souvent son pays—Borges n'est pas un représentant de la littérature argentine, il est un monstre et un génie" (We do not seek an Argentinean writer in him—even if he loves and often evokes his country—Borges is not a representative of Argentinean literature, he is a monster and a genius), wrote a reviewer (Molloy, *Diffusion* 219). Borges did not match French expectations of a Latin American specificity and was, therefore, a monster (albeit a brilliant one) devoid of nationality. Darío, had he written "regional" poems, probably would have matched those expectations. Alejo Carpentier certainly did, partly because of magic realism (to which I shall return) and partly through reverse snobbery: he was erroneously believed to be Afro-Cuban. "M. Alejo Carpentier qui, sauf erreur de ma part, est un écrivain noir" (Alejo Carpentier who, unless I am mistaken, is a black writer), wrote Max-Pol Fouchet in his enthusiastic review of *The Kingdom of This World* (Molloy, *Diffusion* 191). Parallel to the construction of the "Orient" there was a very active fabrication of a Latin American "South," one that had to be, of necessity, free of Western alliances so that Western fantasies could generously play themselves out.

I have gone back to personal history, and to that first shock of recognition—I was, on the one hand, the native informant, on the other, the native spoken for—because some aspects of that same vexed construction of Latin American literatures and cultures (I use the plural deliberately) is often at play today in a different but not unrelated setting, that of departments of literature and/or comparative literature in the United States, intent, if not on "exoticizing" Latin America, at least on acritically, even ahistorically, "postcolonizing" it and channeling it through magic realism. The two gestures have more in common than it would, at first, appear.

Mexican anthropologist Jorge Klor de Alva has written astutely on the pitfalls of applying post-1960 constructions of colonialism, imperialism, and postcolonialism retroactively and anachronistically to the Americas in general, and to Latin America in particular. I will not go into his arguments in detail, but will retain what is obvious to historians and is often neglected by theoreticians and literary scholars, namely, the specificity of the Latin American colonial experience both temporally, politically, and ideologically. With the exception of parts of the Caribbean, Spain's colonies seceded very early in the nineteenth century; the confrontation was not between indigenous peoples and metropolitan colonizers (although it may have been that too) but between Euro-Americans (*criollos*), Westernized *mestizos,* and even some Europeans (*Peninsulares*) against other Europeans; an experience more akin, say, to the North American experience, than to that of the British colonies a full century later. As Latin Americanists working on nineteenth-century literature know full well, the points of contact and friction between the two Americas, their literatures and cultures in the nineteenth century, even in their relations to Europe, are many and fruitful, yet remain largely underexplored. In the nineteenth century that Latin American cultures "write back," then they plagiarize, translate and misread, with the difference that there is no real "empire" to write back to nor to substantially dissent from.[1] Even before secession, Spain, a decaying metropolis already superseded by its energetic colonies, was no longer a model to subvert; she had long been replaced by France (and, to a point, by England) in the cultural imaginary of Latin America. So, if Latin America is "writing back" anywhere—and, given the identification of its new national cultures with Enlightenment models, one wonders whether the expression applies—one could argue that it is writing back to the "wrong" address. It is not striking back, in name of a recuperated indigenous past,[2] but constructing itself afresh, as an alternate, transculturated West.[3]

The distinctiveness of Latin American postcolonialism, which does not necessarily exclude neocolonial situations within its very boundaries (a situation the United States itself should not be unfamiliar with), does not have a place, however, in the legitimating narrative the U.S. academy usually tells itself about Latin America. Instead, in that narrative, Latin American literature "begins" at another time and in another place, is made to "emerge" ("emerge" into U.S. awareness, as in "emergent" literatures which always seem to emerge when the First World discovers a need for new cultural goods) in the early 1960s, an emergence coinciding, roughly, with the Cuban revolution—a "new" beginning—and with the publication of *One Hundred Years of Solitude*—a "new" genre, magic realism, a genre against which *all* Latin American literature would be read in a sort of ahistorical, postcolonial present. This is a literature endowed with a new, snappy genealogy and new interlocutors: Perry Anderson "dates" *One Hundred Years of Solitude* by calling it a typically Third-World "shadow configuration" of First-World modernism (García Canclini 44) and relates García Márquez's novel to Salman Rushdie's *Midnight's Children* and Yilmiz Güney's *Yol*. "It is necessary to question above all the mania that has almost fallen out of use in Third World countries: to speak of the Third World and include in the same package Colombia, India, and Turkey," observes Néstor García Canclini of Anderson's homogenizing gesture (45), echoing the concerns of other Latin American critics and not a few postcolonial theorists from non-Western countries.[4] Above all, it is necessary to question the short-sighted view that García Márquez's novel, in this new configuration, is the symptom of Latin American modernism when that modernism, as García Canclini rightly argues, has been the subject of cultural reflection and aesthetic experimentation in Latin America since the turn of the century. Familiar to any Hispanic reader, this earlier modernist experimentation, however, was only spottily translated into English.

Crucial in this recycling of Latin America into a "new" postcolonial, which sacrifices the thick texture of a process to the superficial similarity of its effects, is, I think, a problem of language, more specifically, *with* language. Critiquing the metropolitan urge to homogenize so-called "Third-World Literatures" and contain their representations, leveling them with "the rhetoric of Otherness," Aijaz Ahmad, in a by-now famous essay, reflected on the problematic availability of certain cultural traditions. These texts may become available directly, through translation, wrote Ahmad; more often, however, they arrive indirectly, in critical essays about those texts that offer "versions and shadows of texts produced in other spaces of the globe" (127). Despite an admirable effort to tease apart "Third-World Literatures," Ahmad drew a not altogether convincing distinction between these unavailable texts (mainly from the Indian subcontinent) and Latin American literatures, whose "direct" availability he stressed:

> Literatures of South America and parts of the Caribbean are *directly* available to the metropolitan critic through Spanish and Portuguese, which are after all European

languages. *Entire* vocabularies, styles, linguistic sensibilities exist now in English, French, Italian, for translations from these languages. Europeans and American theorists can either read those literary documents *directly,* or in case one is not entirely proficient in Spanish or Portuguese, he/she can nevertheless speak of their literatures with *easy familiarity* because of the *translatability* of the originals. (127; my emphases)

The notion of easy familiarity is both rich and problematic here, since it appears to be based on a translatability that is presented, *at the same time,* as a trope and a linguistic reality. As we know only too well in foreign languages departments, linguistic competence is a highly charged ideological issue and nothing is "easy." If Spanish and Portuguese are "after all" European languages, they may be a little less European than others. And, even if they are "after all" European, I would argue that they are certainly not considered metropolitan languages and that their complex cultural traditions, on both sides of the Atlantic, are largely ignored. In this country, the purported "easy familiarity" and "translatability" of Spanish (Portuguese, a less "familiar" language is in a different situation), usually work to its detriment, crediting the language with an unwarranted transparency that seriously limits its range. Rarely, if at all, does the academy view Spanish as a language of authority or of intellectual exchange: Latin American critics who have debated long and hard on postcolonialism *from* Latin America, specifically addressing Latin American difference—say Nelly Richard in Chile, Néstor García Canclini in Mexico, Jesús Martín Barbero in Colombia, to name but three—are rarely if ever brought into general debates about postcolonialism, even when their texts are available in English, i.e., when "real" translations of their works exist. Despite this very direct availability, their interlocutors in this country (with a few notable exceptions) seem to be other Latin Americanists working on postcolonial issues, such as Walter Mignolo, Mary Louise Pratt, George Yúdice, or John Beverley, scholars who, themselves, are not always recognized as productive participants in the more general postcolonial debates.[5]

Let me then render Ahmad's statement a little more complicated and say that Latin American texts appear to offer the *illusion* of an easy familiarity, the *illusion* of translatability, and thus create the *illusion* of cultural competence, not to mention the *illusion* of institutional expertise, usually based on a smattering of texts. This apparently "easy" translatability is further complicated by ideologies of reception that "choose," as it were, certain vehicles (but not any vehicle) for that translatability, certain representations and texts (but not any representation or text). Selected Latin American texts are thus uncoupled from their particular mode of functioning within their respective Latin American traditions *and then* turned into a corpus that purports to be "fully" representative of an "entire . . . sensibility" called "Latin America," "Third-World modernism," or "postcolonial literature." (What exactly does it represent, who selects the criteria of representativity, and from where, ideologically speaking, is that selection being made, are of course the key questions that should be asked here). What is missing from these reductive attempts at reconstructing "entire . . . sensibilities," is the understanding of culture as *relation*. "El libro no es un ente incomunicado: es una relación, es un eje de innumerables relaciones. Una literatura difiere de otra, ulterior o anterior, menos por el texto que por la manera de ser leída," writes Borges (*Obras* 747). "A book is not an isolated being: it is a relationship, an axis of innumerable relationships. One literature differs from another, prior or posterior, less because of the text than because of the way it has been read" (*Labyrinths* 214). The experience that Borges proposes across time should be equally possible across space. Yet the end result of the presumably "direct" contact with Latin America literature is not modes of reading but a dehistoricized, "manageable" corpus, deprived of cultural genealogies or theoretical speculation.

Many years ago, Juan Goytisolo, in a melancholy piece in the *New York Times Book Review,* pondered on the politics of cultural representation in general, the reception of Spanish-language literatures in particular, and their place in a dialogue of literatures and, importantly, the marketing tactics of publishers. He spoke mostly of Spain, a country, he said, that was doomed to being a single-faced culture, allowed only one image that would "translate well" in the international market and "represent" Spain. The image might change with the passing of time but there was always a quota: one image. Latin America, in itself a more fluid cultural composite, suffers from readings that are even more reductive, at least when they come from the North. Real geographical proximity seems to increase the cultural divide; the nearer the border, the more anxious the containment and policing of cultural representativity becomes.

The history of magic realism has been written elsewhere, and it is not my intention to retrace its long and tenacious life. It should be recalled, however, than from its very inception, this figuration of Latin America was a self-conscious, literary effort by a self-conscious, literary writer, Alejo Carpentier. An excrescence of French surrealism transculturated to Cuba and, by extension, to the rest of Latin America, magic realism was a strategic, polemical element in a transnational literary quarrel, it was Carpentier's response both to the Surrealists' conception of poetic image and to the Avant-Garde's discovery of "primitive" art. More than sprouting then "naturally," from Latin American "reality," as

Carpentier himself, in a burst of nativistic fervor, would have his reader believe, magic realism was born on the same operating table on which Lautréamont's umbrella hobnobbed with the sewing machine.[6] A transculturated mode, in the way Fernando Ortiz and Angel Rama (two other Latin American critics rarely cited in postcolonial debates) understood the notion of transculturation, one more product of what Gustavo Pérez Firmat has called Latin America's "translation sensibility" (1), magic realism in Latin America is a mode of literary figuration *among many others;* yet it has been singled out by First World readerships to signify, as surely as Carmen Miranda's fruity cornucopias, "Latin America." What magic realism loses, in this cultural transaction that privileges one form of representation to the detriment of others, is precisely its relational quality. Latin American magic realism becomes a regional, ethnicized commodity, a form of that essentialized primitivism which continues to lurk in the minds of even well-intentioned First-World critics.[7] For a country which persists in representing itself as a Western country (I speak of the U.S.), it is also a handy way of establishing spatial distance and, perhaps more importantly, temporal distance vis-à-vis a region that may be too close for comfort, a way of practicing what Johannes Fabian has called "the denial of coevalness." Magic realism is refulgent, amusing, and kitschy (Carmen Miranda's headdress; José Arcadio Buendía's tattooed penis)—but it doesn't happen, couldn't happen, here.

With its exotic connotations, its potential for stereotypical casting, its "poetic" alienation into the realm of the "magical" i.e., the *very far away,* the *very other,* magic realism has become, for the United States, a mode of Latin American *representation,* not a mode of Latin American *production.* As such—as representation, not as production—it is used to measure Latin American *literary* quality. It is used to both effect and confirm First-World "discoveries" of undetected Latin American talent: readerly expectation (abetted by canny publishing strategies) explains, for example, the huge success of Isabel Allende *outside* Latin America, a phenomenon akin to the reception of Jerry Lewis in France. Applied retrospectively, magic realism may be used to enhance past texts: witness the way in which, in many reviews written in this country, magic realism rubs off on Borges, recycled as a "precursor" of sorts, the scope of his work considerably diminished. More alarmingly, magic realism serves to banish many Latin American writers to the wasteland of the "different-but-not-in-the-way-we-expect-you-to-be-different" or, even worse, to the ever-expanding purgatory of the forever untranslatable. I particularly remember a book review of a novel by Adolfo Bioy Casares, one of Argentina's most subtle, ironic and inventive writers. The review, negative in a half-hearted sort of way, concluded that Bioy, who occasionally collaborated with Borges, was not a very good disciple of the master. Furthermore, it also concluded that, although dealing with the fantastic, Bioy Casares was really not a very good practitioner of magic realism.[8] In sum, the author was found wanting on both counts. He did not confirm the expected image, he was somewhere in-between, and his literary distinction, quite literally, could not be read.

That perception of Latin American literatures should primarily be confined to an essentialized magic realism is unfortunate; that, by extension, magic realism should be seen as the expression of a homogenized postcoloniality exclusively representative of "Latin America" is additionally regrettable.[9] Post-colonial studies should afford a way of teasing apart differences instead of erasing them, of unpacking preconceived notions instead of pre-packaging cultural commodities. Unfortunately, they seldom do.

I would like to mention very briefly the predicament of the Latin American writer in the complicated reception scene I have described, a scene ignoring the heterogeneous composition of Latin American literature, its distinctive, mediated relations to its diverse metropolitan centers, its transculturated Westernism. A well-meaning observer, Timothy Brennan, notes, for example, that among Third World writers there "has been a trend of cosmopolitan commentators on the Third World, who offer an *inside view* of formerly submerged peoples for target reading publics in Europe and North America in novels that comply with metropolitan literary tastes. Some of its better known authors have been from Latin America: for example, García Márquez, Vargas Llosa, Alejo Carpentier, Miguel Asturias [sic], and others." (63) This notion of a metropolitan "taste" waiting to be satisfied with "an *inside view* of formerly submerged peoples," a view so redolent of an imperialist anthropological approach, does not even contemplate (cannot even imagine) that the target reading publics of Latin American writers are, primarily, Latin American; that it is for the literary taste of those publics, and not to comply with metropolitan demands, that the Latin American writer primarily writes. Awareness of the conditions of production and reception of texts *in Latin America,* awareness of what Spivak calls "the staging of the language as the production of agency" (187), would show precisely how the text functions in relation to its many contexts and not as a token commodity.

Reduced often to the role of the native informant by First-World unawareness, the Latin American writer, in his or her dealings with that readership, has often no recourse but ironic assent and creative distortion. An early example of this ironical "writing back," this pandering to First-World preconceptions the better to explode them, may be found in Jules Supervielle, the Uruguayan-born French poet, who invented a *Créolopolis* for his French readers, an "Amérique d'hyperbole," as he describes it in a poem pointedly entitled "Le Goyavier authentique." Hyperbole, of course, reigns supreme in the fictions of García Márquez, who turns the imposture of magic realism into high art. The downside of such Latin American posturing, however, is that the writer may end up caught, for whatever reasons—fame and acclaimed authority being two important ones—in the very hyperbolic fiction he has contributed to create. Carlos Fuentes, for example, writing in the *New York Times* on the uprisings in Chiapas, and giving one more tired turn to the reality-imitates-fiction cliché, referred to the history of this repeatedly oppressed region as "something invented by the great-grandfather of Gabriel García Márquez" (January 9, 1994).

I am not proposing quick fixes, just calling attention to these operations in the hopes of generating a more thoughtful debate on Latin America from within the U.S. academy, a debate (and exchange) recognizing in Latin American cultural production not only multiple representational strategies and aesthetic practices but also a theoretical and critical agency that, until now, has gone unnoticed. This appears particularly urgent at a time when the growth of Spanish has reached uncalculated highs in this country, when it is no longer possible to dismiss it as a merely utilitarian language, although the temptation to do so may persist; particularly urgent when border-crossings and bilingualism are no longer "mere" sociological issues but have become, in many cases, aesthetic choices demanding competent readings; particularly urgent, finally, because Latin American literature, both as creative and institutional practice, and its relation to other literatures, are also being reformulated in specifically Latin American settings, and those "outside" reformulations ("outside" the US academy) should be an integral element of a truly transnational debate.[10] If the U.S. academy, and within it, not just Departments of Spanish and Portuguese but Departments of Literature at large, cannot relate to such reformulations and debates and cannot engage in exchange, if only to realize the importance of the local in any transnational dialogue, then we will have little more than incidences of cultural tourism.

Notes

1.   See Molloy, "Scene," and Sommer.
2.   Carlos Alonso persuasively reflects on the "narrative of futurity" that informs Latin America's secession from Spain and blots out the recuperation (or in some cases the invention) of an indigenous past: "[T]he indigenous populations received the same treatment in this ideological narrative of Creole hegemony as their erstwhile Spanish oppressors: they as well as the Spaniards were simply written out of it by being

subsumed under the mantle of the preterit, by being assigned to what from the perspective of the narrative of the future could only be described as the *non-place* of the past" (16). The fact that *mestizaje* was a most distinctive effect of Spanish colonialism in Latin America further complicates the notion of recuperating a "pure" indigenous past.

3.   I take this notion of alternate Westernness from George Yúdice's excellent essay, "We Are *Not* the World." He writes: "There is a well-founded reaction against Eurocentrism within multiculturalism that seeks to valorize other, non-Western cultural experiences. The transfer of this tendency to Latin American cultures, however, can produce serious distortions, not the least of which is to argue that Latin America is non-Western. . . . Latin American cultural experiences, I would like to argue, constitute *alternate* was of being Western. . . . [It] is not that Latin American cultures are Western in the same way as the U.S. or France but, rather, that they are inscribed in a transcultural relation to Western modernity just as much as, say, Eastern Europe (or for that matter multicultural U.S.)" (209–10).

4.   As Gayatri Chakravorty Spivak writes, "[A]ll the literature of the Third World gets translated into a sort of with-it translatese, so that the literature by a woman in Palestine begins to resemble, in the feel of its prose, something by a man in Taiwan" (180).

5.   None of these names appear, for example, in the "Postcolonial theory" bibliographical section of Susan Bassnett's *Comparative Literature*. As a matter of fact, there are only three entries related to Latin America in that bibliography: Carlos Fuentes (who can hardly be claimed as a theoretician), a rather old anthology of Chicano fiction (Sommers-Ybarra Fausto 1979), and a more recent collection of essays in Chicano cultural studies (Calderón-Saldívar 1990). The pertinence of the last two to Latin America is, at best, indirect. The inclusion of Fuentes as a Latin American postcolonial thinker is one more case of what Yúdice calls "a politics of reception of so-called Third World figures that gives priority to high profile positions and gestures and neglects the contradictions of those figures in their national settings" (204).

6.   A position murkily echoed by Miguel Angel Asturias, in an interview after receiving the Nobel Prize, in which magic realism is strangely equated with social justice (See Morris).

7.   To give but one example: Susan Bassnett, when speaking of Nicolás Guillén's book, *Motivos de son,* concludes that these are "'sound' poems"—misinterpreting the word *son* which refers to a highly sophisticated musical composition and not to mere sound. Carrying the primitive sound motif even further, she adds that in Alejo Carpentier's *The Lost Steps,* the protagonist is "led to the primeval forests of his origins ostensibly by the search for a primitive instrument" (84). The observation is worthy of Cassou's demand for forests and native pampas from Rubén Darío. For an acute analysis of Cuban *son* as a transculturated form, see Pérez Firmat, 67–79.

8.   This exemplary exercise in non-recognition, doubled by testy efforts to classify Bioy Casares no matter what, brings to mind a wonderful passage in Borges: "[E]n 1403

[una sirena] pasó por una brecha en un dique, y habitó en Haarlem hasta el día de su muerte. Nadie la comprendía, pero le enseñaron a hilar . . . Un cronista del siglo XVI razonó que no era un pescado porque sabía hilar, y que no era una mujer porque podía vivir en el agua. In 1403, [a mermaid] slipped through an opening in a dam and lived in Haarlem till the day she died. No one understood her but they taught her how to spin . . . A sixteenth-century chronicler reasoned that she was not a fish because she knew how to spin and that she was not a woman because she could live in the water" (*Obras* 228).

9. To quote Spivak again: "[T]he interesting literary text might be precisely the text where you do not learn what the majority view of majority cultural representation or self-representation of a nation state might be" ("Politics" 187). The apparent lack of interest in "non-representative" Latin American texts in this country is reflected in its particularly problematic translation politics.

10. "Departments of Spanish may flourish, but not because of the attraction of Latin American literature courses," contends William Moebius (253). While this may or may not be true, the mere possibility that cultural reasons and not base pragmatism might explain the success of Spanish departments seems to worry the author. Interestingly, in quoting the MLA statistics for English and foreign language majors in the year 1993–1994, Moebius only reports statistics for French, German, and English.

Works Cited

Ahmad, Aijaz. "'Third World Literature' and the Nationalist Ideology," *Journal of Arts and Ideas* 17–18 (1989): 117–36.

Alonso, Carlos. *The Burden of Modernity. The Rhetoric of Cultural Discourse in Spanish America.* Oxford and New York: Oxford University Press, 1998.

Bassnett, Susan. *Comparative Literature. A Critical Introduction.* Oxford: Blackwell, 1993.

Borges, Jorge Luis. *Discusión.* Buenos Aires: Emecé, 1964.

———. *Obras completas.* Buenos Aires: Emecé, 1974.

———. *Labyrinths. Selected Stories and Other Writings.* Donald A. Yates and James E. Irby, eds. New York: New Directions, 1962.

Brennan, Timothy. "The National Longing for Form," in Homi K. Bhabha, ed. *Nation and Narration.* London and New York: Routledge, 1990: 44–70.

Fabian, Johannes. *Time and the Other: How Anthropology Makes Its Object.* New York: Columbia University Press, 1983.

Fuentes, Carlos. "The News," *New York Times.* January 9, 1994.

García Canclini, Néstor. *Hybrid Cultures: Strategies for Entering and Leaving Modernity.* Trans. Christopher L. Chiappari and Silvia L. López. Foreword by Renato Rosaldo. Minneapolis and London: University of Minnesota Press, 1995.

Klor de Alva, Jorge. "Colonialism and Postcolonialism as (Latin)-American Mirage." *Colonial Latin American Review* I:1–2 (1992): 3–23.

Millington, Mark. "On Location: The Question of Reading Crossculturally," *Siglo XX/20th Century Critique and Cultural Discourse* 13: 1–2 (1995): 13–39.

Moebius, William. "Lines in the Sand: Comparative Literature and the National Literature Departments," *Comparative Literature* 49: 3 (1997): 243–58.

Molloy, Sylvia. *La diffusion de la littérature hispano-américaine en France au XXe siècle.* Paris: Presses Universitaires de France, 1972.

———. "The Scene of Reading," *At Face Value: Autobiographical Writing in Spanish America.* Cambridge and New York: Cambridge University Press, 1991: 13–76.

Morris, Ira. "Interview with Miguel Angel Asturias," *Monthly Review,* March (1968): 50–56.

Pérez Firmat, Gustavo. *The Cuban Condition: Translation and Identity in Modern Cuban Literature.* Cambridge and New York: Cambridge University Press, 1989.

Sommer, Doris. "Plagiarized Authenticity: Sarmiento's Cooper and Others," *Foundational Fictions: The National Romances of Latin America.* Berkeley-Los Angeles-Oxford: University of California Press, 1991: 52–82.

Spivak, Gayatri Chakravorty. "The Politics of Translation," in Michèle Barrett and Anne Phillips, eds. *Destabilizing Theory: Contemporary Feminist Debates.* Cambridge: Polity Press, 1992: 177–200.

Supervielle, Jules. *Poèmes.* Paris: Eugène Figuière, 1919.

Yúdice, George. "We Are *Not* the World," *Social Text* 31–32 (1992): 201–16.

Mules and Snakes:
On the Neo-Baroque
Principle of De-Localization

Alberto Moreiras

Baroque Practice

The baroque *theoria* or procession, not only attends to the passion of the god. Fundamentally, as the *saetas* show, it is also an adventure, an exposure to the open. The baroque *paso,* as a passion in the open, is the site of an event. Something happens (*pathos*) that establishes a relationless relationship with the outside. The baroque pathos, if St. Teresa of Avila or St. John of the Cross can offer a possible model, is the trace of an undefined pilgrimage against the background of a lit house or of a dream of community. The protagonist of Peter Handke's *On a Dark Night I Left My Silent House,* a novel written after a long stay in Castile and in deep reference to St. John's experience, has two dreams: "In one of them, adjacent to the small cellar in his house were suites of underground rooms, one grand hall leading to the next, all sumptuously decorated, festively lit, yet all of them empty, as if in expectation, awaiting a splendid, perhaps also terrible event, and not just recently, but since time immemorial" (40). In the second dream, "the hedge barriers to the neighboring properties were suddenly gone, removed by force or simply fallen away, and people could see into each other's gardens and onto each other's terraces, and not merely onto them, but also into every corner of their houses, now suddenly laid bare, and likewise one neighbor could see the other, which in the first moments caused immense mutual embarrassment and shame, but then gradually gave way to a kind of relief, almost pleasure" (40–41). On the basis of that second dream, we must perhaps reinterpret Vélez de Guevara's "devil on two sticks" as a cipher of the longing for a transparent community, a baroque utopia, whose sinister reverse is the anticipation of the society of control as prefigured in sixteenth-century Spain. But the first dream inverts utopia and gives us its key: the community is empty, it is only the potential site of the drive towards an event that does not happen. The baroque pilgrim—the pilgrims, in Handke's novel—"outside the community, tied to no community" (29), start their banishment in the awareness that it has always already happened. "What they shared, however, was their condition, or their consciousness: of an adventure, dangerous in some unspecified way, one in which a great deal, indeed, everything, was at stake, an adventure, furthermore, on the verge of the forbidden, the illegal, even of a criminal offense. Against the law? Against the way of the world? And none of them could have said where this shared consciousness came from. In any case, what they were doing, or especially would be doing in the future, could bring punishment down on their heads, a punishment without mercy. But turning back now was out of the question for them. And accordingly, in spite of everything, they really experienced their journey as something new and unprecedented" (72–73).

The step of the pilgrim, "ship-wrecked, and love-sick though spurned," in Luis de Góngora's famous description, is de-localizing. Its relation with any possible community is de-localizing. Hence the necessity, also baroque, of its containment. Or it is perhaps containment itself that forces the pilgrim to be a pilgrim—hence the danger. Everything can bring on punishment, but without risking punishment, there is no adventure. If localization seeks in every case tendentially the constitution of a community, and if all community seeks communion—a communion regarding the localizing parameters—then the step or the work of de-localization is against communion: it moves towards the invention of a countercommunitarian or de-communitarian space, towards a relationless relation. As a relationless relation, the baroque *paso* is also a love relation: "Write nothing but love stories from now on! Love and adventure stories, nothing else!—Someone went away. The house became silent. But something was still missing: I hadn't heard a certain door close" (186).

How can we think de-communication politically? How does one de-communicate or excommunicate politically? Through exodus, or affirmative renunciation. There is perhaps a way in which the renunciation or abandonment of positions, rather than antipolitical, unconceals the disciplining conditions of the political and can thus claim a repoliticization. In the name of what? One can only think of an absolutely precarious response to that question: in the name of a principle of affective freedom, of a liberation of affect, in the name of biopolitical de-disciplining, in the name of a refusal of what is, what will be, what was, because temporality itself has come to be experienced as lack, as debt: sad passions.[1] A sad passion is, for Spinoza, the passion that cooperates in its own enslavement—on the basis of a perverse compensation for an absence.[2] If our academic practice is or can be thought as a sad passion, then our academic practice is a sinister university passion for self-discipline and self-domination: an antipolitical passion. In that case, the only properly political thing regarding our academic practice is renunciation and exodus. Where to? Is there an exteriority to university discourse? If our academic practice is nothing but a localizing and disciplining apparatus of capture, can renunciation and exodus determine a non-capturable exteriority? Can the Neobaroque be one of its names?

It would not be just any name. For some decades the Hispanic Baroque has been theorized, on both its Spanish and its Latin American sides, as a cultural principle of modernity, of a certain modernity in our socio-political traditions. Rehearsing the history of that critique, John Beverley extracts from the deep imbrication of the Baroque with the Spanish modality of imperial reason the conclusion that the Baroque may be a sort of non-erasable Latin American cultural unconscious, in its many manifestations as "American baroque, mestizo baroque, creole baroque, new-world baroque, 'real-marvelous' baroque, neobaroque, postmodern baroque" (9). The Baroque is for Beverley the trace of a curious structure in double register: if on one side, it responds to its determination as the cultural form of Spanish imperial domination, both in the colonies and in the metropolitan space, on the other side, it generates a lettered excess or supplement that moves towards the dissemination of sense and makes it work towards a radical immanentization of experience: "the paradox of baroque art is that it is an aristocratic-absolutist technique of power and at the same time an awareness of the limitations of that power" (24). For Beverley, following Louis Althusser, the ideological state-apparatuses are the sites of a conflict, and contradictory as such. To think on the Baroque is to think about literature and the state in early Modernity. The very contradiction at the heart of baroque practice turns the baroque field into a field of immanence, that is, into the possibility of a theoretical practice that will not be reducible, to use Alain Badiou's terms, either to an archi-aesthetics or to an archi-politics.[3] The Baroque announces rather the metapolitical conditions of a practice of truth. As a truth procedure, the Baroque is the site of a subject-constituting struggle. The baroque subject, if it truly dictates the Hispanic appropriation to/of modernity, marks both its self-inscribing possibilities and its possibilities for de-inscription or ex-surrection.

But the ex-surrected subject is a subject in exodus and a subject in self-dissolution: a subject in crisis of faith, the baroque subject-in-withdrawal. Already in Góngora, the pilgrim of *Soledades,* like Handke's pilgrim, is a subject in withdrawal: "he is a hero . . . whose action consists of becoming different than he is" (Beverley 46–47). The baroque field of immanence constitutes a subject whose peculiar form of presence is its withdrawal, "confused solitude." "That is why the ruin comes to symbolize *Soledades* itself" (54). And thus, concludes Beverley,

> At the end of *Soledades* we have not yet reached the direct description of the court or the empire. Both will become the tragic fatherland of the pilgrim 'the following day.' The historical experience of usurpation and disaster tacitly conditions the form of *Soledades.* In baroque narrative legitimacy necessarily implies an immersion in the bucolic that will serve the Prince as an apprenticeship in the rules of prudence and virtue. In order to govern his own people well, he must know the capacity for freedom of the latter, the extension and kind of the people's suffering, the vital and communitarian alternatives that survive in the country. The geometric and social labyrinth of the city hides all of that from him, so he must abandon it, together with his identity and his class, in order to become 'one of them' . . . [I]n Góngora the pastoral golden age is no longer a landscape outside of history, that is, an impossible dream of totality and naturalness, but rather an intra-historical landscape, a painting that must be read in the court's walls, where its social and moral redemptive value will need to be deciphered. Soledad/edad de sol: the deluge that will abolish present disorder and prepare the return to the golden age is the poem itself, by erasing the normal terms of experience and by sending us back to our origins, by atomizing and reforming. (69)

This is one of the two faces of the Baroque: the excessive face, the back face or the immanent antagonism of the Baroque against the containment that situates it as an imperial instrument for state affirmation. From this face, in Góngora, for instance,

> the work that remains is the creation of a fragmentary sense of the hispanic, delinked from an ideology of exploitation and repression . . . perhaps for this reason Latin American writing carries Góngora's strong influence, since it shares with *Soledades* the function of seeking a possible culture and society departing from the mutilation that colonialism and imperialism have inflicted upon their subjects. For Góngora and the Spain of his time, such an appeal was unfruitful; the poet will withdraw to the night of exile and the sad wisdom of disappointment. But the appeal will have to be repeated, since the disappearance of the pilgrim at the end of the work will reveal that we ourselves occupy the stage of the present. (75)

What would the conditions of appropriation be of this baroque practice of the imperial subject in withdrawal for the present? Hispanism, like any other epistemic apparatus, is a site of expropriation. If Hispanism seeks, in every case, something like an appropriation of the Hispanic object, the distance between the object and the appropriative intention remains irreducible. Expropriation happens on both sides: the gaze does not fully capture the object and the object does not exhaustively resist its partial appropriation. We can call that distance *constitutive fissure*. The fissure between theoretical discourse and the field of reflection is constitutive. There are moments in the history of knowledge when the fissure remains in the background and is practically forgotten or disavowed. But there are moments when not just the fissure but its very denegation come to be thematized as proper objects of reflection. It is true that thematizing the fissure and thematizing the denegation of the fissure are different things—one can do the former without the latter, although not the latter without the former. But one can do both at the same time, and that would be the properly baroque fold in academic practice. We are in one of those moments. They are always paradoxical times because they are times of epistemic deconstitution, when knowledge comes to understand itself through its very default or withdrawal, that is, as a relation to non-knowledge. Knowledge understands itself then in its nakedly expropriatory relation—it understands itself as an expropriating relation. This has some inconveniences, but it also has advantages.

The conditions of possibility of Hispanist university discourse have shifted over the last two decades. Only a few years ago, Hispanism was still fairly stabilized at the crossing between our-Americanist drives—we can give José Martí's expression its full appropriative force—or, in the case of Spain, drives that were exceptionalist regarding the history of Europe, and the centripetal forces of scientific universalism. The Baroque has been overwhelmingly understood that way: as a field of identitarian expression concerning the peculiar Hispanic experience of modernity. Our academic practice could still understand itself as the systematic application of identity discourse at the crossing of specific histories and general epistemologies, or of general histories and specific epistemologies. Poststructuralism and postcolonial studies have harshly attacked, if in different ways, the very concept of a general epistemology. There is a dimension of that critique which is not always duly acknowledged: the shadow of the reflexive subject has always fallen upon the object of reflection. Just like Nietzsche told us that the disappearance of the "true" world would end up destroying the very possibility of thinking appearance, the failure of epistemic certainty at the hands of poststructuralist and postcolonialist critique also buries the very possibility of thinking the specificity of the specific.[4] So postcolonialist critique cannot open the way to a re-appropriation of the object: the destruction of a general critical subject implies the dissolution of the specific critical object. We were able to recognize the constitutive fissure between theoretical discourse and field of reflection, but we were unable to sustain that first intuition and we moved towards a new denegation: we buried our head in the illusory sand of a new object of re-appropriation. Epistemic deconstitution is erased as such in the contemporary (postcolonialist) repetition of the essentially appropriative—and thus essentially colonizing and colonialist—gesture of modern university discourse.

In its geopolitical or regionalist dimension, we can date that gesture from its American inception in the first baroque, *criollo* attempts to undo European imperial sovereignty in the Americas. Beverley notes that this practice followed a complicated process of colonial reaffirmation that started with the mystifying spread of imperial Gongorism. If Gongorism, considered a heterodox practice in Spain, becomes a sort of official aesthetic discourse in the Colony, this is because it has come to be recaptured by the state apparatus and turned into a "a kind of magical accumulation theory that masks the real 'primitive accumulation of capital' . . . harmonizing it in appearance with the religious, aristocratic, and metropolitan presuppositions of Spanish imperial ideology: a specular discourse that allows the colonizer the luxury of thinking that his situation of privilege and power is a natural and providential phenomenon, that he inhabits a social space which is in principle harmonious and utopian, where all rebelliousness and all dissidence would be automatically disqualified as the product of forces of evil that threaten to destroy that order" (92). *Criollo,* or proto-nationalist, Baroque consists for the most part of the displacement and reappropriation of the very same apparatus of capture by the *criollo* elites. Its precise beginning can be found in the abandonment of the epic forms in poetry, always associated with military conquest or state foundation, and their substitution with forms of "minor" poetry. For Beverley, these minor forms, "occasional sonnets, *romances, villancicos, loas,* satiric *letrillas*" (104), which were assiduously cultivated by Gongorism, offered the possibility of a new literature where practices of everyday life could be represented. The first edition of Juan de Espinosa Medrano's *Apologético* (1662), with its explicit purpose of "founding the ideological (a nascent creole consciousness) upon the aesthetic," marks "the epistemological birth of the lettered city" in Latin America (115).

From those modern beginnings, regional thinking constitutes itself in the Latin America lettered city in three ideological clusters that might turn out to be one and the same: let us call them identity, mimesis, and difference. We can understand all of them to be modalities of self-projection of colonial Gongorism as state apparatus. On the first cluster, identity, the regionalist gesture has been the attempt to transform cultural-historical discourse, that is, the archive, into a machine for the production and containment of identity: we can be more precise, at some cost, and refer to this first moment as "construction of the nation." But identity, in order to become praxis, must undergo a positivization, an embodiment. The embodiment of identity is also the limit of identity and the moment in which identity turns into appropriative mimesis. Mimetic appropriation is always already a critique of the identitarian theft, a critique of translation as always necessarily translation into the dominant, and at the same time, and crucially, a critique of critique: mimetic appropriation is also a restoration of identitarian theft and a celebration of translation. We can call this second moment cultural anti-imperialism if we do not forget that anti-imperialism lives off what it is against, in the same way in which colonial Gongorism was made possible by its previous heterodoxy: state reason always moves through the incorporation of its own critique. A third moment then ensues, the moment in which identity reasserts its right against mimetic appropriation: the moment of difference. We no longer need identitarian representations but rather differential representations. Identity is now difference, and it is no longer major and national, but minor and fragmented: translation is self-translation, and subjectivity is now transcultural and hybrid. Its stasis, the point of closure of this ideological formation, is now the essence without essence of the local in resistance, that is, the merely representational against other representations, where representation represents nothing but the representational struggle itself, brings nothing new to presence, only re-presents (itself) against. Let us call this moment: globalization, or the moment of cultural studies.

Can we retain the notion that these three gestures are in fact not sequential from a historical or chronological perspective, although that too, but rather co-incidental and co-temporal? No identity without mimesis and difference; no mimesis without identity and difference, and so forth. These are the three gestures of the regionalist intellectual—or rather, the three gestures of the regionalist ideologue, since thinking is somewhere else, always in a fourth gesture which is, as such, much more difficult to identify, since it remains beyond identity, and which would constitute, precisely, what one could call the disaster of the first three, their dis/aster, that is, their dis-orientation, their de-teleologization, their ruin. Thinking would be on the side of the Baroque pilgrim, of his (her) exposure to the open. Thinking is on the side of the always ongoing epistemic deconstitution that does not cease being active for being disavowed. It is the site of the disaster of the three constitutive gestures of modern university discourse in its regionalist dimension. But if disaster is an interval of being, and if crisis is what transforms disaster into possibility, into the possibility of a passage, a passage towards an alternative projection of historical time, towards a new temporality, then disaster is the dawn of a fourth gesture. The constitutive fissure between theoretical discourse and field of reflection already always keeps in reserve the possibility of the fourth gesture, which allows for the turning of a certain abandonment, of a certain banishment, into the de-localizing *paso* towards joyful passions. This is the always implicit *paso* in the constitution of the Baroque: not just a form of power, but also the awareness of the finitude of power. A specific tradition in contemporary Latin American literary thinking has called that *paso* Neobaroque. The recuperation of the Neobaroque form of experience, itself already a recuperation of the Baroque, is a necessity for contemporary theoretical practice, not in the name of a re-appropriation of tradition, but rather in the name of de-appropriation, in the name of an affirmative exodus out of university discourse as a sad passion of self-enslavement. The Neobaroque is one of the forms in which reflection asserts itself anti-ideologically, as a principle of de-regionalization. Thinking is, for the Neobaroque *paso* or passage, the interruption of the principle of regionalization, a pilgrimage towards the outside.

But Beverley resists what he calls "literatura neobarroca," and wonders whether it is itself something other than the superstructural expression of a declining and desperate Latin American petty bourgeoisie attempting to hold on to some kind of residual symbolic power. No doubt Neobaroque literature or criticism can be forms of more or less reactionary privilege and cultural exclusivity, can effectively connive with contemporary forms of imperial control, can serve the establishment of conditions of hegemonic domination in the direct or indirect, intentional or counter-intentional repression of subaltern expressive forms. No doubt this is the main ideological interest in so much of current Latin Americanist pro-Baroque or pro-Neobaroque critique—there where Latin Americanism is still understood, or lived, as a sad passion.

Polemizing against his antagonist Roberto González Echevarría, Beverley states that Espinosa Medrano's historical accomplishment, his inaugural contribution to the foundation of the Latin American lettered city, was not just an act of liberation. Chiasmus (retruécano), to which González Echevarría assigns in Celestina's Brood an emblematic character as the essential trope of baroque practice, will find in Beverley a complex, even dangerous and destructive condition of possibility. For González Echevarría, "the retruécano is an equivalency in the process of displaying itself both in its inherent repetition and difference, in its reiteration and desired simultaneity. The chiasmus can be read in either direction, both ways meeting somewhere in a virtual center where appearances are reversed . . . American history, American writing, and therefore the reading of American writing, must allow for the manifestation of such inversions, must practice such inversions; chiasmus is the system of American history" (181). Espinosa Medrano's work brings to its epochal accomplishment, for González Echevarría, the Baroque chiasmus by placing Gongorism in America and thus giving it its full paradoxical truth:

> The Baroque has a heightened consciousness of the model's prestige and power; hence baroque poetic practice consists in an ambiguous homage to the model, since its monumental presence is still nothing but the setting for the new. The baroque text is a kind of filigree, a jewel in which the setting is highlighted instead of the precious stone. The strange in the Baroque is not the unknown, but the known displaced and blown out of proportion. . . . The Baroque does not suffer from an anxiety of influence so much as from an anxiety of confluence and affluence, an excess in which the new is merely one more oddity. The Baroque consists of an accepted and assumed secondariness and belatedness, which are capable of absorbing the geographic and temporal displacements of the Antartic poet and can even flaunt it like an emblem. (164)

By uniting *criollo* self-awareness and a vindication of Gongorism, Espinosa Medrano founds the Latin American lettered city in chiasmus itself: "the creole lives in a world of art in which he is the artifact par excellence. That is his oddity. He is a trope incarnate" (16). This is the beginning of Latin American poetic language, which González Echevarría presents as the paradoxical accomplishment of a particularist universality, that is, as the first, hence inaugural, American coincidence of being and thinking, or writing, and thus as the establishment of a tradition which will become the very tradition of American hemispheric modernity. But this defense of Americanness as secondary originality and thus properly baroque originality against metropolitan precedence carries within a repressed or disavowed chiasmus—this is the chiasmus that Beverley turns against González Echevarría. If it is true that the becoming-official of Gongorism in America succeeds in incorporating heterodoxy into American life as the genuine mark of an inchoate our-Americanism against the imperial position, it is also true that such an our-Americanism includes, and is even based upon, a founding repression where what is excluded is the very possibility of an indigenous counter-hegemony, which is always already outside the game of models and copies. In the creation of the American lettered city, "the opposition civilization/barbarism has shifted from a racial differentiation (European/indigenous) to a cultural one (cultured/ignorant) which is essentially equivalent to the one that sets Góngora against his opponents in *Apologético*" (Beverley 125). As a consequence, however, "the idealization of literary practice . . . sets up a (precarious) creole or mestizo-creole identity not just in the face of the anterior-ity/authority of European or peninsular culture, a stratagem that will move to-wards a refunctionalization of the literary canon . . . as a register of possibilities for that identity. It also establishes that identity in a differential relationship . . . with a subaltern social subject: subaltern precisely given its lack of access to or presumed incapacity for cultured literature, which can, however, adequately 'represent' or 'speak for' that subject" (Beverley 126–27).

Sad passions appear in González Echevarría through that originary denega-tion that enthrones the Baroque as the condition of possibility of Americanness without noting that the notion of everything that is American is then constituted through its very definition as a mechanism of contention and enslavement of what remains beyond the definition (and not just indigenous discourse). Litera-ture, the site of baroque practice, incorporates in González Echevarría's version of it a dominant character as an ideological state apparatus, understanding state in a wide sense as the set of discursive practices conforming the social. In other words, the Baroque, in González Echevarría's version of it, cannot be but colo-nial Baroque. It cannot go beyond its status as regional ideology at the service of the constitution of the local as a differential/mimetic/identitarian apparatus of social capture. This limit of conceptualization is both a limit and the very condition of possibility of González Echevarría's general project of reflection, which consists of positing the Baroque as a mark of continental identity from its metonymic installation in the so-called Boom of the Latin American novel. "Why the Baroque? From outside the cultures of the Spanish-speaking world it is difficult to fathom why a movement that is so apparently European should be of any concern to modern Spanish-American writers. . . . And yet a host of [them] have made of the Baroque a banner for their new art, calling it the Neo-Baroque" (195–96). González Echevarría is a critic of the Boom, which also means: his critique is necessarily contained within the discursive parameters as-signed to and by the Boom. The Boom explains him, as much as he explains the Boom, because his critical practice would seem to seek the determination of the Boom as a literary apparatus at the service of a differential/identitarian construc-tion where what is truly at stake is the ancestral question of Latin American belonging. For whom is or must Latin America be? For those who make Latin American identity. Who makes it? Whoever has hegemony. The problem is not the answer, in a strong sense tautological and thus unavoidable, but the ques-tion itself. But the question is not simply González Echevarría's: the question of Latin American belonging, of Latin American appropriation, is the very question of Hispanist or Latin Americanist constitution as an apparatus of regional appro-priation. One could only proceed, as Handke suggests, "against the law, against the way of the world" by turning Hispanism around and understanding how appropriation is always simultaneously expropriation and theft, as it is always the case and the general strategy for any epistemic apparatus. One could then seek the critical constitution of an ex-surrected subject of non-knowledge, a subject in withdrawal, in exodus, in crisis of faith and of fidelity, in epistemic deconstitution: a neobaroque subject, against the containment of the Neobaroque as a practice of identitarian belonging. Nothing further, perhaps, from González Echevarría's mind, voluntarily contained in a practice of belonging radicalized into a practice of self-belonging, and thus devoted to a policing and disciplining of borders whose excess coincides with one of the faces, but only one, of the baroque subject itself: "I, the critic, am the border. Nothing outside myself has a valid existence. Nothing I do not approve of is Latin Americanism."

What about Beverley? How does he solve the problem he detects in González Echevarría? Their two positions have largely determined, within North American Hispanism at least, the parameters of critical practice for over a decade. It is not that they have invented their respective positions: rather, the polemic between them sets the historical limit in our professional errancy for the long decade of the 1990s, that is, during the period between the exhaustion of the Boom of the novel and the end of the group project of the Latin American Subaltern Studies group. This is also the moment prefigured by the publication of Rigoberta Menchú's testimonio. In order further to define Beverley's position, one would have to refer to the totality of *Against Literature* and later texts, but I will limit myself to the last chapter of the book I have been quoting from, *Una modernidad obsoleta. Estudios sobre el barroco* (1997). This book could be understood in its totality as a response to González Echevarría's *Celestina's Brood*. Its last chapter reproduces, with significant changes, an essay that was originally read in 1991 and published in 1993: "Post-literatura: Subjeto subalterno e impasse de las humanidades."

In reference to texts on the *tupamarista* and *katarista* rebellions of the late eighteenth century, Beverley points out a forceful critical disjunction: "if the historian chooses literature as a representative instance of rebellion (in the sense of both mimetic and political representativeness), he or she sees an essentially creole-reformist movement, conceived within the very same legal and humanist codes imposed by colonization; if the historian chooses the non-literary practices of rebellion he or she sees a revolution from below, above all of the indigenous popular masses, with conjunctural mestizo and creole allies, willing to reestablish a millenarian and utopian Inca state, or even to reestablish pre-Incaic forms" (145). The force of that disjunction goes, of course, well beyond suggesting an alternative between literary historiography and historiography of social movements. Chiasmus acts here in another way, through the clear view that all textualism, whether literary-critical or properly historiographic, is always already situated within the total interpretation of history as the history of the dominant classes. Prose, and especially colonial prose, is in this view always already, as Ranajit Guha put it, prose of counterinsurgency. All literature is then also seemingly prose of counterinsurgency, in a context in which the implications are not merely political: if the critical apparatus is an apparatus for the interpretation of the prose of counterinsurgency as prose *tout court,* then the critical apparatus is not only counterinsurgent itself, but must abandon all pretensions of aspiring to historical truth. Thus, a critical epistemology based directly or indirectly on textualist or literary resources automatically becomes a bogus epistemology: mere ideology. "From this perspective, to look at texts written by leaders of the rebellion for a creole reader as representatives of the rebellion not just darkens the fact of an indigenous national-popular, non-liter-ary (or not entirely based on cultured literature) production; it is also an act of appropriation that excludes the indigenous subject as a subject conscious of his or her own history and incorporates it as a contingent element in another history (a history of the nation, of emancipation, of Peruvian or Latin American litera-ture) with another subject (creole, Spanish-speaking, lettered)" (147). A for-tiori, if this is the case for texts written by indigenous leaders of an indigenous rebellion, it is even more the case for non-rebel texts, that is, for the majority of texts that make up the Latin American literary archive. The Latin American historical archive appears then as the archive, not of a revelation, but of a con-cealment of experience regarding which the ideological apparatus of university discourse can only appear as collaborationist. What is there to do, then, in order to restitute revelation, not concealment, to the archive? How can we imagine a critical practice that may at least give us, to use words that Maurice Blanchot thought for another context, "the revelation of what revelation destroys" (47)?

Beverley's insistence on subaltern representation leads him to wonder whether literature is hopelessly trapped in processes of social inequality that constitute it as much as it helps constitutes them. His insistence on developing a non-literary concept of the literary represents what is perhaps the fundamental position of what one could consider the Latin Americanist humanities left in the last few years. At the end of his book on the Baroque he asks: "Is it possible to transgress the Kantian distinction between aesthetic and teleological judgment? Does literature depend on the existence of social inequality? " (154). One may wonder if the questions themselves are also baroque or if they are thoroughly exterior to their field of inquiry. Beverley presents us with an apparently apo-retic situation that he calls "the impasse of the humanities," where all possible

its fetid juice or "alpechín," what the olive cries or exudes. But *murga* is also the procession or "company of bad musicians that, upon Christmas or Easter, on birthdays, etc., knock on the door of wealthy households with the hope of receiving some presents" (*Diccionario de la Real Academia*). Let us imagine a *murga* without hope, a *murga* that either arrives or fails to arrive, a murga in imminence, a bad *murga* of improper festivities, invisible, inaudible, but one which, precisely in view of its inadequacies, becomes the transferential horizon, the relationless relation, the abyssal support of the Lezamian "insular night" or of Sarduy's unnameable feast. That *murga* is the trace of the Baroque that Perlongher defines in the following way in the poem titled "La murga, los polacos":

> It is a procession, it marches in the Warsaw night, it makes miracles with the masks, it confuses the Polish public. The Krakow students look at it stunned: They have never seen anything similar in their books. It is not Carnival, it is not a Saturday, it is not a procession, they are not marching, nobody sees. There is no fog, it is a procession, it is streamers, it is confetti, the cold ether like snow in a street in a city in a Poland that is not, that is not. Which is not to say it has not been, or even that it no longer is, or even that it is not being in this instant, Warsaw with its processions, its disguises, its harlequins, and its Caroline bears, its famous peace—we talk about the same, the one that rules leaning on the Vistula, the troubled river where the procession falls, with its whistles, its colors, its meaty cha-cha-chas, producing in the roiling waters a noise like a splashing that nobody pays attention to, since there is no procession, and even if there were one, it would not be in Warsaw, and that every Pollack knows. (23)

If we imagine an intellectual practice based upon the relationless relation with that *murga* that does not quite exist but that, through its not existing, exists in its omission and its void, we will have to imagine that such an intellectual practice would go beyond the enjoyment of words towards the site where words break off their relation with enjoyment and open to a surplus of enjoyment, to a *plus de jouissance* which is always other than enjoyment, in the same way capital is more than money. Do we have ears for such a *murga* in our academic practice? Or is our academic delight nothing but what is meant in the third meaning of *murga,* as in *dar la murga,* that is, "to bother with words or actions that produce tedium through their excess or impertinence"? Against the tedious *murga* the neobaroque *murga,* the disquieting one of the unheard-of leap into the waters of Perlongher's river, of which Peter Robb says or could have said that, in order to read it, "you need a feel for the unsaid, for the missing file, the cancelled entry, the tacit conclusions, the gap, the silence, the business done with a nod and a wink" (np). Robb is talking about the paradigmatic baroque painter, Caravaggio, whose life can only be reconstructed through unworked fragments—"they're lies to the police, reticence in court, extorted confessions, forced denunciations, revengeful memoirs, self-justifying hindsight, unquestioned hearsay, diplomatic urbanities, theocratic diktat, reported gossip, threat and propaganda, angry outbursts—hardly a work untainted by fear, ignorance, malice or self-interest" (np). On seeking the most difficult, in the Lezamian way, one could not hope for a better definition of the baroque archive.

The baroque archive is the non-localization of the theoretical *murga,* of the unnameable, disconcerting and confusing procession of ambiguous ontological status in Perlongher's poem. It is the opposite of the ontopological localization of thinking, its dirty atopics, its suspicion—hardly a word untainted by fear, ignorance, malice, or self-interest. Hardly a word without a body, but where body as well as word sustain their glory in the refusal of localization, of ontopologization, of entrapment and capture. Hardly an untainted word, but where the taint is the name of the very possibility of thought. In "Rapsodia para el mulo" Lezama will refer to that powerful stain in the eye of the mule as *paso:* "Step is the step of the mule in the abyss" (I.165). Lezama writes: "Sitting on the eye of the mule, vitreous, blind, the abyss slowly goes over its invisible. In the sitting abyss, step by step, one can only hear the questions that the mule lets fall over the stone in the fire" (I.165). The mule is the theoretical animal in Lezama, the cipher of neobaroque practice. The mule goes through "the obscure, progressive and fugitive" (I. 163) as it falls in the contemplative abyss, in love with the "four signs," earth and sky, mortals and gods, the signs visible from the temple, from the roof of the temple, from the *contemplatio* or *theoria* that gives us those four signs if only we are willing to fall without wings, like Talos in the Greek myth, or the mule in the abyss, "the saved wings inexistent in the mule" (I. 164).[10] And Lezama warns against the tedious *murga* that projects its own sterility, its own nihilism, its own radical, desolate de-habitation into a darkness that is no longer "the obscure with its four signs" (I.165) of abyssal dwelling but rather the simple deprivation of light at the ontopological house of private resentment:

> This secure step of the mule in the abyss is usually confused with the painted gloves of the sterile. It is usually confused with the beginnings of the obscure negating head. It is usually confused by you, vitreous outcast, by you, hip with patent-leather-like ribbons. It seems to tell us I am not and I am not, but it also penetrates in the mansions where the homely spider no longer gives off light, and the portable lamp translates from one horror to another horror. It is usually confused by you, vitreous outcast, that it is a step the step of the mule in the abyss. (167)

Whoever confuses the mule's *paso* with nihilism and sterility, whoever fails to understand the mule's movement to an alternative region ("step is the step of the mule in the abyss") is, for Lezama, the one who suffers from deprivation of light. This bad *murga* that thinks one must always think from somewhere (hence, not from the abyss), that thought must always have a ground, must always have an identifiable location, that writing can only be autographic—one should not simply disagree with it. There is no disagreement with tedium. It is rather more urgent to ask what happens when those two minor intuitions against the mule's *paso* find no resistance and reach their radicalization: brutal stasis, locationalism, final ontopologization of thinking. Locationalism, from its beginnings as a defense against colonial or imperial expropriation, fails to the precise extent it succeeds. It turns expropriation into property, and turns property into the ultimate horizon of thinking—ontopology is what Karl Marx used to call the social form of money, the inverted projection of exchange value into the ideal foundation of the social. Locationalism, ontopological radicalization—which is the dominant form of ideological thinking today—marks the moment of absolute subsumption of intellectual labor into capital and is therefore absolutely functional to the neoliberal model, even to the extent that it presupposes itself against it.

In some splendid pages of the *Grundrisse,* Marx mentions greed as the fundamental affective tonality of the mode of social production ruled by capital. He discovers a religious element in what he terms greed or monetary mania, a curious historically-produced "en-thou-siasmos," since it is the result of a social change: money, "from its servile role, in which it appears as mere medium of circulation, it suddenly changes into the lord and god of the world of commodities. It represents the divine existence of commodities, while they represent its earthly form" (221). When that happens, when that new god is born in the mutation of the second into the third stage of money, Marx says, "monetary greed, or mania for wealth, necessarily brings with it the decline and fall of the ancient communities [*Gemeinwesen*]" (223). There is no option, Marx says, money becomes the community, *Gemeinwesen,* in the absolute substitution of the old community. As the translator adds in a footnote, *Gemeinwesen* means, beyond community, "common essence," "common system," and "common being." Money becomes being, ontological foundation, "and can tolerate none other standing above it" (223). There is no option: "Where money is not itself the community," once it appears in its third role or third stage, 'it must dissolve the community" (224). And this presupposes, Marx says, "the full development of exchange value, hence a corresponding organization of society," that is, capitalist society (223). "The decay of [the] community advances" (223) to the same extent that exchange value becomes constitutive of the ontological foundation of the social. When capital and wage labor come to full existence "money thereby directly and simultaneously becomes the *real community [Gemeinwesen]*, since it is the general substance of survival for all, and at the same time the social product of all" (225–26).

And greed is simply the affective correlate to the real community whose ontotheology is now constituted by money. Are money and the intellectual production of the regionalist intellectual, then, the same thing? Is money the same thing as identity, mimetic appropriation, and difference? Probably so. In their social function, money and cultural production have a *Gemeinwesen,* a community, a common essence, which is what Marx will call somewhere else in the *Grundrisse* "a vanishing mediation" (269). That is, in their social function, money and cultural production, cultural production and money, mediate a relation, and they do it in such a way that, in the mediation, their common essence vanishes in order to assume the form of the relation itself. An ontotheological equivalency between the regionalist intellectual's modality of university discourse and the social form of money is thus established.

In the *Grundrisse,* concretely in the pages of Notebook II where Marx analyzes the social system that corresponds to the mode of bourgeois social production, Marx is furious at those "socialists" who want to present socialism as "the realization of the ideals of *bourgeois* society articulated by the French revolution" (248). Marx says: "the proper reply to them is: that exchange value or, more precisely, the money system is in fact the system of equality and freedom, and that the disturbances which they encounter in the further development of the system are disturbances inherent in it, are merely the realization of *equality* and *freedom,* which prove to be inequality and unfreedom. It is just as pious as it is stupid to wish that exchange value would not develop into capital, nor labour which produces exchange value into wage labour" (249). The social mode of production ruled by capital, that is, the bourgeois mode of production, although ideally based on equality and freedom, is really based upon the exploitation of wage labor by capital. Proudhonian socialists—and one could add, all manners of social democrats, including their representatives in contemporary university discourse—are characterized by their "utopian inability to grasp the necessary difference between the real and the ideal form of *bourgeois* society, which is the cause of their desire to undertake the superfluous business of realizing the ideal expression again, which is in fact only the inverted projection of this reality" (249).

Marx is pointing out an impassable difference between intellectual positions. One of them departs from and absorbs the Marxian notion of crisis understood as "the general intimation . . . towards the presupposition [namely, the system of production now established upon the 'world market'] and the urge . . . towards a new historic form" (228). The other one is represented by the utopian desire to undertake "the superfluous business of realizing the ideal expression again, which is in fact only the inverted projection of this reality [of inequality and unfreedom]," of the mirage that makes us understand inequality and unfreedom as true equality and true freedom. This is the greed, the reverence, and sanctity of our habitual three gestures, ideologically mediated and offered as the inverted projection of our thirst for money. The three fundamental ideological gestures of our regional-intellectual field are maniacal gestures, always already the result of a possession by the ontotheological foundation mediated by the monetary god, by the social form of money. So, what is common to those three gestures, that is, the only gesture within those identitarian, mimetic, and differential gestures? It is the reduction of the world to the subject of production, and the enthroning of the subject, regional or not, as the only possible exchange value of general interest. In other words, it is the capitalization of the regional subject, be it a continental, a national, or a minoritarian subject. Yet this means that the unique gesture that sustains us, and that, by sustaining us, founds university discourse in our times, is the reduction of the social relation to a relation between things, since the relation between regional subjects, understood on the basis of their "natural" or historical difference, is understood as a relation between subjects of equivalence, who are therefore reified into their equivalence and turned into commodities. The regional subject, turned into a commodity, guarantees in the last instance the right of the region to partake of the universal community, the world market, and to an equality and freedom within it which is the ideal (and ideological) foundation of the social system based on exchange value. Thus understood, the identitarian and anti-imperialist horizon of differential representation in regionalist university discourse has a generalized equivalence of subjects as its implicit goal and final horizon. Identitarian liberation is thus another name for oppression and enchainment, for the inverted projection of the real social relation, which transforms social relations into relations between things. Regional liberation is the transformation into a thing, a commodity, of the regional subject—a subject that is only a thing, an instrument of exchange in the general operation of paying reverence to the god of greed. This is the Marxian analysis—a stunning critique of identitarian politics whose active erasure of the discursive map today is not just casual. Through our discourse as regionalist intellectuals, and through our tendencies, we could say we do what Marx said we did in 1857:

With that, then, the complete freedom of the individual is posited: voluntary transaction; no force on either side; positing of the self as means, or as serving, only as means, in order to posit the self as end in itself, as dominant and primary; finally, the self-seeking interest which brings nothing of a higher order to realization; the other is also recognized and acknowledged as one who likewise realizes his self-seeking interest, so that both know that the common interest exists only in the duality, many-sidedness, and autonomous development of the exchanges between self-seeking interests. The general interest is precisely the generality of self-seeking interests. Therefore, when the economic form, exchange, posits the all-sided equality of its subjects, then the content, the individual as well as the objective material that drives towards the exchange, is *freedom*. Equality and freedom are thus not only respected in exchange based on exchange values but, also, the exchange of exchange values is the productive, real basis of all *equality* and *freedom*. As pure ideas they are merely the idealized expressions of this basis; as developed in juridical, political, social relations [and we could add: in relations ruled by university discourse], they are merely this basis to a higher power. And so it has been in history. (244–45)

Regional intellectuals, in the last two hundred years of history, have been the purveyors of the general interest through their function in preserving the generality of self-seeking, self-localizing interests. They have turned the projected inversion of the social form of money into their task. The identitarian politics of area studies as we know them are not the interruption but the radical reaffirmation and consolidation of the sovereignty of capital over the region, the posited identity between capital and region. How then to think, on the basis of the crisis, towards the interval of being, that is, towards the outside of ontotheology, and towards the abandonment of greed as community, and as the basis of community? How to think towards the fourth gesture, and towards the invention of a new temporality? Is it possible to conceive of a situation where, if the fourth gesture were not itself the community, it would dissolve the community? Is it possible to imagine a principle of dissolution of university discourse for the regionalist intellectual? A way of thinking the outside of university discourse from university discourse? That outside, if it marks the disaster of regionalist dialectics, can it be something other than an obscure murmur, a clamor or a noise of being, only undetermined, and as undetermined empty, and as empty wild, threatening, and destructive?

Dirty Atopics

But it is not so difficult to imagine an affirmative response to the latter questions. Against the ontopological radicalization of cultural studies, the neobaroque practice of dirty atopics. Translation, transculturation, locationalism are not the ultimate horizons of thinking. Dirty atopics dwells in a supplement to locationalism, and traces a program of thought that refuses to find satisfaction in expropriation as much as it refuses to rest on appropriative drives. It is dirty because there is no disembodied thinking, and it is atopic because no genuine thought can be exhausted by its conditions of enunciation. In the foundational work of Lezama, Haroldo de Campos, Sarduy, or Perlongher, and in so many of their inheritors today, whether in literature, the visual, or the theoretical, the Neobaroque becomes an attempt, a murky or dirty attempt, to find the possibility of an interruption of the regional, and to establish that interruption as a category of general thinking. The Neobaroque is a war machine against that other paradigm, the dominant ideological paradigm in the history of Latin American modernity: the identitarian or locationalist paradigm which is still affecting, if in different ways, projects such as those of Beverley (a critic of transculturation in the name of subaltern identity) or González Echevarría (a disavower of subaltern identity for the sake of the self-constitution of the *criollista* critic as the posited master of language). From the days of Angel Rama's translation of Fernando Ortiz's concept of transculturation, there has developed a whole industry of transculturation in academic writing—now merged with the hybridizing industry. In its worst facticity, its most common one, the transculturators and the hybridizers posit as the end of their task to show that there is transculturation in the cultural process, and that transculturation, or hybridity, is, generally speaking, a good thing: the way in which subaltern culture contaminates and subverts dominant culture. We know that there is transculturation, and we know that, for better or for worse, transculturation is not just the form in which subaltern culture subverts dominant culture: it is also the opposite. In any case, transculturation studies, which originated as the great Latin American(ist) response to the threat of a cultural homogenization imposed by global imperialism, have come to be little else than glorified tautologies. This is not to say that it is not absolutely necessary to research and trace as exhaustively as possible the practical and real processes of transculturation: we can call that the study of the historical labor of transculturation, without which there can be no specificity of any kind to understand cultural transformation.[11] But it is to say that there is a huge difference between the study of the labor of transculturation, through piecemeal monographs and case studies, and the endless repetition of the fact that there is transculturation, as if we had somehow forgotten it or ever denied it. There is transculturation, there is hybridity: nobody will deny it. But hybridity is not liberatory per se, and transculturation is not simply the glorious response of the weak to the theft of time by the powerful. The task of thinking starts in a critique of transculturation. Where can we establish the possibility of a critique of transculturation? In a double articulation that I have called subalternist in the past and that I do not hesitate to call neobaroque as well: in its first register, it requires the study of the labor of transculturation; in its second register, it critiques the labor of transculturation. Both must proceed in mutual articulation: without it, the second register cannot exist, and the first register does not matter. We must create a horizon of possibility for a critical perspective that will remain irreducible to the factical study of the processes of cultural transformation. The notion of a double articulation enables us to keep the horizon open to the horizon itself, that is, it permits the affirmation of a beyond of transformational facticity that does not reify it into a specific prescription or a specific dogma. The second register transculturates transculturation: that is the savage inscription that opens history to endless questioning, in the absence of which everything gets refunctionalized at the service of the dominant factical model.

Dirty atopics: the name for a theoretical practice that disrupts the region of thinking for the regionalist intellectual, whose region is then uncannily doubled. Region is quite a word, and it has a king at the center. The Latin rex, the principle of personalized—we could say, regionalized—sovereignty, colonizes the region. The region makes a claim to sovereignty, and it is indeed the claim itself. Region is a claim to sovereignty, the claim to sovereignty in its formal truth. So what is the regional intellectual to do? Is the regional intellectual nothing but the ideologue of the (regional) sovereign? Yes, if the regional intellectual remains within the regional confines of the region; but there is another possibility, in fact, one in which the regional intellectual seeks the interruption of the sovereign claim, and thinks out of the claim and outside the claim: within and without the claim. A regional intellectual who, therefore, seeks a non-regional region within the region: a non-sovereign sovereignty, a groundless ground. I think this is about the only way in which the regional intellectual can be something other than an ideologue of the sovereign; the only way in which the regional intellectual can become something like a thinker, because thinking only happens in the interval of sovereignty, and against it, or rather, outside it, which sovereignty cannot accept as anything but against itself.

But this already says that the regionalist intellectual can only think in the crisis, if crisis is the interval of being, if crisis is whatever turns disaster into the possibility of a passage, a *paso* into an alternative projection of time, and into a new temporality. "Crises are then the general intimation which points beyond the presupposition, and the urge which drives towards the adoption of a new historic form." A general intimation, an urge: a particular kind of basic affective tonality or structure of feeling for the regionalist intellectual as thinker, the mandate to think the interruption of the sovereignty of the region, that is, to go "beyond the presupposition" and to go "towards the adoption of a new historic form." The university discourse of modernity in its regionalist dimension is or wants to be localizing thought. The destruction of programmatic Latin Americanism, of the tedious *murga,* seeks the interruption of localist sovereignty and thus an a-local, atopic, an-archic constituent principle.

This non-principled principle or dirty atopianism is neobaroque irruptive force. Not coincidentally, historical Baroque refers to the moment previous to the final dissolution of the old community at the hands of money in its third stage. The Neobaroque refers to the crisis of the ontotheological community constituted as the social form of money in the moment of postmodernity; that is, when Latin America becomes firmly integrated into the world market under the Keynesian regime of capitalist development, which is also the moment of its failure, as dependency theory has demonstrated. That is the time when Lezama posits the poetic possibility as a "being for resurrection" following the Pascalian norm: "since true nature is lost everything can be supranature"[12] Lezamian *sobrenaturaleza* is the space of constitution of an alternative real, against the regime of productionist accumulation of the real, against Heideggerian "machination," which is the reverse of the ontotheological coin whose other side is culture as the realm of life-experience under capital.[13] But neobaroque nature is not the place of culture—it is the place of the withdrawal of culture, of the renunciation to the cultural, of the exodus from the cultural, now experienced as the biopolitical instance of domination and as a sad passion.

That is the neobaroque *paso: paso* of the mule in(to) the abyss beyond the ontotheological foundation. But the baroque bestiary includes another animal that is for Lezama equally emblematic: the snake. Perlongher speaks of the "step of the snake" in his poem of that title as an explicit supplement to the Lezamian "step of the mule": "a streamer of cobras in the mohave ballet getting wet in the shade of spiralling araucarias marking in the ivy the lightness of a step which is in truth the step of the grass through the air damp with the circles of empty eyes in salty glass ribbons of macramé scanning the pupilar cythar, the cornea horns its humming bird in love simulating in the moss carpet in the humid of the air that dew of the smoke in its dehiscence" (289).

The snake's *paso*—"its hump in unreading brush erases almost forgetting the legends of the soap." What remains is only "the lucidity of the step" (289).

Only the lucidity of passage? We must think of the charcoal sequence in the famous Chapter 9 of *Paradiso* in order to understand what is luminous in that lucidity. There the "master incorporator of the snake," in his full ecstasy of incorporation, causes "the final hecatomb of the charcoal shop"(355). "Charcoal dust flowed like a river at dawn, then the charcoals of regular size, those which have not been made smaller by the shovel, would roll like in the cave of Polyphemus. The noise of the cakes of vegetable charcoal, rough black honeycombs, was louder and more frequent. Through the smallness of the place, the full variety of charcoal bounced off, hit, and left irregular black lines in the bodies of these two ridiculous gladiators, joined by the softened iron of the alienation of the sexes" (355–56). "Through the smallness of the place, the full variety of charcoal bounced off . . ."—as a consequence of the mobilizing and de-localizing passage of the snake. *Carbón* is of course an imperfect or dirty anagram of *barroco*.

Notes

1. Severo Sarduy's interpretation of the Baroque as "operativity of the efficacious sign" (591) already points to the inversion of all sad passions based upon lack. Furthermore, if the object "is also that which splits the unity of the subject and marks in it an invisible lack, a lack to him/herself," Sarduy tells us that in José Lezama Lima's *Paradiso,* an emblematic work of Latin American Neobaroque, a "a particular hilariousness" is its foundational characteristic. Hence "that little . . . laughter, violent but choked, with the same virulence, the same energy . . . as guffaw, but never reaching explosion." I will give the original, rather untranslatable Spanish: "esa risita cejijunta, violenta pero ahogada, que tiene la misma virulencia, la misma energía de choteo y de impugnación que la carcajada, pero que nunca llega al estallido, a la explosión, al grafismo caricatural y sincopado" (595). In Lezama's wake, Sarduy is the first to theorize the Latin American Neobaroque as joyful passion.

2. See the Third Part of Spinoza's *Ethics,* "Of the Origin and Nature of the Affects." In Postulates 54 and 55, for instance, "The mind strives to imagine only those things which posit its power of acting" (182), and "When the mind imagines its own lack of power, it is saddened by it" (182), it is already understood how sadness is the passage to "a lesser perfection" from the joy of affect (188). Sadness is not deprivation, but an act in itself, "a man's passage from a greater to a lesser perfection" where the power of mind is diminished or restrained (188). The sad passion is the mind's act of self-enslavement.

3. Cf. Bruno Bosteels's essay, "Antagonism, Hybridy, and the Subaltern in Latin America," where the terms "archi-politics" and "archi-aesthetics" are used to criticize the Latin Americanist subalternism which is at the basis of my own essay.

4. "We have abolished the real world: what world is left? Perhaps the apparent? . . . But no? With the real world we have also abolished the apparent" (*Twilight* 51). I must also say that poststructuralist and postcolonialist critique are not at all the same. It would be useful to establish the specific history of what I must leave as summary affirmation.

5. Far from wanting to be exhaustive, I must cite at least other analyses of the Baroque that are related to the positions that interest me in this essay: Maravall, of course, and also Moraña, Naranjo, and Echeverría.

6. Lea says of the Inquisition, using a strictly aporetic tropology, that it is "a power within the state superior to the state itself" (357).

7. In "El heredero" Sarduy uses as his epigraphe the following passage from Jacques Lacan: "If I tell you all of this it is because I am returning from the museums, and because, in sum, the Counter-Reformation meant a return to the sources, and because the baroque is the exhibit of that return. The baroque is the regulation of the sould through bodily scopy . . . I am only speaking, for the moment, of what one can see in every church in Europe, what hangs from the walls, everything that leaks, everything that . . . delirates. What I have called obscenity, but exalted" (Lacan 104–05; citado por Sarduy 593).

8. My use of the notion of exodus is indebted to Paolo Virno, who says, for instance: "Exodus is the foundation of a Republic. The very idea of 'republic,' however, requires a taking leave of State judicature: if Republic, then no longer State. The political action of the Exodus consists, therefore, in an engaged withdrawal. Only those who open a way of exit for themselves can do the founding; but, by the opposite token, only those who do the founding will succeed in finding the parting of the waters by which they will be able to leave Egypt" (196). The disciplinary exodus I mention is not shy about the possibility of an alternative foundation.

9. It is difficult not to quote Néstor Perlongher's famous poem on Teresian transverberation, entitled "Luz oscura," and which I will leave without translation: "Si atravesado por la zarza el pecho/arder a lo que ya encendido ardía/ hace, el dolor en goce transfigura,/fría la carne mas el alma ardida/en el blanco del ojo el ojo frío/cual nieve en valle tórrido: el deseo/divino se echa sobre lanzas ígneas/ y muerde el ojo en blanco el labio henchido" (304). Cf. also in Lacan, *Encore,* the references to St. Teresa's mystical experience as a baroque form of knowledge, and its metonymic relation to a possible notion of feminine knowledge, or of knowledge as feminine.

10. On the relation of Talos' myth and theoretical practice see Alberto Moreiras, Interpretación y diferencia (102–18), and an expansion of the same argument in "Pharmaconomy."

11. See for instance John Kraniauskas' "Globalization is Ordinary" and "Hybridity in a Transnational Frame," where he argues the need for explicit attention to the labor of transculturation.

12. En "Preludio a las eras imaginarias:" "poetry had found letters for the unknown, had situated new gods, had acquired the potens, the infinite possibility, but its last great

dimension remained: the world of resurrection. In resurrection the potens culminates, exhausting its posibilitéis" (Obras 819), and "Only the poet, master of the act operating upon the germ, which is nevertheless still creation, can be casual, can reduce the totality, through metaphor, to comparative matter. In this dimension, perhaps the most incommensurable and powerful that can be offered, the poet is the casual being for resurrection" (*Obras* 819–20). On "supranature" Lezama says that in Pascal's image he found a "terrible affirmative force" that decided him to "place the image at the site of lost nature. In that way, against nature's determinism, man responds with the total freedom of the image. And against the pessimism of lost nature, man's invincible joy in the reconstituted image" (*Obras* 1213). Note that "el total arbitrio de la imagen" places the invention of the image beyond culture as an organic response to human separation from nature.

13. See in *Contributions,* Heidegger's comments on "machination" (88–100). For instance, "Be-ing has so thoroughly abandoned beings and submitted them to machination and 'lived-experience' that those illusive attempts at rescuing Western culture and all 'culture-oriented politics' must necessarily become the most insidious and thus the highest form of nihilism" (97–98).

Works Cited

Beverley, John. *Una modernidad obsoleta. Estudios sobre el barroco.* Los Teques [Venezuela]: Fondo editorial ALEM, 1997.

———. *Against Literature.* Minneapolis: University of Minnesota Press, 1993.

Blanchot, Maurice. "Literature and the Right to Death." *The Gaze of Orpheus and Other Literary Essays.* Trans. Lydia David. New York: Station Hill, 1981.

Bosteels, Bruno. "Antagonism, Hybridity, and the Subaltern in Latin America." *Disposition.*

Echavarren, Roberto. "Prólogo." In Néstor Perlongher, *Poemas completos,* 7–16.

Echeverría, Bolívar. *La modernidad de lo barroco.* México: Era, 2000.

———. *Modernidad, mestizaje cultural, ethos barroco.* México: El equilibrista, 1994.

González Echevarría, Roberto. *Celestina's Brood. Continuities of the Baroque in Spanish and Latin American Literature.* Durham: Duke University Press, 1993.

Handke, Peter. *On a Dark Night I Left My Silent House.* Trans. Krishna Winston. New York: Farrar Strauss Giroux, 2000.

Heidegger, Martin. *Contributions to Philosophy. (From Enowning).* Trans. Parvis Emad and Kenneth Maly. Bloomington: Indiana University Press, 1999.

Kraniauskas, John. "Globalisation is Ordinary: The Transnationalisation of Cultural Studies." *Radical Philosophy* 90 (1998): 9–19.

———. "Hybridity in a Transnational Frame: Latin Americanist and Postcolonial Perspectives on Cultural Studies." *Nepantla-Views from South* 1.1 (2000): 111–37.

Lacan, Jacques. Encore. *Le Séminaire XX.* Paris: Seuil, 1975.

Lea, Henry Charles. *The Inquisition in the Spanish Dependencies.* New York: MacMillan, 1922.

Lezama Lima, José. *Obras completas. II. Ensayos/cuentos.* Madrid: Aguilar, 1977.

———. *Paradiso.* Eloísa Lezama Lima ed. Madrid: Cátedra, 1980.

———. *Poesía completa.* 2 vols. Madrid: Aguilar, 1988.

Maravall, José Antonio. *La cultura del barroco.* Análisis de una estructura histórica. Barcelona: Ariel, 1975.

Marx, Karl. *Grundrisse. Foundations of the Critique of Political Economy.* (*Rough Draft*). Trans. Martin Nicolaus. London: Penguin, 1993.

Moraña, Mabel. *Viaje al silencio: exploraciones del discurso barroco.* México: Facultad de Filosofía y Letras, UNAM, 1998.

Moreiras, Alberto. *Interpretación y diferencia.* Madrid: Visor, 1991.

———. "Pharmaconomy: Stephen and the Daedalids." In Susan Stanford Friedman, ed. *Joyce: The Return of the Repressed.* Ithaca: Cornell University Press, 1993. 58–86.

Naranjo, Rodrigo. "La recaída al barroco. Imagen y clase a fines de la modernidad." Unpublished.

Nietzsche, Friedrich. *Twilight of the Idols/The Anti-Christ.* Trans. R. J. Hollingdale. London: Penguin, 1990.

Perlongher, Néstor. *Poemas completos* (1980–1992). Ed. Roberto Echavarren. Buenos Aires: Seix Barral, 1997.

Robb, Peter M. *The Man Who Became Caravaggio.* New York: Henry Holt, 1999.

Sarduy, Severo. "El heredero." In José Lezama Lima, *Paradiso.* Cintio Vitier ed. Madrid: Archivos, 1988. 590–97.

Spinoza, Benedict de. *A Spinoza Reader. The Ethics and Other Works.* Ed. and trans. Edwin Curley. Princeton: Princeton University Press, 1994.

Virno, Paolo. "Virtuosity and Revolution: The Political Theory of Exodus." In *Radical Thought in Italy. A Potential Politics.* Eds. Paolo Virno and Michael Hardt. Minneapolis: University of Minnesota Press, 1996. 189–209.

◆ **9**

Keeping Things Opaque:
On the Reluctant Personalism
of a Certain Mode of Critique

Brad Epps

For L.C.-H.
Of course, principally,
for A.M.

Disciplines, Institutions, Nations, and Selves

Posicionalidad, locación y memoria . . . son los centros
del debate político e intelectual de este fin de siglo

(Positionality, location, and memory are the centers
of political and intellectual debate at this century's end)
— Hugo Achugar, *Leones, cazadores e historiadores*

When we speak of literature, or culture, or the queer, or the subaltern, or so much else, do we not also speak of our disciplines, or institutions, or nations, maybe all together?[1] Are we not spoken, at least in part, *by* our disciplines, institutions, or nations as well, even when we represent them as intermixed? For that matter, when we speak of ourselves, when we deploy the "we," are we not also speaking, again in part, of a fragmented, yet insistent, "I"? And is this "I" not also spoken by someone, or something, beyond it, too? The questions are largely rhetorical, at least as I turn them. They may be less rhetorical for others, which is to say that they may be answered, if they are answered, with a "no," resounding, nuanced, or otherwise. No, we are not spoken by our disciplines,

institutions, or nations, or not in any consequential manner, and certainly not—
and I would agree—exhaustively. No, we do not speak individually when we
speak in the plural, for representation does obtain. And so on. The debates that
mark much academic inquiry, the debates between, say, literary studies and
cultural studies—the former subsuming, and virtually erasing, philology and
literary history, and the latter involving, often quite tensely, postcolonial and
subaltern studies—turn on such questions. So, for that matter, do the debates
between Hispanism, however understood, and other disciplines, but also *within*
Hispanism, its trans-Atlantic vortices, its national factions, its essentialist and
anti-essentialist maneuvers, its hegemonic fantasies and para-hegemonic aspirations, its turgid reconfigurations, and its struggles for visibility, fame, and
power. As my own language suggests, it often seems as if Hispanism—or any
"ism"—were an entity endowed with agency, something above and beyond the
individuals who variously contribute to it, participate in it, and are interpellated
by it. The appearance of something transcendent, or perhaps alienating, might
provide, however, the occasion for a return to the material grounds from which
thought—including so-called groundless thought—is at least *partly* produced.
The ideologies of Hispanism are, among other things, the institutionalities and
(inter)nationalities of Hispanism, the places where people work and from which
they speak and write.

As for me, working at Harvard University is not exactly unobtrusive—particularly when I call attention to it, something I have never before done *in writing*. Then again, publishing habits are such that an institutional affiliation, when
there is one, almost always accompanies the author's name. The persistence of
the proper names of individuals and institutions in critical work bears reflection,
perhaps especially when said critical work presents itself as radical. For amid
all the ethico-political proclamations, it is as if intellectual recognition entailed
institutional recognition, as if thought could only circulate by presenting itself
as tethered to a relatively delimited, individualized site: a particular person, or
group of people, in a particular place, or in particular places. The independent,
free-lance critic is still a minor player in academic circuits, particularly in the
United States. And as for academic circuits, the flow is hardly free: whatever
elective affinities allow for the formation of study groups, associations, alliances, or cliques, a principle of selection fractures them as well. Selection is
at the core of the U.S. academic system, where applications and admissions
vary from institution to institution. Harvard prides itself on its ability to admit
only the "best and brightest," and many, if not most, of those admitted endorse
the principle of selection, assume it as their own. Admission is thus a multi-
faceted and ideologically charged process, one whose effects are potentially

unending. A powerful multinational corporation that profits from its non-profit status, Harvard continually seeks to increase an already enormous endowment by capitalizing on a fetishized aura, the self-replicating illusion of select knowledge, expertise, and truth, of the ever-so grand *Veritas* emblazoned on its gates, stationery, caps, and tee-shirts. Harvard is jealous of its name and insignia, and administrators and professors alike worry about dissemination, diffusion, and depletion: both name and insignia are guarded, quite explicitly, as trademarks, as signs of value, but also of wealth.[2] Wealthy, Harvard is not alone; like many other universities and colleges, it capitalizes on the nostalgia and melancholy attachment of its alumni and would-be alumni, binding them together in a select collection of donors and would-be donors. It benefits more materially by making supposedly savvy investments and by acquiring, sometimes in less than transparent manners, more and more of the surrounding communities often only to disregard the standards of these communities, including, rather notoriously, the adjusted standard of living or "living wage."

The preceding statements, if they are to be more than the sour grapes of a disenchanted insider recently given a lesson in political and economic justice by students and workers, are themselves attached to some idea of truth, verily.[3] My knowledge, including the essay that you now have before you, is implicated in its site of production—a partly movable site that inheres in funded sabbaticals, summers, and travels elsewhere—and carries a stamp of privilege that at once credits and discredits it. Something similar holds for those teaching at other rich, private institutions, say, Yale or Stanford or Duke, the latter being a place where students and teachers, fuzzily evoking a Civil War past, sometimes still refer to Harvard as the Duke of the North. All sites, with all their rivalries, perforce condition—not determine, but condition—what is there or, as both Mabel Moraña and Hugo Achugar insist, *from there* produced.[4] Alberto Moreiras may be on solid ground when he states that "[t]he university, in view of the shrinking of the intellectual public sphere, has become one of the last institutional sites where a critical practice is not just theoretically possible, but also practically existing" ("Global Fragments" 82). Yet it is important to recognize, without reifying them, that there are differences not only between and within universities but also between and within "intellectual public spheres." One can certainly assume that Moreiras has in mind what earlier in the essay just quoted he calls "western universities," but the university *and* the public sphere that are most densely adumbrated are those of the United States of America, where both Moreiras and I are employed. The critical practices that "the university" makes possible are conditioned, that is, by the particularities of universities (in the plural) and of the people (again in the plural) who work in them. If a critical practice is "practically existing" in "the university" it is in a way that is, as Moreiras must surely know, far from even. Power is such that it produces powerful imbalances, and the U.S. academic system, with its principle of selection, its leagues, tiers, hierarchies, stars, awards, prizes, grants, investments, tenure concerns, contracts, and contacts—what Pierre Bourdieu might call social capital—is perforce a *questionable* site for critique, theoretically *and* practically. In some sense, it may be one of the *most questionable* sites for critique imaginable.

The problems and paradoxes that attend radical or progressive critique in privileged places are obviously not new, and Noam Chomsky and Fredric Jameson are obviously not the only ones implicated. But a lack of novelty does not make for a lack of significance, and old, onerous, and obvious as it may be, it is again necessary, I believe, to consider what is at stake in the institutional site of the discipline(s), particularly when it is a site of financial privilege. Hispanism—which John Beverley has called an "ideological *minifundio*" (10)—is undoubtedly institutionalized, but it is so, as indicated, in uneven ways that recall, *without necessarily duplicating,* the unevenness of international configurations. Latin Americanism, as a now dominant, if contested, mode of Hispanism (itself contested too), raises questions of *economic* unevenness that do not hold, at least not with the same intensity, for Peninsularism. True, arguments about economic contributions and political representation mark debates about the unevenly recognized languages and cultures of the Spanish state, but the differences between Catalonia and Andalusia, economically speaking, are not of the same order as the differences between Spain and any country in Latin America. Indeed Spain, like the United States, is a powerful investor and creditor in Latin America, especially in banking, telecommunications, and utilities, and *that* fact makes no mean difference in the debates by which Hispanism replicates itself. And yet, Latin Americanism—an ideality arguably more operant, or at least operant differently, in the United States than in Latin America proper—is profitable in the United States in a way that now tends to outstrip the ideality known as Peninsularism. Some scholars, and even some departments, take great stock in the decline of Peninsularism, as if the injustices of a colonial past were somehow, in some tiny way, corrected. The reaction is understandable—and I speak as one formed as a Peninsularist. After all, Peninsularism long dominated and often denigrated Latin Americanism, as if the latter were to the former as a copy to a model. Such a situation endures, albeit in a softer mien, in the representation and promotion of the Spanish language as the felicitous legacy of an effectively sanitized process of conquest and colonization.[5] Linguistic "patrimonio" remits, that is, to the "madre patria" [literally the mother fatherland], and the violence of history is accordingly "redeemed" in the form of a universal or international "gift"of communication and commerce. The defense and celebration of Spanish is by no means unique to Spain (nor can it be reduced to a Spanish national project), but the Spanish government, and more than one of its intellectual representatives, would capitalize nonetheless on a genealogy which accords a place of privilege to Spain. Triumphant as they may at times appear, the cultural politics of the Real Academia de la Historia and the Instituto Cervantes, for example, signal an anxiety about the place of Spain in the Spanish-speaking world, which is also an anxiety about the place of Spain in the English-speaking world. After all, in international Hispanism, particularly in the United States, Spain does not enjoy the position of dominance that many once considered its due.[6] The tables have turned but in a manner that bears consideration. Spain is increasingly strong economically, but it is an increasingly hard "sell" in the U.S. academy, even though economic and political difficulties in parts of Latin America (most recently in Argentina) have entailed the closing of some U.S. programs and the compensatory move of some U.S. students to Spain. Such moves do not mean that interest wanes; quite the contrary, they may even stimulate interest. Demographics and immigration—positionality, location, and memory, in Achugar's formulation—doubtlessly play crucial roles in the construction of interest, but Renato Rosaldo's critique also seems germane: in the land of the rich, cultural vibrancy, economic hardship, and academic interest often go hand in hand.[7]

The "success" of Latin Americanism in the United States has been described, as Moreiras remarks, as a "sell-out" ("Order" 126), an assessment that is not, for all its harshness, without reason. I will return to the question of a "sell-out," but for the moment suffice it to say that the "success" of Latin Americanism in the United States, only partly measured in positions, grants, salaries, study abroad programs, and publishing opportunities, exists alongside the "difficulties" of much of Latin America itself. The "difficulties" of Peninsularism in the United States exist alongside the relative "success" of Spain. Clearly, however, things are not so simple; success and hardship are relative and highly debatable, and the situation in one Latin American country is not the same as in another. But within the trends, the status, in the United States, of Latin Americanism and Peninsularism—let alone of what Moreiras calls "first" and "second Latinamericanism" ("Global Fragments" 85) or "neohispanism" ("Neohispanism")—varies from institution to institution, even within a given institution. Still and all, as a general rule, academics (like myself) who attempt to wrench themselves from one formation into another or who attempt to reconfigure longstanding disciplinary divisions contend with the shadow of opportunism, that is to say with the shadow of suspicion—as if a late arrival troubled belonging. So-called Trans-Atlantic Studies are constituted in such a shadow, and so, for that matter, are both Latin Americanism and Peninsularism (indeed, Hispanism in general) *outside* of Latin America and Spain. Suspicion also attends Latin Americanism and Peninsularism *inside* Latin America and Spain (which clearly does not saturate a peninsula), for their conceptual unity is contested by an array of indigenous and peripheral endeavors, likewise subject to suspicion. Suspicion, in short, may well be a mainstay of both the construction of disciplines and their deconstruction, of both essentialist and anti-essentialist postures, of work here, there, and at all points in between.

The critique of identity, which necessarily bears on difference, has been successful in promoting suspicion, its own included. For the critique of identity, though pushing most forcefully at the established disciplines, *at once consolidates and fractures* less established disciplines such as subaltern studies, post-colonial studies, queer studies, women's studies, ethnic studies, cultural studies, Latino studies, and (other) so-called area studies, varying, again, from institution to institution. And varying from nation to nation: for the proliferation of disciplines, differences, divisions, and debates, bound up in the relative success of the critique of identity, does not mean that certain reductive gestures, evident in "North/South" or "U.S./Latin America," become impossible or even unadvisable. Granted, "it would be *wrong* to *reduce* [the] debate [over studies, knowledge, and power] to an issue of relatively disempowered professionals from the Latin American semiperiphery confronting their comfortably settled brothers and sisters from the capitalist core" (Moreiras, "Order" 127, emphasis mine).[8] But it would also be "wrong" to brush reduction, relativity, or even a reductive relativity aside, to assume that the specific site of questioning is *not* in question, that it is *not* part, maybe even a *big* part, of the problem. However reductive it may seem, relative (dis)empowerment obtains—no less than relative (dis)comfort—and it does so in ways that no amount of theorization can gainsay, at least if we accept the implications of "an accomplished globalization" (Moreiras, "Order" 125)—no pun with "accomplished" necessarily taken. As Walter Mignolo accurately notes, "globalization has neither erased nor supplanted [the] distinction" between center and periphery (183). Indeed, globalization, as thus far accomplished, means precisely that there *are* relatively disempowered professionals (let alone non-professionals) in Latin America and relatively comfortably settled professionals in the "developed" nations, that there *is* a "reduction" of the world, fraught with complexities, into a "semi-periphery" and a "core."

Moreiras's critique of reductive geopolitical maneuvers entails, logically enough, their reiteration: "objections concerning unequal exchange bear heavily upon metropolitan-based institutional intellectuals, who may very well have tried to incorporate a certain amount of self-reflexivity in their work but who still see themselves constrained by their own institutional location into types of discursive behaviour which they are unable to control" (126). Though it may indeed be the case, it is unclear if the burden and the constraints to which Moreiras refers are also his own, and to what degree, if any, they shape his reflections. One can certainly assume that they are, and that he knows that they are, but it is just this lack of clarity, part and parcel of an elliptical evocation of self-reflexivity in which the personal, as soon as it is "thematized," is recast, rather abjectly, as the personalist, that I would like to consider in the pages that follow. I will be doing so mainly by way of Moreiras, because he proffers a critique that is notable for its theoretical density, its relative visibility, and, more specifically, its claims to radical para-hegemonic legitimacy in a transnational frame. Furthermore, I will be engaging the personal not as a solution but as a *problem* that hounds what might be called the refusal to engage the personal in a "conventionally" or "identifiably" personal way, a refusal whose history as a token of seriousness (where seriousness is always opaque and obscure) is as lengthy as it is complex. Inasmuch as I will be examining the problem of the (im)personal by way of Moreiras, whom I personally know and respect, I inevitably risk representing him as representative of a self-consciously unconventional critical practice which is arguably, even defiantly, still minor within Hispanism. I also risk representing myself, by way of so many situated, quasi-anecdotal references, as representative of another critical practice, largely essayistic and also rather minor, that would lay claim to legitimacy by way of fragility, insufficiency, partiality, and so on. The divide, like any divide (including that of North and South), is vexed, and arguably specious, but it insists, in its relative inconsequentiality, all the same. It insists, as Moreiras himself indicates, as objections, burdens, constraints, and controls (or the lack thereof) that complicate the flow of critique and of capital, symbolic and otherwise. More pointedly, however, some sort of divide is the very condition of possibility for the debates and competitions on which critique and symbolic capital depend.

According to Moreiras, "the ongoing debate [here specifically the debate between literary and cultural studies] has been initiated by scholars whose association with the *transnational* academic sphere is longstanding, which *automatically* turns their interpellation into a matter of intellectual not social position" ("Order," 126, emphasis mine). And yet, not only are automatic interpellative turns and a transnational academic sphere likewise *debatable* (How transnational is transnational? How is interpellation rendered automatic?), it seems more than likely that the intellectual and social are inextricably intertwined. Whether or not Moreiras means to suggest that they are not (his sentence structure, at any rate, does), a non-social intellectual interpellation is untenable. The intellectual *is* a social and, no less importantly, an economic position that may vary according to any number of material and psycho-symbolic factors, also intertwined, but that nonetheless obtains for all "intellectuals," regardless of how they "understand" contextualization, historicization, and identification. It is also, as I have been insisting, a disciplinary, institutional, and national position (even when it situates itself outside disciplines, institutions, and, more anxiously, nations). Self-proclaimed international, transnational, or postnational intellectuals (the new cosmopolitans[9]), many of whom champion dislocations and disjunctions, still contend with national laws and borders; they still *stop* before crossing (the repositioning of borders in the European Union, for instance, only reinforces their power elsewhere). Moreiras, who has advocated a "second Latinamericanism" purportedly "[n]o longer caught in the search and capture of 'positions, fixed points, identities' [the terms are Michael Hardt's]" ("Global Fragments" 88) and who appears to have positioned himself in the "non-position" of rifts, fissures, and disjunctions—when not ever so tendentiously *beyond* position—is thus not without *real* motivation. After all, as someone who was not born in the United States, Moreiras surely has dealt with some aspect of the Immigration and Nationalization Service (recently subsumed within the Bureau of Citizenship and Immigration Service, BCIS), some control, some demand to assume a "fixed point" or "identity" and to "justify" his presence in the United States. His colleague, Walter Mignolo, who has "no problem saying that I am Argentinean and Latin American, although I live in the United States and am a naturalized American [sic]," has also had to assume, if only performatively, a fixed point and an identity that *allow* him to "balk at saying that I am American when the implication is 'from the United States'" (182), while staying *in* the United States. Different as they are, both men are interpellated by specific governmental agencies that effectively make their intellectual positions social, economic, and national positions as well.

Living on the hyphen, holding two passports, switching codes, deconstructing "identity politics," and so on, may complicate, but certainly do not obviate, the force of geopolitical boundaries, brutally reinvigorated in the wake of September 11, 2001. Nationality may not be determinative in the last instance, but national governments often function as if it were—which is why it is incumbent for critical thinkers to engage "fixed points and identities" rather than to dispense with them, almost telegraphically, as so many benighted populist ruses. In the United States, the newly created Bureau of Citizenship and Immigration Services and the Directorate of Border and Transportation Security, both of which are part of the newly created Department of Homeland Security, have concentrated their efforts on the enforcement of existing laws and the creation of new ones. As a result, all sectors of society, including the Academy, have been compelled, and constrained, to be more "vigilant" with respect to the identity and ideology of its members. The machinations of the BCIS and other governmental agencies not withstanding, the Academy is still *not* easily *reducible* to national identity, as if all universities in the United States were the same, indeed as if all nursery schools or dance academies were the same. Clearly they are not, and the relative poverty of one may be the relative wealth of another. This may allow us to say that the nation is not one, that the United States is not quite so united and uniform as many of its supporters *and* detractors claim. Class continues to divide (and even to divide academics), even if it does not do so with the clarity of days gone by; indeed, need-based scholarships effectively blur class divisions even as they acknowledge them. But this nation that is not one (the U.S.), and that has been constructed by way of the fractured disavowal of class, nonetheless functions as if it were one, and often as not with a vengeance. Nationality, and its reductive charge is not superseded, even when the turning towards the one that is at the root of the "university" is wittily, or cynically, recast as the turning towards the many, the "polyversity." The multinationalism that implicates higher education in the United States does not, in other words, translate seamlessly into transnationalism, let alone postnationalism, for it is *still* replete with highly delimited national implications and investments in sweatshops *abroad,* outsourcing at *home,* and the military-industrial complex in *strategic locations.*

Part of being "comfortably settled" may in fact entail both a nagging sense of discomfort at the intractability of uncomfortable, even deadly, differences and divisions the world over and an obstinate attempt to complicate said differences and divisions as "always already" complicated—all the while sidestepping or downplaying complicity. I do not mean to affirm a binary logic, but *at the same time* I do not mean to deny it, as if it, or some trace of it, were no longer operant. What is more, anti-binary logic becomes binary itself when it consigns binary logic to the "wrong"—read "reductive"—"side" of things, when it winnows out binarism and reductionism from hybridity, heterogeneity, and pluralism or, more cryptically, from excess, openness, exteriority, and infinitude. All of these signs—hybridity, pluralism, openness, and excess—have been employed not only in radical anti- or para-hegemonic projects but also in a relatively loose project, implicating citizens *and* non-citizens, of U.S. national self-affirmation, what Frederick Buell calls "the reconstitution of U.S. cultural nationalism in an interesting, new, 'postnational' form" (551). There is, still and all, a more tenacious problem here, that of materiality. As Bourdieu notes, a "dual economy" of both local and global proportions is far from obsolete, and a "small privileged minority of stable workers endowed with a permanent salary" exists alongside, and yet largely separate from, "an enormous army of industrial reserve, comprised of a non-professional sub-proletariat" (*Contre-feux,* 48). Bourdieu, who was certainly not the most vulnerable of intellectuals, notes that duality entails "an economic regime that is inseparable from a political regime, a mode of production that entails a mode of domination founded on the *institution of insecurity,* domination by way of precariousness" (*Contre-feux,* 46, emphasis original). Duality and division, reductive as they may be, mark the entire "transnational" academic system.

Duality marks the academic system variously, to be sure: public and private institutions with greater or lesser endowments (and some private institutions are more financially embattled than some large public institutions), but also tenured and non-tenured positions. As a tenured faculty member, I enjoy stability, and I do so in a way that structurally separates me from many of my actual and potential interlocutors as well as those who have few "pretenses" or little "desire" about being engaged at all. The same, more or less, goes for all tenured faculty members, for tenure, as a guarantor of stability, effectively puts the tenured in a "safe" place (one might even say, more cryptically, that it encrypts them). Little wonder that attacks on tenure at specific institutions, or by way of specific individuals, organizations, or state governments, generate anxiety among many of the tenured for they indicate that the place is not *that* safe. Indeed, it is not that tenured faculty members do not experience economic insecurity and precariousness, but rather that they experience it as a fantasy, or nightmare, of *institutional disruption, not* as business as usual. The dining workers, janitors, security guards, and others who "share" our academic space—the "subalterns" who guard the grounds, clean the offices, and serve the food—belong to a work force whose major signs *are* insecurity and precariousness. In this, they are arguably closer to non-tenured faculty, though some of the latter, presumably through "hard work" and "dedication," may still aspire to, and attain, security as tenure, which is basically, for all the intellectual rationalizations, a "stable salary" that underwrites the aforementioned "practically existing" critical practice.

I say this, belabor it even, to call into question my own intervention as well as—at once more tentatively and more brazenly—those of many of my colleagues. This calling into question is not, as Moreiras seems to think, tantamount to abstention or renunciation or to the notion that the subject is "exhausted" by location and that "locationalism" is perforce reactionary, quite the contrary (abstention, after all, can assume the guise of a highly involute theorization, a fetishization of theory). Tenure in a wealthy U.S. university does not account for the subject in his or her entirety, as in some game of all or nothing, but it does "count" *for something*. To claim that tenure does not alter the charge of the subject's utterances, or to claim that tenure is a mere matter of luck (the right person in the right place at the right time), is to underestimate, even misunderstand, the structure of burdens and constraints as well as of rewards and privileges. The irony—which is, of course, the "fact"—is that even the present critique, duly signed and published, will expand my *curriculum vitae* and fold (itself, me) back into an academic system in which value is measured by way of publications. To borrow a phrase from Nelly Richard, mine is a "centrist signature," but one whose "power of auto-referentiality" does not reside in its invocation of the self as much as in the self's situation in a place of privilege (222). "Even when their current hypothesis is that of de-centering," Richard writes, "those who formulate it continue to be surrounded by the reputation, academic or institutional, that allows them to situate themselves in 'the center' of the debate at its densest point of articulation" (222). Richard's signature itself is hardly minor, but it is not centrist or not as centrist as the signature of those, like me, who live and teach, with tenure, in rich universities in the United States. Anonymity, writing to have no name, or no face, remains a utopian gesture associated, in the putatively more sophisticated circles, with the names of such famous writers as Blanchot, Barthes, and Foucault. The radicality of anonymity is such that it cannot be "duly cited" or "named" without being compromised. In fact, true anonymity in the academy is more typically reserved for the subjects whom academics figure as "subaltern" and who give a sense of urgency and importance to our work. Academic entities such as the Latin American Subaltern Studies Group may challenge the power of the proper name, but do not, perhaps indeed cannot, dispense with it entirely. The "Founding Statement" of the group is, after all, reprinted in *Dispositio/n* "with the kind permission of Duke University Press, who [sic] published it in *boundary 2* 20:3, 1993" (1, note). Others, including many of those who have participated in the group, have publicized the names of the participants; indeed, the names are listed later on in the original publication. The point may be petty, but that is precisely why it matters; for it gives the lie to some of the more grandiloquent gestures of professional academics. This is not to say that those who participated in the aforementioned group—or indeed any group—are the same or that their work is the same, for clearly it is not. Instead, it is simply to say that academics, regardless of our affiliations, continue to be marked by any number of external signs of (in)validation. It is also to say that the day that our exchanges take place *without* copyright, proper names, and institutional affiliations will be the day that a certain radicality has finally taken root, that utopia has finally found its place. In the meantime, academic work will proceed, *more or less,* as it has.

One of the ways that such work proceeds is by casting itself in a heroic, risk-ridden, cutting-edge role. Risk, precariousness, and insecurity, often abstrusely figured, function as an ethical principle for many academic endeavors. And abysses, fissures, breaches, and other such signs function as the abstrusely figured spaces of said endeavors. Moreiras's invocation of a "second Latinamericanism"—attesting both to the inadequacy and stiffness of Latin Americanism *per se*—constitutes an *assertive radicality* that spins in just such a space:

> [a second] Latinamericanism does not primarily work as a machine of epistemic homogenization, but rather against it: a disruptive force, or a wrench, in the epistemological apparatus, an anti-disciplinary instance or Hegelian 'savage beast' whose desire does not go through an articulation of difference or identity, but rather through their constant disarticulations, through a radical appeal to an epistemic outside, to an exteriority that will not be turned into a mere fold of the imperial interior. In this sense, Latinamericanism seeks an articulation with alternative localities of knowledge production to form an alliance against historically constituted Latinamericanist representation and its attendant sociopolitical effects. ("Global Fragments" 87)

An entity apparently endowed with its own agency, its own "desire," this "second Latinamericanism" not only sets straight the "first" by twisting it inside out, it also maintains a principle of order and progress—first that, then this—that trumps teleology, however twisted, by rendering it ghostly. What any of this has to do with anything Latin American (rather than, say, Asian or European or African) remains to be seen. Repeatedly, Moreiras cites Latin America, appeals to it (or rather beyond it), but rarely offers anything "precise" or "specific" about it. To do so, of course, would presumably be to fall prey to a benighted "articulation of difference or identity"—or to a "sociological and literary conventionalism"—that would keep the imperial machine working smoothly, wrench-free.[10]

Of course, the idea that Moreiras's own critique is not also smoothly at work, and that its "beasts," "wrenches," and "radical appeals" are not also standard fare in a highly theorized U.S. academic setting rife with its own conventions, is specious, to say the least. Moreiras's work, which I obviously take seriously, moves me, but also gives me pause. In many respects, it is work that engages Latin America as a concept or idea within parameters that are, disciplinarily speaking, more philosophical than literary, historiographic, sociopolitical, or economic. As such, it is entirely "legitimate" and both addresses and raises important questions that push at the limits of materialist analysis. A lack of material specificity is not, *in itself,* problematic, and I do not mean to suggest that Moreiras's work does not make a significant contribution to the field, quite the contrary. Rather, I would resist the assertiveness that would erect a particular approach or line of study into *the* approach or line of study for Latin America, even as concept or idea. It is the tendency to emit something like a *prescriptive, assertive* overview in which materiality is adduced in the most general and "philosophical" of terms that concerns me. Bourdieu makes much of the play of words over things, or realities, and criticizes "the propensity to a revolutionariness with object and without effect" (*Contre-feux,* 35). His critique rings in important ways, as does his advocacy, articulated at none other than the 1999 MLA in Chicago, for a committed scholarship or, as he also puts it, an engaged knowledge (*Contre-feux,* 33–41). His call for efficacy, clarity, and self-critique is one that I take seriously, and impresses much of what I have to say here. Antonio Cornejo-Polar makes a similar critique, but does so, importantly, as part of a critique of the preponderance of a limited critical canon that is not written in Spanish (343). More explicitly localized than Bourdieu, Cornejo-Polar also grapples with the play of words and reality. His call for a critical practice in Spanish is also one that I take seriously, *though I do not heed it here,* largely because I want to intervene in the debate as practiced in the United States, where the dominance of English remains undeniable (as the present volume indicates). There is another reason, of course, and it hardly has the same intellectual or professional veneer as the former: English is *my* native language, and *my* sense of its limits and possibilities, *my feeling* of its rules, regulations, and their abrogation, is especially acute.

I will return to affective linguistic investments later on, but for the moment I want to underscore what is so obvious as to go often noticed. Differences and divisions among and within universities and academics matter, but they still, within a fractured generality, allow for contrasts between the United States and Latin America. They matter in ways that outstrip the presence or absence of particular lines or programs of studies, of particular subjects presumed to know, indeed of particular disagreements and debates. They matter not just symbolically but also materially. And yet, the material value of academic institutions, including their physical plants, libraries, laboratories, investments, endowments, portfolios, contracts, pay scales, salaries, financial benefits and perks are elided or ignored in a number of essays that assert their radicality (and the radicality of their authors). Different as cultural studies, subaltern studies, postcolonial studies, queer studies, literary studies, Hispanic studies, and Latin American studies (first, second, or whatever) may be, they all have something in common. To state the obvious, *they are all studies.* The debate over them, for all its exilic, migratory, cosmopolitan, or radical gestures, for all the fervor it stirs and all the ink it spills, is housed, *especially in the United States,* in particular institutional sites, primarily universities, many of which have outposts and investments overseas. Achugar is on to something when he argues that the debate itself is debatable, that the debate is not the same in the United States as it is in Latin America in part because the relations between the academy and civil society (or the intellectual public sphere) are different. That said, it is not that the sites where, or from which, academics work can account for us in our entirety (that would indeed be reductive in the "wrong" sense), but rather that we cannot leave these sites entirely behind. In a so-called globalized era, a system of symbolic *and* material profit necessarily implicates us all, differently, unevenly, unequally, and at times, quite divisively.

However radical the appeals to exteriority, our nationality, and that of other academic critics who participate in intellectual "debates" (Sarlo, Achugar, Moraña, Mignolo, etc.), is at stake in ways that the nationality of *most* immigrants is not. As I have previously intimated, the "non-native" or foreign professionals that manage to secure academic or other "prestigious" forms of employment in the United States typically need their employers, whose papers are already in order, to vouch for their skills, their *unique* skills. The rhetoric of skills recently made an appearance at my place of employment, when the then president of Harvard University, Neil Rudenstine, confronted with a student protest that included a three-week occupation of his office, used it to "justify" outsourcing, downsizing, and low wages for non-unionized, largely immigrant employees. He even went as far as to point out that Harvard was "humane" enough to provide "free" English classes (note the importance of a *de facto* "national" language) so that the workers could find better employment, more than likely *elsewhere.* The point is important, for it underscores the degree to which the employed academic intellectual, whose skill is ratified as unique by the institution, is separated from those *with* whom, but more commonly *for* whom, he or she would speak and whose history he or she would "restitute." A visa, green card, or passport is a mighty thing, and it enables all sorts of legally sanctioned speculations on legality and illegality, nationality and postnationality, hegemony and anti-hegemony, locations and dislocations—all sorts of balking and talking. It is a document that enables, despite its burdensome constraints, a rather materially comfortable settling and critical practice in the brutally unequal core of capitalism.

To deconstruct nationality, however commendable a project, can be to disavow it, to make as if it did not matter or, perhaps, as if it mattered too much.

Whatever the case, such deconstruction tends to be yet another sign of privilege, the surplus effect of a relatively unencumbered time and place in which thought, reflection, and theory can come to be. For those who are beaten at the border, or who drown or suffocate in the crossing, or who are interned in camps, or who "dream" of leaving home for a "better life," the debate between cultural studies and literary studies, or Peninsular studies and Latin American studies, or subalternism and aesthetic value, is indeed academic. This is not to say that the difference does not signify and is ultimately indifferent (though it is to say, once again, that it may be relatively inconsequential), but rather that it is institutionally and nationally circumscribed, shot through, moreover, with questions of economic class. And yet, literary and cultural critics, Peninsularists and Latin Americanists, subalternists and aesthetic theorists, are arguably more alike than not. If they can be said to constitute a transnational community, it is against the background of others whose transnationality, less prone to skillful institutional validation, is decidedly more vulnerable, when not downright inoperant. Whether or not "we" academics call these others—usually without really calling them—"subaltern," we almost invariably call ourselves, in our fractured individuality, in the process. Nationality works yet its divisive magic, roughly and ever so peacefully, so much so that its overcoming, undoing, negation, or erasure is in some dogged sense national, too. The critique of nationality *is* important and might take the form, from time to time, of a self-critique, a critique of the location, positioning, and memory—to use Achugar's words—of the critic, his or her signs of identity and his or her interrogation, or refusal, or such signs.

The Nameless Project

> *In order not to be authoritative, I've got to speak autobiographically.*
> —Stuart Hall, *Cultural Studies and its Theoretical Legacies*

In what follows, I want to focus my attention on a more delimited disagreement and debate, the previously invoked exchange between Alberto Moreiras and Beatriz Sarlo which appeared, in English, in the *Journal of Latin American Cultural Studies* in 1999. A first version, in English, of Sarlo's piece was presented in 1996 at Duke University; it was first published, in Spanish, in 1997 in *Revista de Crítica Cultural;* it was then translated by Lucy Phillips and published as indicated. Moreiras's much longer piece bears no marks of translation and was evidently written in English: there is no note, as is the case with Sarlo's piece, which indicates that it has a cross-cultural, bilingual history. The distinction is not insignificant. As Moreiras declares: "Sarlo's essay . . . must be read in the context of a developing discussion of what Mabel Moraña calls 'international Latinamericanism' or theory about Latin America at an international level" ("Order" 125).[11] Sarlo's piece, which is a defense of literature, literary criticism, and aesthetic value(s), antedates Moreiras's piece, which thus functions as a response or rebuttal—not just to Sarlo but also to Achugar, Moraña, and others who are not primarily, or as resolutely, concerned with a defense of aesthetic value(s). Both pieces engage literary studies and cultural studies or rather, as Moreiras recasts it, literary studies and the modality (or anti-modality) of cultural studies that he champions: subaltern studies. The twists and turns of studies, by which "cultural," "subaltern," "postcolonial" and so on are now tied together, now torn apart, are as complex as they are common. Sarlo's intervention is unquestionably less demanding—in more than one way—than Moreiras's and, interestingly, less artfully wrought.[12] What most strikes me about Sarlo's piece is, however, what strikes Moreiras: its instances of personal reflection, location, and interpretation, what Sarlo designates as "personal experience." Moreiras, who *here* avoids drawing on any personal experience of his own, or in his own name, maintains a stance of critical distance, a semblance of objectivity, autonomy, and radicality whose measure is an absence of grounds, fundamental, in turn, to his understanding of accomplished globalization ("Order" 125).[13] Despite a few caveats regarding the complexity of meaning and the lack of satisfactory answers to the questions that cultural studies poses, Moreiras's response to Sarlo is confident and, moreover, rigorously anti-anecdotal. It rehearses no personal story, no little incident, no subjective moment, and virtually no point of location, *except by way of others.* Sarlo's "personal experience" accordingly occludes what the reader can only *imagine* as Moreiras's "personal experience;" it functions under his pen as a pettiness that inhabits, like some benighted negativity, Moreiras's theoretical speculation, itself immersed in negativity of a more dazzling sort.

Such dazzling negativity reminds me—*toutes proportions gardées*—of what Keats, referring to Shakespeare, called "negative capability" and what Paul de Man, glossing Keats, celebrated as "a life so buried under the wealth of its own inventions that it has ceased to exist as a particular experience" (xxv). Moreiras might be similarly, if less sumptuously, buried, if only what he celebrated did not entail here something like the burial of poetry itself, its encryption under a wealth of subalternist inventions. Rhetorically, it is by way of Sarlo's "personal experience" that Moreiras incorporates into the body of the text that bears his name and that forms part of his *curriculum vitae* personality and experience as other than his, as not his, as *nameless.* Said namelessness is *essential,* it seems, to the subaltern, or rather to the subalternist studies, that

Moreiras advances. Pursuing "the possibility of raising questions in the name of nothing," Moreiras asserts "the question about asking under no name, in the name of nothing: a nameless thinking or a nameless asking" ("Order" 136). The question, he assures us, has to do with the subaltern and, though he certainly does not put it so, with its institutionalized maintenance in and as subaltern or subalternist studies, especially in the United States. Sarlo had already noted the conditioned profitability of cultural (and subalternist) studies, whose "growing popularity . . . has provided employment for countless retrained literary critics" (115)—and retrained philosophers, I am tempted to add. But Moreiras, in responding to Sarlo, is not interested in addressing such questions as employment, and labors instead to make a more philosophically compelling argument invoked by Sarlo herself. And here, in the shadow of labor and the market, we return to the ever so constrained burden of selling, or selling-out. Moreiras takes on those "Latin American intellectuals" who "have sharpened their critical knives on what they regard as a major Latinamericanist sell-out of Latin America into the global market taking place primarily if not exclusively through the U.S. academy, and in particular through Latinamericanist subaltern and postcolonial studies" ("Order" 125–26). Compelling as it is, Moreiras's argument for namelessness, groundlessness, and subalternist critique finds itself shaped by the very "knives" that would be sharpened against it. It also turns, at times even decisively, on a number of slippery, universalizing premises of its own.

Adducing Bové's claim that "'history has been the principle within and according to which modern state systems organize knowledge,'" Moreiras goes on to declare that "we must also realize that value thinking has been the principle of that principle" ("Order" 133). The dutiful tenor of the sentence—in which the I disappears behind a collective "we must"—and the penchant for meta-theoretical repetitions—the "order of order, the value of value, the reason of reason" with which he begins ("Order" 125)—are two of the more insistent features of Moreiras's prose. But imperatives and polyptoton—the employment of the same word in various cases—are not what is most at stake. For what is at stake is nothing less than the configuration of the world and the value of the configuration of the world, and, of course, of value itself. For Sarlo, the value at stake is aesthetic, a value in need of rescue and protection by the Left (which needs to rescue and protect it from wholesale appropriation, or sell-out, by the Right). But values, which Moreiras identifies as "consubstantial to state thinking" ("Order" 133), are supposedly "without a ground when at stake is, not the need to rebuild a previous state form as a defense against transnational capital, but rather the necessity [sic] to think through what Bové calls 'the transnational space between state and superstate (or no state) and the national and transnational forms of capital'" ("Order," 133). What happens when, and if, there *is* a "need to rebuild a previous state form" is unclear, though still more unclear is what happens when there is a "need" to build a state that has no previously existing form or a form whose previous existence is long past. Moreiras does not consider that value, if identified as consubstantial to state thinking, might *vary* according to the state or would-be state in question. Whatever the transnational space may be, there is little space in Moreiras's conceptualization for any state in abeyance, in protracted projection, in erasure, or even in danger: the "no state" is not, then, just a possible end but also a seemingly impossible beginning. Tellingly, Moreiras names no state or states and deploys instead the nonstate, or non-superstate, of Latin America even as he criticizes the presumably more homey *nuestro americanismo* (literally, "our Americanism') of others.

The lack of attention to specific states and non-states, to specific moments and events, distinguishes Moreiras's defense of subalternist studies from work by Dipesh Chakrabarty, Ranajit Guha, and other subalternist critics who relate events in a manner that does not entail the deletion of history and historiography as heretofore practiced. For that matter, it distinguishes it from the work of other members of the Latin American Subaltern Studies Group such as Ileana Rodríguez as well as that of Guillermo Bonfil Batalla, Manuel Burga, and others working in Latin America. Moreiras's ethico-philosophical interests, perhaps his ethico-philosophical formation, may partially account for both his apparent unwillingness to name (he does not, quite rightly, aim to speak *for* the subaltern or *in* its/his/her name) and his apparent disinterest in historical "details." Such "details" turn on him, as author, all the same. For the nameless thinking or nameless asking, when asserted by one who has a name and whose name is known, smacks of what Bourdieu calls the oracle effect, an assumption of ever greater authority by abolishing the self and by speaking in the name of others or an ideal. For Bourdieu, "it is when I become Nothing . . . that I become Everything. . . . The oracle effect is a veritable *splitting of personality:* the individual personality, the ego, abolishes itself in favour of a transcendent moral person" (*Language* 211). Although Bourdieu himself is no stranger to the oracle effect (perhaps "no one" who publishes is), his work puts the ground back, if only provisionally, under the groundlessness that has become so dear to much self-designated radical critique. Bourdieu's work does so, I might add, not by simply denying groundlessness, but by indicating that groundlessness, not unlike globalization, is easier said than done, let alone lived. Moreiras, however, presents groundlessness as an all but indisputable truth and, furthermore, as a value in its own right: its truth entails the impossibility of securing truth and its value, the impossibility of securing value. The upshot, so thick with paradox (as Moreiras knows), includes not just idealist moves against idealism, but also a developmental logic against developmental logic. Tracing a line of ascendant, developmental, hierarchical truth-value (precisely what he claims not to trace), Moreiras impugns a "retrenchment into past forms" (128) and an attempt to "resuscitate" nationalist projects "from the ruins of state-centered *desarrollismo* (developmentalism)" (129). More significantly, he holds that some critics hold on to "the dying (which remains spectral)" while others embrace "the emergent" (134). It almost goes without saying that Moreiras (implicitly) situates himself among, and maybe at the forefront of, the emergent.

For someone as given to spectral thinking as Moreiras is elsewhere, it is curious that he does not dally with the possibility that the specter of the dead and dying might haunt the emergent or that the emergent might be a rehearsal, with a difference, of the dead and dying. The closest he comes is when he writes that "this is not to say that these forms [of value thinking] will not return: they will, necessarily, but always under the guise of unavoidable farce, in the well-known Marxian sense" (136). Moreiras does not gloss what is "well-known," and so the would-be Marxian designation of farce here functions as a dismissive accusation in its name. Be that as it may, the complication of critical positions appears less important than a reaffirmation of their division. For all its philosophical and political trappings, the aforementioned division between the dying and the emergent (which ironically, if not farcically, supports a *desarrollismo* of its own) signals also, and perhaps primarily, a *competitive ethos* in which ideas, projects, and persons, truths and values, vie for critical ground, or groundlessness. In this, it "necessarily" shares more than a little with capitalism and the so-called market of ideas.[14] Mabel Moraña's sense of *déjà vu* with respect to much postmodern theorization (218) is borne out, I believe, in Moreiras's formulation of critical positions that recall previous divides—never exactly neat—between decadents and regenerationists, traditionalists and avant-gardists, and so on. Without naming names, Moraña criticizes the penchant to "hacer de América Latina un constructo que confirme la centralidad y el vanguardismo téorico globalizante de quienes la interpretan y aspiran a representarla discursivamente" (make of Latin America a construct that confirms the centrality and globalizing theoretical avant-gardism of those who interpret it and aspire to represent it discursively) (219). Moraña refers to the *boom* in subaltern studies, by which she indicates the imbrication of theory in literature and of both in the market. Just as the "boom" in Latin American literature was *partially* designed in Barcelona, so might the "boom" in Latin American subaltern studies be understood as *partially* designed in Pittsburgh and Durham (in both cases, Latin American production is downplayed in order to be "discovered" and promoted from a metropolitan site). Moraña is considerably more discreet in her allusions than I am, but Moreiras seems to be engaged nonetheless. He counters, more directly (by citing her), with a discourse of displacement that has little patience for the ostensible pettiness of placement. Championing a nameless, ground-less, radical thinking, Moreiras styles himself, but *only implicitly,* as among the emergent but also as in the "interregnum," another concept he borrows from Paul Bové (135). The interregnum designates an in-between whose exaspera-tion with "populist-historicist" projects apparently leaves its denizens little time to recall, at least in Moreiras's version, the regal, dynastic dimensions of what was, once upon a time, a between kingdoms. At any rate, the name, the history of names, is here out of the question, as if its recognition could only entail the misrecognition or, worse still, the disrespectful evacuation of the subaltern.

The division, if nothing else, seems clear. Those who hold on to the dying are, in Moreiras's words, "tendential neo-Arielists . . . by and large engaged in a salvaging movement of what is past" ("Order" 134). So engaged, the "neo-Arielists" (like the *nuestroamericanistas*) are eminently melancholy, mired in a movement past and forever backward, mired, in fact, in non-movement. So engaged, the "neo-Arielists" can hardly be viable challengers in the "patterned disputes," or debates, with the people "they critique," some of whom "place themselves in the interregnum" ("Order" 134). The *voluntarism* of such a pro-nouncement, tendentious in its own right, is indicative of a refusal to confront the *insufficiency* of the will and, hence, the *difficulty* of self-placement and the *insistence* of preexisting structures of placement (the burdens and constraints already noted). In contrast to such willfully oblique self-placement, Sarlo's "re-course to 'personal experience'" is openly conditioned by disciplinarity, institu-tionality, and nationality. Her "adoption" of the position of art critic is in some very significant sense *out of her hands* and takes the form of an exasperating, at times exhausting, negotiating of terrain. If Sarlo's position is one of delimited negotiation and struggle, in which recourse to personal experience can be an act of resistance, Moreiras's place, despite his claims to openness, untimeli-ness, and infinitude (indeed perhaps *because* of them), seems uncannily more secure. True, Moreiras does not place himself *by name* among those who place themselves in the interregnum (he refers to "some of the people"), but it seems all but clear that the interregnum is his place and that he is one of the people that the "tendential neo-Arielists" critique. It seems also all but clear that he need not and indeed *should not* name himself.

The lack of the name is not always the same, however. Moreiras's liter-ary-theoretical study, *Tercer espacio,* is a *deeply personal work* that includes a lengthy reflection on a photograph of a young child, held in the arms of a young woman, looking into a mirror. The photograph is duly reproduced, apparently in order to give more credibility—dare I say "ground"—to the written description. The woman and child are described in the third person, their names withheld, in a manner that ostensibly strengthens the photograph's allegorical charge. The photograph might thus appear to be *any* old photograph, a found object, a piece of a personal past that becomes impersonal or extrapersonal or, as Moreiras prefers, "desprivatizado" (deprivatized) (*Tercer* 34) because it can only partially be remembered and never, with any exactitude, named. The date of the photograph, however, is given at the very outset: 1957. Only a bit later does the reader "see" that the child in question is the author and that the woman is the author's mother. The index does not mention the mother and refers only to the "foto del autor" (author's photo), but the entire work is explicitly dedicated to her, *in memoriam,* as well as to the author's father, whose first name only is given. It is a compelling strategy, this withholding of the name, for it casts the photograph into the sphere of something like the universal, though the fashion, faces, and frame of the mirror, let alone the date, impose a more localized impression. The strategic withholding permits Moreiras to hold forth in some powerfully reflective ways. "Mirar ese espejo (in the photograph) es un anticipo de lo imposible" (to look at that mirror is to anticipate the impossible) and, for the photographed child as author, "una lección en todo lo que le desborda" (a lesson in everything that exceeds him) (*Tercer* 33). Despite the annunciation of what might pass as a universal impossibility, the lesson is arguably more pointed, and more poignant, for the subject therein depicted. To make that perfectly clear, however, might risk wrecking a lesson for the reader. For "en este texto la foto se desprivatiza y deviene no sólo lugar de escritura, sino emblema o alegoría fundacional" (in this text the photo is deprivatized and becomes not only a place of writing but also a foundational emblem or allegory) (*Tercer* 34). With just the right spin, the author's personal, private baby picture becomes a place for writing and an allegory, apparently for us all.

In Moreiras's allegorical lesson, Roland Barthes—the dead author whose writings about the death of the author are supplemented by autobiographically touched speculations on his love for his (dead) mother—is mentioned by name, as is Iván Zulueta, director of *Arrebato.* Interestingly, in *La chambre claire (Camera Lucida)*, Barthes does *not* show his best-loved photograph of his mother, a photograph of her as a child, before he could ever be *seen* (by us at least) in her arms. For Marianne Hirsch, "Barthes *cannot* show us the photograph because we stand outside the familial networks of looks and thus cannot *see* the picture in the way that Barthes must. To us it would be just another generic family photograph from a long time ago" (2, emphasis original). Moreiras proceeds differently, showing us a baby picture, his own, but refusing to deploy a proper name or first person pronoun of his own. Then again, Moreiras's name graces the cover of the book, and perhaps any repetition would have seemed unseemly; after all, books, with their editors, copyrights, and ISBN numbers, are already such delimited, personally marked products. The "deprivatization" of the photograph thus runs against the privatization of the book, but it also spins the allegorical into something generic, just another family photograph from a (fairly) long time ago. For Hirsch, the generic spells the end of poignancy, and yet *for me,* there is something poignant in Moreiras's open self-retention, such showing without quite telling, such mournful determination to be taken away without being taken away, or "arrebatado." It is almost as if the author were embarrassed by his authority, his name, and his publicly uttered I, embarrassed or all too proud to give it up easily.

But this is mere speculation, pregnant with emotional markers, the writerly afterlife of reading and seeing. What is less speculative is that even at his most intimate, Moreiras remains (touchingly) distant. There is a lesson here—*Tercer espacio* is not part of a debate, but of a monograph, of which more later—and it whispers to us that we might show ourselves, but not speak of ourselves, at least not by way of a proper name or a first person pronoun. The mother tongue is, nevertheless, at play, and it comes through amid considerable confusion, its dramatic quotient benefiting in the process. Moreiras recounts his "duda entre redactar sus palabras en la lengua que le compete pública y profesionalmente, dada su afiliación, o en la lengua que, a fuerza de distancia y desgaste, ha acabado por no hacerse suya, a pesar de su filiación, pero en cuya extrañeza cree entrever a veces todavía una genuina posibilidad de escritura" (doubt between composing his words in the language which, given his affiliation, is of his public and professional competence or in the language which, despite his filiation to it, has by dint of distance and wear turned out to not be his, but in whose strangeness he believes that he at times still glimpses a genuine possibility of writing), (*Tercer* 36). Never abandoning the third person, which seems to be the person best suited to the "third space," Moreiras explains, in Spanish, his doubt about explaining anything, including himself, in Spanish, or perhaps in English, or perhaps in yet another language. Emotion rears its head again, if only to cast down its eyes. What Moreiras writes in his response to Sarlo about his Latin American Latin Americanist colleagues and their affective investment in Spanish may go for him, at least in *Tercer espacio,* though only up to a point. And what Moreiras writes, in a footnote, is that "emotion may be the very heart of the matter under discussion" ("Order" 142, n. 14). He does so in acknowledgment of what he calls the "affective investment" in the Spanish language by

Cornejo-Polar, Achugar, Moraña, Sarlo, and other Latin Americans ("Order" 142, n. 14).

Recognizing the affective investments in Spanish and other languages, I want to stay with Moreiras's own affective, autobiographical gesture, fraught with strangeness, *extrañeza*. The strangeness that Moreiras claims to glimpse as offering *a genuine possibility of writing*—of writing, if of nothing else—also carries a charge of estrangement. Moreiras is from Spain, at times still called by some the mother country, though from a corner of the mother country where Spanish is not always the mother tongue (the mother tongue of Moreiras's mother, *though not of his father,* seems to be Spanish; cf. *Tercer espacio,* 36). Whatever place Galician may have in Moreiras's account of public and professional competence, affiliations and filiations, remains, however, opaque.[15] I have been drawing on personal knowledge, admittedly limited, and not on the shaky provenance of a name—in which the "ei" of "Moreiras" might be taken as a mark of identity, i.e., Galician—or on the possible wordplays to which the proper name may lend itself (in such play, *mor*tality would necessarily be shadowed forth). As a result, something no less suspicious—i.e., my limited personal knowledge of, and fractured affection for, another person—wriggles its way ever more flamboyantly into play and leaves me with no less clarity than before. Galician might, in some way, here signify, and, in signifying, might push at the either/or formulation of a linguistic dilemma, and decision, that runs along more established international lines. The third space and the third person might implicate a third language, one less inclined to hegemonic success than *either* English *or* Spanish. And yet, "Galician," as is well known, functions in parts of Latin America as a virtual synonym, or perhaps metonym, for "Spanish." The exilic history of the Galicians, itself stamped by Castilian hegemony, wrinkles the transatlantic relations between languages, places, and identities, including stereotypes. Moreiras's own relation to such historically layered relations might matter, I suspect, but I simply do not know for certain.

The logical effect of such suspicious uncertainty might be silence, my keeping quiet about what I do not know and, for that matter, what I know. Silence certainly has its place in critical endeavors, but Moreiras is hardly a silent critic. That said, the place where Moreiras places himself without quite naming himself, the interregnum, is purportedly "a logical place, the obverse of hegemony, a place of silence without a permanent positivity of its own" (141). That this "logical place" is "the subaltern position" might be one thing, I suppose, but that it is also, and in the same stroke, the subalternist position, the position of the practitioner of subaltern studies, is another. The two positions—subaltern and subalternist—are not commensurate, and Moreiras's involute prose, demanding (if seductive) for even the most theoretically engaged of critics, brings that incommensurability home. For my part, I do indeed "feel . . . a certain de-historicizing [is] at stake" in such speculation. And yet, how I "feel" about de-historicization, historicism, or history, seems to be beside the point, or rather it seems to be a point beyond speculation. Moreiras adduces the charge of de-historicization as a sort of reactive formation—"perhaps some of the critics of subaltern studies react to what they feel is a certain de-historicizing" (141), but he brings it up only to set it aside. "But with this," he writes, "we have reached a point that no amount of metacritical commentary and no lengthy theoretical statement could ever trespass. Monographs are needed, since there are not enough of them, to show that the subalternist critical perspective in Latin American studies can restitute history as history" (141). At the close of his piece, *as its close,* the theoretician of the emergent, placed in the interregnum, declares theory to be at a dead end, a site that cannot be trespassed. We have traveled far, up to a point where only a return or entrenchment is possible. Arriving at this point, beyond which we cannot perform any more metacritical commentary or theorization, we either stop dead or turn back to produce . . . monographs.

Monographs are needed, Moreiras tells us. And monographs, which the dictionary defines as "learned treatises on a particular subject," seem to be on *this side* of a theoretical limit. Whatever else monographs may accomplish, they will at least show something powerful and productive about "the subalternist critical perspective in Latin American studies" (141). Moreiras's call to monographic action implicitly recalls Gramsci's, for whom "this kind of history [subaltern history] can only be dealt with monographically, and each monograph requires an immense quantity of material which is often hard to collect" (55). Florencia Mallon cites the preceding passage from Gramsci in her 1994 examination of Latin American Subaltern Studies, its "promise and dilemma." She does so in order to support her insistence on a "laborious and methodologically complex task" that draws on "semiotics, literary criticism, and many forms of textual analysis" (1497) without "dismissing earlier traditions and works as irrelevant and passé" (1501). For Mallon, the dismissal of earlier traditions entails the dismissal, or at least avoidance, of "the archive and the field" (1501), whose demands are difficult "in today's academic world, with it notorious overproduction" (1502). Waxing rapturous about the quasi-revelatory joys of "getting one's hands dirty in the archival dust" and "one's shoes encrusted in the mud of field work" (1507), Mallon, nonetheless, reminds us of the neatness of some of our more theoretically informed speculations and programs. She also warns against a literary-philosophical habit by which historiographic monographs are elided, forgotten, ignored, or declared to be nonexistent. Criticizing Patricia Seed for failing to "demonstrate an awareness" of previous work by Latin Americanists on subaltern subjects (1500), Mallon implicitly submits that showing is knowing, a dubious proposition that, still and all, has an effective, and affective, charge when placed alongside Moreiras's call for (more) monographs.

For Moreiras, apparently writing after Mallon, what the much-needed monographs will show is the subalternist perspective as that by which history is restituted as history, in "an absolute, that is, non-arbitrary way" (141). History restituted in *an absolute, that is, non-arbitrary way:* the assertion is strong, and it comes without any qualifier such as Gramsci's *"this kind* of history." The qualifier "absolute" remits to Moreiras's presentation of Jameson's "absolute historicism" which "grounds the possibility of a comprehensive theory of past societies and cultures in the structure of the present, of capitalism" (qtd. in Moreiras, 131). Moreiras continues to quote Jameson, who refers to "honoring" "existential historicism" as "an experience" (131), but he does not unpack either "existence" or "experience" and moves immediately "to claim the status of absolute historicism for that which subaltern studies attempts to do" (131). Against absolute historicism, as its *insufficient* rival, he declares that he "will retain the name of populist historicism to refer to an always insufficient kind of historicism, thwarted by its confusion of the part and the whole, and intent on hegemonic seizure" (131). Moreiras's own possible confusion of parts and wholes, his own possible intents on hegemonic seizure, do not quite figure, but neither do the "repressive strategies" and "collusion" that Dipesh Chakrabarty mentions in a passage that Moreiras quotes as supporting his presentation of "absolute historicism" as a "motto for subalternism" (131). And what Moreiras quotes from Chakrabarty is his request "for a history that deliberately makes visible, within the very structure of its narrative forms, its own repressive strategies and practices, the part it plays in collusion with the narratives of citizenship in assimilating to the projects of the modern state all other possibilities of human solidarity" (qtd. in Moreiras, 131). Even if it is admitted, by way of an appeal to disciplinarity, that Moreiras is writing not history but a critique of history, the critique of history is not yet beyond history (or historiography), and, hence, not yet beyond its own repressive strategies and its own forms of collusion. Within that, it remains unclear, and perhaps deliberately so, what it would mean for Moreiras's own subalternist, or meta-subalternist, practice to ask—by way of a previous authority whose relation to subalternity is *not* Moreiras's—for a history that *deliberately makes visible* such things.

All told, if this is not how subalternist studies fall "prey to itself by, precisely, not being subalternist enough," then I either have no idea what the academy is or I have no idea what the subaltern is. *Who* the subaltern is, or might be; and whether he or she can speak; and whether it depends on whether we have been listening or not; and whether there is indeed a history here to be restituted; and whether restitution will alleviate misery, injustice, exploitation, and suffering, I do not know. At least I do not know any of this after so much metacritical commentary and so lengthy a theoretical statement, so much "unmasterable excess" that "constitutes [Moreiras's] personal investment" (140) and that sends me packing back to monographs, to another kind of study, more focused, more delimited, more specific. Or perhaps it is more in touch with the archive and/or the field. Whatever the case, Moreiras's gesture is a strong one, a slap in many a face already de-faced as hegemonic because it is not subalternist in the manner that Moreiras puts forth. The gesture mimics, as in an inverted glass, that of those, like myself, who would take Moreiras to task for being intent on hegemonic seizure in *his* own right (as if hegemonic seizure were always already "wrong"). Whatever the plays of Gramsci (whom Moreiras does not cite), Jameson, and Chakrabarty, the idea that a *line of study,* duly practiced by "transnational" intellectuals employed in U.S. universities, could restitute history as history in an absolute, non-arbitrary way, might indeed best be answered with silence. And yet, second best to silence, it does lead me to raise the question as to why restitution, *so figured, should be* the objective.[16]

Sarlo, for whom "art is about . . . something extra" (123), helps me, however, to see Moreiras's highly theoretical piece on subalternity as *artful* in its excess. That it is also a mode of academic power and a perspective of study is, I guess, just something extra. There is of course more. Moreiras writes with unwavering seriousness, not stopping to deal with the messiness—or as Stuart Hall might put it, the "nastiness"—of materiality, not stopping to unpack such loaded terms as "absolute" and "non-arbitrary," "experience" and "existence," "repression" and "collusion." Such seriousness is, as Sarlo might say (and I would certainly agree), Moreiras's "right," and it would be frivolous of me—or all too serious—to bend, or want to bend, his writing into something else. yet, I am struck by a certain *excessive effect of seriousness.* In an unwitting reiteration of conventional gender divisions, Moreiras plays the man's part (selfless, general, forward thinking, philosophical) while Sarlo, at least in Moreiras's response, is made to play, ever so implicitly, the woman's part (self-concerned, specific, bound to the past, given to art). Interestingly, Sarlo's own deployment of gender leads her to present "white males" as given to art and art criticism and women and (other?) subalterns as relegated, by the aforementioned men, to the production of cultural objects. However philosophy, art, and culture are sliced, gender and race are sliced in, too. But Moreiras does not really engage either category, and limits himself to saying "and so it is so" (133) to Sarlo's assessment. That said, he returns directly to debunking "value thinking as the right medicine for cultural-studies-based racist orientalism" (133), taking up Sarlo's explicit reference to racism and ignoring her only implicit reference, or non-reference, to sexism. Insofar as Moreiras insists on attending to the "great debate of the end of the century," and insofar as said debate "is not a debate on values, but rather on that which values obscure" (136), it is interesting that he does not attend to what is obscured in Sarlo's summation.

Gender, race, class, and nationality, as categories of identity and difference, are what Moreiras would push away, or behind, in the great debate on values; or rather, they are what he, concerned about reductive maneuvers, would reduce to populist articulations resolutely at odds with critical articulations (135).[17] Asserting a division between populism and criticism that effectively subsumes and trumps all other divisions, Moreiras positions himself (ostensibly against all positions) firmly on the side of the later. He is, after all, a critic, and *that* designation, *that* position, *that identity,* obscured as it may be, is not without so-cio-symbolic ramifications. Maintaining a consistently high level of discourse, Moreiras would keep us centered on the crisis of the value of value, the ground-lessness of grounds, radical openings, social infinitudes, "ruptural horizons," interruptions, and "unmasterable excesses." The latter, as I have already inti-mated, is the closest Moreiras comes to acknowledging his own critical person-ality. "That the social only gives itself to us under the form of an unmasterable excess," he writes, "constitutes my own personal investment in subalternism" (140). The confession, if such it may be called, is telling. Not the plight of the poor, or the injustice of unequal economic distribution, or the destructive ef-fects of globalization, or the denial of representation and self-representation, or any of the other issues one might *expect* (all too humanistically?) from subal-ternism, or from a *personal investment* in it, is sufficient. Rather, excess alone is enough, more than enough, and it apparently exceeds all attempts, all expecta-tions, to ground it, to situate it, to pin it down, if only for an arbitrary moment, and take it to task. The rhetoric of radical openness that Moreiras deploys seems to close his critique off from critique and to close him off as a situated social subject. For to open him and his critique to critique would violate not only a principle of delicacy, it would throw the one who makes such an overture (*moi*) into what Moreiras scripts as a retrogressive position, prone to populist histori-cist platitudes and identity politics presumably indistinguishable from "the old metaphysical objection to post-metaphysics" (138).

Validating the valueless value of values, the groundlessness of grounds, as the newest, latest, most historically *adequate* way of thinking (and of thinking inadequation), Moreiras presents himself as more in tune than Sarlo, Achugar, and Moraña with what he calls, without any appreciable irony, "the spirit of our times" (136). "*Zeitgeist*" haunts 'the spirit of our times,'" and does so in a way that disturbs its "untimeliness" (140). For "*Zeitgeist*" drags "the spirit of our times"—no doubt kicking and screaming—back into a line of high historicist thinking and brings to the fore, by way of contrast, the presence of a collectivity appreciable in "*our* times." The spirit of the times, or the spirit of time, that is one of the most internationally recognizable terms in German contains no mention of the equivalent, in German, of "us" or "our," and Moreiras's invocation of it at least allows "us" to see "our" implication in it. In that respect, Moreiras does "us" a service. The spirit of our times, however, is an effect of subjectivity amassed and monopolized, recast, forgotten, and remembered as more than subjectivity—again I want to say estranged—and taken as if in excess of any and all closure of personality. I would nonetheless *open* the "our" back up to its *petty, particular closures,* especially to those closures that, oracle-like, claim themselves to be so unidentifiably open. My point here is not, however, to criticize Moreiras's rhetoric as if something social could thereby be redeemed (the very thought is absurd). For within my disagreement with Moreiras, I am in agreement with many of the points he makes. I too am troubled—that ubiquitous word—by the invocation of value as aesthetic value and of aesthetic value as the reason, or ground, for preserving literature as a redemptive social practice, redemptive of the social precisely because it would remove itself, in Sarlo's formulation, from the social.

The culture of redemption, as Leo Bersani argues, relies on "apparently acceptable views of art's beneficently reconstructive function" that rely, in turn, "on a devaluation of historical experience and of art. The catastrophes of history matter much less if they are somehow compensated for in art, and art itself gets reduced to a kind of superior patching function, is enslaved to those very materials to which it presumably imparts value" (*Culture* 1). Bersani does not pit art against society, or make one the horizon of the other, and in that respect his suspicion of redemption dovetails Moreiras's (and mine). The difference is that Bersani does not concern himself with art in Latin America, or Latin American art, but with art *per se,* which is here, as so often is the case, Western art or, more precisely, a Western conceptualization of "art." Sarlo's "recourse to 'personal experience'" (Moreiras, 132) hinges on this difference, one that she finds repeated in institutional settings and professional practices worldwide. "We have had trouble," she writes, "in establishing common ground on which to make decisions" (122). Generalizing from personal experience in an exemplary manner, Sarlo claims that *non*-Latin Americans look at things produced in

Latin America, by Latin Americans, with "sociological eyes" (122) while she, a Latin American, assumes the "perspective of an art critic" (123). Moreiras, a non-Latin American, does not grapple with the way such a claim implicates him, and proceeds to deride personal experience—or at least to be suspicious, unflinchingly suspicious, of the *recourse* to it—as indicative of an inability to be in sync with the spirit of our times. Among the things that "trouble" me, *personally as well as professionally,* is the refusal, on the part of Moreiras, here to acknowledge, even if to deconstruct it, his elliptical, "extimate" relation to the reiterated site of his interest, competence, expertise, and investment: Latin America.

As a non-native Peninsularist, I am struck by the conceptual vagueness with which Moreiras insistently adduces Latin America. Disciplinarity will yet have its way, and Moreiras, despite his professed interest in "raising questions in the name of nothing" (136), raises them in the name of Latin America *and* the subaltern, a Latin American subaltern. His authority, however, is neither separable from, nor reducible to, his recognized disciplinary and institutional status as a Latin Americanist, the insistence with which he, like it or not, identifies himself and is identified by others as such. My authority, for whatever it is worth, is neither separable from, nor reducible to my disciplinary and institutional status as a Peninsularist, one whose discontent with said recognition has increasingly lead him down a different path, Catalanist and Latin Americanist—curious as the conjunction may seem to some. The conventions of disciplinarity require, for a valid assumption of the position of the subject assumed to know, both the erasure and the expansion of particular traits, qualities, or signs of identity, both their remembrance and their forgetting. Manuel Burga, in an interesting article on "lo andino" (the Andean), makes a similar—but of course quite different—observation: "negar lo andino y sentirlo propio, . . . sentirlo muy presente y darlo por ausente, son las paradojas y contradicciones de nuestra alma nacional" (to deny the Andean and to feel it as one's own, to feel it to be very present and to give it as absent, is one of the paradoxes and contradictions of our national soul) (68). My uneasiness with such a phrase as "nuestra alma nacional" (our national soul) might be, among other things, a symptom of my own national, institutional, and disciplinary formation, but what I find compelling is the paradox of the negation, or erasure, and the affirmation, or (re)writing, indeed the expansion, of identity. Burga signals a sort of intellectual inhibition—though it is also possible to speak of intimidation—whose markers are something like "theoretical sophistication" and "globalization." And theoretical sophisticated in an age of "accomplished globalization" tends to cast feeling into a reactive, regressive, benighted regime of essences, spirits, and identities.

In order to "estar a tono con los tiempos de un nosotros diverso y de la global-ización" (be in tune with the times of a diverse 'we' and of globalization), feel-ing must assume a mask—Burga speaks of "disimulo" (dissimulation)—that closes more than it opens dialogue.

If I find it difficult to forget my past, it is in part because family, friends, and colleagues, as well as unknown people in the street, in a bar, or in a store, remind me of who I am or, rather, who they think I am. I am told, often by people I have never before met, and almost always after I have answered their question as to the place of my birth, that they could indeed "tell" that I was, and apparently still am, a Southerner because they could "hear" it in my voice. They are generally pleased with such a state of affairs, not only because it reaffirms their discerning linguistic competence but also because, I venture to say, it reaf-firms a longstanding sense of place, language, identity, and, yes, destiny. I am what I sound like, and no amount of vigilance seems sufficient to suppress the shibboleths that *give me away,* that offer me up to them as a quasi-familiar, or unfamiliar, identity. Lest I be mistaken for misspeaking, I will add that I often engage in the same activity, pricking up my ears to see if I can tell something about the place, and "identity," of a person from the opening of a vowel or the duration of an onset consonant.[18] I will not be brash enough to say that "we" all "hear" identity, but I will say that many of us still try, still listen. And the listening obtains even for those whose "hybridity" or native or near-native bi-lingualism makes their tongue slippery in the extreme. What my name is, and what language or languages I speak, and what I sound like when I speak them (maybe even what I sound like when I write), are so many variables that are far from inoperant in the academy or, for that matter, in society at large. The re-course to personal experience is indeed not as easy as it sometimes seems, but it is not as difficult, benighted, or moribund as Moreiras maintains in his response to Sarlo. As has often been noted (an impersonal way of putting it, of course), personal experience is an experience not just of personality, but of a *persona,* a mask, an act or performance. Sarlo's recourse to personal experience is also recourse to a mask, a performative gesture, one that, in its explicit reference to students, acknowledges other spaces, less hypothetical than the transnational spaces between state and superstate (or no state), and perhaps, from a limited institutional and disciplinary perspective, just as pressing.

Here, as I come to an inadequate close, I cannot but admit to a certain exasperation that may resemble resentment—at least as Moreiras formulates it. Moreiras, after all, marshals forth a series of resentful practices, specifically citing three:

first, national and/or regional particularisms resenting reductive representational practices coming from the metropolitan location standing in as a signifier of universality; second, local interests resenting what they perceive as an overwhelming colonization of their discursive space by intellectual and political agendas emanating from other locations that cannot be made their own without a varying but always present degree of violence; and third, personal histories resenting powerful interpretative frameworks which are felt as a threat to the moral right of self-interpretation. (126)

Moreiras's is a powerful interpretative framework that does its best to give a full account by emptying itself of any mention of particularisms, local interests, or personal histories except in general, that is to say, as categories without content. Lest my own personally styled intervention be consigned forthwith to the dust heap of resentment, I will venture the following: it is not that I "resent" but rather that I "feel again" what Moreiras and others, in accord with the "spirit of our times," have declared dead or dying. All this I feel again because, in a distressingly self-implicating sense, I have incorporated it within me as one of the conditions of possibility of an I that I might, more or less improperly, call my own through, for, and against what Sarlo calls "cultural inheritance" (121). Far from constituting an essentialist position, I would submit that said "inheritance" can be constructivist and progressive, even in some of its "conservative" gestures, such as the gesture of love. The love of literature, something that even Sarlo does not dare to name, "conserves" it as a cumulative and disperse effect of the lives of others. It is, moreover, an effect of lives often lovingly, and hatefully, recounted in "little" languages that most of us, even in a politically oriented Hispanism, do not know or take the time to learn. Said effect, which is also an affect, does not rely perforce on either aesthetic value or social efficacy, but on both and neither, sometimes at once.

In his rebuttal of Sarlo, Moreiras does not really tarry with the possibility of what Sarlo suggests: *literary and cultural studies* or even *literary cultural studies;* much less does he mention his own highly theorized work on literature. Instead, he reiterates their division in now classical fashion, in order to make the debate more of a debate, one in which differences are strong and clear even when arguments may be weak and muddled, and which might give way, as here, to a debate on a debate. All of which brings me looping back to that from which Moreiras, by way of Sarlo, started: the order of order, the value of value, and so on. It is no doubt revealing that I have quoted no literary texts, whether from Latin America, Spain, the United States, or anywhere else. Just as Moreiras, in his response to Sarlo, says nothing specific about the subaltern, or Latin America, I have said nothing specific about literature or, I admit, Latin

America. There is a paradoxical agreement here. It is time, I think, to get back to work, each in his or her own way, the so-called dying and the emergent *at the same impossible time*. But that is what *I* think. I would be done—even though I know that I will not be done—with such highly theorized proclamations, such abstract debates, such metacritical turns, such confidently rendered time lines, such self-concerned negations of the self. Monographs are needed, indeed.

Notes

1. I wish to thank José Antonio Mazzotti, Luis Cárcamo-Huechante, and Nelly Richard for their comments and suggestions. But I also wish to thank, in the most profound way possible, Alberto Moreiras himself, whose dialogic openness, amid all the ostensible opacity and obscurity (perhaps indeed *thanks* to all the ostensible opacity and obscurity), is exemplary in its complication, if not rejection, of exemplarity. My desire, if of desire I may speak, is to engage, even at the risk of disengaging, a densely theoretical critique that has been caricaturized and dismissed, when not met with silence, on the part of many, not all, of those with whom I am in agreement: the so-called locationists. In so doing, I also desire—and no doubt this may seem more jarring than anything I write about Moreiras—to open, or reopen, location to reflection and critique, to take it as *other* than a given, to rehearse, "essayistically" and even anecdotally, its fragility and strength. I do not know if I accomplish this, but in this *question* of accomplishment I come close, I want to believe, to Moreiras, even as I come close, I also want to believe, to those who may be less ambivalent about some of their proximities, and distances, than I am. Such closeness, needless to say, cannot (but) hope to be reciprocal, and may indeed be at its most intense when it is denied, pushed away, set at naught by way of so many locations, whether "strategically" essentialized or not, that I can never have or hold.
2. Harvard University's "Policy on the Use of Harvard Names and Insignia" states that "the University and its members have a responsibility to protect its assets by seeking a fair share of the economic value that the use of the Harvard name produces." It goes on to state: "'Harvard University' is one of the most widely known and respected trademarks of any kind. The commercial fruits of this fortunate reputation are largely attributable to the contributions of many generations of faculty, students and staff, and therefore should be allocated for the benefit of the University as a whole. Any use of the Harvard name that may depreciate its long-term value should be avoided." It remains to be seen if a critique of such rhetoric—in which the University is explicitly likened to a commercial enterprise and its name to a trademark—qualifies as "depreciation."
3. In the spring of 2001, a group of students, many of them affiliated with a group called The Progressive Student Labor Movement, occupied the president's and provost's offices in one of the venerable old brick buildings in Harvard Yard to demand a "living wage" for out-sourced, non-Unionized, largely immigrant workers. Both Cambridge

and Boston city councils had enacted a living wage, significantly higher than the national standard, for all city government employees.

4. Moraña asks: "¿Cómo redefinir las relaciones Norte/Sur y el lugar ideológico desde donde se piensa y se construye América Latina como el espacio irrenunciable de una otredad sin la cual el 'yo' que habla (que *puede* hablar, como indicaba Spivak) se des-centra, se des-estabiliza epistemológica y politícamente?" (how to redefine North/South relations and the ideological place from which Latin America is thought and constructed as the unremitting space of an otherness without which the 'I' that speaks [and that *can* speak, as Spivak indicated] is decentered and destabilized epistemologically and politically?) (218). Achugar stresses the importance of "un lugar desde donde se habla y desde donde se lee" (a place from which one speaks and from which one reads) (383). One might just as well add "desde donde se escribe y desde donde se escucha" (from which one writes and one listens) to the range of locations.

5. Responding to a welter of recent Spanish works on the legacy of colonialism, Silvia Bermúdez confronts the symbolism of "debt" in Hispanic trans-Atlantic culture. "Frente a la noción de que es España, como agente colonizador, quien está 'en deuda' con los países que hoy constituyen lo que denominamos Latinoamérica, la nueva articulación establece que es en realidad América Latina la que supuestamente está en deuda con España. España, en realidad, no debe nada a Latinoamérica por el pillaje, las matanzas, y la destrucción de la colonización. De hecho, perspectivas históricas negacionistas como las que se formulan en *La mentira histórica desvelada. ¿Genocidio en América?* de Juan Luis Beceiro se utilizan para re-escribir los devastadores efectos del proceso colonial de la conquista de América" (Against the notion that it is Spain, as colonizing agent, which is 'in debt' to the countries that today constitute what we call Latin America, a new articulation maintains that it is Latin America which is supposedly in debt to Spain. Spain, in reality, does not owe anything to Latin America for the pillage, massacres, and destruction of colonization. In fact, revisionist—or 'negationist'—historical perspectives such as those formulated in Juan Luis Beceiros's *The Historical Lie Unveiled: Genocide in America?* are used to rewrite the devastating effects of the colonial process in the conquest of America) (349). This "nueva articulación" (new articulation) is, as Bermúdez knows, scarcely "new" and has a lengthy history. In a similar vein, L. Elena Delgado responds to the 2002 Premio Príncipe de Asturias de la Concordia, whose recipient was Edward Said, by noting that "la figura de Said es apreciada por su papel de crítico del colonialismo ajeno (sobre todo anglosajón e israelí) pero, aunque su obra está traducida al español, sus conclusiones no se aplican para analizar también el colonialismo *propio*" (Said is appreciated in Spain for his role as critic of foreign colonialism [especially Anglo-Saxon and Israeli] but, even though his work is translated to Spanish, his conclusions are not applied to analyze Spain's own colonialism) (329, emphasis original).

6. As James Fernández indicates, U.S. Hispanism has been interested, since its very inception, in Latin America.

7. According to Rosaldo: "as the 'other' becomes more culturally visible, the 'self'

becomes correspondingly less so" (202). In much of Moreiras's work *neither* the self *nor* the other becomes "visible." Such double invisibility may hold a promise, but the promise is shadowed forth in a highly wrought manner that renders it *also* other than promising.

8. In *The Exhaustion of Difference,* Moreiras writes: "Look now at stereotypical Latin American Latin Americanists and you will realize that they are by no means off the hook: if the problem of their alien friend was an excessively comfortable installation in the privileges of Northern knowledge, and if such sinister installation in knowledge (sinister because 'excessively comfortable,' and thus not comfortable at all) was inverted as a mark of unredeemable ignorance, Latin American Latin Americanists may find a dubious legitimation in the positioning of location as final redemption" (6). Whether Moreiras finds a dubious legitimation of his own remains unclear. What is less unclear is, however, the gainsaying of *material* comfort by way of epistemological and ethical discomfort.

9. Moreiras's professed aim in his response to Sarlo is "to show that there is a certain 'essentialism of anti-essentialism' at work in her essay, which *limits the cosmopolitan scope* of her words and might even reintroduce, through the back door, and possibly counterintentionally, just as in the case of Moraña or Achugar, a sort of anti-populist populism as the ultimate horizon of critical thinking" (129, emphasis mine). That cosmoplitanism is, or should be, unlimited, indeed that it should be a value, is itself not beyond questioning. As Bruce Robbins notes, "any cosmopolitanism's normative or idealizing power must acknowledge the actual historical and geographic contexts from which it emerges" (2).

10. The latter phrase is from Richard's blurb on Moreiras's *The Exhaustion of Difference.*

11. The reference is to Moraña's "El *boom* del subalterno" (50).

12. Sarlo also writes of demands: "Literary criticism not only asks questions but makes, in a strong sense, demands of texts" (122).

13. Later on, however, Moreiras seems to question the accomplishment of globalization: "In globalization (provided it could ever be accomplished) . . ."(133). Later still, he states, glossing Paul Bové's concept of the "interregnum," that "temporally, it [the interregnum] occupies rather something like a time gap—the time gap of unaccomplished globalization, which will remain our host for a long time to come" (140). The question then arises: if one of the paradoxes of an accomplished globalization is that it leaves us without a ground to question its very ground, does something *less* than an accomplished globalization leave us with less groundlessness? Leave us, that is, with just a bit of ground?

14. As Hall says with respect to the Gramscian-inspired problem of the organic intellectual, "the problem is that it appears to align intellectuals with an emerging historic movement and we couldn't tell then, and could hardly tell now, where that emerging historical moment was to be found" (281). Wherever or whatever the emergent may be, Moreiras seems to know that he is "with it."

15. Moreiras does not make things easy for his reader. If "la lengua que le compete pública y profesionalmente, dada su afiliación" (the language which, given his affiliation, is of his public and professional competence) is English, then the act of writing in Spanish is indeed more "daring." Or, if not daring, it is consonant with some of Cornejo-Polar's observations about language and scholarship: "los textos críticos en inglés suelen utilizar bibliografía en el mismo idioma y prescindir, o no citar, lo que trabajosamente se hizo en América Latina durante largos años" (343).

16. That Moreiras invokes the restitution of history as history right after he tells us that we have reached a point that no theory can *trespass* reminds me of his criticism of Gordon Brotherston's criticism of Brett Levinson's reading of Rigoberta Menchú and *testimonio*. Defending Levinson's "intellectualization" of Menchú's text, which supposedly "managed to operate a concrete historical restitution that may have no precedent or continuation," Moreiras offers an impressive reproof of empathy. For Moreiras, empathy forestalls or forecloses "interlocution" and maintains a divide as profound as that wrought by intellectualization (*Exhaustion* 218). Moreiras sides with Levinson, his former student, and upbraids Brotherston for suggesting, as Moreiras styles it, that "third world or resistant texts should only be treated abjectly, with 'affect, empathy, or commiseration' (*Exhaustion* 218–219). It is interesting that Moreiras renders empathy—not sympathy, but empathy—as a mode of abjection and that he advocates, however implicitly, a mode of non-empathetic, intellectual solidarity. But no less interesting is Moreiras's claim that "restitutional excess can . . . choose to negate itself as such; [that] it can look for its own point of closure in an attempt to come to the end of itself, *as in Brotherston's response to Levinson*" (*Exhaustion* 221, emphasis mine). Moreiras is not alone in linking restitution to excess, which he calls "restitutional excess," but what strikes me is how his rendition of Brotherston's essay (i.e., a restitutional excess that leads to negation and to closure) resembles his own "final words" on Sarlo. Whatever his intentions, Moreiras's language encrypts the subaltern as *that* which only the subject who assumes the subalternist perspective can "know." The subaltern is, from this perspective, a disciplinary construct, a thing of the academy, and it is the discipline that seems to come out on top. If "the discipline cannot be abolished by its object" (*Exhaustion* 222), it may just be that the object can be abolished by the discipline.

17. Moreiras's expressed desire "to help move the debate beyond *merely* situational parameters" (131, emphasis mine) is one I share, but only if it does not entail the absolute erasure of said parameters.

18. I have in mind Sean Crist's article on so-called gay speech in American English.

Works Cited

Achugar, Hugo. "Leones, cazadores e historiadores, a próposito de las políticas de la memoria y del conocimiento." *Revista Iberoamericana* 63.180 (1997): 379–87.

Barthes, Roland. *La chambre claire: Note sur la photographie.* Paris: Etoile, Gallimard, Seuil, 1980.

Bermúdez, Silvia. "De patriotas constitucionales, neoconservadores y periférficos: ¿Qué hace una España como tú en un entre siglos como éste? *Revista de Estudios Hispánicos* 37 (2003): 341–55.

Bersani, Leo. *The Culture of Redemption.* Cambridge: Harvard University Press, 1990.

Beverley, John. "Can Hispanism Be a Radical Practice?" *Ideologies and Literature* 16.4 (1983): 9–22.

Blanchot, Maurice. "La Littérature et le droit à la mort." In *De Kafka à Kafka.* Paris, Gallimard, 1982. 11–61.

Bonfil Batalla, Guillermo, introd. *Utopia y revolución: el pensamiento político contemporáneo de los indios en América Latina.* México DF: Editorial Nueva Imagen, 1981.

Bourdieu, Pierre. *Contre-feux 2: Pour un mouvement social européen.* Paris: Raisons d'Agir, 2001.

———. *Language and Symbolic Power.* Trans. Gino Raymond and Matthew Adamson. Ed. John B. Thompson. Cambridge: Harvard University Press, 1991.

Bramen, Carrie Tirado. *The Uses of Variety: Modern Americanism and the Quest for National Distinctiveness.* Cambridge: Harvard University Press, 2000.

Brotherston, Gordon. "Regarding the Evidence in *Me llamo Rigoberta Menchú.*" *Journal of Latin American Cultural Studies* 6 (1997): 41–58.

Buell, Frederick. "Nationalist Postnationalism: Globalist Discourse in Contemporary American Culture." *American Quarterly* 50.3 (1998): 548–91.

Burga, Manuel. "Lo andino hoy en el Perú." *Quehacer* 128 (2001): 65–68.

Cornejo-Polar, Antonio. "Mestizaje e hibridez: Los riesgos de las metáforas. Apuntes." *Revista Iberoamericana* 63.180 (1997): 341–44.

Crist, Sean. "Duration of Onset Consonants in Gay Male Stereotyped Speech." *U. Penn Working Papers in Linguistics* 4.3 (1997): 53–70.

Delgado, L. Elena. "La nación (in)vertebrada: razones para un debate." *Revista de Estudios Hispánicos* 37 (2003): 319–40.

De Man, Paul, ed. *John Keats: Selected Poetry.* New York: Signet, 1966.

Fernández, James. "Longfellow's Law: The Place of Latin America and Spain in US Hispanism, circa 1915." In *Spain in America: The Origins of Hispanism in the United States.* Ed. Richard L. Kagan. Urbana and Chicago: University of Illinois Press, 2002. 122–41.

Foucault, Michel. *The Archeology of Knowledge.* Trans. A. M. Sheridan Smith. New York: Pantheon, 1972.

Gramsci, Antonio. "Notes on Italian History." In *The Prison Notebooks: Selections.* Eds.

and Trans. Quintin Hoare and Geoffrey Nowell Smith. New York: International Publishers, 1971. 44–120.

Guha, Ranajit and Gayatri Chakravorty Spivak. *Selected Subaltern Studies.* New York: Oxford University Press, 1998.

Hall, Stuart. "Cultural Studies and its Theoretical Legacies." In *Cultural Studies.* Eds. Lawrence Grossberg, Cary Nelson, and Paula Treichler. New York: Routledge, 1992. 277–94.

Hardt, Michael and Antonio Negri. *Empire.* Cambridge: Harvard UP, 2000.

Hirsch, Marianne. *Family Frames: Photography, Narrative and Postmemory.* Cambridge: Harvard University Press, 1997.

Latin American Subaltern Studies Group. "Founding Statement." *Disposition* 19.46 (1994): 1–11.

Levinson, Brett. "Neopatriarchy and After: *I, Rigoberta Menchú* as Allegory of Death." *Journal of Latin American Cultural Studies* 5 (1996): 33–50.

Mallon, Florencia E. "The Promise and Dilemma of Subaltern Studies: Perspectives from Latin American History." *American Historical Review* 99.5 (1994): 1491–1515.

Mignolo, Walter. "Human Understanding and (Latin) American Interests-The Politics and Sensibilities of Geohistorical Locations." In *A Companion to Post Colonial Studies.* Eds. Henry Schwarz and Sangeeta Ray. Malden, Massachusetts: Blackwell, 2000. 180–202.

Moraña, Mabel. "El *boom* del subalterno." *Cuadernos Americanos* 67.1 (1998): 214–22.

Moreiras, Alberto. *The Exhaustion of Difference: The Politics of Latin American Cultural Studies.* Durham: Duke UP, 2001.

———. "Global Fragments: A Second Latinamericanism." In *The Cultures of Globalization.* Eds. Frederic Jameson and Musao Miyoshi. Durham: Duke UP, 1998. 81–102.

———. "Neohispanism: A Program for Tongue Dispossession." In *Intellectuals and Global Culture.* Eds. Charlie Blake and Linnie Blake. Oxford, U.K.: Angelaki, 1997. 29–40.

———. "The Order of Order: On the Reluctant Culturalism of Anti-Subalternist Critiques." *Journal of Latin American Cultural Studies,* 8.1 (1999): 125–45.

———. *Tercer espacio: Literatura y duelo en América Latina.* Santiago: LOM Ediciones/ Universidad Arcis, 1999.

Richard, Nelly. "Cultural Peripheries: Latin America and Postmodernist De-centering." In *The Postmodernism Debate in Latin America.* Eds. John Beverley, José Oviedo, and Michael Aronna. Durham: Duke University Press, 1995. 217–22.

Robbins, Bruce. "Introduction Part I: Actually Existing Cosmopolitanism." In *Cosmopolitics: Thinking and Feeling Beyond the Nation.* Minneapolis: University of Minnesota Press, 1998. 1–19.

Rosaldo, Renato. *Culture and Truth: The Remaking of Social Analysis.* Boston: Beacon Press, 1989.

Sarlo, Beatriz. "Cultural Studies and Literary Criticism at the Crossroads of Values." *Journal of Latin American Cultural Studies,* 8.1 (1999): 115–24.

Part IV
Hispanism/Latin Americanism:
New Articulations

◆ **10**

Xenophobia and Diasporic Latin Americanism: Mapping Antagonisms around the "Foreign"

Idelber Avelar

(translated by Ignacio Sánchez-Prado)

The "Foreign" among Us

The set of problems to be framed in this essay—discursive battles taking place within and around the category of the "foreign" as well as the status of Latin Americanism in them—does not start on September 11, 2001 but is the result of a contradictory historical process. These questions have been, however, formulated differently in the wake of the attacks and the ensuing war, the limitless war that lacks a concrete, identifiable, visible enemy but not countless victims. In this context, literary and cultural studies in Spanish cannot be absent from the conversations and negotiations on what gets defined as "foreign" within and outside the university. Spanish here again deserves specificity as the language, amongst the ones studied as "foreign" in the United States, most obviously in contradiction with that pedagogical status. In a previous piece, I argued that the demographic importance of the Spanish language in this country is of a centrality impossible to explain if one holds on to the ideology (dominant both in Hispanism and in Anglophone studies) that affirms, or at least silently assumes, a belated arrival of Spanish to an already constituted American identity and, parallel to that assumption, that of an organic and essential relationship between Spanish and the territory geopolitically designated as "Latin America" ("Clandestine"). That text was an attempt to think the current state of literary/cultural studies in Spanish through this double determination: a domestic language that gets studied as a foreign language, while its literary and cultural components inhabit an indeterminate zone in programs of comparative literature and theory, between the post-romantic Western canon and postcolonial literatures. Latin Americanism in the United States operates in this "in-between" space, one that cannot, however, be satisfactorily thought out within Latin American Studies, due to this interdisciplinary field's endemic, proverbial lack of self-reflexive theorization.[1]

But in-between academic spaces do not remain unaffected by wars, especially by a war like this, with invisible, virtual, presumed or yet-to-become actual enemies, accompanied by an unprecedented mobilization of state, media, and intelligence apparatuses as well as orchestrated restrictions to immigration and civil liberties of non-American citizens, with repressive measures directed specifically to the student body. If anybody still conducted debates within the university recurring to the derogatory label "ivory tower" (which supposedly protected the academic subject, and according to a commonly heard argument, disqualified entire discourses by the alleged security enjoyed by those within the university against the harassment of the "real world"), the events of the past few months in the U.S. have made visible the anachronism and naiveté of such binarism. As the market value of trustworthy translators from Arabic rises, so does the demand for classes that could introduce the young elite to the understanding of a world globalized not only by capital but also by terrorism. Vis-à-vis the in-between space occupied by Latin America and Latin American studies, situated in the interval that separates the West from its other, the suspicion remains: Are they with us or with them?

The various stories of Mexicans recently being objects of hostile attacks in the U.S.—by being or not confused with Middle Easterners—are emblematic: not white enough, the Latin American *mestizo* is subject to the xenophobic attack by evoking the image of the feared other, the dark, the impenetrable, the Eastern. The darker other today takes the place of the necessarily excluded, that outside without which the subject—the Subject of American bellicose patriotism—could not constitute itself. This is a particularly eloquent instance both of what Ernesto Laclau has called "constitutive outside" and what Judith Butler has theorized as the unspeakable, the nonhuman, never to be confused with a hidden substance, but rather understood as the abjected whose exclusion sustains the field of the possible (the readable, the speakable)—a field that ceaselessly remakes itself by abjecting other bodies and reappropriating bodies previously abjected.[2] The politics of social abjection today revolves around skin color, hair texture, facial traits, garments, all of them signs that must be read beforehand, as a foundation for the action to be taken. The foreigner has to be identified in order to be catalogued in the continuum of dangerousness, in an operation that effectively denies him/her access into the political, while the ongoing war redefines the very notion of politics, now equated with a crusade of Good against Evil over and above any international law and any identifiable goal. Danger is thereby decreed to be outside politics, and becomes itself that which dominant politics—through its war machine—must seek to destroy. But an implacable dialectical law continues to organize that movement: a mighty and powerful military operation to eliminate danger cannot be deployed without making proliferate more and more of the very danger it presumably attempts to erase. The operation we witness today attempts, of course, to circumscribe that danger outside "our" borders, by ceaselessly producing corpses, widows, orphans, and disabled throughout the "Third World," as the abject, unrepresentable, unspeakable bodies.

In the continuum of intolerance installed in the wake of September 11th, some are clearly more "foreign" than others. In a discussion on racial profiling as a necessary or desirable security measure in airports—the U.S. media already discusses the need or desirability of torture as a questioning tool, as attested by the odious article published in *Time* by Charles Krauthammer and many other written and televised pieces—a CNN commentator explicitly defended the practice by indicating that a Mrs. Smith, with two kids, will never be as likely to be a terrorist as a Middle Eastern man, traveling in Arab garments and with a Syrian passport. By being confronted with the question of how to differentiate, only by sight, the universe of possible terrorists from the "good Arab-American citizens" (in the end, a community numbering in the millions), the same commentator recurs to the lapidary comment: "but those are not American citizens and are not seeking citizenship." The commentary assumes that an American passport automatically exempts anyone of any possibility of ties with terrorism. It is to be expected, of a CNN commentator, the forgetting of examples such as Oklahoma City. Most logically contradictory, however, is the move from the sphere of the visible (features, garments) to the sphere of the initially invisible (citizen of what country? What passport does he carry in his pocket?). It is in this zone where xenophobia operates and disseminates: How to identify and catalogue the other? How to establish beforehand the border between the citizen and the non-citizen without recurring to racism?[3] What if racism is founded in this very distinction?[4]

In the wake of September 11th, then, the distinction between citizen and non-citizen manifests, more than ever, its instability, its reliance on racist premises, necessary for sustaining the binarism's imaginary solidity. In other words, not only are we amidst a wave of racist and xenophobic violence in the U.S. but also alongside such repressive offensive there are the many everyday operations, the various micro-interventions of power through which bodies, habits, voices, and accents are identified, marked, imprinted, and called by the law. This law is not (it has never been) a consensual system of democratically defined regulations, in some sort of utopian, Habermasian exercise of communicative competence. Neither is a written-in-stone law with transcendental origins and authority, unchangeable by political intervention. It is a law that evolves, transforms, and becomes another, and whose trajectory is the object of a political struggle with implications for university life, from the negotiations of disciplinary boundaries to admission and hiring policies.

Ethnic, cultural, and area studies programs, as well as those of foreign languages and literatures, are probably the institutional sites more directly vulnerable to this rearticulation of the limits of legality in the U.S. Regarding the national composition of its scholarly body, these programs share with some of the natural sciences the status of being demographically more suspicious for the bellicose and xenophobic Right. In the sciences, at least, the institution already has at its disposal a solid technical apparatus that constrains the uses of the knowledge produced there. Such control is never equivalent to an absolute and uncontested monopoly, as proven by the technological knowledge displayed by the terrorists of September 11th. As the sciences witness a significant offensive to instrumentalize new forms of scientific knowledge for the war machine deployed in the country, in the humanities, things happen on a much smaller scale. But a renewed demand for translators, historians, and anthropologists of the Arab world followed September 11th, as did promises to reconfigure both student choices and research priorities. As Andrew Ross pointed out in the early 1990s, "as humanists and social scientists, we have also begun to recognize that the often esoteric knowledge we impart is a form of symbolic capital that is readily converted into social capital in the new technocratic power structures" (104). Most certainly this remains true, but it is the nature of this convertibility that must be investigated: what kinds of laws are governing the interpellation to a historian, for example, to explain on television the nature of "Islamic belief"? What operations can we carry out to short-circuit this fake invitation to dialogue and put the real problem on the agenda, i.e., the terms in which the question is posed?

Refraining, then, from any illusions about the stability of a binary between a science controlled by monopolies versus the presumably "counter-hegemonic" humanities, it seems that humanities programs more immediately identifiable as "foreign" will become objects of a differentiated scrutiny, based on a strategy not yet agreed upon within the political, military, and financial elites, much less in the universities' administrative sub-elite (which remains, as always, deeply derivative, fearful, and uncreative in its response to ruptures, breaks, and crises in the texture of the social, such as the one experienced today). The demand for a self-justification, for an explicit declaration of objectives, methods, and principles has always weighed heavily on those humanities programs. The history of the appropriation of this demand by a morally traditionalist and geopolitically bellicose Right is an important chapter in this country's cultural wars of the last twenty years.[5] The fact that such programs lack a unified, consensual declaration about their missions has often put them in a defensive position against attacks by self-appointed spokesmen for the "Western canon," "traditional and family values," and "Judeo-Christian civilization." Everything indicates that such offensive returns, framed by other tactics and rhetoric: the call to understand "fundamentalism," "Islamic mentality," "anti-Americanism," and a series of other notions that are scholarly fragile, but no less important or operative because of that.

"Fundamentalism" rhetoric masks a polarization between an "us" and a "them" in which the latter are assigned a series of mutually contradictory attributes, that of being cowardly kamikazes, primitive barbarians and tech wizards. As far as the discursive articulation of that "them" takes place entirely around the category of the foreign, our context begs the question: what intervention opens for cultural, ethnic, and area studies programs, beyond the mere struggle for self-preservation and autonomy in which we will doubtlessly have to engage? Will we be limited, as was the case in the cultural wars of the 1980s, to a defensive position that stops on the mere affirmation of the obvious, that is, that September 11th has nothing to do with the admission policies for foreign students in our universities? What will be the form taken by the ideologeme "foreign" within and outside the university campus? In the debate about the cultural dimension of the latest events, have the terms of the conversation already been determined by the racist right-wing? Or can one hope to displace, however minimally, the axis of this debate through a pedagogical and scholarly practice carried out in the university?

Border of Excellence

Indian historian Dipesh Chakrabarty, in a piece on the relation between diasporic and area studies, quotes Robert Redfield, an advocate of the latter in the 1950s in an influential book, *The Primitive World and its Transformations*. Redfield concluded his book, Chakrabarty reminds us, with a quote from J.C. Furnas, who "proved" that the accusation that "Western man does not understand the savage," can only take place because "the two sets of cultures work unmistakably in two levels." Furnas's reasoning was that "the Western man" possesses something that the rest does not, something that "imposes the privilege and complicating obligations of intellectual integrity, self-criticism and generalized selflessness." J.C. Furnas concluded his "comparative anthropology" with the statement: "if there is something we may call the white man's burden, this is it." We know that within the academic apparatus to which Redfield and Furnas belonged, these statements were never seen as scandalous or aberrant, but on the contrary, represented the hegemonic view in centers of area studies.

Chakrabarty comments, insightfully, that it was the fact that they referred to cultures defined as foreign that made the Eurocentrism of their premises invisible. If the term already was fully loaded with ideology in the 1950s, if it masked a series of internal contradictions to what was defined as the "West," the migratory fluxes of the last decades have made it even more inadequate. The CNN commentator's difficulty, when trying to identify who should be the targets of the racial profiling she defended for airports, functions here as a revealing allegory. The form taken by such confusion in the media has been, as we have seen, the insistent reminder that "the enemy can be among us, within our borders." The foreigner, even within the dominant ideology, turns out to be less foreign than one expected.

Debates on borders within area studies have recently acquired a considerable protagonism.[6] The last few years have witnessed the publications of various writings, such as Chakrabarty's, devoted to the mapping of the many and contradictory filiations of the subjects involved in area studies as a result of migratory fluxes.[7] As usual, cultural/literary studies in Spanish arrives belatedly to the discussion, despite the fact that it is impossible to understand the discipline's trajectory in the U.S. without a history of the migrations caused first by the Spanish Civil War and later by Latin American dictatorships. In recent years, the constitution of a "diasporic Latin Americanism"—a growing community of Latin Americans that operates professionally outside of their countries of origin—has produced visible effects in the discipline and redefined what is understood as foreign, both in the United States and in the Latin American academies.[8]

Regarding the consciousness on how disciplinary problems are affected by the international division of labor, cultural, and literary studies in the U.S. are still poorly equipped.[9] Nothing in our discipline better illustrates the absolutization of an exclusively national paradigm than the processes of tenure in Departments of Spanish and the discourses on standards that accompany them. Whatever one position on the desirability of tenure, and in what forms, it is indisputable that Spanish language publications, in Latin American or Spanish presses, do not regularly receive the same treatment as publications in American university presses. Since we know that the latter do not publish in any language other than English—even though everything seems to indicate that an academic market in Spanish will soon be constituted in this country, following what is already going on in other publishing areas—many U.S.-based Latin Americans confront the election of either writing in a language, English, that they use on an everyday basis but in which, for whatever reasons, they may not feel comfortable writing, or risk being professionally punished for choosing to publish in Spanish.

This takes place, we must not forget, while these young faculty are evaluated as members of a Spanish department (or a Department of Romance Studies, or Foreign or Modern Languages, as the case may be). The devaluation of Latin American publications, of course, is never accompanied by any explicitly xenophobic or racist statement, but by a very "reasonable" question about the standards of the press in question, allegedly unknown due to the fact that the process of evaluation of manuscripts does not include proof of peer review. This question is, invariably, asked in bad faith, since those putting it forth within Spanish departments know, or should know, that the peer-review system as standardized in this country is not, nor has ever been, a universal practice, and that the discipline in Latin America, Asia, Africa, and most of Europe has opted for other methods of evaluation—other methods, not the absence of methods. They also know that one should expect a junior faculty in a Spanish department to be allowed, vis-à-vis the mechanisms of professional reward, to establish his/her scholarly reputation in that language. In a context in which publishing in Spanish still means to publish exclusively in Latin America or Spain, it would be expected that the mechanisms of professional reward—for those who work in that language—had already included a consideration of this geopolitical difference and an appreciation of the evaluation methods used by other publishing traditions. If those methods are regarded as insufficient by the standards of any American institution, the minimum obligation of these institutions would be to inform the interested parties at the beginning of their probationary period, instead of waiting seven years to destroy a tenure case with the ill-intentioned question: "Where are the readers' reports?"

The work carried out over the past three years by the MLA Committee on the Future of Scholarly Publishing has shown the complexity of the problem. The profession's mechanisms of reward are in blatant contradiction with the economic possibilities of scholarly publishing today, as measured by the (growing) number of manuscripts produced, the (declining) number of publication slots in university presses, and the (declining) average of copies sold of every scholarly book that does see print—the latter decline accentuated by a budget crisis in libraries as well as the systemic flux of funding away from humanities purchases to science journals.[10] For those publishing in "foreign" languages such as Spanish, the absence of explicit peer-review mechanisms in Latin American presses becomes an issue all-too-easily manipulated against junior faculty, even though it is well known that in any reputable press publishing scholarly work in Latin America manuscripts are also evaluated, generally by specialists employed by the publisher.

The undemocratic (imposed) universalization of this particular paradigm has served as a justification for disqualifying countless academics from Latin America and elsewhere, many of them with a curriculum superior to those disqualifying them. As I write this text, another excellent assistant professor of Latin American literature has received an unfavorable notification on her tenure case, despite being recommended enthusiastically by her department and by all of the external reviewers contacted by the university. The case in question is typical: its protagonist is the author of two well-reviewed books and a finished manuscript under contract, not to mention a respectable corpus of articles in some of the most recognized journals in the profession. The external reviewers recommended her unanimously. To her surprise and indignation, and to the surprise and indignation of all of us who evaluated her within the discipline, her university's promotion and tenure committee rejected her. One of the recurrent arguments was the lack of "evidence" of the "scholarly standards" of the press where this young scholar had published her two books. The press in question was the Universidad Nacional Autónoma de México (UNAM).

If it is tacitly accepted that an American biologist or mathematician sitting on a tenure committee does not have to know the UNAM, it is also tacitly accepted that the final word, in those cases, will belong to the specialists in the field (Spanish)—a field within which few people ignore that the Autonomous National University of Mexico maintains standards superior or equivalent to the American university presses held as norms of excellency. Within the discipline, this young professor—punished for publishing in Spanish—was evaluated enthusiastically, but the discipline does not seem to have enough political strength to impose its decision on university administrations. The framework is complicated by the fact that the discipline is inhabited by a group of scholars who more and more resent the loss of cultural capital of their subfields and what they perceive as an "invasion" of methods, discourses, subjects, and accents with which, until recently, they did not have to deal. These are the ones who invariably pose the question "where are the readers' reports?" with the bad faith proper to those who ask rhetorical questions in order to corner their interlocutors into silence.

Another conflict takes place around the writing styles brought by Latin American students coming to graduate programs in American universities in increasingly large numbers. In Anglo-America, both the humanistic disciplines and the social sciences have followed, for decades, the protocols of one particular genre, the paper. The introduction of diasporic Latin American students—some of them already mature and with considerable academic experience in their countries of origin—to this genre has not taken place without controversy, one in which the terms of the debate are plagued by "misunderstandings" (or in fact untranslatability) on all sides. The criticism leveled against the essay—the privileged genre within humanistic disciplines in Latin America—is well known: from the point of view of the paper, the essay is a vague, impressionistic genre that lacks consideration for evidence, and where statements are made without reference to the relevant bibliography, thus generating unconscious repetitions of studies already published by others, redundancies within the same text, and logical leaps without the pertinent links. I do not deny that such accusations are often true. To defend the essayistic tradition en bloc and propose the essay as an alternative model of writing is not something I am ready or willing to do, at least not until a significant displacement is imposed on some protocols of that tradition. It is a matter, instead, of critiquing and remaining on guard against formulations of the problem that implicitly endow the Anglo-American genre of the paper—a genre based on paraphrase and Aristotelian syllogism—a monopoly on "rigor." This tendency is particularly harmful in the context of a discipline that has lacked consensual mechanisms whereby "rigor" could be defined and where the very vague, accident-plagued trajectory of this notion—one devoid of any rescuable "rigor"—could be unveiled, studied, interrogated.

If the criticism flung at the essay from the point of view of the paper is well known, the reverse is not any less true: looked at from the standpoint of an essayistic tradition, the paper is a boring accumulation of reading notes, hiding the author's lack of creativity or originality and her/his choice of taking refuge in the shelter of quotes of authority. It is a model of writing that has found a safe haven in the social sciences of the Anglo-American world, and against which countless Latin American students manifest a resistance that is understandable, even when it is not well articulated. To those who later experience migration to the American academy, the conflict, however implicit and silent, is unavoidable. They will be evaluated within a discursive genre with which they have had an antagonistic relationship. This would not be necessarily a problem if the discipline had built a more generalized understanding of the historicity and geographic specificity of the genre, but such understanding is the exception and not the rule. The most common reasoning, amongst those in charge of guiding students coming from other traditions, is that the syllogistic-paraphrastic model of the paper should simply be assumed as a given, eternal, ahistorical ideal of academic writing, as if the profession's standards could never be questioned by their members and changed by their political and intellectual practice.

The worst one can do, then, with the essay vs. paper controversy is to entrench oneself in one of the two positions, thereby maintaining intact the imaginary purity of the two genres and giving up the true task, that of inhabiting these two traditions without blinding oneself to a genealogical understanding of both, to a critique of both, to a practice of writing that could unsettle the borders of both. This task—that we might call deconstructive—consists in not taking borders for granted but as contingent operations of enclosure that can be rethought, redrawn, remade, even if one concedes (or precisely because one concedes) that one's discourse is never simply external to those limits but is, in fact, contained by them. For those of us working in an English-speaking university, it may be valid to point out to Latin American students that access to the mechanisms of professional reward here depend, to a great extent, on one's mastery of the writing codes proper to the paper (the genre's particular understanding of what "evidence" is, its conception of empirical grounding of argument, its teleological structure). This guidance, however, ought to be accompanied by an intellectual practice that includes a critique of the genre itself, and of the history through which these codes established themselves. This is nothing other than the indispensable metadisciplinary interrogation: how democratic have the election and consecration of the discipline's mechanisms of professional reward been? How open to the scrutiny by its members have their standards and patterns of excellence been? Which voices have been silenced by those conceptions of excellence? To what extent can the unearthing of these voices unsettle the very rules of the game, the very field of the visible and the speakable?

Conclusions

These are questions that have recently gained a renewed urgency. The task today is to combine attention to the politics of exclusion (recent repressive measures directed against the university and against specific programs or voices within the university) and attention to the epistemological debates on paradigms that are, in many cases, complicit with the racism and xenophobia implicit in those measures being taken in society at large. In the case of Spanish, an open and well-informed debate on the globalization of the process of publication and its relations with the standards of tenure in the U.S. is a particularly important item on the agenda. The tradition that diasporic academic subjects bring with them, instead of being disqualified (or at best taken as a tabula rasa on which to imprint a new model) should instead be addressed as a tradition with which to engage in mutual knowledge and critical dialogue, no more and no less, in order that the specific labor on the deficiencies of each particular student can take place without resort to ethnic, national, or religious stereotypes.

If cultural wars in this country have left a legacy of special interest to cultural and literary studies in Spanish, it is the conclusion that the democratization of cultural capital in the discipline not only lies on the canon and its expansion. If it was once possible to believe that canon renewal was the great political intervention one could make from within the discipline, and if at that same point it was possible for others, like John Guillory, to believe that the expansion of the canon did not alter at all the mechanism of distribution of cultural capital in the discipline, it seems clear that both positions are now insufficient. The former need to be reminded that the belief in the necessarily democratic potential of curricular revision ignores the ways in which power absorbs and appropriates those inclusions without necessarily altering the Real antagonisms that structure the field. Guillory and followers have to be reminded that canons are never altered without setting in motion other social and institutional forces, and that an alteration of the canon never is simply a replacement of content. Thus, we must keep pursuing initiatives of curricular renewal, but without the illusion that the horizon of possible intervention is exhausted there: "values" and "the canon" are both concepts that name—imperfectly, as it is proper to the concept—zones of struggle for access to the production and distribution of cultural capital in the discipline. In times like these, to consider values and canons as the "fundamental crossroads of our time" is at worst, a mistake, and at best, a metonymy. And to the young, epistemologically and institutionally fragile disciplines, mistaking the part for the whole can be particularly harmful.

Notes

1. The notion of "in-between" ("entre-lugar") was coined by Silviano Santiago in a canonical essay in 1971. It does not designate, as some paraphrases have led to believe, a celebration of the "middle of the road," but an argument on how postcolonial binarisms are constituted and how aporetic choices are confronted by intellectuals inhabiting these interstitial spaces. The paradigmatic binarism against which Santiago raised his voice was the false opposition between imitation and autochthony that plagued Latin American criticism in the 1960s. For an excellent translation of Santiago's writings with a very useful introduction, see *The Space In-between,* a recent volume edited by Ana Lúcia Gazolla.

2. By ceaselessly remodeling its borders, the field of power thereby *opens* itself up to politics. In other words, the open-ended and mobile conception of power proposed by Foucault and sharpened, critiqued, and developed by Judith Butler has nothing to do with the political quietism that would argue that "power will always reappropriate everything," "there is no room for real oppositional/transformative action," etc. For Butler on the dialectic of gender performativity and power, see *Gender Trouble,* the original book (1990) and the indispensable preface to the 1999 edition. For a refined, careful reworking of what may have remained complicit with a certain voluntarism in *Gender Trouble,* see her tour de force *Bodies that Matter,* especially the introduction (1–23) and the critique of Lacan (57–119). For Ernesto Laclau's notion of the constitutive outside, see especially the classic study coauthored with Chantal Mouffe, *Hegemony and Socialist Strategy,* as well his reassessment in *New Reflections on the Revolution of Our Time.* On the theory of the subject, the role of hegemony, and the continuing relevance of a certain concept of universality, see Judith Butler's contributions in *Contingency, Hegemony, Universality,* a remarkable compilation of written debates among Butler, Slavoj Zizek, and Ernesto Laclau in which alliances are slowly, patiently, and carefully theorized: a Butler-Zizek alliance against Laclau, attempting to show the centrality of the Hegelian dialectic for a theory of the social; a Butler-Laclau alliance in the defense of the irreducibility of the deconstructive practice, identified by Zizek with a relativistic and ultimately quietist multiculturalism; and, finally, a Zizek-Laclau alliance against Butler's critique of the transcendental or quasitranscendental status ascribed by Lacanian theory to the Phallus and to the Real of the trauma. As Zizek points out in the book, the "gap that separates the three of us is impossible to define in neutral way," i.e. the very formulation of each disagreement necessarily will involve "taking sides" (213–14).

3. For an insightful argument about the Greek distinction between citizen and non-citizen, see Page DuBois' *Torture and Truth,* a study of the origins of the practice of torture in Greek courts, sanctioned as long as the tortured was not a citizen but a slave. DuBois' argument is that the juridical sanctioning of this practice is of a piece with the understanding of truth that comes to be hegemonic in Western philosophy. I have briefly discussed DuBois' revolutionary book in "Five Theses on Torture."

4. This is the point that well-meaning but imperialistic First-World liberals continually miss when they speak of "ethics" and "cosmopolitanism." For the most obvious example, see Martha Nussbaum's profoundly North American, upper-class liberal definitions of "humanity" in her *For the Love of Country,* a book that also features critical responses by over a dozen scholars and a reply by Nussbaum, in which she chooses to ignore the only response, that of Judith Butler, that critiques the heart of her project (her dependence on a mythical notion of the "universal"). As Butler points out, "What constitutes the community that might qualify as a legitimate community that might debate and agree upon this universality? If that very community is constituted through racist exclusions, how shall we trust it to deliberate on the question of racist speech?" (49). For my critique of Nussbaum, see "The Ethics of Criticism."

5. Amongst the wide bibliography I singularize, for the clarity and forcefulness of its arguments, Michael Bérubé's *Public Access* and the compilation of articles by Bérubé and Cary Nelson, *Higher Education under Fire.* As Peggy Kamuf has pointed out in *The Division of Literature,* the characterization of academic work as "too specialized, technical or obscure" operated doubly in the cultural wars as a mark of respect and distinction for the sciences and as a mark of disdain for humanities. For a theoretically and historically indispensable argument on the restructuring of the university around the interests of monopolist capital, see Bill Readings, *The University in Ruins.* All anglophone and francophone bibliography of the past seven years has been written, as expected, in ignorance of the most complete and radical analysis of the modern university recently published, Chilean philosopher Willy Thayer's genealogical tour de force, *La crisis no moderna de la universidad moderna.*

6. The border studies endeavor has played a key role in establishing this as a central question. Yet it is also necessary to make a clarification on what is understood by "border." As Robert Irwin shows in a recent article, an Anglocentric map of the border has systematically been privileged, a fact that "often seems to paradoxically perpetuate or even reinforce barriers that prevent both dialogue with Mexican scholars based in Mexico and the study of Mexican texts that speak to issues of U.S.-Mexico relations and border culture" (511). For Irwin, José David Saldívar's focus on the border as a land extending all the way to Seattle (as if it could only extend towards the North), is symptomatic. See Irwin's argument in "Toward a Border Gnosis."

7. A capital text on the diasporic as locus of enuntiation for contemporary cultural practices is Homi Bhabha's introduction to *The Location of Culture.* On the recent transformations in the field of English-language postcolonial studies, see the excellent article by Gaurav Desai "Rethinking English."

8. I will leave for another opportunity the debate with all the Latin American critics that have hypostatized an enemy in the "foreign" paradigm of Cultural Studies, thereby reproducing the mythification we critique here. The most nuanced critique remains that of Beatriz Sarlo, who insists on recuperating "values" presumably essential to political practice and ignored by the "relativism" of Cultural Studies. For a particularly unfortunate example of a resentful classicist lamenting the passing of the times

when canons were stable and universal, see the foremost Brazilian Barthesian, Leyla Perrone-Moisés. For an identitarian recourse to an "us" vs. "them" rhetoric that attempts to put forth a critique of US multiculturalism while refusing to engage the aporias of the Latin American tradition, see Hugo Achugar.

9. The phenomenon is not, again, exclusive of our discipline: in a previous piece ("Ethics") I tried to observe how the Anglo-American bibliography on the topic of the Ethics of criticism—produced by both literary critics and philosophers—is written without attending to their position in the international division of intellectual labor, an ignorance that profoundly affects, of course, whatever they have to say about "cosmopolitanism," "humanity," and the like.

10. The MLA Committee on the Future of Scholarly Publishing was composed of Judith Ryan, Idelber Avelar, Jennifer Fleissner, David E. Lashmet, J. Hillis Miller, Karen H. Pike, John Sitter, and Lynne Tatlock. The report that it has produced includes a detailed analysis of the economics of scholarly publishing today and a set of recommendations to all parties involved, from departments to libraries, from university presses to administrations. The report is published in the 2002 issue of *Profession*.

Works Cited

Achugar, Hugo. "Repensando la heterogeneidad latinoamericana (a propósito de lugares, paisajes y territorios)." *Revista Iberoamericana* 62 (1996): 845–61.

Avelar, Idelber. "The Clandestine *Ménage à Trois* of Cultural Studies, Spanish, and Critical Theory." *Profession* (1999): 49–58.

———. "The Ethics of Criticism and the International Division of Intellectual Labor." *SubStance* 91 (2000): 80–103.

———. "Five Theses on Torture." Trans. Philip Derbyshire. *Journal of Latin American Cultural Studies* 10.3 (2001): 253–71.

———. "Tres signos vacíos y el 11 de septiembre." *Revista de Crítica Cultural* 23 (2001): 66–67.

Bérubé, Michael. *Public Access: Literary Theory and American Cultural Politics.* London and New York: Verso, 1994.

Bérubé, Michael and Cary Nelson, ed. *Higher Education under Fire: Politics, Economics, and the Crisis of the Humanities.* New York: Routledge, 1995.

Bhabha, Homi. *The Location of Culture.* London: Routledge, 1994.

Butler, Judith. *Bodies that Matter: On the Discursive Limits of "Sex."* London and New York: Routledge, 1993.

———. *Gender Trouble: Feminism and the Subversion of Identity.* Second ed. London and New York, 1999 [1990].

———. "Universality in Culture." Nussbaum et al. 45–52.

———. Ernesto Laclau, and Slavoj Zizek. *Contingency, Hegemony, Universality: Contemporary Dialogues on the Left.* London and New York: Verso, 2000.

Chakrabarty, Dipesh. "Reconstructing Liberalism: Notes Toward a Conversation between Area Studies and Diasporic Studies." *Public Culture* 10.3 (1998): 457–81.

Desai, Gaurav. "Rethinking English: Postcolonial English Studies." *A Companion to Postcolonial Studies*. Ed. Henry Schwarz and Sangeeta Ray. Malden, Mass. and Oxford: Blackwell, 2000. 523–39.

DuBois, Page. *Torture and Truth*. New York and London: Routledge, 1991.

Guillory, John. *Cultural Capital: The Problem of Literary Canon Formation*. Chicago: University of Chicago Press, 1993.

Irwin, Robert. "Toward a Border Gnosis of the Borderlands: Joaquín Murrieta and Nineteenth-Century U.S.-Mexico Border Culture." *Nepantla: Views from the South* 2.3 (2001): 509–37.

Kamuf, Peggy. *The Division of Literature, or the University in Deconstruction*. Chicago and London: University of Chicago Press, 1997.

Krauthammer, Charles. "In Defense of Secret Tribunals." *Time Magazine* 158.23. November 26, 2001.

Laclau, Ernesto. *New Reflections on the Revolution of Our Time*. London and New York: Verso, 1990.

Laclau, Ernesto and Chantal Mouffe. *Hegemony and Socialist Strategy: Towards a Radical Democratic Politics*. London: Verso, 1985.

Nussbaum, Martha et al. *For Love of Country: Debating the Limits of Patriotism*. Boston: Beacon Press, 1996.

Perrone-Moisés, Leyla. "Que Fim Levou a Crítica Literaria?" *Folha de São Paulo*. Suplemento Cultural "Mais!" 25 de Agosto de 1996.

"Report of the MLA Committee on the Future of Scholarly Publishing." *Profession 2002*. New York: MLA, 2002.

Ross, Andrew. "Defenders of the Faith and the New Class." *Intelectuals: Aesthetics, Politics, Academics*. Ed. Bruce Robbins. Minneapolis: University of Minnesota Press, 1990. 101–32.

Santiago, Silviano. "O Entre-Lugar da Literatura Latino-Americana." *Uma Literatura nos Trópicos*. São Paulo: Perspectiva, 1978. 11–28.

———. *The Space In-Between: Essays on Latin American Culture*. Ed. Ana Lúcia Gazzola. Intro. Ana Lúcia Gazzola and Wander Melo Miranda. Trans. Gazzola, Tom Burns, and Gareth Williams. Durham: Duke UP, 2001.

Sarlo, Beatriz. "Los estudios culturales y la crítica literaria en la encrucijada valorativa." *Revista de Crítica Cultural* 15 (1997): 32–38.

Thayer, Willy. *La crisis no moderna de la universidad moderna: Epílogo del conflicto de las facultades*. Santiago: Cuarto Propio, 1996.

11

Hispanism in an Imperfect Past and an Uncertain Present

Nicolas Shumway

The notion of "Hispanism" will never be an easy sell in the United States academy. Nor should it be. It is a term fraught with intellectual weaknesses and marked historically by ideological agendas that do it little credit. In the Anglo-American world, no broad movement exists in support of an analogous term for the culture of England and its former colonies. Anglicanism has been claimed by religion; Englishism, Commonwealthism, or Britishism sound as weird as the concept they invoke; and "Americanism" calls to mind a kind of right-wing zealotry that few of us would support.

Yet, despite such reservations regarding *Hispanism,* I consider myself a Hispanist and remain extremely enthusiastic about Hispanic Studies, i.e., the study of all things pertinent to Spain, Spanish American nations and peoples, and Spanish-Latino populations in the United States. Indeed, studying and teaching about the Spanish-speaking world have occupied most of my professional life. I came to this world in my late teens when I first studied Spanish in earnest. This was the beginning of a life-long fascination that continues to shape my research, teaching, and travel. My career as a Hispanist has also blessed me with numerous Hispanic friends who enrich my life in countless ways. I therefore rejoice at skyrocketing enrollments in courses dedicated to Spain and Spanish America, and am delighted to participate in the opportunity the present moment affords for Hispanists to renegotiate for ourselves and for our students a more prominent place in the U.S. academy.

So why does the term "Hispanism" make me so nervous? For starters, Hispanism is not a field. Like most terms ending in -ism, Hispanism suggests an ideological, political, or even religious agenda. My initial contact with this sense of the term put me on guard very early in my career. It occurred in one of my first teaching positions where a senior faculty member specializing in Spanish Medieval literature insisted on reviewing all readings used in first- and second year-Spanish language classes to assure that junior-faculty course supervisors like myself included sufficient material from Spain. As I grew more familiar with the workings of the department, it became apparent that his worries in this regard extended all the way through masters and doctoral reading lists. In his view, titles on such lists should be approximately 60 percent from Spain and 40 percent from Spanish America. Sensing my disagreement, he explained that we should never lose sight of Hispanism, which in his view meant the spiritual centrality and dominance of Spain. Of course, a curriculum designed around this notion of Hispanism also meant a majority of faculty appointments in Peninsular literature and guaranteed enrollments in this particular individual's courses. It also meant a subservient departmental role for anything involving Spanish America.

This article looks at Hispanism from six vantage points. First, I consider how Hispanism developed in the nineteenth century as a strategy for replacing a political empire with a spiritual one. Second, I look at how the newly independent Spanish-American nations throughout most of the nineteenth century wanted nothing to do with any kind of Spanish empire, spiritual or otherwise. Third, I give brief overview of the pronounced anti-Hispanic bias one finds in Anglo-American thinking and historiography, from Elizabethan times to well into the twentieth century. Fourth, I analyze how in the early twentieth century the idea of Hispanism became more respectable throughout the Spanish-speaking world as a counterweight to U.S. hegemony. Fifth, I consider some of reasons why Hispanism is now an important agenda item for U.S. universities. And finally, I conclude where I began: explaining why Hispanism continues to strike me as a bad idea.

Consolation Imperialism

As it turns out, I had good reason to be wary of my senior colleague's view of Hispanism, for Hispanism—as an ideology and not an area of study—was in some sense a strategy created to save a dying empire, to affirm a spiritual empire in place of the political empire that had just collapsed. Consider for example the critical note on José Joaquín de Olmedo's famous poem, "Ode to Bolívar" (Canto a Bolívar) that appeared in 1826 in the London-based *Ocios de Españoles Emigrados,* a cultural review published by Spanish liberals exiled by the reactionary Ferdinand VII. Olmedo's poem praises two of the most decisive defeats dealt Spain by the Spanish American insurgents: the Battle of Junín and the Battle of Ayacucho, both fought in 1824. In discussing Olmedo's poem, the Spanish critic (either Joaquín Lorenzo Villanueva or Pablo Mendíbil according to Luis Monguió from whose article I quote) had a problem. On the one hand, he laments the "unpleasant memories" of a defeated Spain "that wound our national pride."[1] He further mourns that those same events "have forever separated from the lap of the mother we hold in common those . . . brothers of our own people . . ." On the other hand, however, he claims that this poem that celebrates Spain's defeats paradoxically sings of Spanish triumph, for the poem brings glory to "Castillian poetry" by being "one of the compositions that most pays it honor" (cited in Monguió, 230–31).[2] The critic's gambit, then, is basically identical to that of my senior colleague. Whatever their political differences with the mother country, Spain's former colonies in the critic's view will always be spiritual children of Spain and members of that grand Hispanic family evoked by the term "Hispanism."

No one waxed more eloquently in creating and defending this notion of spiritual Hispanism than the Spanish romantic scholar and nationalist, Marcelino Menéndez y Pelayo (1856–1912). Menéndez y Pelayo was such a prolific researcher that few elements of Hispanic culture, from the Spanish Middle Ages to Spanish philology to Spanish American literature, escaped his attention. Yet, despite the breadth of his erudition, his studies of Castilian literature and history always arrive at a similar conclusion: that only Spain gives cultural and spiritual unity to all things Spanish and Spanish American. And not just Spain, mind you, but don Marcelino's particular vision of Spain which is firmly rooted in the Spanish Middle Ages. In weighty tome after weighty tome, Menéndez y Pelayo argues against political liberalism and shows no qualms in defending the Spanish monarchy and ultramontane Catholicism. In sum, his is not just a defense of Hispanism; it is also an attack on a modern world whose material and scientific success would seem an affront to Spanish glory.

Menéndez y Pelayo is clearly arguing against the Spanish liberals of his own time, men like Benito Pérez Galdós and Pío Baroja who wrote withering critiques of Spanish backwardness and cultural provincialism. But the foundation of his argument is Hispanism. He maintains that all true Hispanists must resist foreign imports like liberalism and return spiritually if not literally to those things that made Spain great and unique in the first place, to wit, the crown, the church, and the cultural empire of Hispanism. Along with Free Masonry and Protestantism, much of the modern world is, in his view, inimical to the Hispanic essence. The Spanish sixteenth century in his view "withstands comparison with most glorious ages of the world. . . . Not since the times of Judas Maccabeus was there a people that could so justly believe itself the chosen people to be the sword and arm of God; and everything, even their dreams of greatness and universal monarchy were referenced and subordinated to one supreme goal: one faithful flock and one pastor" (Menéndez y Pelayo, 264–65).[3]

Currents in Menéndez y Pelayo's thinking found new proponents in the Spanish Generation of '98 when the loss of Spain's last American colony in the Spanish-American War forced an entire generation to ponder Spain's decline from a world power to one of the least developed countries in Europe. Even more sobering for the Generation of '98 was the fear that Spain had actually contributed little to the modern world, that in a society dominated by science and commerce, Spain, Spanish culture, and Spain's colonial offspring had become marginal and even irrelevant to the mainstream of Western culture. Although no single attitude towards these questions emerges in the Generation of '98, some of its members—notably Ramiro de Maeztú in his *Defensa de la Hispanidad*—continued Menéndez y Pelayo's attacks on liberalism. Not surprisingly, such ideas became key features of Spanish fascism. Franco's dictum that "Spain is different" masked many disagreeable ideas, chief of which was the notion that the Spanish spirit demanded strong, Catholic leaders who must resist liberalizing tendencies that would betray true Hispanism. In a word, Franco himself. Not surprisingly, the strapped Franco government found ample funds to republish much of don Marcelino's work.

Spanish America as Non-Spain

Meanwhile, back on the American continent in Spain's former colonies, a much different story was unfolding. No one should be surprised that Spanish American independence leaders had little good to say about Spain. After all, who speaks well of an enemy in times of revolution? In his widely read "Letter to a Jamaican Gentleman," for example, the Liberator Simón Bolívar denounced Spain as "an old serpent that only seeks to satisfy its poisoned fury" by trying to reclaim its lost American colonies (71–72).[4] Bolívar fully supports Bartolomé de las Casas' highly jaundiced version of the Spanish conquest (63). But, more importantly, he claims that Spain had kept its colonies in a state of "permanent infancy" which made the new Spanish American nations incapable of modern self-government and in some sense predestined to failure (63). In short, he considers the Spanish legacy an impediment to be overcome rather than embraced.

Much more surprising is how this anti-Spanish animus informs the thought of liberal leaders and reformers in Spanish America for virtually all of the nineteenth century, long after independence was won. Indeed, one could argue that, in great measure, modern Spanish America actually defined itself against Spain rather than descended from Spain. For example, in his *Facundo* of 1845, the Argentine Domingo Faustino Sarmiento claims that Spain's only legacy to the Americas was "the Inquisition and Hispanic absolutism." Spain for him is "the backward daughter of Europe" (2).[5] Later, when he visited Spain in 1847, Sarmiento found a retrograde and paradoxical country where all democratic tendencies had been crushed by popular despots and Counter-Reformation fanaticism. While aware of the former glories of the Spanish empire, Sarmiento saw them as old and worn, symbolized by El Escorial, which in his words is "a still fresh cadaver, that stinks and inspires disgust" (Viajes, II, 49).[6] Similarly, the Chilean essayist and novelist, Vitorino Lastarria, succinctly noted in 1844 that progress for Spanish America was synonymous with de-Spanishization (19–20). In sum, with great difficulty does one find among nineteenth-century Spanish American liberals anything akin to "Hispanism." Rather, their attitude towards Spain seems frankly Oedipal. They could hardly wait to cast off their embarrassing Spanish parent and adopt new cultural models in Northern Europe and North America. Even well into the twentieth century, the obligatory youthful journey of all Spanish American elites was to France, not Spain. In fairness to some Spanish intellectuals, let it be said that a chief influence in this denunciation of Spain and Spanish culture were Spanish liberals like Mariano José de Larra who were just as damning in their indictments of Spanish provincialism and absolutism.

Which is not to say that reverence for Spain did not survive among *some* Spanish Americans, but hardly among liberals, positivists, and believers in progress. Among religious and political conservatives—the kind who brought Maximillian to Mexico, for example—reverence for Church and Monarchy did indeed endure. But who looks to them for cultural models today? For the fact is that what we call modernity and enlightened thinking had only timid echoes in Spain. Of course, Spain experienced an enlightenment of sorts, but it was a movement so respectful of the Church and the Monarchy that it hardly compares with the radical reforms being proposed in Northern Europe and North

America. Moreover, up until the fall of Franco, liberal ideas in Spain were regularly denounced as imported French perversions, out of sync with the Spanish soul.

Hispanism and the Anglo-American Tradition

In the meantime, how was Hispanism faring in England and the United States? Not at all well it turns out. The Anglo-American tradition is marked by a profound and abiding anti-Hispanic bias whose roots go back at least as far as Reformation England. When Henry VIII, hoping for a male heir, defied the Pope and discarded his Spanish wife Catherine of Aragon to marry Anne Boleyn, he set England against Rome and earned the undying enmity of the Spanish Hapsburgs, beginning with Catherine's nephew, Charles I (also Charles V of the Holy Roman Empire). Without Spanish interference, the Pope would have surely granted Henry the annulment he requested; after all, previous popes had granted annulments on grounds even more specious. But Spanish-led intrigue in the Vatican made such accommodation impossible.

Things got worse when Henry died without a male heir. Mary, daughter of Henry and of the spurned Catherine, assumed the English throne. A devout Catholic, she tried to return England to Rome, murdering as many real and imagined heretics as she could get her hands on, including the revered Thomas Cramner, primary author of the first *Book of Common Prayer,* which in modified form is still used in Anglican worship throughout the world and remains a monument of English prosody. She thus earned the sobriquet "Bloody Mary" by which she is still remembered in history, legend, and song. For English reformers and their descendants, she typified the best one could expect of a Spanish Catholic ruler: authoritarian, fanatical, and ruthless.

English enmity for Spain reached new intensity under Mary's eventual successor and half sister, Elizabeth I, the Virgin Queen for her loyal subjects, the Bastard Queen for Roman Catholics who never recognized Henry's marriage to her mother Anne Boleyn. Her irregular birth did not, however, prevent Phillip II from courting her, knowing that things with the Vatican could be straightened out with well-placed favors and proper politicking. Elizabeth apparently realized that marital union with any man would diminish her powers and was quite happy to flirt with many powerful suitors but bind herself to none. She was just as fickle in religious matters and skillfully sought a middle ground between Rome and Geneva. Frustrated at her elusiveness and England's continued disuse for the papacy, Phillip launched the Invincible Armada in 1588 which proved anything but. Humiliated in battle by the smaller but more mobile English fleet, the Armada eventually succumbed to a storm hailed by the English as God-sent. Ten years later, in response to rumors that Phillip was planning a second assault, Elizabeth's navy launched a surprise attack on the Spanish fleet anchored at Cádiz. Clearly, the stage had been set. For the next two centuries, Spain and England would contend mightily as Europe's leading colonial powers —and the English empire would eventually eclipse its Spanish rival.

Their enmity was ideological as well as political and economic. Demonizing Spain became one of England's favorite parlor games. An unwitting ally in England's vilification of all things Spanish was no one less than the Catholic reformer, Bartolomé de las Casas. His *Brevísima historia de la destrucción de las Indias* was promptly translated into English. The London edition of 1689 carried the following description on the title page:

> Popery truly Display'd in its Bloody Colours: Or a Faithful Narrative of the Horrid and Enexampled Massacres, Butcheries, and all manner of Cruelties, that Hell and Malice could invent, committed by the Popish Spanish Party on the Inhabitants of West India . . . Composed first in Spanish by Bartholomew de las Casas, a Bishop there, and an Eye-Witness of most of these Barbarous Cruelties . . . (cited in Herring, 176–77)

To be sure, the English colonizers treated the Indians just as badly, if not worse, than the Spanish. But that was no reason for the anti-Spanish, anti-Catholic English to not use de las Casas' history as a useful instrument for discrediting their country's chief colonial rival.

This anti-Spanish animus in Anglo-American historiography gained strength in the nineteenth century and, to some degree, has never quite disappeared. Although he died in 1859, the histories of the conquest of Mexico and Peru by Boston-born William H. Prescott still stand as monuments of U.S. historiography and figure among the very few nineteenth-century histories to continue in print. His low opinion of Spanish culture, however, pulsates on virtually every page he wrote. Consider how in his *History of the Reign of Philip II, King of Spain* he tells us that "The Inquisition succeeded in Spain, for it was suited to the character of the Spaniard" (1:379), or that "Spain was shut out from the light which in the sixteenth century broke over the rest of Europe. . . . The genius of the people was rebuked, and their spirit quenched. . . . Every way the mind of the Spaniard was in fetters. His moral sense was miserably perverted" (1:446). He later argues that "The same dark spirit of fanaticism seems to brood over the national literature. . . . The greatest geniuses of the nation, the masters of the drama and of the ode, while they astonish us by their miracles of invention, show that they have too often kindled their inspiration at the altars of the Inquisition" (1:447). Or consider this concluding paragraph from Henry Charles Lea's 1922 study of the Inquisition and his depiction of Spain as a national failure:

> Thus the conclusion that may be drawn from our review of the causes underlying the misfortunes of Spain is that what may fairly be attributable to the Inquisition is its service as the official instrument of the intolerance that led to such grave results, and its influence on the Spanish character in intensifying that intolerance into a national characteristic, while benumbing the Spanish intellect until it may be said for a time to have almost ceased to think. (4:508)

Not until the somewhat revisionist histories of Lewis Hanke and Lesley Byrd Simpson do the Spaniards in U.S. history books start getting more sympathetic treatment. But in the popular mind, Hispanism, fanaticism, authoritarianism, and the Inquisition seemed to go hand in hand. The one area where Spain got slightly better press among Anglo-American writers was in folklore and literature. Washington Irving's popular "Tales From the Alhambra" presented a human side of Spain while English romantics like Shelley and Coleridge found much to admire in Calderón de la Barca. And, of course, folkloric Spain found enduring representation in Carmenesque operas and music. Dancing gypsies, romantic guitars, bullfights—these became the only images of Spanish culture that could rival those of tyrannical rulers and grand inquisitors—which of course was not much of a victory for Hispanism since being admired for folkloric value hardly earns one a better place in academe.

Anti-Spanish bias in the United States also influenced politics. Manifest Destiny was in the air the day the Pilgrims landed at Plymouth Rock. Like the Spanish to the south, the early English settlers claimed American lands by divine right. The United States' early and main territorial expansion came through legitimate political means (if we disregard Indigenous peoples). The Treaty of Paris of 1781 gave the fledgling country all territory claimed by Great Britain up to the Mississippi River, and the Louisiana Purchase of 1803 allowed claim to territories through the Pacific Northwest to the Pacific Ocean. However, when it came time to claim Mexican territories that now comprise the U.S. Southwest—the United States' first real imperialistic enterprise—anti-Spanish sentiment proved crucial. Consider, for example, how Senator William Preston in 1847 sought to justify the U.S. War against Mexico:

> This invader [Santa Anna] had come at the head of his forces, urged by no ordinary impulse—by an infuriate fanaticism—by a superstitious Catholicism, goaded on by a miserable priesthood, against that invincible Anglo-Saxon race, the van of

which now approaches the del Norte. It was at once a war of religion and of liberty. And when the noble race engaged in a war, victory was sure to perch upon their standard. (Cited in *Tureson,* 151)

Clearly, Senator Preston felt that the war against Mexico was justified since Hispanism represented darkness while Anglo-Saxon Protestantism represented light. Things Hispanic imbued by a "superstitious Catholicism" and led by "a miserable priesthood" deserved to be replaced. The Mexican War was, therefore, not imperialist but liberating—and from what the southwestern territories needed liberation was precisely the ideologies of Hispanism.

Roughly a half century later, similar attitudes nurtured United States expansion into Cuba, Puerto Rico, and Panama. Theodore Roosevelt and his co-religionists had little trouble persuading most U.S. citizens that such expansion was done in the name of civilization, since things Hispanic just were not that civilized. Consider the following lines from 1899 in which Roosevelt urges Congress to sign the treaty with Spain and continue the war in the Philippines:

> To refuse to ratify the treaty would be a crime not only against America but against civilization. To leave the task half done whether in the East or the West Indies would be to make the matter worse than if we had never entered upon it. We have driven out a corrupt medieval tyranny. In Cuba and Porto Rico we are already striving to introduce orderly liberty. We shall be branded with the steel of clinging shame if we leave the Philippines to fall into a welter of bloody anarchy, instead of taking hold of them and governing them with righteousness and justice . . . (16:471–72)

For the soon-to-be president, Spain in 1899 was still a "corrupt medieval tyranny" that the United States routed in the name of civilization, not to mention, that time-worn trinity of Anglo-American Puritanism: liberty, righteousness, and justice. Not all North Americans agreed with "Teddy." Mark Twain, among others, famously dissented from Rooseveltian imperialism, but theirs was a voice crying in the wilderness.

Making Hispanism Respectable

In odd ways, however, United States imperialism became a rallying point for Hispanism and helped make it more respectable over a broad cross-section of Spanish and Spanish-American intellectuals. Menéndez y Pelayo's paeans to the spiritual riches of Hispanism seemed less quaint against the backdrop of the Spanish-American War, the War in the Philippines, and the proxy war by which the United States seized the Panama Canal Zone. While virtually no one in Spanish America felt sad about Spain losing its last American colonies, increasing numbers saw the United States and U.S. culture as an enemy against whom Hispanics from both sides of the ocean and of varying political stripes could rally.

One of the most peculiar texts in this regard was also the most popular: the book-length essay *Ariel,* published in 1900 by the Uruguayan writer José Enrique Rodó. Rodó argues that the descendants of Greece and Rome, whom Rodó calls the Latin race, already possess a spiritual and aesthetic superiority over the *yanquis*. He incongruously chooses the native-born, earthbound, and ultimately treacherous Caliban from Shakespeare's *The Tempest* as the symbol of U.S. vulgarity, materialism, and "utilitarianism." Likewise, he sees the winged Ariel from the same play as the marker of the aesthetically sensitive Latin peoples. Rodó is particularly critical of his Spanish American forebears who blindly idolized the United States while failing to appreciate the wealth of their own cultural heritage. Rodó also waxes eloquent in defending leisurely contemplation and talent-based aristocracies while expressing a lofty disdain for democratic systems that confer undue authority on the untutored masses, producing not democracy but *mediocracia* (from mediocre). He thus echoes arguments being presented concurrently in Spain that not only defended Hispanism and Latinidad but also identified U.S. cultural hegemony as Hispanism's chief enemy. Oddly, Rodó denounces U.S. cultural hegemony without mentioning the more immediate dangers of U.S. military and commercial expansionism. Two years earlier, the U.S. had occupied Cuba, Puerto Rico, and the Philippines, yet the best Rodó can come up with is an assertion of Spanish America's spiritual and aesthetic supremacy.

While Rodó says little about Spain, his defense of "latinidad" and his attacks on liberal society as seen in the United States are at one with emerging currents in early twentieth-century Hispanism on both sides of the ocean. In 1913, the Argentine writer Manuel Gálvez published an essay entitled *El solar de la raza* in which he argued that Argentina had sacrificed its Hispanic and Catholic birthright for a mess of liberal potage. In Spain, José Ortega y Gasset worried about the rebellion of the masses and the wealthy untutored who trampled good taste. Back in Argentina, Manuel Ugarte saw the United States as the New Rome. And in Mexico, José Vasconcelos echoed now familiar currents in Hispanism in his unabashed admiration of Spanish culture and Catholicism and his disdain for the United States as a disgusting, vulgar, materialistic society. Be not surprised that Vasconcelos found much to admire in Spanish fascism.

Hispanism and Hispanic Studies in the United States

These discussions, however, had little effect on United States universities until the 1930s. There had, of course, always been courses in Hispanic studies in literature and history departments, but largely as also-rans. The history of Spain and Spanish America was not considered central to the U.S. experience, and literature in Spanish acquired at best a tenuous secondary status in Romance Language departments where French was clearly the favored partner. In short, while U.S. scholars included in their ranks people who might be called Hispanists, they were a minority presence.

After World War I, several forces combined to make Hispanic Studies more visible in the United States. European scholars and artists began immigrating to the United States, drawn first by the muscular young country's prosperity but later by the deteriorating political conditions of Europe. Among these were exiled Spanish intellectuals fleeing fascism, many of whom found homes in United States universities. While unsympathetic to fascism, these scholars were nonetheless quite nationalistic in their desire to place the literature of Spain at the center of Hispanic studies in the U.S. academy. And in fairness to them, it was the literature they knew best. It was largely under their tutelage that the first generation of North American Hispanists studied and wrote dissertations, often reflecting similar preferences for the literature of Spain.

Scarcely ten years later a new influx of Spanish-speaking intellectuals came to U.S. universities, but this time they were Argentines fleeing Perón. While often politically sympathetic to their colleagues from Spain, Spanish departments soon became the locus of an unending tug-a-war between Spanish Americanists and Peninsularists that to this day has not ended. The Argentines brought with them a new awareness of Spanish American literature as seen in the work of critics like Pedro Henríquez Ureña, who although a Dominican realized his pivotal histories of Spanish American literature in Argentina. Later Argentine scholars of this generation, men like Enrique Anderson-Imbert, Aníbal Sánchez Reulet, and Raimundo Lida, came to powerful academic positions in leading U.S. universities from which they insisted on a greater place for Hispanic literature generally and equal representation for Spanish American literature in the Hispanic canon. Then, beginning in the late 1950s, another social upheaval brought to the U.S. academy significant numbers of Cubans, who quite naturally insisted on equal treatment for excellent writers like Alejo Carpentier and José Lezama Lima while objecting strenuously to the often pro-Fidel sympathies of their older Spanish colleagues.

Concurrent with these developments, from the end of World War II through the 1970s, red scares and sputnik envy caused state and federal governments in the United States to invest heavily in higher education. Through the Title VI programs of the National Defense Education Act (now the Health and Education Act), support for graduate students interested in Latin America became increasingly available. Title VI National Resource Centers and wealthy foundations, such as the Ford and the Rockefeller Foundations, also brought financial backing for research, conferences, and lecture series on topics related to Latin America. Hispanists clearly benefited from these programs, particularly those of a Latin American persuasion.

Student enrollments also climbed steeply, so much so that since 1985 more U.S. students study Spanish than all other foreign languages combined. Student interest was partly driven by a growing sense that Spanish was becoming the second language of the United States, given the growing numbers, influence, and visibility in the U.S. academy and the society at large of so-called "heritage" speakers of Spanish. These groups influenced the U.S. curriculum in two significant ways. First, they helped fill classrooms of traditional Spanish language and literature programs, giving Hispanic studies political clout in the U.S. academy that it has never had before. Second, they claimed a place for the study of United States Latino literature and were primary movers in expanding literary studies to include cultural studies, a shift from the study of texts to the study of cultural contexts. Through this second endeavor, they brought new pressure on a curriculum designed primarily with a focus on Spain, yet in their political stance they could be just as damning of Anglo-centric academe as the Menéndez y Pelayos or Vasconcelos of yesteryear.

Because of these numbers, the study of Hispanic cultures has never been better situated in the U.S. academy. We have numbers, we have political clout, we have students, and we have faculty. The question now is How much can this new situation borrow from the Hispanism of yesteryear? Or said differently, is there anything in the *ideology* of Hispanism that those of us dedicated to promoting Hispanic Studies might find useful? I conclude with some tentative answers to these questions.

Hispanism or Hispanic Studies?

Obviously, Hispanism must occupy us as an object of study. The study of the debates on collective, national, and cultural identities that underlie notions of Hispanism must concern us, whether they be Larra's critique of Spain or

Maeztu's and Gálvez's proto-fascist defense of *hispanidad.* No overview of Hispanic cultural history and production can ignore such ideas. I would also hope that the study of Spanish cultural nationalism might lead to deliberation on nationalism in general including that of the United States. Indeed, the counterpoint Hispanism offers in its critique of U.S. cultural hegemony and middle-class self-satisfaction can lead to very fruitful discussions. I have also found that North American students are frequently drawn to Rodó's fulminations against U.S. culture, perhaps because Rodó, surely without knowing it, wrote in the tradition of the Jeremiad, a Puritan preaching tradition in which listeners perversely enjoyed being upbraided for their manifold imperfections.

But to teach an idea is not to defend it much less be persuaded by it. Indeed, questioning central currents of Hispanism and examining where its essentialism and anti-liberal sentiment led in some instances (e.g., fascism) must not avoid scrutiny. We must also be bold in recognizing the ways Spanish-centric Hispanism continues to distort the curricula of Hispanic studies. Consider for example how in Spanish language literature programs only Spain seems to have the right to teach its literature as a national literature. Spanish American literature more often than not is framed as well Spanish American literature. Our literature programs seldom teach national literatures of Mexico, Argentina, Cuba, or Chile, although all these countries have highly developed traditions of writers, publications, and criticism that lend themselves to being studied in a national framework. Moreover, writers from those countries, including even the cosmopolitan Borges, can often be understood only in dialogue with their national traditions. Lumping all Spanish American literature together also hides vital differences in those literatures. For example, Andean and Mesoamerican literature will surely say more about indigenous peoples than the literature of the River Plate, just as Caribbean literature will necessarily speak to issues of negritude to a greater degree than that of the Southern Cone. Despite such differences, nonetheless, we continue to teach courses with titles like "Introduction to the Spanish American Novel" or "Spanish American Vanguardism." Such course titles suggest that literature programs are still organized with Spain at the center and everyone else in a marginalized amalgamation that recalls terms like *las colonias* or *las Indias.*

Now before anyone gets too annoyed, let me quickly say that I love much of the literature of Spain and that any student of Spanish language literature needs a firm grounding in the Spanish classics from the Middle Ages through the Golden Age. But I must also note that after Independence, Spanish American literature becomes increasingly disconnected from Spain. There are, of course, moments of rapprochement, for example, during Modernismo or among some of the vanguardist poets. But students of twentieth-century Spanish American fiction would do better reading Tolstoy, Dostoyevsky, Joyce, Faulkner, and Proust than Galdós, Miró, Cela, or Goytisolo.

Traditional notions of Hispanism also seem ill-equipped to accommodate recent developments in Spanish language literature resulting from globalization. Two of the most significant anthologies published in recent years are *McOndo* and *Se habla español,* both of which give visibility to expatriate writers who, although from various Spanish-speaking countries, have been partly educated in the United States. What greatly distinguishes these young writers is the degree to which they are in dialogue with the United States, not as *aficionados* a la Sarmiento or anti-hegemonists a la Rodó, but as bright, creative young people who recognize that some element of U.S. culture now forms part of their individual and collective identities. In short, quite unlike the anti-imperialist left that people of my generation supported, these new writers see globalization as an identity to be embraced rather than a hegemony to be resisted.

Nor is it at all clear how traditional Hispanism might accommodate the literature of U.S. Latinos. Spanish departments in the United States have often been notoriously inhospitable to U.S. Latino literature, partly because much of it is written in English and partly, I suspect, because U.S. Latinos raise hackles among people educated in Ortega's fear of the masses. Yet, there it is, a rich, diverse and burgeoning literature that can claim Hispanic roots as much as any literature of Spanish America.

So how do I conclude? Hispanic studies is an exciting field, or better said, an exciting current within many fields. Moreover, there has never been a better time to be a Hispanist in the United States precisely because of the opportunities this moment affords. *Hispanism* on the other hand strikes me as an outmoded idea based on essentialist, ideologically driven, and Spain-centric notions that will ultimately do more to divide than to promote. I began this essay saying that Hispanism would never be an easy sell in the United States. I haven't changed my mind.

Notes

1. "ingratos recuerdos que hieren el amor nacional."
2. Respectively, los sucesos que han separado para siempre del regazo de la madre común a unos pueblos, hermanos del neustro, a quines no podemos menos de desar tanta ventura como a nostros mismos," and "defraudar . . . a la poesía castellana de un homenaje debido por una de las composiciones que más la honran."

3. "¡ . . . resiste la comparación con las edades más gloriosas del mundo! . . . Nunca, desde el tiempo de Judas Macabeo, hubo un pueblo que con tanta razón pudiera creerse el pueblo escogido para ser la espada y el brazo de Dios; y todo, hasta sus sueños de engrandecimiento y de monarquía universal, lo referían y subordinaban a este objeto supreme: Fiet unum ovile et unus pastor."
4. "una vieja serpiente, por solo satisfacer su saña envenenada."
5. "la hija rezagada de Europa."
6. "un cadáver fresco aun, que hiede e inspira disgusto."

Works Cited

Bolívar, Simón. *Escritos políticos.* Ed. Graciela Soriano. Madrid: Alianza Editorial, 1969.

Gálvez, Manuel. *El solar de la raza.* Buenos Aires: Sociedad Cooperativa *Nosotros,* 1913.

Hanke, Lewis. *Las Casas and the Spanish Struggle for Justice in the Conquest of America.* New York: Columbia University, 1966.

Herring, Hubert. *A History of Latin America from the Beginnings to the Present.* Second edition. New York: Knopf, 1965.

Lastarria, José Victorino. *Miscelánea histórica y literaria.* Valparaíso: Mercurio, 1855.

Lea, Henry Charles. *A History of the Inquisition of Spain.* 4 volumes. New York: Macmillan, 1906–1907.

McOndo. Ed. Alberto Fuguet y Sergio Gómez. Barcelona: Mondadori, 1996.

Menéndez y Pelayo, Marcelino. *La conciencia española.* Ed. Antonio Tovar. Madrid: EPESA, 1948.

Mongiuó, Luis. "Las Tres Primeras Reseñas Londinenses de 1826 de *La Victoria de Junín.*" *Revista Iberoamericana* 30 (1964): 225–37.

Paz Soldán, Edmundo y Alberto Fuguet. *Se habla español: voces latinas en USA.* Miami: Alfaguara, 2000.

Ortega y Gasset, José. *La rebelión de las masas.* 1929; Madrid: Ediciones de la Revista de Occidente, 1970.

Prescott, William H. *History of the Reign of Philip the Second, King of Spain.* Philadelphia: Lippincott, 1855; Rpt. 1869.

Rodó, José Enrique. *Ariel.* Montevideo: Impr. De Dornaleche y Reyes, 1900.

Roosevelt, Theodore. *The Works of Theodore Roosevelt.* 21 volumes. New York: Charles Scribners and Sons, 1925.

Sarmiento, Domingo Faustino. *Civilización y barbarie: Vida de Juan Facundo Quiroga.* Ed. Raimundo Lazo. [1845] Mexico City: Editorial Porrúa, 1977.

———. *Viajes por Europa, Africa y Estados Unidos.* 3 volumes. Ed. Julio Noé. [1845–1851] Buenos Aires: La Cultura Argentina, 1922.

Simpson, Lesley Byrd. *The Encomienda in New Spain: the Beginning of Spanish México.* Berkeley: University of California Press, 1950.

————. *Many Mexicos.* 4th ed. Berkeley: University of California Press, 1967.

Tuveson, Ernest Lee. *Redeemer Nation: The Idea of America's Millennial Role.* [1968] Chicago: University of Chicago Press, 1980.

Ugarte, Manuel. *El destino de un continente.* Madrid: Editorial Mundo Latino, 1923.

Vasconcelos, José. *La raza cósmica: misión de la raza iberoamericana.* Paris, Agencia mundial de librería [1920?].

12

Hispanism and Its Lines of Flight

Román de la Campa

The era in which Hispanism stood as an organic principle governing the study of Spanish and Spanish American letters seems like a dim and distant memory. Whether we like it or not, humanistic fields of study such as Hispanism have been supplanted by a disciplinary practice in a constant state of flux, less a community of established texts and methods than an aggregate of wholly disparate elements in which innovation, transgression (or even a reluctant tweaking of tradition), must somehow concur in the pursuit of new packaging for disciplines and scholars. The same could also be said for newer articulations of related fields such as Latin Americanism, or even Latino studies, a more distant cousin. Some would argue that such a state of disciplinary affairs only pertains to the American (U.S.) academy, but one can't help but notice the degree to which other historically influential sites of Hispanism—Britain, for example, or even Spain itself—must now respond to the same logic of knowledge production.

The pull of the American research apparatus currently engaged with what was once the province of Hispanism has evolved into an expansive institutional nexus that trains and supports a growing body of transnational, middle-class, professional academics with potentially lifelong positions, in numbers that are simply unthinkable anywhere else. This new class of intellectual began to emerge in the United States during the cold war, with its emphasis on area and international studies as a form of national defense, but it grew into much larger and more influential sphere through the 1980s, as postmodernism, cultural studies and globalization steadily voiced a North American view of humanistic endeavors that supplanted the European paradigm of modern aesthetics.[1]

It, therefore, seems particularly important to note that projects engendered in the American academy betray certain propensities, as they do everywhere else. Generally speaking, they reveal a tendency toward a historical sweep, often with proposals that seek to redefine the past, present, and future in one fell swoop, a symptom not only of the reach and ambition of work possible under the auspices of an extraordinary research university system, but also of the mounting pressures for inventive productivity faced by humanist intellectuals in this era of privatization. In the case of Spanish-related topics, this new field of force vastly intensified during the last four decades. It reached that magnitude not necessarily as a primary site of theoretical or artistic origination—no one would deny the import of high European theory and Latin American literature during this time—but as part of an impulse given to remapping disciplinary paradigms, an energy comparable to software design that constantly alters the domain of fields, areas, and objects of study. Equally important, this timing also coincided with the advent of deconstructive modes of reading and writing, arguably the most productive common denominator behind the myriad sequence of theoretical frameworks evidenced during this period, a fertile register for an epistemology of turns, breaks, and interstices that gathers strength through poststructural praxis and postmodern experience.

It is possible to intuit that most, if not all, of these methods and approaches share a common challenge of considerable proportions: How to incorporate the legacy of Western culture into a new world order being presently promoted by neoliberal capitalism, particularly after 1989? Not only was the aesthetic utopia of Western postmodernity advanced during the 1980s deeply challenged by the subsequent crudity of global economies, but the teleological project inspired by Third World modern narratives lost even more prestige, as evident in Latin America and other areas demarcated as peripheral or compromised modernities. This led either to deep disenchantment or muted resistance amongst scholars and artists who continued to have a stake in imagining the world as a safer, fairer place, particularly those for whom migration to the United States or Western Europe was not an option or a wish.

Therefore, it seems paramount to constantly scrutinize the radical changing nature of knowledge and value production prevalent today. Does it augur a lamentable sliding slope of dispersion, or a moment of theoretical dissemination worthy of celebration? Are those two opposite viewpoints implicitly linked? Do they promise more than a new strand of inchoate pluralism where value resides largely or solely in the will to produce, inspired by the pull of sub-specialties or even smaller groups of scholars capable of continuously launching and establishing their own new paradigms in the globalized American (U.S.) academy? Has the emphasis on conceptual design claimed a new terrain no longer dependent on high-low divide and national traditions? Could it have led to certain aversion toward literary studies and the aesthetic realm?

One thing seems clear: It has become much more difficult to sustain areas of study through single meta-signifiers such as Hispanism, or, for that matter, Latin Americanism, given the plethora of conflictive elements contained by the latter term. In his most recent book Néstor García Canclini asks, with a considerable degree of consternation, just how we might continue to think about Latin America today.[2] Similar questions apply to the field of study known as English, a thoroughly globalized sphere best conceived as a transnational or diasporic entity whose disciplinary object can only be grasped as lines of flight in constant movement amidst linguistic, cultural, and national traditions.[3] For the cluster of Spanish/Latin American/Latino discourses, the question is not just what each of its fields can add to the archive at this point—say, new or forgotten authors, regions, epochs, conceptual frameworks, or even traditions—though these are important pursuits. The larger question, it seems to me, would be whether this opportunity can be seized to recast the fleeting lines of Humanism itself, with a more central role for the new constellation of disciplines associated with Hispanism. After all, Spanish language and literature always held a secondary rank in the Humanist hierarchy of value fashioned by European national literatures; and Latin Americanism came into its own rather late in the game. Moreover, even though post-Hispanist discourses may no longer rely on the pillars of philological foundation, their heterogeneity may help unfold new interdisciplinary endeavors that bridge humanistic disciplines and the lettered social sciences (history, sociology, cultural anthropology), or at least help erase the way in which those two cultures of research have been so drastically severed in the last half century.[4]

Equally important, and perhaps more dramatic, are the momentous changes undergone by departments otherwise known as Spanish (often with Portuguese barely clinging to the title) in the United States. These are units whose growing importance deserves special attention in a nation reluctantly assuming a condition of de-facto bilingualism throughout its major metropolitan areas. English may have turned into the *lingua franca* of globalization, but the links between language, literature and nation have been undermined like never before. English departments, for example, must now account for an increasing body of literature by authors who write in English, but whose cultural and national bearings reside elsewhere, (India, South Africa, Asian American, U.S. Latino, among others). In that contradictory terrain, Spanish now awakens to the destiny of a second national language in the United States, in spite of that nation's deep-seated disinterest in foreign languages, a symptom that has only grown in the past few decades. Spanish departments must, therefore, not only brave the fragmentation of their traditional disciplines, but also come to grips with their own set of rising entanglements.

These administrative units of academic capital, once the guardians of Hispanism as a foreign language and literature, must now ask what it means—culturally, linguistically and theoretically—to live and work in the midst of 40 million citizens of Hispanic and Latin American background in the United States, with a buying power projected to approach one trillion dollars by the end of this decade?[5] No longer the cultural embassies of Hispanism in American (US) academia, Spanish departments now rehearse the possibilities of an unexpected global realm with uncertain yet profound implications for the potential links between Spain, Latin America, and the growing U.S. Latino community. The latter's demographic, cultural, and political profile has not only seen tremendous gains in coastal cities like New York, Chicago, Miami, Los Angeles, but also in Minneapolis, Atlanta, Denver, and many other southern and mid-western areas, both urban and suburban.[6]

Mapping such a global terrain would comprise an equivocal but extraordinary economy of Hispanic and Latino cultures: texts, services, products and styles, as well as languages. Indeed, Spanish now claims the attention of all English speakers in the United States (and some parts of Canada), at least as a means to gain employment, but the path of post-Hispanism is not far removed from a bilingual condition. Migrant multitudes from Latin American countries are bound to learn English in the United States, but they nonetheless continue to retain a relationship with Spanish and their nations of origin (which includes small, but significant, numbers of Spaniards or their descendants as well). It may seem farfetched for Hispanism to rethink itself through this growing bilingual register in the Americas, indeed, there may even be a certain irony implicit in that destiny if one realizes it came about in the site where the two most ambitious colonial histories crisscrossed with their respective languages. Be that as it may, it also seems clear that this bilingual condition contributes to a global sense of Spanish in which Spain has found a unexpected re-entry of sorts, one that is not defined by a sense of national or linguistic colonial empowerment, but rather by the opportunities of investment in cultural and linguistic dissemi-

nation, a sort of postnational Spanish marketing that is intrinsically transnational, with its main theater of consumption in the Americas.[7]

Most critics concede that globalization and postmodern constructs impact
various nations differently, but it seems fair to say that few critical paradigms
take such complications to heart. Sifting through these events and their impact
on theory has been a difficult and challenging task, as one can plainly see in
two of the most highly cited contemporary attempts to address the crisis in the
field of humanistic endeavors: Jacques Derrida's *Specters of Marx* and the more
recent *Empire* by Michael Hardt and Antonio Negri.[8] The question one draws
from both, after thirty years of deconstructive work, is whether deconstruction
can critically address the post-1989 global scene, or at least draw a clear line of
resistance from postcapitalism, the other force of designification.

It seems crucial, therefore, to examine the contradictory ways in which
deconstruction figures as a nondifferentiated common denominator in many of
today's critical discourses. Regardless of the diverse and often opposing ways
in which it is deployed, deconstruction imbues modalities of reading, writing,
and even speaking that inevitably turn toward de-signification of presence, and
logocentrism, in short, an incessant commitment to problematize how cultures
and histories establish notions such as reality, identity, and worldviews. Due
to its apparent negativity, it is often said that deconstruction only aims to tear
down critical paradigms once sacred to the humanities, yet one could argue it is
equally capable of rebuilding or reconceptualizing them. After all, humanistic
endeavors gained considerable prominence as an uncertain interplay between
aesthetics and epistemology, particularly through the postmodern aesthetics of
the early and middle 1980s.

It is therefore important to note that as a body of theory that looks upon
writing as a self-referential domain, deconstruction remains closer to artistic
practice, often distant from engaging how its critiques apply to the social, a disciplinary perspective that, in spite of its unquestionable possibilities as radical
epistemology, basically retains the pattern of the humanist researcher engaging
texts in isolation, banking on its pertinence in the postmodern lettered order
or awaiting a call to action through distant connections to the social. For those
involved in what was or may still be humanistic work after 1989, such an approach has increasingly become insufficient. The plane of concrete differences
has increased beyond the reach of models that define difference as particularism, as well as those that critique modernities in the abstract, usually on the way
to claiming a new postmodern, subaltern or colonial overarching logic.

To move past this cul-de-sac, new comparative work may well be necessary, the type of approach that will conjure new links between the production

of empirical and discursive knowledge, indeed, a reconfiguration of disciplines capable of articulating the richness of the living social text in its constructive, as well as deconstructive, realms. Examples of this kind of work can already be found in texts such as *The Politics of Culture in the Shadow of Capital,* edited by Lisa Lowe and David Lloyd, or the recent work of cultural critic Antonio Méndez Rubio, or that of Andreas Huyssen, a leading figure in the area of comparative literature.[9] They chart new paths beyond the openings propounded by deconstruction, either with a very attentive ear to the exigencies of the social text—concrete nationalisms, emancipation movements, different types of feminist struggles—or invoking a renewed aesthetic realm decoupled from any nostalgia for the old order, one perhaps not envisioned by the cultural studies hegemony.

Without these engagements, we attend to a postmodern order that values only economic data or epistemic speculation, a new order of knowledge anchored exclusively in the digital revolution and the stock market on one hand, and epistemological indeterminism on the other. Then again, perhaps these two forces mirror each other in ways totally unforeseen up to this point, ways that perhaps slip from writing as a self-enclosed deconstructive domain. The critique of the nation may well provide a case in point, since it has thus far shown much more socioeconomic pertinence than critical acumen. There may be no doubt that global capital finds collective identities such as the nation somewhat anachronistic to its ever-widening drive toward new and unobstructed markets, but the work of differentiating how this applies across the plane of varying types of nation-states remains largely unexplored, particularly among literary and cultural critics.

To say that identity critique, multi-temporality, and multiculturalism have been made tangible in nearly all parts of the world only confirms the commonplace, celebratory side of postmodernism and cultural studies. Indeterminacy, on the other hand, is now a global condition that requires elucidation through conceptual proximity to entanglements such as split-states, permanent diasporas, postnational imaginaries, and the intensive realm of consumer subjectivity. New insights will obviously be needed for differential approaches to cultures and nations, particularly those with divergent or discomforting modernities, but these pressures continue to startle academic structures, at times leading to surprising but revealing proposals that must somehow redraw the boundaries of the universal within national frameworks, be they linguistic, philosophical, or literary. Among these efforts, Harold Bloom's call for a literary canon may be the most notable example. Western, North Atlantic, American, European, Latin American, ethnic, universal, each imaginary must now field unprecedented strains, not only from migration waves that disturb the national identity like never before, but, what is more important, from the techno-mediatic performance industry, which has proven capable of designing a rich array of multicultural products on its own.

A postnational understanding of Hispanism could perhaps begin by tracing the following contours: a) the awakening national multiplicity of Spain that has been steadily unveiling itself since the death of Franco; b) the large scale migration from half of the Latin American nations to the United States and Europe; and c) the onset of Hispanic enclaves—a majority in some instances—in the major urban centers of the United States. Each case reveals a splitting of the nation-state equation, albeit in widely different forms that correspond to circumstances encountered by Spain, Latin America and the United States in the last few decades. It is not, therefore, an end of the nation in a rigorous sense, as many have augured, but rather a symptom of its dispersal that deserves special attention by those who study culture and literature, since it also implies opportunities for shaping the links between transatlantic and new American Studies, without abandoning discourses pertaining to Peninsular and Latin American traditions. Indeed, one might even suggest that new comparativism within the postnational sphere could renew our understanding of the Humanist past, as evidenced in Derrida's suggestive re-reading of Shakespeare, as well as Negri's and Hardt's poignant re-articulation of Renaissance thought. Nevertheless, such a disciplinary reorientation will also entail a more detailed look at culture industries whose main products today engage the manufacture of desire through television production and computer technologies. This impulse has succeeded in fusing the culture of marketing with the realm of performativity, creating a new epistemic niche in direct competition with universities and other institutions for the best creative talents. Commercial products must go to the market endowed with artistry and self-conscious performativity at the same time that artistic and cultural products must assume market logic in order to survive. Even the academy and its practitioners must now respond to this logic. As such, it constitutes a deeply contradictory element, since it bridges the culture of globalization and academic production precisely at the time that schools are becoming secondary agents of education—indeed, at a moment in which mass media service industries have managed to bring the acquisition of practical knowledge and training closer to the interests of corporations.

It all points to an intricate nexus that links citizenship with consumption, thereby comprising new forms of distributing and packaging the symbolic capital necessary to enter middle class status. It remains unclear, however, whether or how critical discourses will respond to this challenge. The aesthetics of imaging—television, videos, advertisements, the Internet, performative arts, and other media constructions of consumer citizenship—clearly exact a totally new relationship with academic intellectuals. The space once known as "the street" now breaks into the fold with a new force and legitimacy, no longer just an intruder that overturns the high-low cultural divide. The place of the researcher, or intermediary, becomes irremediably more public and ultimately more anxious, because capitalism itself demands it.

How, then, does one bridge the growing gaps between academic disciplines, their object of study, and the new phenomena I have attempted to summarize in this essay? Some might allege that it cannot be done, given that objects of knowledge are necessarily by-products of disciplinary thinking, and that the latter have been dissolved by the twin forces of deconstruction and global reordering. Others prefer to look upon universities as places of resistance from which to reclaim disciplinary order. A third position might insist on a new approach in which critical theory explores a new role within, not outside, the growing nexus of cultural markets and the arts. A comprehensive and suggestive example of this position has been articulated by Andreas Huyssen. I offer, by way of conclusion, a summary of its most *salient points,* each followed by a brief commentary of my own:[10]

a) *Abandon the traditional split between high and low culture that opposes serious art and literature to mass culture.*

This challenge, one suspects, may well prove equally difficult for critics who opt to remain exclusively within literature as well as those who seem to have abandoned it altogether. The same could be said for critics quite at home with the idea of a theoretical discourse that takes everything on board but remains far removed from the specific analysis of both, literature, and mass cultural forms.

b) *Substitute that vertical relationship (high/low divide) with a lateral or horizontal one that would recognize that scholars are also subject to market pressures.*

At stake here would be the role of the academic intellectual in the research university, particularly in the United States, an institutional space that has obviously changed, some would say drastically, during the past decade or so. If we ourselves are prone to market pressures, can we still address our object of study in terms of a tradition immune from such exigencies? If not, the question would not be how to dispense with that tradition, but rather to learn new ways of reading it, fully aware of the fact that our own subjectivity is being rehearsed in the process.

c) *Approach the topic of media in all its historical, technical and theoretical complexity.*

Much of the scholarship dealing with cultural studies continues to emanate from scholars with literary training who embark upon the brave new world of global or mass culture somewhat lightheartedly. We seem to bank on the weight of our symbolic capital, particularly our command of theory, to talk about film, television, architecture, music, and many other forms of contemporary culture. Often we remain closer to textual analysis than to actual exploration of new forms. Needless to say, such an approach, its limitations notwithstanding, often yields new and refreshing work, but even if one concludes that it is a necessary extension of the literary enterprise in today's academy, one must wonder if it is sufficient to meet its own claims and aspirations.

d) *Reintroduce issues of aesthetic quality in the analysis of cultural forms and products.*

Much has been said about the category of "the aesthetic," particularly as regards to the authoritarian hermeneutic tradition it has left behind, laden with universal value claims that often went unquestioned. But how will distinctions based on quality be articulated or accounted for henceforth? Can literature retain any particular value as a distinct practice of verbal exploration and polysemy in the contemporary critical domain? Even market-driven cultural production often involves a complex process of discernment among artistic performances. One cannot help but wonder if the critique of universal aesthetic claims has been displaced by a universal disclaimer of aesthetic discernment whose ideological pretenses remain unchallenged.

e) *Abandon the notion that the well-deserved critiques of elite cultures will play the role in political and social transformations that was reserved for the avant-garde. Look instead for the ways in which cultural products and practices link to political discourses in specific instances.*

All contexts have their internal shapes, needs and economies of value, even if the institutional expansiveness and wealth of the North American academy makes it possible to envision and theorize humanistic discourses as if they were devoid of localized propensities. Indeed, those of us working in the United States may be more prone to conceive our object of study as a transnational community of discourses able to absorb all difference through theoretical paradigms. But such a literary order, no doubt an interesting and timely symptom, deserves particular scrutiny. A pivotal example would be the work of Argentine master Jorge Luis Borges, for many, a model of the twenty-first century post-symbolic imaginary. There is no doubt that his short stories advanced the deepest challenge to literary conventions held in the late nineteenth and early twentieth centuries, many of which favored surrendering the uniqueness of individual texts to the tedium of literary history. It is also true, however, that by the end of the twentieth century his oeuvre took on a new symbolic meaning. Indeed, it became a primary point of reference for postmodern official aesthetics, a restoration of sorts within literary values that goes beyond the Western to perhaps a global appreciation. Borges's mastery may well lie precisely in having taken literature to an aesthetic plane that knows, or values, only the probing of its own making, a state of immanence eminently capable of turning what was once an aporia into its own metaphysics.

f) *Map a new comparative approach to cultural studies able to link disciplines such as cultural history and anthropology with literary and artistic histories.*

Literary and cultural studies would be well served by conceiving more comparative frameworks able to approach the differential application of literary studies, postmodernity, feminism, postcolonialism and queer theory—among others—as well as the growing disconnect between the humanities and social sciences. The question of difference seems paramount here. Today we are witnessing new ways of mapping multiple contradictory textual and cultural practices difficult to encompass from national or regional paradigms. But old habits are hard to break, even when driven by the spirit of innovation and radical ambition. New mapping may well require a deeper understanding of the relationship between literary studies and the lettered social sciences, particularly if we are to move beyond reductionist tendencies to cast these approaches as necessarily driven by either relativism or factualism.

Notes

1. Andreas Huyssen makes a significant attempt to distinguish the date of the first stage of postmodernism and distinguish it from the contemporary moment. "Literatura e cultura no contexto global."
2. Nestor Garcia Canclini, *Latinoamericanos buscando lugar en este siglo.*
3. The extent of this phenomenon has become quite evident in England, where there is now a new national emphasis on studying the future of English studies. See Elaine Showalter's "What Teaching Literature Should Really Mean."
4. For an englightening discussion of disciplinary history, see Immanuel Wallerstein, et

al., 1996. Open the Social Sciences: Report of the Gulbenkian Commission on the Restructuring of the Social Sciences.

5. This figure comes from television industry calculations, as reported in the *New York Times* by Mireya Navarro.

6. For data and cultural commentary of the Latino urban pressence in the United States, see Mike Davis's *Magical Urbanism.*

7. Néstor García Canclini details how Spain has strategically positioned itself in the new cultural economy of globalization while Latin American governments have failed to do so. Op. Cit. pp. 20–48.

8. Jacques Derrida, *Specters of Marx.* Antonio Negri and Michael Hardt, *Empire.*

9. Lisa Lowe and David Lloyd, *Politics of Culture in the Shadows of Capital,* Antonio Méndez Rubio, *Encrucijadas: Elementos de critica de la cultura,* and unpublished manuscript: "Cultura y Desaparición." Andreas Huyssen, op. cit.

10. Huyssen, Andreas, op. cit. This is a summary of his five main points outlined in pages 29–31.

Works Cited

Bloom, Harold. *The Western Canon.* New York: Harcourt Brace, 1994.

Canclini, Nestor García. *Latinomamericanos buscando lugar en este siglo.* Buenos Aires: Paidos, 2002.

Davis, Mike. *Magical Urbanism.* London: Verso, 2000.

Derrida, Jaques. *Specters of Marx.* London: Routledge, 1994.

Huyssen, Andreas. "Cultura y Desaaparición." Unpublished manuscript.

———. "Literatura e cultura no contexto global" in *Valores: Arte, Mercado Política.* Eds. Reinaldo Marques and Lucia Helena Vilela. Belo Horizonte, Brazil: UFMG, 2002.

Lowe, Lisa and David Lloyd. *Politics of Culture in the Shadows of Capital.* Durham: Duke University Press, 1997.

Méndez Rubio, Antonio. *Encrucijadas: Elementos de la crítica de la cultura.* Madrid: Catedra, 1997.

Navarro, Mireya. "Promoting Hispanic TV, Language and Culture," *New York Times.* December 30, 2002. C7.

Negri, Antoni and Michael Hardt. *Empire.* Cambridge: Harvard University Press, 2000.

Showalter, Elaine. "What Teaching Literature Should Really Mean," *The Chronicle Review of Higher Education.* January 17, 2003.

Wallerstein, Immanuel et al. *Open the Social Sciences: Report of the Gulbenkian Commission on the Restructuring of the Social Sciences.* Stanford: Stanford University Press, 1996.

◆ Afterword

Nicholas Spadaccini

In her introduction to this volume, Mabel Moraña argues that the concept and practice of Hispanism ought to be reexamined from a multidisciplinary and transnational perspective, keeping in mind the academic *loci* from which the dissemination of knowledge related to this field emanate. This very point is also emphasized by several contributors, all of whom are either Peninsularists or Latin-Americanists who practice their craft in the United States. It is the U.S. university system of private and public institutions with their extraordinary resources (some of which, however insufficient, do seem to trickle down to Humanities departments, including Spanish) and the visibility of Spanish as the second most widely-spoken language of the United States, and with the highest language enrollments other than English at our universities, which serve as a backdrop for some of the exchanges that take place in these pages.

Moraña underscores the importance of taking into account the role of scholars and writers "in the production of critical discourse related to categories of colonialism, national formation, modernity and identity politics" and stresses the need to reflect on "the project and practices of hispanization. . . . both in Spain and Spanish America, throughout the process of formation and consolidation of national states, and, nowdays, in the context of globalization" (x). And these issues are indeed dealt with by many of the contributors, some of whom focus on the traditional use of the Spanish as both a practical and symbolic device of subjugation within the Latin American and Spanish contexts. Such of course is not the case within the U.S. where Spanish is the language of a large and diverse minority population and the favorite "second" language at the university level.

The question of language colonization is dealt with explicitly in several essays, beginning with Lydia Fossa's "Spanish in the Sixteenth Century: The Colonial Hispanization of Indigenous Languages and Cultures," in which it is argued that the hispanization of Andean indigenous languages and cultures in the Sixteenth century went well beyond purely linguistic change as indigenous peoples were required to assume the language, habits, and religion of the colonizer. Fossa points to the pragmatic appropriation by missionaries of indigenous languages such as Aymara, Puquina, and especially Quechua through the importation of Spanish words and concepts, all to the detriment of other indigenous dialects and languages, in order to carry out evangelization (21–22). Her focus on the colonizer's strategies of domination through the colonization of language leads her to conclusions which are substantiated by meticulous analysis of well-known texts and legal documents. Yet, something equally important is left unsaid, namely, that while the indigenous peoples were often required by colonizer to "cease being themselves" (29), they were by no means passive subjects void of resistivity.

The discussion in these pages on language colonization demonstrates the extent to which Spanish is viewed both as a common language between people of various ethnic and cultural background in both Spain and Latin America and as an obstruction to greater autonomy and presence for "other" indigenous languages and cultures. This very point is made by several contributors, among them Ignacio Sánchez-Prado who in his essay, " The Pre-Columbian Past as a Project: Miguel León Portilla and Hispanism," analyzes the "Hispanist and nationalist foundations of nahuatl literary studies" in the work of the well-known Mexican historian which focused on the recovery of Bernardino de Sahagún's methodology, on the appropriation of Las Casas' advocacy of indigenous causes, and on the role of Spanish as *lingua franca,* as a unifying force among different ethnic groups (53). Sánchez-Prado is careful to point out that in a later defense of the Spanish language in *Pueblos originarios y globalización* (México: El Colegio nacional, 1997, 57) León Portilla distances himself from "the exaltation of the linguistic and cultural *mestizaje* he endorsed in 1962" (53) while continuing to argue that the use of Spanish as a common language between cultures does not negate their cultural specificity (53). Sánchez Prado's point seems to be that, despite León Portilla's reassessment, there remains a basic problem: since Spanish is the only language of political interaction in present-day Mexico, bilingualism can be viewed as an obstruction to cultural independence. From the postcolonial perspective which Sánchez-Prado seems to favor (in line with well-known debates on national identity among intellectuals such as Bonfill Batalla, Florescano, and Villoro) this sort of nationalist appropriation of pre-Columbian history and cultures in the Mexican national narration is seen as being tantamount to epistemological violence, while others (León Portilla among them) could well find this assessment somewhat reductionistic.

The privileging of Spanish at the expense of other indigenous languages and cultures is also criticized by Joan Ramon Resina ("Whose Hispanism? Cultural Trauma, Disciplined Memory, and Symbolic dominance") for whom Hispanism implies nothing less than the voiding of various traces of cultural and historical memory. Cognizant of the differences between the market-driven Hispanism of the United States and the so-called state Hispanism of Spain, Resina questions the privileged place accorded to Spanish on both sides of the Atlantic at the expense of a recognition of difference in the multicultural and multilingual realities of Spain and Latin America (183). His diagnosis of the problem is both cogent and difficult to refute on the theoretical level. Yet, a solution to the conundrum is elusive, especially within the U.S. context. How does one generate demand for those "other" living languages of Spain and Latin America within the undergraduate curriculum of a U.S. university? It is well known that Spanish has become the second language of the United States with extraordinary appeal for a large majority of students who fulfill second language requirements and see it as a vehicle for enhancing future employment. It is also irrefutable that Spanish is the most popular "foreign" language in U.S. high schools and that demand for Spanish is continuing to grow at a vertiginous pace. For these very reasons, it seems clear that university administrators respond to the marketplace and little can be done in practice about this reality. This, of course, does not negate Resina's arguments but does point to the difficulties of translating a democratic debate—one that might have resonance within the specific historical and current political contexts of Spain and certain Latin American countries—into practice within the more complex and largely market-driven environment of the U.S. university in which Spanish is viewed by administrators as "cash cow."

Resina and others also remind us, correctly, that Hispanism is bound up with cultural nationalism, with all of its negative implications. Thus, Sebastiaan Faber ("'La hora ha llegado': Hispanism, Pan-Americanism, and the Hope of Spanish/American Glory [1938–1948]) questions the usefulness of the concept and argues that despite its transnational ambitions, Hispanism does not reflect the concerns and struggles of different social classes, ethnic groups, and communities across Spain and Spanish America (89). His conclusions are based on the use of unitary concepts as well as ideological slips in three key journals published in Mexico City between 1938 and 1940: the *Revista Iberoamericana, Romance,* and *España Peregrina.* Faber finds it ironic that the *Revista* should embrace a "pan-nationalist connection to the United States, with . . . invocation of cultural uniqueness, shared destiny, and future glory" (74), even while asserting Latin-American literature's independence from Spain's "universal mission" and, therefore, distinct from Peninsular literature (73); or that *España peregrina* should postulate that America was the redeemer of mankind and repository of Western civilization while proclaiming that such a phase was inaugurated by "the sacrifice of the Spanish people" (81); finally, a similar slippage is detected in the journal *Romance* and its proposal of "a unitary concept of Hispanic culture . . . covering the whole of the Spanish-speaking world, with Pan-Hispanic folk tradition as its strongest bond" (83). Farber's conclusion seems to be that, even with the best of intentions, the concept called Hispanism is likely to be misused and is, therefore, unredeemable.

Another essay that touches on the problem of using unitary concepts within multicultural and multigual contexts, is Thomas Harrington's "Rapping on the Cast(i)le Gates: Nationalism and Culture Planning in Contemporary Spain," which argues that the castilianist model of culture planning articulated by Nebrija toward the end of the Fifteenth century was virtually unchallenged for nearly four hundred years—until the *Sexenio Revolucionario* (1868–1874) and the establishment of the First Republic when the castilianist discourse was temporarily disrupted (117) only to regain momentum with Cánovas (*Discurso sobre la nación,* 1882) and the philological work of Menéndez y Pelayo "whose cultural project and that of his political correlate, Cánovas, might be compared with those of the Sixteenth-century Jesuits and the twentieth-century members of *Opus Dei*" (119). Harrington traces the efforts at culture planning by various nationalist movements since the end of the Nineteenth century, pointing as well to the inevitable counterattacks by castilianist politicians and intellectuals. His essay ends with a rhetorical statement that has the flavor of exortation: "Would it not be easier for everyone involved if the Neo-Castilianists of today would simply admit, and base any and all negotiations over the future of Spain's civil society, on the unassailable fact that today's Spain contains not just three, but four major, historically-defined movements of national identity?" (134)—Castilian, Basque, Catalan and Galician. Harrington, a Hispanist writing from the United States, presumably with no identity ties with any of movements in question, ventures such a statement after having outlined the practice of castilianist culture planning from Nebrija to Aznar. At the same time the essay recognizes, implicitly, that in today's Spain culture planning is not the exclusive province of castilianists and that the various nationalities have varying degrees of autonomy in the cultural and political spheres.

Several other essays in this volume address questions related to specific discussions within the field of Hispanism and, in some cases, propose certain correctives. Thus, referring specifically to the so-called Siglos de Oro or Renaissance and Baroque periods, Anthony Cascardi ("Beyond Castro and Maravall: Interpellation, Mimesis, and the Hegemony of Spanish Culture") calls for a Hispanism that goes beyond the existential historicism of Américo Castro and José Antonio Maravall's emphasis on ideas and institutions to focus on subjectivity on the concrete level. Cascardi seeks to remedy this situation through the use of Althusser's notion of ideology and interpellation to see how subjects were "fashioned through their interactions with various cultural institutions and 'Ideological State Apparatuses'" (149). Yet, Cascardi also recognizes the conundrum posed by the culture that emerges under Spanish Absolutism which is "less than a perfect mirror of state ideologies" (149) and argues that subject formation was rooted in a "process of cultural (re)production that involved in the fracturing of mirrored images'" (150), using concepts from Lacan, Braudrillard, and Fuentes.

In the particular case of Maravall, it is important to recall that he is a historian of social mentalities and political institutions and that he speaks of a "transpersonal subjectivity" linked to a kind of "protonational political evolution" (*Estado moderno* 33; 490). The modern state with its centralized, absolutist political system is dependent upon interpersonal bonds—what William Egginton has recently called "*theatrical identification*," an active ingredient "of the modes of subjectification analyzed by critics from Althusser to Foucault to Butler" (141). Eggington also makes the case that the notion of a transpersonal collectivity can exist only in a "world" "whose spatiality is theatrical" and finds a sociological correlate: Jurgen Habermas's theory of the public sphere (144). The point is that if—as Maravall argues—in the urban society of the Seventeenth century, the "mass-oriented" nature of society led to a pervasive anonymity, in which "bonds of neighborhood, friendship and kinship" are seriously diminished (*Culture of the Baroque* 14), these bonds are gradually superseded by an arena in which the "transpersonal collectivity" is played out in practical, everyday ways. In Maravall's case, it must be said that despite his basic emphasis on ideas and institutions and, therefore, on the excercise of power from above rather than a focus on subjectivity on a more concrete level, his writings also make clear that one cannot understand the complexities of Baroque culture without taking into account the discrepant voices that are raised against its conservative programs. This position is made clear in several of his major books—*La oposición política bajo los Austrias, La literatura picaresca desde la historia social* and even *La cultura del Barroco,* in which he explicitly says that there are "instances, even frequent ones, of repulsion against what is proposed. The background of conflict and of opposition in the Seventeenth century is there for all to see, and without taking it into account—one must also insist on this point—nothing can be understood" (198, my translation).

This does not negate the importance of Cascardi's suggestion but merely points out that Maravall's interpretation of the baroque as a "guided," "conservative," "urban," and "mass-oriented" culture which saw the dominant segments of society and their surrogates use persuasion and socio-political propaganda in their drive to preserve their privileges, seems to be especially compelling when one examines certain mass-oriented cultural artifacts (the comedia, the auto sacramental, etc.) within the more immediate context of their production/ reception in the 1600s (see Spadaccini and Martín-Estudillo; and Castillo and Spadaccini).

Another essay which focuses on a somewhat specific issue is Sylvia Molloy's "Latin America in the U.S. Imaginary: Postcolonialism, Translation, and Magic Realist Imperative," which calls into question how Latin America is constructed in the U.S. academy, especially within the postcolonial framework. Molloy's main contention is that Spanish is dismissed in the U.S. academy as a language of intellectual exchange, claiming that well- known critics from Latin America are generally not brought into the larger debate on postcolonialism while other Latin-Americanists working at U.S. universities are, with some exceptions, usually absent from the larger debates (195). To underscore her point Molloy discusses the reception of magic realism as a univocal representational strategy and questions the lack of recognition of multiple aesthetic practices and strategies as well as theoretical and critical agency within Latin-American cultural production (198).The major point of this essay is compelling. Yet, as one reflects on how Latin America is constructed in the U.S. academy, one also senses the tensions and differences that exist between some U.S. based Latin-Americanists and those writing from Latin America as Emil Volek has recently pointed out in his introduction to his edited volume *Latin America Writes Back. Postmodernity in the Periphery* (xvii-xx) where he speaks of academies "on different tracks": "There may be a lot of apparent interaction, even mimicry, between the two, and, as always, a good number of Latin American intellectuals of the first order work full- or part-time in the U.S. But this only covers up the fact that the two academies are on different tracks. Those Latin Americans who are not mimicking current fashion in the North seem oddly out of place here, are ostracized or find themselves in the category of provincial 'subalterns' who really don't and cannot speak for themselves, and need the right interpreters" (xvii). While this particular take may well be controversial, some of the specific issues raised by Volek cannot be easily dismissed such as, for example, his observation regarding cultural studies in the U.S. and Latin America respectively; the former tied to the Humanities and much of it focused on identity politics; the latter oriented toward the Social Sciences and influenced by the Birmingham School (xviii; see also Larrain). These examples show the complexity of discussing concepts such as Latin Americanism or Hispanism even if one takes into account the particular *loci* of enunciation.

The status of Latin Americanism within the U.S. is also dealt with in Idelber Avelar's "Xenophobia and Diasporic Latin Americanism: Mapping Antagonisms around 'the Foreign'" in which he specifically addresses problems encountered by colleagues who write in Spanish rather than English and goes on to review the general status of Latin Americanism within the category of the "foreign" both within and outside the American (U.S.) academy. For this critic, Latin Americanism occupies an "in-between" space (using Silvano Santiago's concept) which in post-September 11 is said to be affected by the war on terrorism and the erosion of civil liberties. Avelar goes on to caution us to beware of a politics of exclusion at U.S. universities and to keep an eye on academic practices which might be complicit with racism and xenophobia. Such practices are often masked by the language and rhetoric of "standards" and by the lack of interest in other methods of evaluation (280).One could argue, of course, that the American (U.S.) academy is not a monolith and that the kinds of difficulties encountered by people writing in a language other than English in tenure decisions vary considerably from one university to another. One might also cite the cases of the many *exiliados* or expatriates from Spain and more recently Latin America who have had—and continue to have—extraordinary careers at U.S. universities. Yet, Avelar's cautionary notes cannot be easily dismissed. The examples he cites are compelling and are often replicated in subtle ways. In a recent search at a major research institution ("de cuyo nombre no quiero acordarme") a truly splendid candidate, a non-U.S. citizen from a Spanish-speaking country, was eliminated from the competition after a campus visit because his English was not deemed to be not sufficiently "native," despite the fact that the language of instruction in that particular department is Spanish and that the person in question is conversant in four languages, has published five books, and came highly recommended from specialists both from within and outside of the U.S. university system. By those standards, few, if any, of the outstanding intellectuals from Spain and Latin America who have shaped generations of graduate students in the U.S. would have survived this particular competition. Avelar seems to have a point: in post-September 11 (and within the realities of identity politics), beware of the "foreign" among us.

Roman de la Campa's essay, "Hispanism and the American academy in the Postnational Era" offers a broad reflection on the disciplinary changes that have taken place within Hispanism, Latin Americanism and Latino Studies during the last several decades and argues one can no longer think in terms of organic principles. He points to large-scale immigration from Latin America to the U.S. and Europe, as well as to the large Hispanic enclaves in urban U.S. cities, and the affirmation of multiple nationalities in Spain in order to call for a postnational understanding of Hispanism/Latin Americanism. De la Campa also calls for new theoretical approaches to the production/consumption of knowledge toward an exploration of "the growing nexus of cultural markets and the arts" (311). While it is difficult to argue with De la Campa's call for renewal, one wonders to what extent Hispanism and Latin Americanism are thought about today in terms of the organic principles that defined them in the past, prior to poststructuralism and postcolonial studies and prior to the extraordinary changes alluded to by De la Campa in terms of large scale migrations, globalization, and the "post national" condition.

Alberto Moreiras's essay ("Mules and Snakes: On the Neo-Baroque Principle of De-localization"), also speaks indirectly to some of these issues, as it points to the shifts in university discourse and the challenge to the notion of a general epistemology by poststructuralism and postcolonial studies. His essay reflects upon the understanding of the Baroque as a "field of identitarian expression concerning the peculiar Hispanic experience of modernity" (207) and engages in dialogue with the respective interpretations of Roberto González Echevarría and John Beverley. He takes issue with the former for positing the Baroque "as a mark of continental identity" and locating it "metonymically in the so-called Boom of the Latin-American novel" (212), while, in fact, not going beyond the Colonial Baroque or "its status as regional ideology at the service of the constitution of the local as a differential/mimetic/identitarian apparatus of social capture" (212). Moreiras also questions Beverley's view of literature as superstructure and as a mechanism of control by the dominant classes (215) and defines him "a critic of transculturation in the name of subaltern identity." In the end, Moreiras distances himself from the so-called regionalist, identitarian paradigms, to embrace the concept of the Neobaroque, which implies an "interruption of the principle of regionalization" and a kind of passage or "pilgrimage toward the outside" (210). The Neobaroque is mobilized in the name of a "freedom of thought" (218): thought marked by interruption in the line with the foundational work of Severo Sarduy, Lezama Lima, and others (225).

Moreiras's own critical practice as exemplified in one of his books (*The Exhaustion of Difference. The Politics of Latin American Cultural Studies,* Duke, 1991) is scrutinized by Brad Epps in his essay "Keeping Things Opaque: On the Reluctant Personalism of a Certain Mode of Critique" in which he explores the question of locality—the institutional, political, and rhetorical site of enunciation of critical discourse. Of particular interest in this discussion is the American (U.S.) university as a privileged place for academic exchange. Epps's critique of de-localization seems to aim precisely at what Moreiras in this volume calls Neobaroque thinking—a "pilgrimage toward the outside" which, in line with Epps' arguments, could also be circumscribed by institutional considerations.

Finally, in an largely upbeat essay (despite its title) "Hispanism in an Imperfect past and an Uncertain Present," Nicolas Shumway reflects on the state of Hispanic Studies in the United States and sees Hispanism as an arcane idea which fails to accommodate new trends in Spanish-language literature within the context of globalization. Among the examples he cites in this respect are those of a young generation of expatriate writers, partly educated in the United States, who are represented in recently-published anthologies (*McOndo* and *Se habla español*) and who, to a great extent, are in dialogue with their adopted country without shedding the identity of the countries and continent of provenance. Shumway also asks what one does with Latino literature, much of which is written in English, if old assumptions and paradigms about our field are retained.

If Shumway and others are correct that Hispanism is an arcane idea, the same problem surfaces in conjunction with the appellation Hispanic which, in the U.S., is widely used and politically charged. On the one hand, it is rejected in certain quarters because of its ethnocentric European connotation; on the other hand, it continues to be used by the federal government for administrative/demographic purposes (Giménez Micó). This appellation encompasses people who in the recent census identified themselves as either "White," "Black," or "some other race," with the former having the highest income, followed by those in the category of "some other race" and "Black" respectively, despite the fact that the latter indicated the highest level of education ("How Race Counts for Hispanic Americans," Lewis Mumford Center for Comparative Urban and Regional Research at SUNY, Albany; cited by Fears). What does it mean to be a Hispanist or a Latin Americanist in the U.S. academy which, despite the advances of interdisciplinary studies, is still largely organized around traditional disciplines, both in the Humanities and the Social Sciences? What does it mean to be called Hispanic given the complexity of the phenomenon of migration from so many different places, with their own multicultural and multilingual realities? What is it that we do as academics, in our teaching and research, to address these complexities?

The debates undertaken in this volume point to a profession in flux and to an extraordinary range of reflection about concepts (Hispanism/Latin-Americanism) which may no longer be as relevant as they once were. In the world of the "Post-" what do we do with Hispanism and Latin-Americanism? Most of the essays in this volume engage these questions and provide suggestions on how rethink our disciplines.

Works Cited

Castillo, David and Nicholas Spadaccini. "Cervantes y la comedia nueva: lectura y espectáculo." *Theatralia* 5 (2003). 153–63.

Egginton, William. *How the World Became a Stage: Presence, Theatricality, and the Question of Modernity.* Albany: State University of New York Press, 2003.

Fears, Darryl. "Race Divides Hispanics, Report Says." *Washington Post,* July 14, 2003, Page A03.

Giménez Micó, José Antonio. "Calibán in Aztlán: from the Emergence of Chicano Discourse to the Plural Constitution of New Solidarities." In *National Identities and Sociopolitical Changes in Latin America.* Ed. Mercedes F. Durán-Cogan and Antonio Gómez Moriana. New York and London: Routledge, 2001. 320–51. (Hispanic Issues, vol. 23).

Larraín, Jorge. *Identity and Modernity in Latin America.* London: Blackwell Publishers, 2000.

Maravall, José Antonio. *Estado moderno y mentalidad social.* 2 vols. Madrid: Revista de Occidente, 1972.

———. *La cultura del barroco. Análisis de una estructura histórica.* Barcelona: Ariel, 1975. English ed., *Culture of the Baroque,* trans. Terry Cochran. Minneapolis: University of Minnesota Press, 1986.

———. *La literatura picaresca desde la historia social.* Madrid: Taurus: 1986.

———. *La oposición política bajo los austrias.* Barcelona: Ediciones Ariel, 1974.

Santiago, Silvano. *Latin American Literature: The Space in Between.* Trans. Stephen Moscov. Buffalo, N.Y.: Council on International Studies, State University of New York at Buffalo, 1973.

Spadaccini, Nicholas and Luis Martín-Estudillo. *Libertad y límites: el barroco hispánico.* Madrid: Ediciones del Orto, 2004.

Volek, Emil. "Introduction." *Latin America Writes Back. Postmodernity in the Periphery.* New York: Routledge, 2002. xi-xxviii. (Hispanic Issues, vol. 28).

◆ Contributors

Idelber Avelar is Associate Professor of Latin American Literature at Tulane University. He is the author of *The Untimely Present: Postdictatorial Latin American Fiction and the Task of Mourning,* which was revised and extended for a Spanish version entitled *Alegorías de la derrota: la ficción postdictatorial y el trabajo del duelo.* He has published articles on topics such as dictatorship, transculturation, and torture. He is currently working on a book on the genealogy of Latin Americanism.

Román de la Campa is Professor of Latin American Literature and Comparative Literature at Stony Brook University, of the State of New York, where he also holds the position of Chair of the Hispanic Languages and Literature Department. He has published numerous books and essays in the United States, Latin America, and Europe. His most recent books are *América Latina y sus comunidades discursivas: cultura y literatura en la era global* (1999), *Latin Americanism* (1999), and *Cuba On My Mind: Journeys to a Severed Nation* (2000). His next book, *Latin, Latino, American: Split States and Global Imaginaries,* will be published by Verso. He was born in Havana and now resides in New York.

Anthony J. Cascardi is the Richard and Rhoda Goldman Distinguished Professor in the Humanities and Professor of Comparative Literature, Spanish, and Rhetoric at the University of California, Berkeley. He is author of, amongst others, *Consequences of Enlightenment: Aesthetics as Critique, Ideologies of History in the Spanish Golden Age* and *The Subject of Modernity,* as well as of over fifty articles on Spanish literature. He has also been recipient of numerous awards, such as the Andrew Mellon Foundation Publication Award for *The Bounds of Reason.*

Brad Epps is Professor of Romance Languages and Literatures and Women's Studies at Harvard University. He has published over fifty articles on modern literature, film, and art from Spain, Latin America, Catalonia, and France and is the author of *Significant Violence: Oppression and Resistance in the Narratives of Juan Goytisolo.* He is currently editing two collections of essays, one with Luis Fernández Cifuentes, titled *Spain Beyond Spain: Modernity, Literary History, and National Identity* and another with Keja Valens, titled *Passing Lines: Immigration and (Homo)sexuality.* He is also working on two books-length projects: *Daring to Write,* on gay and lesbian issues in Latin America, Spain, and Latino cultures in the United States, and *Barcelona and Beyond,* on the modernization of Barcelona from the Renaixença to the present.

Sebastiaan Faber is Assistant professor of Hispanic Studies at Oberlin College. His interests are Nineteenth and Twentieth-century Spanish and Latin American literature, Pan-Hispanism, Pan-Americanism, and Spanish Civil War exile. He is the author of *Exile and Cultural Hegemony: Spanish Intellectuals in Mexico, 1939–1975* (2002) and has published in *Hispania, Journal of Latin American Cultural Studies, Journal of Spanish Cultural Studies, Bulletin of Spanish Studies,* and *Revista de Estudios Hispánicos,* among other journals. He is currently writing two books; one on the impact of the Spanish Civil War on Hispanism in the United States, Britain, and the Netherlands; and one on the representation of Hispanic/Latino identity since 1810.

Lydia Fossa is Assistant Professor of Spanish and Portuguese at the University of Arizona. Recently, she has finished the manuscript entitled *Narrativas problemáticas: los Inkas bajo la pluma española* to be published by the Instituto de Estudios Peruanos in Lima, Perú. She is also preparing the electronic version of the third part of "Glosas Croniquenses: Glosarios tempranos Quechua-Castellano." She has recently published the following articles: "Autorestempranos, intérpretes e informantes: primeras interacciones para describir a los andinos," and "L'interlocution dans la culture andine."

Thomas Harrington is Associate Professor of contemporary Iberian Culture at Trinity College in Hartford, Connecticut. The prime focus of his research in recent years has been on the dynamics of "cultural commerce" (the strategically inspired transfer of cultural goods from one national cultural system to another) in early twentieth century Spain and Portugal. He has also published studies on the history and function of Hispanism in North America, Galician thought, Catalan cinema and ideas, the development of Spanish Cultural Studies, the journalistic enterprises of José Ortega y Gasset, and the Spanish emigrant/exile communities of Cuba.

Sylvia Molloy is Albert Schweitzer Professor in the Humanities, Spanish and Portuguese Languages and Literatures and Comparative Literature at New York University. Amongst her books are *Signs of Borges* and *At Face Value: Autobiographical writing in Latin America*. She has also written extensively on Modernismo, feminist, gender and queer theory and questions of Comparative Literature and Cultural Studies.

Mabel Moraña is Professor at the University of Pittsburgh and Director of Publications of the Instituto Internacional de Literatura Iberoamericana. She is the author of *Literatura y cultura nacional en Hispanoamérica, 1910–1940* (1982), *Memorias de la generación fantasma* (1988), *Políticas de la escritura en América Latina. De la Colonia a la Modernidad* (1997) and *Viaje al silencio. Exploraciones del discurso barroco* (1998). She has edited *Relecturas del Barroco de Indias* (1994) and co-edited *La imaginación histórica en el siglo XIX* (1994). She has coordinated special volumes on colonial literature for the *Revista de Crítica Literaria Latinoamericana* and the *Revista Iberoamericana*. In recent years, she has coordinated multiple volumes on indigenism, Latin American cultural criticism, modernity, and postcolonialism.

Alberto Moreiras is Anne and Robert Bass Professor of Romance Studies and Literature and Director of the Center for European Studies at Duke University. He has published *Interpretacion y diferencia, Tercer espacio: Duelo y literatura en America Latina, The Exhaustion of Difference: The Politics of Latin American Cultural Studies,* and has coedited with Nelly Richard *Pensar en/la postdictadura*. He is a coeditor of the *Journal of Spanish Cultural Studies*.

Joan Ramon Resina is Professor of Romance Studies and Comparative Literature at Cornell University. He is the author of *La búsqueda del Grial* (1988); *Un sueño de piedra: Ensayos sobre la literatura del modernismo europeo* (1990); *Los usos del clásico* (1991); *El cadáver en la cocina. La novela policiaca en la cultura del desencanto* (1997). He has edited five volumes: *Myhtopoesis: Literatura, totalidad, ideología* (1992), *El aeroplano y la estrella: el movimiento vanguardista en los Países Catalanes (1904–1936)* (1997), *Disremembering the Dictatorship: The Politics of Memory since the Spanish Transition to Democracy* (2000), *Iberian Cities* (2001), and *After-Images of the City* (2003). He has published nearly one hundred essays in professional journals and in collective volumes.

Ignacio M. Sánchez-Prado is currently a doctoral candidate in Hispanic Languages and Literatures at the University of Pittsburgh. He is the author of *El canon y sus formas: la reinvención de Harold Bloom y sus lecturas hispanoamericanas* (2002) and editor of *América Latina: Nuevas perspectivas desde los estudios literarios y culturales* and, with Adela Pineda Franco, *Alfonso Reyes y los estudios latinoamericanos*.

Nicolas Shumway is Tomás Rivera Regents Professor of Spanish American Literature at the University of Texas at Austin, where, since 1995, he has also been the director of the Teresa Lozano Long Institute of Latin American Studies. He has published widely on Latin American literature and intellectual history, with particular emphasis on Argentina. His book, *The Invention of Argentina,* won international recognition and was selected by *The New York Times* as one of the notable books of the year. In 1994, Emecé Editores published a Spanish translation of the book in Argentina and a revised edition in 2002. He is currently completing a book on thought and literature of the early national period in several American countries, including Argentina, Mexico, and the United States.

Nicholas Spadaccini is Professor of Spanish and Comparative Literature at the University of Minnesota. He has published numerous books, editions, and collective volumes, with an emphasis on early modern Spain and Latin America. His most recent study (co-authored) is *Libertad y límites. El barroco hispánico* (2004) and he is currently completing a book on Cervantes and the culture of crisis of Baroque Spain. He is editor in chief of the Hispanic Issues series.

Index

Compiled by Gerardo Garza

VOLUMES IN THE HISPANIC ISSUES SERIES